RAND McNALLY

WORLD
FACTS
& MAPS

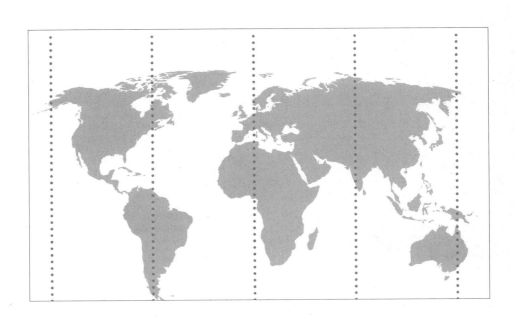

Contents

Hot Spots: Current Events in Focus

Rand McNally *World Facts and Maps*
Copyright © 1996 by Rand McNally &
Company. All rights reserved.
ISSN 1057-9834
ISBN 0-528-83695-1

Published and printed in the
United States of America

Photograph credits:
Hot Spots, page 5: Black Star
Gazetteer, page 69: Viesti Associates

World Gazetteer: Profiles of Nations and Places

HOT SPOTS:
CURRENT EVENTS
IN FOCUS

Bosnia and Herzegovina: Soldiers walk through a village destroyed in the country's ethnic warfare.

Europe

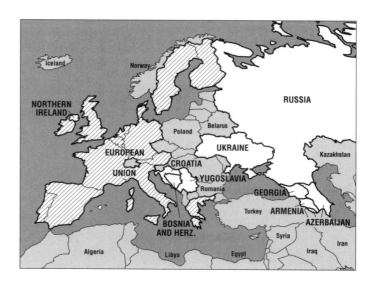

The end of the twentieth century will be remembered as a time when change came to Europe at a dizzying pace. In the east, new political and economic structures replaced the totalitarian Communist governments that were legacies of the two World Wars that occurred in the first half of the 1900s. In the west, nations buried old resentments and worked to forge a Europe unified both politically and economically.

The World Wars devastated much of the continent and ultimately divided Europe into East and West. While the Soviet Union controlled the countries of the East, the countries of Western Europe were allied to the United States, and Germany was partitioned between the two. The "Cold War," an ideological and military standoff that saw massive military buildups and severe restrictions on communications, trade, and travel between the two sides, characterized European politics during this era. The nations of Eastern Europe evolved into Soviet-style, centralized Communist governments dominated by policies set by Moscow, while Western Europe maintained its capitalist systems; each bloc jealously guarded its sovereignty against outside influences.

By the late 1980s it became apparent that the Cold War was coming to an end as the nations of Europe shifted their priorities to the revitalization of their economies. Both the decentralized, capitalist countries and the centralized, socialist countries were suffering from maladies endemic to the world's developed nations—low growth rates, a decreasing standard of living, and an aging industrial base. While inflation, recession, and unemployment plagued the capitalist countries, the socialist countries suffered even more from morale problems within the work force, which resulted in declining productivity and severe distribution problems. Trade deficits became a major issue as light, high-technology industries developed in the United States, as well as in Japan and other Asian countries, and the world market was subsequently flooded with ingenious products which Europeans wanted to own but were not prepared to produce.

Ironically, each of the two opposing sides in the Cold War looked to the other for a new direction in an attempt to dispel its economic woes. The West moved towards centralization while the East has been decentralized; the West experimented with socialism while the East opened the door to capitalism and democracy. These transitions have not been easy, but they are the harbingers of a Europe that will continue to transform itself in the coming decades.

Western European centralization has been taking shape as the European Union attempts to bridge centuries of national and economic rivalries to create a common prosperity. In 1993, the nations of the European Union took a dramatic step towards unity when they removed many trade, enterprise, and mobility barriers between themselves. They are also working towards full monetary union using a single currency. But these moves have not been easy, and the question of full political union has been hotly debated. The United Kingdom, for one, has been very reluctant to relinquish any sovereignty to a supranational European state.

The desire to create more equitable societies has led individual European countries such as Sweden, France, and Greece to experiment with socialist programs that have had varying degrees of success. None of the countries of Western Europe used the Soviet model for development—a monolithic, centralized, single-party Communist state. Instead, socialists rose up within the existing multiparty political framework and exerted their influence to enact socialist legislation.

Overshadowing the affairs of Western Europe have been the astonishing changes that have ripped through the former Soviet Union and the nations it once dominated. Following World War II, policies set by Moscow firmly governed Eastern Europe, which had learned the lessons of the Soviet military invasions of Hungary in 1956 and Czechoslovakia in 1968 following protests for reforms and increased personal freedoms. The Soviet Union, with its vast natural resources, supplied raw materials to the countries in its sphere of influence, which automatically returned manufactured goods to the Soviet Union. This closed economic system, along with declining productivity, resulted in ever-increasing shortages in the entire Soviet bloc.

Mikhail Gorbachev's rise to power in the Soviet Union marked the dawning of a new age. His program of restructuring, or "perestroika," was intended to decentralize some of the decision-making in the Soviet economy and to encourage the development of privately-owned enterprise to stimulate growth and alleviate shortages. Gorbachev also implemented a policy of "glasnost," or openness, the purpose of which was to speed the reform process, stimulate creativity and personal initiative, and prepare the way for more decentralized decision-making. Glasnost resulted in greater personal freedoms, artistic expression, and access to information.

Within the Soviet Union, glasnost had a profound effect, especially on the country's one hundred ethnic minorities who, for the first time, were allowed to express their grievances about Soviet rule. New political parties founded along ethnic lines sprang up across the nation as various nationalities began to press for more autonomy and even independence. Glasnost also fueled rising nationalism which led to renewed animosity between various ethnic groups. Fighting soon erupted between the Armenians and their Turkish rivals in neighboring Azerbaijan.

Another significant change in Soviet policy was the renunciation of the so-called "Brezhnev Doctrine," which asserted the Soviets' right to interfere in the affairs of other Communist countries. Accordingly, the Soviets began to withdraw their troops from many foreign countries, including the nations of Eastern Europe.

Cautiously at first, the countries of Eastern Europe began to test the limits of the new Soviet tolerance. When it became clear that the Soviet military was no longer a threat, reform movements and revolution began to spread across Eastern Europe like wildfire. In 1988 the Communists were firmly in control; by the end of 1989 all of the Communist governments had been either replaced or radically altered. Even the Soviet Union's powerful Communist Party relinquished its stranglehold on the Soviet people by giving up its monopoly on power and establishing political pluralism.

The event which best symbolized the incredible changes was the demolition of the Berlin Wall in 1989 and the subsequent absorption of East Germany into West Germany. By early 1990, all of the countries had restored basic personal freedoms and were moving toward establishing market economies and relations with the West.

Events in the east reached a climax in 1991 with the breakup of the Soviet Union and the rise of Russian President Boris Yeltsin. Predictably, change has not come easy to Russia. Yeltsin has shown remarkable resilience in resisting efforts by the communists to regain power. At times he has resorted to brute force, such as in 1993, when he violently evicted opposition politicians from the Russian parliament. As Russia's economy has been wrenched by change, many citizens are impoverished and out of work. This has given rise to ultra-nationalists who clamor for a return of the Soviet Union and its repressionist policies. Yeltsin faced another major crisis in 1994 when he faced criticism for using military force to defeat the breakaway republic of Chechnya and reclaim the area as Russian territory.

Change has also been difficult for other republics in the former Soviet Union. Georgia, Tajikistan, Azerbaijan, Uzbekistan, Kazakhstan, and Kyrgyzstan have all experienced violent clashes between rival ethnic and political groups. Along the Baltic Sea, Latvia, Estonia, and Lithuania have all found independence complicated by the large numbers of Russians who settled in those nations after World War II. Relations with Moscow have been strained by accusations that these and other former soviet republics are discriminating against their sizable Russian minorities.

Elsewhere in Eastern Europe, former communists have gained renewed strength as people become disillusioned with economic reforms. In most cases, the transition to a market economy has resulted in inflation and unemployment. Many people look back fondly to the days when communist governments tried to provide all of their citizens with food, housing, and employment. In search of greater prosperity, the people of Bulgaria, Hungary and other nations have voted reformers out of office in favor of traditional socialists.

To the south, independence from the Soviet Union led to the break-up of Czechoslovakia at the end of 1992. Remarkably, the division of the nation into the Czech Republic and Slovakia was accomplished peacefully. Since then the two nations have gone in different directions. While Slovakia struggles with the same economic problems that bedevil other former Soviet bloc nations, the Czech Republic has a booming capitalistic economy that is rapidly approaching Western standards.

While the breakup of the Soviet Union was relatively peaceful, thousands have died since the fall of the Yugoslavian federation in 1991. As each of the constituent republics declared its independence, the Serbian-dominated federal government fought to maintain control of Serbian-inhabited areas within the new nations. By 1995, Yugoslavia had bowed to international pressure by distancing itself from Serbian independence movements in the breakaway republics of Croatia, Macedonia, and Bosnia and Herzegovina. However, fighting between Serbians and other ethnic groups in the region continues unabated.

Turmoil in Transcaucasia: Chechnya

Perspective

1817–1864	*Russians consolidate control of Chechnya during the Caucasian Wars.*
1922	*Chechen Autonomous Oblast is formed.*
1934	**January 15.** *Chechnya and Ingushetia are merged.*
1944	*Chechens are deported by Stalin.*
1956	*Chechens are allowed to return to their homeland.*
1991	**August.** *Dudayev overthrows Chechnya's communist government and declares its independence.* **November 10.** *Russian troops sent to Chechnya are forced to withdraw.*
1992	**June 4.** *Russia approves split between Chechnya and Ingushetia.*
1993	**April 17.** *Dudayev imposes presidential rule.*
1994	**September 1.** *Fighting breaks out between Chechen factions.* **December 11.** *Russians invade Chechnya.*
1995	**February 8.** *Russians capture the Chechen capital.* **June 14.** *Chechen terrorists raid a Russian village and seize 300 hostages.*

For almost 300 years the Chechens have longed for independence from their powerful Russian neighbors to the north. In the aftermath of an abortive coup against Soviet president Gorbachev in 1991 by hard-line communists, the Chechen communist government was overthrown by the ambitious Dzhakhar Dudayev. Dudayev promptly declared the independence of the Chechen republic, and for three years the tiny nation was effectively independent until factional fighting prompted a Russian invasion in 1994. It is a testament to the determination of the Chechens that Russia has been unable to defeat this tiny nation, which is about the size of the U.S. state of Connecticut.

Issues and Events

Russia dispatched troops to Chechnya soon after the republic declared its independence in 1991, but they were immediately surrounded by armed Chechens and forced to retreat the following day. Russia, preoccupied with the breakup of the Soviet Union and the outbreak of ethnic conflicts throughout the region, made no further attempts to enforce its rule on Chechnya. In 1992 the Russian parliament approved a formal division of the Ingush and Chechen territories into two republics, because the Ingush people had indicated their desire to remain within the Russian Federation. Russia imposed an embargo against Chechnya in 1991, and the government soon lacked funds to pay teachers, government workers, doctors, and others. By 1993 resentment about Dudayev's government began to erupt into massive demonstrations. Dudayev, a former commander of the Soviet air force, was unwilling to tolerate dissent. He responded by disbanding the legislature and imposing presidential rule. Soon there were reports of hundreds of deaths resulting from sporadic fighting between the Dudayev government and opposition forces. By September the unrest had escalated to full-scale warfare, with both sides employing tanks, aircraft, and heavy artillery.

On December 11, 1994 Russia invaded Chechnya to restore Russian control of the area, an act which was condemned by over three-quarters of the Russian population. After four months of heavy fighting which included massive aerial bombardment of the Chechen capital, the Russians succeeded in capturing all of the main Chechen cities. Although the Russians have established a puppet government, Dudayev and his supporters continue to launch attacks against the Russians from virtually impenetrable strongholds in the imposing Caucasus Mountains. The Chechens vow that they will continue the battle until they are free, and Russians concede that the fighting could go on for years. Increasing terrorist attacks against Russian civilians are expected. In June 1995 Chechens raided a Russian village and captured 300 hostages. Although the hostages were released one week later, the event generated fear throughout Russia.

So far about 25,000 Chechens have been killed, most by the aerial bombardment. Russian troops are accused of massacring entire villages that are suspected of harboring rebels. About one-third of the population has been displaced and there is widespread suffering. About 1,000 Russian soldiers have died in this conflict, the first war to be televised to the Russian people. Opposition to Russian involvement in the conflict continues to mount as people are confronted with images of death and destruction.

Background

Tensions have run high between the Russians and the Chechens ever since the bloody Caucasian Wars of the 1800s. Although the Russians were victorious, the Chechens never accepted the imposition of Russian rule. Their hatred of the Russians was reinforced after Stalin deported the Chechens from their homeland in 1944, resulting in the deaths of more than one-third of the population. The Chechens were not allowed to return to their land until 1956.

The Chechens' language, culture, and religion are all distinct from those of Russia, and most Chechens are fiercely nationalistic. Many Russians are fearful of the Chechens because they have a reputation for ruthlessness, and also because some Chechens are involved in organized criminal activities throughout Russia. Although the region has large oil reserves, most of the nation's 1.2 million people are relatively poor and live quiet lives in rural areas.

Turmoil in Transcaucasia : Armenia and Azerbaijan

Perspective

1921	July. *Nagorno-Karabakh region is awarded to Azerbaijan.*
1987	October. *Street protests erupt in Nagorno-Karabakh.*
1988	February 20. *Nagorno-Karabakh requests transfer to Armenian republic.*
1989	January 8. *Nagorno-Karabakh is placed under direct Soviet rule.* September. *Azerbaijan blockades Armenia.* November 28. *Nagorno-Karabakh is returned to Azerbaijan.* December 1. *Armenia unilaterally annexes Nagorno-Karabakh.*
1990	January 16. *Renewed violence prompts Soviet invasion.*
1991	December 25. *Armenia and Azerbaijan gain independence.*
1992	May 9. *Armenia secures Nagorno-Karabakh.*
1994	May 12. *Cease-fire agreement is reached.*

Throughout history the Armenian people have endured hardship and foreign rule. Some 3.5 million Armenians, out of a total population of 5.5 million, now reside in the independent republic of Armenia. Another one-half million reside in the Nagorno-Karabakh region of neighboring Azerbaijan. Conflict over this region has resulted in a prolonged war between Armenia, which is Christian, and Azerbaijan, which is Islamic.

Issues and Events

In October 1987, an Azerbaijani ruling banning Armenian history in the schools of Nagorno-Karabakh touched off massive demonstrations by Soviet Armenians. In February, the territory requested an administrative transfer to Armenia, but this move was quickly vetoed by the Soviet government. Tensions continued to mount between the two groups and finally exploded in February 1988 when Azerbaijanis killed thirty-two Armenians in Sumgait.

Soviet efforts to end the violence were unsuccessful. In January 1989 the Soviet government placed Nagorno-Karabakh under direct rule, a move which angered both the Armenians and Azerbaijanis.

The enclave was returned to Azerbaijan in November, and Armenia showed its outrage by unilaterally annexing the territory a few days later. Enraged Azerbaijanis responded with renewed attacks. A Soviet invasion did little to end the violence, and the Soviet troops withdrew shortly after Armenia and Azerbaijan gained their independence in 1991.

In 1992 there was a growing threat of foreign intervention after Armenians gained military control over all of Nagorno-Karabakh and opened up a corridor from the enclave to Armenia through undisputed Azerbaijani territory. During 1993, ethnic Armenians from Nagorno-Karabakh with backing from Armenia scored several military victories and occupied twenty percent of Azerbaijan. The Armenian victory prompted Turkey to come to the defense of the Azerbaijanis, who are also Turks, but Russia announced that if Turkey entered the war the Commonwealth of Independent States would fight on behalf of Armenia. Turkey quickly backed down, but the prospect of an expanded war is ever present.

A cease-fire agreement between Azerbaijan and the Armenians was signed in May 1995 but prospects for a negotiated settlement remain dim. Azerbaijan is outraged by the continuing Armenian occupation of its lands, and insists that Nagorno-Karabakh's sovereignty should be determined by mediation between Armenia and Azerbaijan. Armenia has renounced its claim to Nagorno-Karabakh, but has insisted that the people of the enclave should have the right to determine their own future. The Armenians of Nagorno-Karabakh continue to restate their goal of unification with Armenia. Another major concern is the status of more than 500,000 refugees who have been displaced by the war.

Background

The region which now encompasses Armenia and Azerbaijan emerged as a separate country in the first millennium B.C. It reached its greatest extent in the first century B.C. when it encompassed parts of present-day Turkey, Syria, Iraq, Iran, and the Caucasus region. In A.D. 301 Armenia became the first country to declare Christianity as its official state religion. After the late 300s, the region was successively conquered and divided by the Romans, Persians, Arabs, Mongols, and Turks. In 1828 the Russian Empire conquered the northern part of Armenia, leaving the southern part in Turkish possession. At the same time, the region known as Azerbaijan was formally divided between Russia and Persia (now Iran). In 1915 the Turks began a systematic slaughter of Armenians in Turkish territory that resulted in one million deaths and mass emigration to Russian Armenia. After the Russian Revolution, Armenia formally became part of the Soviet Union, along with the Turkish republic of Azerbaijan.

The Armenian-dominated oblast of Nagorno-Karabakh was awarded to Azerbaijan in 1921 because existing transportation and other economic factors linked the territory to Azerbaijan rather than Armenia. Although the Soviets believed that nationalism would eventually disappear under Communist rule, the enmity between the Armenians, Turks and Azerbaijanis continues.

Turmoil in Transcaucasia: Georgia

Perspective

1989	**July 14.** *Fighting between Georgians and Abkhazians prompts a state of emergency.*
1990	**September 20.** *South Ossetia announces its intent to secede from Georgia.* **December 10.** *Georgia abolishes South Ossetia.*
1991	**April 9.** *Georgia declares its independence from the Soviet Union.*
1992	**January 6.** *President Zviad Gamsakhurdia ousted by a military coup.* **February 6.** *Tensions in Abkhazia escalate under military rule.* **October 11.** *Eduard Shevardnadze elected President.*
1993	**September.** *Most of Abkhazia is overrun by Abkhazian rebels.*
1994	**February 3.** *Georgia and Russia sign an accord.* **March 1.** *Georgia agrees to join the Commonwealth of Independent States (CIS).* **June 24.** *Russian peacekeeping forces arrive in Abkhazia.*

Georgia's independence from the former Soviet Union has proved short-lived. Political instability and a series of ethnic rebellions ultimately forced Georgia to sign several accords with Russia that limit Georgian sovereignty. In return, Russia has agreed to back the Georgian government with its military might and end the fighting which has claimed tens of thousands of lives.

Issues and Events

Georgia's recent troubles began in the southern territory of South Ossetia. In late 1990 the Ossetians announced their intention to secede from Georgia and join with the Russian territory of North Ossetia. Ongoing strikes and demonstrations prompted the Georgian government to abolish the territory in 1990. When the Soviet government tried to intervene in 1991, Georgia imposed a blockade against South Ossetia and ultimately declared its independence from the Soviet Union. Amidst the chaos in Georgia following the breakup of the Soviet Union and a subsequent military coup, the war between South Ossetia and Georgia quickly escalated. Talks between Georgia, Russia,

and the Ossetians in 1992 ended the mounting violence and resulted in the establishment of a joint Russian-Georgian peacekeeping force operating under United Nations auspices.

The Abkhazians were agitating for independence from Georgia and recognition as a republic within the Soviet Union as early as 1978. When Mikhail Gorbachev came to power in the Soviet Union and glasnost took effect, Abkhazia was one of the first areas in which nationalist demonstrations took place. Fighting between Georgia and Abkhazia began in 1989 and continued to escalate despite numerous cease-fire attempts.

Abkhazia, which is a popular Black Sea tourist destination, has received arms and other support from Russia. Rebels succeeded in driving Georgian forces from the territory in late 1993. President Eduard Shevardnadze barely escaped when the Georgian stronghold of Sukhumi fell to the Abkhazis in a humiliating defeat. This loss led to a rebellion by forces loyal to former President Zviad Gamsakhurdia. Shevardnadze asked the United States and the United Nations for military intervention but was rebuffed.

Faced with the many challenges to his rule, Shevardnadze was forced to turn to Russia for help. Georgia joined the CIS and signed a series of agreements that gave Moscow significant influence over Georgian military and economic affairs. In June 1994, Russia ordered thousands of troops into Abkhazia to stop the growing bloodshed, and subsequently began establishing military bases throughout Georgia. Ties with Russia continue to strengthen, much to the disdain of many Georgians whose hopes for a truly independent Georgia have been shattered.

Background

Georgia was incorporated into the Soviet Union in 1921, but only after several years of violent resistance. The Georgians argue that Abkhazia and South Ossetia are truly part of Georgia and that the territories were created by the Soviet Union to divide Georgia and diminish its importance. Both South Ossetia and Abkhazia are run by conservative governments and remain committed to communism despite the breakup of the Soviet Union. The Georgians gained independence in 1991 and were fiercely determined to preserve their territorial integrity. Georgia was one of the last former Soviet republics to join the Commonwealth of Independent States.

Russia's interest in Georgia dates back centuries. Traditionally the Russians have been wary of their southern borders and have been suspicious of the many ethnic peoples living there. By exerting influence over Georgia, Russia maintains its links and controls in the region. Georgia also serves to buffer Russia from Turkey, an important factor during the Cold War. Now, Georgia helps buffer Russia from Iran and its potential for destabilization.

Ukraine: Crisis in Crimea

Perspective

1783	*Russia annexes Crimea.*
1944	*Tatars are exiled.*
1954	*Soviets award Crimea to Ukraine.*
1989	*Tatars are allowed to return to Crimea.*
1991	**December 21.** *Soviet Union is dissolved; Ukraine gains independence.*
1992	**May 5.** *Crimea declares its independence from Ukraine.*
1993	**July 9.** *Russian parliament lays claim to the Crimean port city of Sevastopol.*
1994	**March 27.** *Crimean referendum shows strong support for Crimean autonomy.* **August 23.** *Sevastopol declares itself a Russian city.*
1995	**March 17.** *Ukraine annuls Crimean constitution and asserts its claim to Sevastopol.* **April 1.** *Ukraine assumes direct control over the Crimean government.* **June 25.** *Tatar rioting spreads to six towns.*

With its mild climate and scenic location on the Black Sea, the Crimean Peninsula was the premier resort area of the former Soviet Union. Since the demise of the USSR, sovereignty of the region has been contested among Russia, Ukraine, and the indigenous Tatars.

Issues and Events

Russia's claims to Crimea date back to 1783 when it originally annexed the region. Although the area was awarded to Ukraine in 1954, most Crimeans are Russian nationals and identify with Russia. When Ukraine proclaimed its independence from the Soviet Union in 1991, Crimean leadership quickly began working for reunification with Russia.

Ukraine tried to placate Crimea by granting it a certain amount of political autonomy, but Crimean leadership declared its independence from Ukraine in May 1992. Later in the month the Russian parliament further complicated the situation by voting to repeal the 1954 transfer of Crimea to Ukraine. Crimea's main port city, Sevastopol, declared itself to be part of Russia in 1994.

In 1995 the Ukrainian president asserted his authority by putting the Crimean local government under his direct control until it recognizes Ukrainian sovereignty. If this measure fails, Ukraine has threatened to disband the parliament completely.

Crimea is of special strategic importance to both Russia and Ukraine in part because the naval base at the city of Sevastopol is the headquarters of the Black Sea fleet of the former Soviet Union, the status of which is yet to be determined. Both nations lay claim to the entire fleet, and efforts to reach a permanent settlement have been unsuccessful.

So far there has been little inducement for Crimeans to want to remain under Ukrainian sovereignty. Even Crimeans of Ukrainian descent speak Russian rather than Ukrainian. Another problem is that the economy of Ukraine is in much worse shape than Russia. Also, it seems likely that Russia will ultimately obtain control of most of the Black Sea Fleet.

None of this matters to Ukraine's Tatars, who were expelled from their homeland in 1954 and barred from returning until 1989. Today many Tatars have migrated back to Crimea, where many are living in dire poverty in shantytowns. These conditions led to a major Tatar demonstration in June 1995 which resulted in two deaths. The Tatars have demanded their own state, special autonomy, a ban on non-Tatar immigration, and restitution for property that was seized from them.

Although the future status of the Crimean Peninsula inflames the passions of many, so far there has been little violence. Relations between Ukraine and Russia continued to thaw throughout 1994 and 1995 as both nations realized the extent to which they depend on each other. Russia is dependent on Ukraine, the former "breadbasket" of the Soviet Union, for food and other agricultural products. In turn, Ukraine needs Russian fuel. Both nations rely on the good will of the other as they implement the terms of an agreement regarding the disposal of Ukrainian nuclear weapons. Hopefully peace will prevail as the future of Crimea unfolds.

Background

The histories of Ukraine and Russia have been intertwined since the founding of the Kievan Rus Dynasty around the year 808. After suffering from several invasions by various groups, Ukraine turned to Russia for protection in 1654 and became a Soviet Republic soon after the founding of the USSR. Agricultural collectivization imposed by the Soviets resulted in mass starvation after most of the farmers were killed. The country gained independence in 1991 at the time of the breakup of the Soviet Union.

Tatars arrived in the Crimea in the 1200s and established their own state in the 1400s. The area was soon overrun by the Turks and remained under Turkish rule until it was annexed by Russia in 1783. During the Crimean War in the 1850s, Russia fought to retain control of the peninsula when the Turks, British, and French tried to overtake it.

Crimea has historical significance because it is a major crossroad between Europe and Asia. The peninsula has historically been home to Bulgarians, Greeks, Armenians, Germans, Italians, and many other peoples. Today most of the inhabitants are of either Russian or Ukrainian descent.

Russia: Struggling with Democracy

Perspective

800s	*Russian empire begins with the emergence of the state of Kiev.*
1800s	*Pre-Communist military expansionism ends.*
1917	*Bolshevik Revolution brings Communists to power.*
1922	*Union of Soviet Socialist Republics is formed.*
1985	**March 11.** *Mikhail Gorbachev is appointed general secretary of the Communist party.*
1988	**February 28.** *Armenians and Azerbaijanis clash, resulting in thirty-two deaths.* **November 16.** *Estonians enact "Home Rule" legislation.*
1990	**March 11.** *Lithuania votes to secede from the Soviet Union.*
1991	**June 13.** *Boris Yeltsin is elected president of Russia.* **August 19.** *Communist hard-liners launch an abortive coup against Gorbachev.* **December 8.** *Russia, Belarus, and Ukraine initiate the Commonwealth of Independent States.* **December 25.** *Gorbachev resigns.* **December 26.** *The Soviet congress acknowledges the dissolution of the Soviet Union.*
1992	**February 23.** *Anti-Yeltsin protesters clash with police.* **March 31.** *Russian Federation Treaty is signed by most of Russia's republics.*
1993	**April 25.** *Referendum gives Yeltsin a mandate for continued rule.* **October 2.** *Hard-line parliamentary deputies stage an unsuccessful armed revolt against Yeltsin.* **December 12.** *Russian voters approve new constitution backed by Yeltsin, while electing many hard-liners to parliament.*
1994	**February 14.** *Russia and Tatarstan reach an autonomy agreement.* **December 11.** *Russia invades Chechnya.*

While a nervous world looks on, Russia has begun the delicate process of emerging from the tumultuous post-Soviet years and laying the foundations for permanent democracy. President Boris Yeltsin continues to face down challenges to his rule from hard-line former communists on the right and disenchanted reformers on the left, while a new constitution has allowed a rough system of checks and balances within the government to develop. Western nations have actively supported Yeltsin, whom they see as Russia's best hope for the immediate future. Meanwhile, many problems continue. Agricultural and industrial production are down, inflation and unemployment levels are high by Russian standards, and an armed conflict in Chechnya threatens to drag on for years.

Issues and Events

As president of Russia, Boris Yeltsin replaced Mikhail Gorbachev as the leader of the largest portion of the former Soviet Union. Yeltsin wasted no time in implementing a rapid economic reform program to transform the nation from a centralized, communist economy to a free market, capitalist one. Hardship ensued in the form of massive inflation, crime, corruption, and political instability.

A dangerous power struggle between Yeltsin and the conservative Russian parliament quickly escalated. In March 1993 the legislature voted to curtail Yeltsin's powers, and he retaliated by invoking presidential rule and calling for a special referendum. Weeks later the Russian people voted in support of Yeltsin and his economic reform program, and also indicated that fresh parliamentary elections should be held. However, the parliament, dominated by communists appointed in the waning days of the Soviet Union, continued to block Yeltsin at every move.

The situation reached a breaking point in October 1993 when Vice President Aleksandr Rutskoi and Parliamentary Speaker Ruslan Khasbulatov led an armed rebellion from their headquarters in the Parliament building in Moscow. Yeltsin responded harshly, ordering loyal army troops to storm the building. The ensuing battles were broadcast around the world.

December elections resulted in the approval of a Yeltsin-backed constitution that restructures the Parliament with a new upper house called the Federal Assembly. However, the voters also elected many independents and extremists who promised to oppose the President at every turn. The most notorious of the new deputies was Vladimir Zhirinovsky, whose open racism and calls for a restoration of the Soviet Empire were viewed with alarm in the West. In January 1994, Yeltsin announced changes to his cabinet that included the departure of many economic reformers such as Yegor Gaidar in what was seen as an effort to mollify those hard hit by the economy's fitful shifts to capitalism.

In his continuing battle with rival politicians, Yeltsin has enlisted the support of Russia's ethnic-based republics by granting them greater autonomy. This new, looser relationship was defined in the Russian Federation Treaty, which was approved by 18 of Russia's 20 republics in March 1992. Tatarstan and Chechnya, the two republics that refused to sign the treaty, are both Islamic republics that possess rich oil resources. Tatarstan and Russia settled their differences and approved a treaty in 1994, but war broke out in the republic of Chechnya in the Caucasus region. With its myriad of ethnic groups, Russia is particularly fearful of any further collapse of its empire to independence movements. Nevertheless, Yeltsin was accused of mishandling the Chechnya rebellion when Russian troops were sent to the republic and inflicted devastating damage.

Although the threat of ethnic tensions in Russia should not be underestimated, the shaky economy presents even more peril. So far the economic reforms have brought mostly hardship to the Russian people. Huge and inefficient former state-owned industries continue to fire tens of thousands of people as they try to address the realities of the emerging free market economy.

During 1994 Russia began moving even more rapidly toward establishing a free market economy. Although the economy is still unstable, there are signs that the worst is over and economic recovery may not be too far away. Unemployment seemed to stabilize at about 3%, and inflation was down to about 13% by the end of the year. About one-third of Russia's large state enterprises had been privatized, and the nation maintained a $16 billion trade surplus. However, agriculture has lagged behind. Only about 6% of the agricultural land has been distributed to individuals, and Russia is still unable to produce enough food to meet its needs.

Because Yeltsin's political survival depends upon his ability to improve the economy, he has turned to the West for political and economic assistance. Many nations have provided aid, loans, and technical advice to help the Russians.

This support may not be enough to keep Yeltsin in power. The year 1996 could bring momentous change when the nation holds presidential elections. Should Yeltsin lose in his bid for the presidency, it will undoubtedly present new, complex problems for the nation as it attempts to reintegrate itself with the world political and economic community.

Background

The flowering of the Kievan state in the late 800s marked the beginnings of the first Russian nation. After Ghengis Khan destroyed Kiev in 1240, another Russian state centered around Moscow rose to prominence during the 1300s. By the time Ivan the Great came to power in 1462, the new Muscovy state eclipsed the former Kievan state in importance.

The steady expansion of the Russian Empire began in earnest under Ivan the Terrible in the late 1500s. By 1700 the empire stretched to the Arctic Ocean in the north and the Pacific Ocean in the east. During the end of the eighteenth century, Peter the Great sought to end Russia's isolation and backwardness by opening up relations with Russia's western European neighbors. Catherine the Great further expanded Russia's boundaries to include Crimea, Ukraine, and Belarus. By the mid-1800s, Russia's expansion was essentially complete.

Due to the vast distances involved and the lack of modern communications, the Russians' influence in much of their empire was minimal until the Bolshevik Revolution in 1917 brought the Communists to power. Under the leadership of Vladimir Lenin, the state seized all private property, which resulted in a bitter civil war that lasted until 1922, when the Union of Soviet Socialist Republics was formed.

Lenin advocated self-determination for all of the peoples of the old empire. After Lenin's death in 1924, Joseph Stalin put an end to this policy and extended the Soviet Union to its present size. Stalin's purges in the 1930s and 1940s resulted in the deaths or forced relocation of those whose loyalty was questioned. The Stalinist system did not tolerate dissent, and successive Soviet leaders ruled their regime with an iron fist until Gorbachev came to power in 1985.

Gorbachev inherited a stagnating society. Low productivity, chronic shortages, an obsolete industrial base, and a growing national debt were only a few of the many problems. When Gorbachev implemented reforms to revitalize the economy, he also loosened the bonds that held the Soviet Union together. Cautiously at first, people began to air their grievances and dissident groups began to spring up, each with its own agenda. The empire began to weaken under the strain of rising nationalism among the nation's one hundred or so different ethnic groups. Fighting erupted between neighboring republics of Armenia and Azerbaijan in 1988, resulting in hundreds of deaths, and the Soviet government was unable to help the two groups reach a negotiated settlement. Military force was ineffective in stopping recurrent violence in Uzbekistan, Azerbaijan, Georgia, Kyrgyzstan, Moldova, Lithuania, and Latvia. Led by the Baltic states of Estonia and Lithuania, other republics began to agitate for secession from the Soviet Union, and formed their own armies to repel what they considered to be the Soviet invaders.

When communist hard-liners launched a coup against Gorbachev in August 1991, they were soon defeated by a people's movement led by Russian president Boris Yeltsin. However, the nation was transformed by the chaos, and eleven of the fifteen Soviet republics quickly declared their independence from the Soviet Union. The Commonwealth of Independent States was formed in December, and Gorbachev was ultimately forced to accept the inevitable collapse of the Russian empire. As changes swept the country at a dizzying pace, Gorbachev was swept aside as well, replaced by Yeltsin.

Yugoslavia: The Killing Continues

Perspective

1918	**December 1.** *South Slavic countries unite to create the Kingdom of Serbs, Croats, and Slovenes.*
1929	*Conflict between the Serbs and Croats results in the failure of democracy.*
1945	**November.** *A Communist government is established under the leadership of Josip Tito.*
1980	**May.** *Tito's death renews fears of ethnic disputes.*
1987	*Slobodan Milosevic sparks Serbian nationalism.*
1990	**September 9.** *Police break up riots in Bosnia and Herzegovina.* **September 28.** *Kosovo loses its autonomy.* **October 1.** *Serbs in Croatia declare their autonomy following weeks of escalating violence.*
1991	**February 20.** *Army units are dispatched against rioters in Kosovo.* **March 16.** *Milosevic declares home rule for Serbia.* **June.** *Croatia and Slovenia declare their independence; fighting breaks out.* **December 19.** *Macedonia declares its independence.*
1992	**February 21.** *United Nations approves a peacekeeping force for Croatia.* **February 29.** *Bosnia and Herzegovina declares its independence, sparking fighting between Serbs and Bosnian Muslims.* **April 26.** *Yugoslavia proclaims a new federation consisting of Serbia and Montenegro only.*
1993	**May 6.** *U.N. places six "safe areas" under its protection.*
1994	**February 5.** *Mortar attack on Sarajevo market kills 68.* **March 1.** *Bosnian Croats and Muslims agree to unite their forces.* **April 10.** *North Atlantic Treaty Organization (NATO) launches the first of many air strikes against Bosnian Serbs.*
1995	**May 1.** *Croats invade a Serbian–occupied enclave within Croatia.*

The fragile union of republics known as Yugoslavia seemed hopelessly destroyed by World War II. Croatian fascists and Serbian terrorists brought about the deaths of thousands of their own countrymen and created a legacy of hostility that should have prevented the reemergence of the federation. After the war, Yugoslavia was reunited by force under the dictatorship of Josip Tito. Although the country prospered under his rule, the bitterness that many of the people felt for each other after the war was buried, but not forgotten. Reaching far into the next generation, this hatred resurfaced when economic problems and political changes in Eastern Europe created a climate for resurgent nationalism that ultimately tore the country apart and ignited Europe's bloodiest war since World War II.

Issues and Events

Serbian leader Slobodan Milosevic rose to national prominence by championing the cause of Serbs living in Kosovo, a region of Yugoslavia predominately inhabited by Albanians. The Albanians of Kosovo had long sought elevation of their province to republic status, on an equal basis with Serbia. The Serbs were unable to stop the unrest, and the government assumed direct control of Kosovo in 1989. Milosevic's inflammatory rhetoric aroused nationalist passions in Serbs throughout the country and alarmed all of Yugoslavia's other ethnic groups.

While the Albanians continued their fight in Kosovo, rioting also broke out between Muslims and Serbs in the republic of Bosnia and Herzegovina. Serbs living in Croatia declared their allegiance to Serbia, and Croats and Slovenes became increasingly restless.

The declarations of independence began in 1991. Serbia was the first to declare the supremacy of its laws over those of the federal government. Three months later, the republics of Croatia and Slovenia declared their independence from the central government, and the Serbian army moved in to support rebel Serbs in those areas. The fighting quickly subsided in Slovenia, but the conflict exploded in Croatia. In the next few months over 10,000 people, many of them civilians, were killed. The fighting escalated until early 1992, when the warring nations bowed to international pressure and allowed the United Nations to send in a peacekeeping force to monitor a cease-fire between the two groups.

The clash between the Serbs and Croats did not prevent tiny Macedonia from declaring its independence in December 1991, nor did it thwart the aspirations of the ethnically mixed republic of Bosnia and Herzegovina. After Bosnia and Herzegovina's declaration of independence on February 29, 1992, Serbians from Yugoslavia moved in to protect areas inhabited by Serbs, and fighting erupted among Muslims, Croats, and Serbs in the new nation. Although the United Nations tried to quell the rapidly escalating conflict by imposing an embargo, the Bosnian Serbs continued to receive arms and supplies from Serbs in Yugoslavia. Without similar outside support the Muslims were unable to defend themselves, and the Serbs began driving Muslims out of areas under their control, a tactic that came to be known as "ethnic cleansing."

In May 1993, the United Nations declared six cities to be "safe areas" in Bosnia in an attempt to protect besieged Muslim civilians. The measure was largely ineffective and Bosnian Serbs continued to launch attacks against these cities. In 1994 a mortar shell which killed 68 people in the Sarajevo "safe area" led to an ultimatum by the powerful North Atlantic Treaty Organization (NATO). Although the Serbs withdrew from Sarajevo, NATO soon launched an attack against Serbs who were attacking other safe areas. At first, Russia bitterly protested the attacks on the Serbs. But after a series of ceasefires negotiated by the Russians were violated by the Serbs, Russia changed its policy and began supporting air strikes.

Yugoslavian support for the Bosnian Serbs has also disappeared as a result of international economic sanctions imposed to stop the flow of Yugoslavian arms to their Serbian neighbors. Despite ongoing NATO air strikes and deteriorating relations with all of its former allies and suppliers, the Bosnian Serbs have managed to maintain an upper hand in the conflict and hold all of the territory they seized early in the war.

During 1995 the war heated up on another front when Croatia began to grow impatient about Serbian occupation of about 30% of their territory. Despite the presence of U.N. peacekeepers, the Croatians launched a successful attack and recaptured one Serbian enclave in May. The Serbian Croatians replied by shelling the Croatian capital city of Zagreb in an attempt to inflict as many civilian casualties as possible and prevent further incursions into their territory.

The war in Bosnia and Herzegovina has been a war against civilians. More than 200,000 people have been killed or declared missing since 1992 when the war began, including 10,000 in the city of Sarajevo. Millions have been left homeless. Fierce fighting continues despite ongoing negotiations that have resulted in more than 30 cease-fire agreements.

The Bosnian Serbs, who currently hold about two-thirds of Bosnia and Herzegovina, have stated that their goal is to reunite with Yugoslavia. The Bosnian Muslims refuse to recognize defeat, and vow to regain their lost territory and establish an independent federation with the Bosnian Croats. The Bosnian Croats also envision a federated nation, but also hope to establish some kind of loose federation with Croatia. The Croatian Serbs are seeking independence from Croatia and plan to establish their own country called Krajina.

Even if these conflicts could be resolved, the possibility of even more devastating wars in Macedonia or Kosovo that might involve Greece or Albania still exists. Muslims throughout the world are angered by the plight of the Bosnian Muslims. Radical nations such as Iran and Afghanistan are rumored to be supplying arms to the Bosnians, despite an international arms embargo against both the Muslims and the Serbs.

At present, the future is bleak and will remain so until the people of the region realize that they must inevitably put aside their hatred and learn to protect the rights of minorities in their midst.

Background

Most of the original inhabitants of Yugoslavia were displaced by Slavic people who immigrated in the seventh century A.D. Serbia was established as an independent kingdom in the thirteenth century, and in the next century it gained control of Montenegro. The Ottoman Turks conquered the Serbs in 1389, but the Serbs never ceased to rebel against Turkish oppression. In 1828 Turkey was forced to recognize Serbia as a self-governing nation, and to confer complete independence in 1878. In the mid-1800s a movement arose to advocate the creation of a new nation uniting Serbs, Croats, Slovenes, and other Slavic people in the region, despite vast cultural differences between the various groups. The Croats and Slovenes were predominately Roman Catholic, while the Serbs were Orthodox. Many of the Bosnians were Muslims as a result of years of Turkish rule. Each group had its own Slavic language and culture.

Despite these differences, the movement gained strength, and when a terrorist advocating a Slavic homeland assassinated an heir to the throne of the Austro-Hungarian empire, it served as the spark that led to World War I. After the war, the Kingdom of Serbs, Croats, and Slovenes became a reality. Between the two World Wars, relations between the Serbs and Croats deteriorated steadily. The Serbs dominated the union and advocated a strong central government, while the Croats and Slovenes favored a looser confederation. Unable to find a peaceful solution to the escalating conflict, the Yugoslavian king abolished the constitution, changed the country's name to Yugoslavia, and assumed dictatorial powers in 1929. Angry Croats responded by forming the Ustashe, a fascist separatist movement.

After Germany invaded Yugoslavia in 1941, the country was divided among Germany and its allies, except for Croatia, where the fascist Ustashe were rewarded with control over an independent Croatia. During the war, the Serbs, Jews, and Gypsies were viciously persecuted by both the Croats and the Germans. Meanwhile, another conflict was taking place in the occupied territories of Yugoslavia as two different resistance groups—the Chetniks and the Partisans—engaged in a power struggle. In all, over 1.5 million Yugoslavians died during the war, but perhaps the worst legacy was the hatred that was engendered between the various Yugoslavian people.

Enmity was put aside after the war when a new Communist government was established under the firm leadership of Josip Tito. The new Yugoslavia consisted of six republics—Serbia, Croatia, Slovenia, Bosnia and Herzegovina, Macedonia, and Montenegro. Over the years, the Yugoslavians resisted Soviet domination by practicing their own brand of communism and maintaining contacts with the West. Tito made many efforts to moderate Serbian dominance within the federation by giving each of the republics greater autonomy and establishing Kosovo and Vojvodina as self-governing provinces within Serbia. However, prosperous Croatia and Slovenia continued to protest that they were being exploited by the Serbs.

Northern Ireland: Building Peace

Perspective

1607	*British begin the occupation of Ireland.*
1801	*Irish union with Great Britain is proclaimed.*
1846	*Potato famine prompts increased unrest.*
1858	*Irish Republican Brotherhood is formed.*
1919	*Irish Republican Army (IRA) is formed; war of independence begins.*
1920	*Ireland is partitioned.*
1921	*Southern Ireland gains its independence.*
1968	*IRA begins heavy campaign of bombing British targets in Northern Ireland.*
1972	*Direct British rule is imposed on Northern Ireland.*
1993	**December 15.** *United Kingdom and Ireland sign the Downing Street Declaration.*
1994	**September.** *IRA announces a unilateral cease-fire.* **October 13.** *Loyalist militia join cease-fire.*
1995	**February 22.** *Framework document is signed.* **March 24.** *British troops end Belfast patrols.*

While most of Ireland is an independent state, the six counties of Northern Ireland remain part of the United Kingdom. Most Irish Catholics have never accepted the partition of their island into two parts to accommodate the interests of the Protestant descendants of the British. The Protestants, who are the majority in Northern Ireland, fear for their rights if Ireland were reunited, and remain adamant in their insistence that their region remain part of the United Kingdom. Radical groups from both sides have engaged in bloody violence and terrorism that have claimed nearly 3,200 lives since 1969. There was a glimmer of hope for an end to the conflict in 1994 when a cease-fire was implemented and both sides began working to build a lasting peace.

Issues and Events

The unrelenting conflict between the IRA and various Protestant loyalist groups escalated during the 1990s, while the number of British troops sent to the area increased to eleven thousand. Beginning in 1992, the IRA launched a bombing campaign in London and other areas of England that has targeted police stations, airports, rail stations, and London's theater and financial districts.

A major breakthrough occurred in late 1993 when, after years of negotiations, the United Kingdom and Ireland signed the Downing Street Declaration. This historic accord set out guidelines for beginning peace talks, including a provision that specifically banned groups that use violence from participating in the peace process. The IRA responded to the accord in September 1994 when it declared a unilateral cease-fire. At first the announcement was greeted with skepticism, but after several weeks without a major violation the loyalist militia groups that oppose the IRA also agreed to join the cease-fire.

The peace process deepened when another pact was signed by the United Kingdom and Ireland in 1995 which represented a basis for future discussions. This framework document called for the re-establishment of an elected legislature, the renunciation of Irish claims on Northern Ireland, the right for the people of Northern Ireland to determine their own future, and the drafting of a bill of rights.

There are still many impediments to a lasting peace. The British demand that the heavily-armed IRA turn in its weapons, and the Irish insist that the British end their occupation of Northern Ireland. Loyalist Protestants, who are in the majority and support continuing British rule, have expressed outrage at what they consider to be a betrayal by the United Kingdom.

Although many years of negotiations will probably be needed before the fate of Northern Ireland is determined, the cease-fire has already brought increased prosperity. Perhaps this return to a normal way of life will entice these longtime enemies to fight as hard to establish peace as they have fought to perpetuate war.

Background

The first seeds of the present conflict were sown by the British in the early seventeenth century. In an attempt to consolidate their control over Ireland, they adopted a policy of seizing land from the Irish landowners and awarding it to English and Scottish settlers. The dispute gained religious overtones because the Irish were traditional Roman Catholics, while the British invaders were Protestant.

The Irish were never acquiescent under British rule. Growing unrest following the disastrous potato crop failure and the ensuing famine in 1846 led to the birth of Ireland's first terrorist organization, the Irish Republican Brotherhood, in 1858. When the Irish began agitating for independence, the Protestants in Northern Ireland demanded continued ties with Britain, and the country was subsequently partitioned. The Irish Republican Army was formed in 1919 to drive the British from the island. Today it is one of the world's most dangerous and effective guerrilla groups, and its tactics are closely studied by terrorist organizations throughout the world. It continues to demand the withdrawal of British troops and the reunification of Ireland. In recent years, the IRA's methods have also been adopted by various Protestant paramilitary groups.

European Union: Not So United

Perspective

1951	*European Coal and Steel Community (ECSC) is established.*
1957	*ECSC countries form the European Economic Community (EEC).*
1967	*EEC is renamed as the European Community (EC).*
1973	*Denmark, Ireland, and the United Kingdom are admitted to the EC.*
1981	*Greece joins the EC.*
1985	*Plans for economic union are announced.*
1986	*Spain and Portugal are admitted.*
1992	**February 7.** *Maastricht Treaty is signed.*
1993	**January 1.** *Economic union begins.*
1994	**January 1.** *The EC changes its name to the European Union (EU).*
1995	**January 1.** *Austria, Finland, and Sweden join the EU.* **March 26.** *Freedom of movement between seven European countries begins.*

In the years following World War II, many Western European nations envisioned a new Europe united both economically and politically—a kind of United States of Europe. In 1985 the member nations of the European Community (EC) agreed to a daring plan that called for the elimination of all barriers to free trade among the EC's 350 million people. When trade regulations were eased in 1993, the EC became the world's largest single market. Despite the difficulties in achieving economic cooperation, political unity has been even harder to achieve. Although some important actions have been taken, there are still many formidable obstacles to the creation of a united Europe.

Issues and Events

The steps toward European union envisioned in 1995 were carefully defined in the Maastrict Treaty, signed in 1992. The treaty called for the creation of laws and standards concerning a broad range of topics including industry, education, the environment, economics, health, and other topics. It also called for freedom of movement for all people within the union, coordinated foreign policy, the development of a single European currency, and efforts to equalize the standards of living in all member nations.

The road to European unity has not been smooth. On the eve of economic union in 1993, plans for creating a coordinated European monetary system collapsed because of an unexpected financial crisis. During the first year of economic union, Europe experienced one of its worst recessions in decades. Plans to coordinate European foreign policy were frustrated when member nations could not agree on a strategy for ending the devastating war in Yugoslavia. Free movement of people and goods within the EU was delayed until 1995, and even then only seven states agreed to eliminate their internal border controls, although others are expected to join in.

In 1995 EU member states began preparations for a 1996 conference which will further define the future of the EU. Some nations, like France and Germany, would like to accelerate the pace of European political union, while others like the United Kingdom would prefer to limit the role of the organization to economic cooperation. The Germans have proposed some nations should go ahead with full political union, leaving the others to join in when and if they are ready. The British would prefer to be able to pick and choose the programs in which they would like to participate.

Accession of new members is another contentious issue. Some nations want to see the organization expand to include all of the countries of Europe, while others want to limit the size of the organization and concentrate on establishing political union among the nations already in the EU. Voting laws within the union were established when there were only a few countries, and many kinds of decisions require unanimous consent of member nations. As membership expands, this policy becomes more and more impractical.

In the long run, the fate of European political unity will rest on the success of economic union and whether it brings greater prosperity to its member states.

Background

In 1951 six nations—Belgium, France, Italy, Luxembourg, the Netherlands, and West Germany—signed a treaty establishing the European Coal and Steel Community (ECSC), the success of which led to the formation of the European Economic Community (EEC) in 1957. The United Kingdom became a member in 1973, along with Ireland and Denmark. Greece was admitted in 1981, and Spain and Portugal followed in 1986. The newest members are Austria, Finland, and Sweden which joined in 1995.

The organization has changed its name twice—from European Economic Community (EEC) to European Community (EC) in 1967, and then to European Union (EU) in 1994.

Despite some disputes in which the member nations have indulged, the Common Market is generally considered to be a success. The effects on the economy of Western Europe have been positive.

The Middle East and North Africa

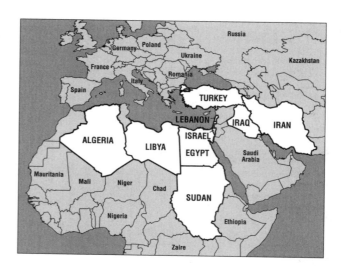

Describing the Middle East as a "powder keg" is a cliché that has never lost its accuracy since it was first used to describe this region in the nineteenth century. Wars have occurred sporadically between Israel and its Arab neighbors ever since Israel declared its independence in 1948. Factional fighting that began in 1975 in Lebanon between rival political groups rendered the country practically uninhabitable. In the 1980s as many as one million people were killed when Iran and Iraq engaged in one of the bloodiest wars in the region's history. In the early 1990s both Iraq and neighboring Kuwait were left in ruins after Iraq's unsuccessful attempt to incorporate Kuwait. The struggle between secular governments and Islamic fundamentalists has left hundreds dead in Algeria and Egypt and threatens the peace and stability throughout the region.

The area known as the Middle East generally includes the countries of the Arabian peninsula and Iraq, Iran, Israel, Jordan, Lebanon, and Syria, as well as the Arabic-speaking countries of Northern Africa. Islam is the majority religion of the area, with the exception of Israel. Arabic language and culture are dominant in all nations except Israel and Iran.

It is often difficult to separate religion from politics in the Middle East. In many countries there is little or no separation of church and state. The region is the birthplace of three of the world's great religions: Judaism, Christianity, and Islam, all of which have become intertwined with the political or cultural problems of the region. Islam, the religion of the overwhelming majority, is mainly composed of two sects: the majority Sunnis and the rapidly-growing Shiite minority. In recent years the differences between these two sects were sharply defined when Shiite fundamentalists in Iran overthrew the government in 1979 and threatened the economic and political stability of the entire region. The Shiites claimed that the Sunni-controlled governments of the region were too closely allied with Western nations and that outside contacts were corrupting Islam. The Sunnis regarded the Iranian Shiites as radicals who would destroy the economy and social order of the region if their brand of religion were allowed to spread. A third Muslim group, especially prominent in Syria and Lebanon, is the Druze. Although the Druze regard their religion as a branch of Islam, other Muslim sects view it as heretical. There is also considerable tension in Israel between the Orthodox and other branches of Judaism. In Lebanon, where Christians, Muslims, and others make their home, political and military groups have formed along religious lines and have seriously fragmented the nation.

The site of some of the world's most ancient civilizations, the Middle East was host to people of many different cultures. The great civilization of ancient Egypt developed on the banks of the Nile, and the area of the Tigris and Euphrates rivers saw the society of Mesopotamia flourish. Invaders and immigrants were diverse — the many peoples coming to the region included Assyrians, Hebrews, Phoenicians, Chaldeans, Medes, and Persians. Islam was founded in the seventh century A.D. and had a profound influence on the culture and politics of the people. As the Arabs expanded their empire, their religion and culture spread throughout the Middle East.

The Arab Empire came to an end about the tenth century and was followed some centuries later by the empire of the Ottoman Turks, who were also Muslim. The Ottoman Empire dominated the region until Turkey was defeated in World War I and control of many Middle Eastern lands passed to France and Britain. The British and French established political boundaries with little regard for the natural boundaries that had arisen from ethnicity or tribal allegiances.

Countries of the Middle East thus came to be demarcated by artificial borders created by treaties and agreements among the colonial powers. The land of the region had fostered a nomadic lifestyle, and the new foreign-imposed boundaries prevented the people from following their traditional way of life. Hardship often ensued.

When independence was finally achieved, the artificial boundaries remained, sometimes uniting diverse peoples into a single nation, as exemplified in Iraq, Lebanon, and Syria. These boundaries sometimes served to separate a single people by an international border, as in the case of the Kurds, who live in the area dividing Iran, Iraq, and Turkey. Dissension was often the result; many borders remain in dispute. Long-standing border disagreements led to both the Iran-Iraq War and the Iraqi invasion of Kuwait.

Attempts by the colonial powers to establish political systems capable of diffusing cultural differences were ineffective. Nowhere was this more apparent than in the effort to establish both Arab and Jewish states in the former British mandate of Palestine. Palestine, roughly corresponding to present-day Israel, was mandated to the British in 1920. Arab outcry about Jewish immigration into Palestine resulted in the division of Palestine into separate Arab and Jewish states. When Israel declared its independence, the surrounding Arab states declared war on Israel; in effect, they rejected the United Nations' vote for partition. The Arab state envisioned by the United Nations never materialized, and Palestinian Arabs became refugees. Major conflicts between Israel and the surrounding Arab states included a 1956 war focused on the Suez Canal, the Six-Day War of 1967, and a war in October 1973. Arab resentment about the establishment of Israel and the unresolved status of the stateless Palestinians has been a major source of continuing tension in the Middle East. Lebanon was nearly destroyed when thousands of immigrating Palestinians upset the delicate political and religious balance and vaulted the nation into war and chaos.

A major step toward regional peace and stability was taken when the Arabs and Israelis joined together for peace talks which began in 1991 and continue today. In 1993 the discussions bore fruit in the form of an agreement resulting in limited autonomy for the Palestinians living in Israeli-occupied territories. Since then there has been growing progress in Arab-Israeli relations, although the region is still subjected to sporadic terrorist attacks by those who oppose the peace process.

In most Arab countries, the response to years of foreign intervention has been fervent nationalism. A distaste for Western institutions, combined with a passionate appreciation for tradition, have hindered the spread of democracy in the Middle East. Some countries, such as Saudi Arabia, Bahrain, and Qatar, are ruled by traditional hereditary monarchies. Others are governed by authoritarian leaders, as is the case of Hussein in Iraq, Assad in Syria, and Qadhafi in Libya.

The majority of the countries in the region share enormous oil resources, while others, such as Jordan, have very little or none. Some nations, like Iran, Iraq, and Libya, have squandered their assets through military adventurism or economic isolation. Political stability in Saudi Arabia, the United Arab Emirates, and many other oil-rich states of the Persian Gulf has resulted in a remarkable level of affluence for the citizens of these countries, although declining oil prices have led to economic decline throughout the region. The income disparities that have developed between countries contribute to growing instability, and the prosperous sheikdoms of the Gulf have become tempting military targets for their poorer neighbors. Iraq's invasion of Kuwait was economic in origin.

Poverty and governmental corruption fueled Iran's Islamic revolution in 1979, an event which had a profound effect on politics throughout the entire region. Empowered by the Iranian example, Islamic fundamentalist movements began to gain strength in almost every corner of the region and are now considered the greatest threat to regional stability.

A return to traditional Islamic values has provided an outlet for the desperation of the poor and powerless. However, it has also spawned violence and chaos. Most of these movements are supported by Iran and Sudan, the two nations where fundamentalists are in control of the national governments. The United Nations has established a "no fly zone" in southern Iraq to protect Shiite fundamentalists from the Iraqi government. In Algeria, the government refused to honor the results of an election that would have brought fundamentalists to power. In Southern Lebanon, peace is threatened by Islamic fundamentalists bent on the destruction of Israel. In Egypt, fundamentalists have declared war against both tourists and the Egyptian government.

Israel: Creating a Palestinian Homeland

Perspective

1897	*World Zionist Organization is founded.*
1920	*British mandate for Palestine is established.*
1947	**November 29.** *United Nations divides Palestine into Jewish and Arab territories.*
1948	**May 14.** *Israel declares its independence.* **May 15.** *Arab armies invade Israel. Arabs flee Israel.*
1949	**January.** *Arab-Israeli War ends; Israel expands its territory.*
1964	**June.** *Palestine Liberation Organization (PLO) is founded.*
1967	**June.** *Israel captures all of Palestine during the Six-Day War.* **November.** *United Nations calls for Israel to withdraw from its occupied territories.*
1970	*PLO moves its base to Lebanon after it is expelled by Jordan.*
1973	**November 9.** *Egypt, Syria, and Jordan launch a third Arab-Israeli war.*
1974	*United Nations recognizes the right of self-determination for the Palestinian people.*
1978	*Israel invades Lebanon to stop Palestinian attacks against Israel.*
1982	**June.** *Israel invades Lebanon; one result is a massacre of Palestinian refugees.*
1987	**December.** *Palestinian uprising, or intifadah, begins.*
1988	**November.** *PLO declares Palestinian independence from Israel.*
1991	**November 1.** *Peace talks between Arab nations and Israel begin.*
1993	**September 13.** *Israel and PLO sign peace agreement in Washington, D.C.*
1994	**February 25.** *Israeli settler kills 48 Palestinians in Hebron mosque.* **May 4.** *PLO leader Yasser Arafat signs agreement with Israel giving Palestinians limited autonomy in the Gaza Strip and Jericho.* **September 30.** *Arab nations begin to lift trade embargo against Israel.*
	October 19. *Hamas bomb kills 23 people in Israel.* **October 26.** *Israel and Jordan sign a peace treaty.*
1995	**January 22.** *An Islamic Jihad bomb kills 19 Israelies.*

When Israeli Prime Minister Yitzhak Rabin and Palestinian Liberation Organization (PLO) leader Yasser Arafat signed an historic peace agreement in 1993 it signaled the beginning of a new era in Middle East politics. After decades of Israeli occupation, the Palestinians were granted limited autonomy in the Gaza Strip and a tiny section of the West Bank. Ironically this accord, which was designed to bring stability to the region, has resulted in an increase in violence as radical Palestinian factions maneuver to derail the peace process.

Issues and Events

After enduring three wars instigated by neighboring Arab nations, the Israelis had good reason to worry about their national security, and they believed it was in their interest to continue their occupation of Arab lands captured during these wars. Palestinian tensions in the occupied territories erupted in December 1987. Scores of Palestinians were killed, and many thousands wounded and arrested in the *intifadah*, or uprising. Increasingly regarded as the oppressor rather than the oppressed, Israelis found themselves under growing pressure by the international community to allow for the development of a Palestinian homeland, just as they were once supported in their own quest for a land of their own.

The Persian Gulf War of 1990-91 had a profound impact on the entire Middle East region. It was not long after the last shots were fired in the Gulf War that the United States began to call for negotiations between the Arabs and the Israelis as a part of an intensified effort to achieve regional peace and stability. The resulting peace talks, which began in 1991 have had dramatic results.

In September 1993 an agreement was signed in which the Israelis and the Palestinians formally recognized the existence of each other for the first time. In May 1994 they approved a plan which gave the Palestinians limited self-rule in the Gaza Strip and parts of the West Bank. According to the terms of the agreement, Israeli troops were required to withdraw from Jericho and the Gaza Strip. The Palestinians were given responsibility for many matters, such as taxation, education, health, and security. Numerous joint committees between the two sides were formed to monitor security and civilian matters affecting the region.

The entire problem of Palestinian political stability and growing factionalism is the greatest threat to the ongoing peace process. The Palestinian government is controlled by Yasser Arafat and the PLO, but the PLO is opposed by many Palestinians who continue to refuse to recognize Israel's right to exist. One powerful group called the Islamic Resistance Movement (Hamas) has been responsible for slaying more than 90 people since the signing of the peace accord between Israel and the PLO in 1993. The Hamas and other groups, like the Islamic Jihad, have launched violent campaigns of bombings and terrorist attacks against Israeli and Palestinian targets. Opposition to the PLO is also fueled by Arafat's dictatorial style, and also by growing reports of possible human rights violations committed by the new Palestinian security forces which have been deployed in the Gaza Strip. The ongoing power struggle will probably result in continuing violence until the Palestinians hold elections, but both the Israelis and the PLO refuse to allow elections as long as there is any chance that the PLO might not win.

There are still many other unresolved issues. The city of Jerusalem is claimed by both the Israelis and the Palestinians. While Israel has indicated that it might be willing to relinquish as much as 70% of the West Bank and all of the Golan Heights in exchange for peace, it has adamantly refused to surrender any part of Jerusalem.

Another important issue involves Jewish settlements and military presence in the West Bank. Israel continues to allow new construction in the West Bank even though it is in violation of the spirit of the peace talks. As long as Israeli citizens live in the West Bank, Israel insists that it has an obligation to provide them with military protection. This is in violation of the autonomy agreement, which requires Israeli troops to end their occupation of the West Bank. The West Bank has also become a breeding ground for violently anti-Arab Jewish radicals. One of these radicals was responsible for the massacre of 48 Arabs at a mosque in Hebron in February 1994.

The Palestinian economy is in very bad shape, and the territory is dependent on Israel for its economic survival. Most Palestinians in the region have to commute to Israel to find work. As a result of increased bombings and security problems during the last year, Palestinian workers were deprived of their livelihoods when they were barred from entering Israel for weeks at a time. Many Israelis believe that their security can be guaranteed only if Israel walls itself off from its Arab neighbors, so they have been turning to other sources of labor and increasing the Palestinian unemployment problem.

Perhaps the most formidable problem remaining is that of as many as 2.5 million Palestinian refugees who currently reside in other countries. These people, many of whom either fled or were forced to leave when Israel became a state, are demanding the right to return to their homes. At the very least, they expect compensation for property that was confiscated from them.

One major benefit of the peace process has been improved relations between Israel and neighboring Arab states. In 1994, Arab nations agreed to a partial lifting of the trade ban that it had long imposed against Israel. Also, Israel and Jordan agreed to put aside their historical enmity and sign a peace treaty.

For the Israelis, especially those living in the West Bank, it is a time of great uncertainty about the future. There is also growing fear throughout Israel about the increasing number of terrorist attacks within Israeli borders. For the Palestinians, the sober realities of every-day life temper any jubilation over self-rule. Poverty and joblessness are rampant in the overcrowded Palestinian territories. Hatred and prejudice on both sides continue to flare up into violence. Despite these obstacles Israel and its Arab neighbors claim that they are firmly committed to establishing a lasting peace in the region.

Background

Conflict between Jews and Arabs has erupted sporadically since the British received a League of Nations mandate for Palestine in 1920. The mandate, which included a provision for the creation of a Jewish homeland, marked the beginning of massive Jewish migration to the area. When they first began arriving in Palestine in 1920, they lived in peace with their Arab neighbors. However, as their numbers began to swell, they were met with increasing hostility by the Arabs, who had dwelled there for centuries and feared that they would be overrun by the newcomers.

In November 1947 the United Nations approved a plan that provided for the partition of Palestine into roughly equal Jewish and Arab states. When the British mandate over Palestine ended in 1948, the Israelis declared their independence, but the Arab state envisioned by the United Nations never came into being. Egypt, Lebanon, Syria, Jordan, and Iraq declared war on the new Jewish state of Israel, but Israel defeated the invaders. Thousands of Palestinian Arabs, fearing for their lives, left their homes only to find that they were not welcome to return. Arab nations boycotted all Israeli goods and refused to recognize Israel's right to exist.

Fighting broke out again in 1956, and again Israel made substantial territorial gains. Israel later traded this territory back to Egypt. The Six-Day War of 1967 was by far Israel's most spectacular victory against the Arabs. During the war, almost twenty thousand Arabs lost their lives, and by the time the war ended, Israel had occupied the former Egyptian Sinai Peninsula, the Gaza Strip, all of Jerusalem, Syria's Golan Heights, and the Jordanian-controlled West Bank of the Jordan River. In 1973, Egypt, Syria, and Jordan attacked Israel but they were driven back by 1974. The Camp David accords of 1979 (in which Israel and Egypt agreed to a peace treaty) provided for the return of the Sinai Peninsula to Egypt in 1982, but all of the other occupied territories remained under Israeli rule.

The Palestine Liberation Organization (PLO) was founded in 1964 to represent and unite the Palestinians, but it became notorious for its terrorist acts. Until 1988, when the Palestinians declared their independence from Israel, the PLO denied Israel's right to exist and refused to try to arrive at any negotiated settlement. First based in Jordan, the PLO was driven into Lebanon in 1970. As a result of PLO attacks against Israel, Lebanon has experienced several Israeli invasions in the last twenty years. Israel and Lebanon are separated by a United Nations-supervised security zone.

Iraq: The Embargo Continues

Perspective

1968	July 17. *Members of the Arab Baath Socialist Party (Baathists) overthrow the government.*
1979	July 16. *Saddam Hussein takes over.*
1980	September 22. *Iraq invades Iran.*
1983	February. *Iraq begins using chemical weapons against Iran.*
1987	January. *Seventy thousand people are killed when Iran attacks Basra.*
1988	July 18. *War with Iran ends.*
1990	August 2. *Iraq invades Kuwait.* August 6. *United Nations organizes economic embargo against Iraq.*
1991	January 16. *"Operation Desert Storm" begins as allied forces bomb Iraqi targets.* February 27. *Iraq surrenders.*
1992	August 27. *The U.N. establishes a "no-fly" zone in southern Iraq.*
1993	January 15. *Allies bomb Iraq.* June 27. *U.S. missiles target Baghdad.*
1994	November 10. *Iraq renounces all claims to Kuwait.*

Iraq under Saddam Hussein is a nation isolated from the rest of the world. After four years of U.N. sanctions, its economy is failing and its people are impoverished. With more than 10 percent of the world's oil resources, Iraq could have claimed its place as a leader of the Arab world without all of the violence and bloodshed that recent years have seen. The country has greater agricultural potential than most nations in the region. Tourism could bring in enormous wealth. Sadly, until Iraq experiences a change in government, it will be treated as a pariah by the rest of the world and its isolation will continue. Meanwhile, throughout the country people suffer from a U.N.-imposed economic embargo that has caused ever-increasing shortages of food, medicine, and fuel.

Issues and Events
Saddam Hussein had held the reins of power for little more than a year when he launched an attack against Iran and thus began the region's bloodiest war in modern times. By the war's end in 1988, more than one million people had been killed, and one-tenth of those killed were civilians.

During the war, Iraq received support from both Arab and Western nations eager to suppress Iran's fundamentalist Islamic revolution led by the Ayatollah Khomeini. Consequently, Iraq acquired the latest weapons from around the world, including technology for chemical and nuclear weapons.

On August 2, 1990, Iraq invaded neighboring Kuwait to gain its vast oil resources and to secure greater access to the sea. The United Nations condemned the invasion, and the United States immediately sent troops to the area. By the time hostilities began in January 1991, troops from more than a dozen countries had joined the Americans against the Iraqis.

The war brought profound hardship to the Iraqis. Perhaps as many as 100,000 died in the war. Unrelenting allied bombing made normal civilian life impossible. Public buildings, roads, bridges, and telecommunications facilities were destroyed. It is estimated that 72,000 Iraqis were left homeless.

After the war, Iraq was required to destroy its biological and chemical weapons, allow U.N. inspections of its nuclear program, compensate Kuwait for financial losses incurred during the invasion, renounce terrorism, and give up its territorial claims to Kuwait. Iraq's failure to comply with these terms of surrender resulted in the continuation of severe economic sanctions that prohibit Iraq from selling its oil and importing vital supplies.

The severity of the embargo and sporadic Allied military actions have gradually coaxed Iraq to comply with the U.N.'s demands. By 1994, much of Iraq's chemical and biological weapons stockpiles had been destroyed and the nation began cooperating with nuclear inspectors. Later in the year, Saddam's growing desperation was evident when he gave up all claims to Kuwait's territory. However, world leaders, wary of Saddam's intentions and mindful of his violent past, seem unwilling to ease the economic stranglehold anytime soon.

Background
In Iraq lies the birthplace of civilization. The ancient Sumerians, who inhabited the region known as Mesopotamia, were the first people in the world to develop written language, agriculture, and irrigation.

Following WW I, the League of Nations took Iraq from Turkey and placed it under British rule. Oil was discovered in 1923, and the country gained its independence in 1932. Political stability has been elusive in Iraq, which began experiencing military coups just four years later. Most of the governments were pro-Western until 1958, when General Abdul Karim Qasim created an Arab nationalist state. In 1963, members of the Arab Baath Socialist Party killed Qasim. The Baathists were ousted later in the year, but regained control in 1968, and Saddam Hussein took over the government in 1979.

Saddam quickly established a ruthless regime, and reportedly used napalm and other weapons of war against dissidents. A powerful secret police was established, and purges were commonplace. Kurds in the north and Shiite Muslims in the south were frequent targets. Despite his renowned brutality, Saddam Hussein enjoys the support of many Iraqis for promoting literacy campaigns; establishing compulsory education for all children; building schools, hospitals, and housing; and eradicating financial corruption in government.

Iraq–Turkey:
Kurdish Uprising

Perspective

1826	*Kurds revolt against the Turks.*
1932	*Independence of Iraq leads to Kurdish uprising.*
1945	**December.** *An independent Kurdish state is created in Iran but it lasts only six months.*
1961	*Kurds begin armed revolt against the Iraqi government.*
1974	*Kurdistan Worker's Party (PKK) is formed in Turkey.*
1979	*Iran's Islamic revolution fails to bring autonomy to the Kurds.*
1989	**June.** *Iraq forcibly relocates 100,000 Kurds to southern Iraq.*
1991	**February 28.** *Iraqi Kurds launch a violent revolt in the aftermath of the Gulf War.*
1992	**May 19.** *Iraqi Kurds hold elections in United Nation's supervised "safe zone."*
1995	**March 20.** *Turkey invades Kurdish territory in Iraq.*

For thousands of years the Kurds have been waiting and fighting for a homeland they can call their own. Numbering 20 million, they are one of the largest ethnic groups without a homeland. Spread out in a region called Kurdistan that comprises parts of Iraq, Iran, Turkey, Syria, Armenia, and Azerbaijan, the once-nomadic Kurds have been pawns in a region that has seldom known peace.

Issues and Events

To quell Kurdish rebels, governments have indiscriminately killed hundreds of thousands of civilians and repeatedly subjected suspected insurgents to forced relocation, torture, and execution. In Iraq, it is believed that the government used poison gas against entire Kurdish villages.

Kurds became the focus of international attention in 1991 in the aftermath of the Gulf War. Encouraged by the United States to rebel against Saddam Hussein, the Iraqi Kurds launched a major rebellion. When their forces were defeated by Iraq, more than 1.5 million Kurds suffered unspeakable hardship when they were forced to flee to squalid mountainous refugee camps.

To lure the Kurds away from the camps and back to their homes, the Americans established a "no-fly zone" in northern Iraq and forbade any Iraqi flights over the region. The United Nations later took responsibility for monitoring the safe zone, and the Kurds seized the opportunity to elect their own government in 1992. Unfortunately for the Kurds, the U.N. has stated that it has no interest in helping the Kurds to establish their own independent state and that its presence in the area is temporary. The Kurds are safe from Iraqi reprisals, but factional fighting among Kurdish groups has perpetuated violence in the region. Iraqi Kurds have also been at odds with Turkish Kurds who use the Iraqi safe haven as a base for organizing attacks against Turkey.

Although the Kurds in Iraq have received more publicity, it is the Kurds of Turkey who have waged the fiercest war for independence in recent times. Living in the southeast provinces of the country, Turkey's 10 million Kurds are divided into multiple factions. The most notorious is the Kurdistan Workers' Party (PKK), which has been at war with the Turkish government for more than a decade. The PKK is blamed for numerous bombings, and has also been linked to killings not just of government forces, but also of teachers, politicians, journalists, and Kurdish civilians who do not share their political views. The PKK obtains its funding by smuggling heroin from Turkey to destinations in western Europe.

For its part, Turkey has waged a brutal war against the PKK. During the 1980s, Turkey engaged in a campaign to eradicate Kurdish culture and assimilate the people and has been accused of obliterating 1,500 villages. In 1994 and 1995, Turkish troops drove thousands of Kurdish civilians into northern Iraqi refugee camps. This most recent campaign culminated with the incursion of a 35,000-strong Turkish force into Iraqi Kurdistan. The Turks have refused to withdraw their troops until some kind of buffer zone is established to prevent the rebels from launching attacks from Iraq.

Iraq has complained that the Turkish invasion is a violation of sovereignty and claims that Turkish troops are killing Iraqi civilians. Alleged human rights abuses, including illegal executions, disappearances, and torture of Kurds have caused the European Union to indefinitely block Turkish membership in their organization. However, Turkey is determined to rid the country of Kurdish rebels no matter what the cost. So far 14,000 people are believed to have died in the violence.

Background

The Kurds are descendants of semi-nomadic Aryan people who have inhabited the mountainous region known as Kurdistan for thousands of years. Located between the powerful Persians and the Turks, the Kurds never have had a nation of their own. Kurdish rebellions became common throughout the 1800s as the Kurds began agitating for independence. They have frequently reached autonomy agreements with various governments, but the promises made to the Kurds have never been met. The British and their allies promised the Kurds their own state in 1920, but never enforced its creation.

Although known for inter-tribal warfare, the Kurds' shared culture, territory, lifestyle and blood ties have also served to unite them through the centuries. While all Kurds speak Kurdish, there are many different dialects. Most Kurds adhere to moderate forms of Islam, and women are not secluded or veiled. Most people rely on farming and shepherding for their livelihood.

Iran: The Revolution Continues

Perspective

650	*Islam is introduced to Iran.*
1908	*Oil is discovered.*
1941	*Mohammad Reza Pahlavi becomes shah.*
1963	*Ruhollah Khomeini is exiled.*
1979	**January 6.** *Shah flees Iran.* **February 1.** *Khomeini takes charge of the government.* **November 4.** *Iranian students seize United States embassy and capture 66 hostages.*
1980	**September 22.** *War with Iraq begins.*
1988	**August 20.** *War with Iraq ends.*
1989	**June 3.** *Khomeini dies.* **July 28.** *Hashemi Rafsanjani is elected president.*
1992	**May 30.** *Rioting breaks out in the holy city of Mashhad.*
1994	**February 1.** *Assassination attempt is made on Rafsanjani in Tehran.* **June 20.** *Bomb kills 25 in Mashhad.*

The Islamic fundamentalist revolution that swept through Iran has been likened to a tidal wave that could engulf the Middle East and plunge the region into a new Dark Age. The death of the Ayatollah Khomeini in 1989 marked the beginning of a more moderate regime in Iran, but the burdens of high inflation and enormous foreign debt have weakened support for the Rafsanjani government. Other signs of discontent include a growing number of terrorist attacks and assassination attempts linked to rebellious factions. Riots have broken out in several cities, and fundamentalists have become more active in criticizing the government.

Despite these mounting problems, millions of the world's Shiite muslims are fighting to establish similar regimes in their own countries.

Issues and Events

In 1979 the Ayatollah Khomeini changed the course of international politics when he established a new, theocratic republic based on the tenets of Islam. An important goal of Khomeini's regime was to spread the new Islamic revolution throughout the world.

When war broke out between Iran and Iraq in 1980, moderate Arab nations feared an Iranian victory could strengthen the appeal of the fundamentalist movement. Consequently, Iraq enjoyed the support of the United States, the Soviet Union, and the oil-rich Arab nations, while Iran drifted deeper into economic and diplomatic isolation. Ending in 1988, the war was one of the worst in the world's history.

Since Khomeini's death in 1989, power has rested with President Hashemi Rafsanjani, a more moderate politician by Iranian standards who has had to contend with Iran's diplomatic isolation and its battered economy. The nation suffers from high unemployment and inflation. Most of the educated work force has left the country, and the gap between the rich and the poor continues to widen. In 1992 poverty was the spark that ignited the worst rioting in Iran since the 1979 revolution. More than 80 government buildings were destroyed in the city of Mashhad by squatters who were forced from their land. Two people were killed, and hundreds more were injured or arrested. In February 1994, riots broke out in Zahedan, and an attempt was made on Rafsanjani's life at a rally in Tehran. In June, Mashhad was once again the scene of violence when a bomb killed 25 and injured many more.

Although many in Iran have become disillusioned by the revolution, the fundamentalist movement started by Khomeini continues to spread throughout the Arab world. Iran has asserted its authority by supporting fundamentalist uprisings elsewhere, supplying arms to Bosnia, seizing several Persian Gulf islands, and maintaining a strong military presence in the region.

Sudan is under the control of a radical Islamic government; other countries that have sizable fundamentalist movements are Egypt, Tunisia, Algeria, Afghanistan, Jordan, and Turkey. For the growing number of poor people in these countries, Islamic fundamentalism provides an alternative to the social systems that have left them with little hope of improving their condition. While revolutionary zeal tends to burn out quickly, Iran is living testament to the damage it can cause in a very short time. Iran's economic recovery and reintegration into the international community will be a slow and painful process.

Background

The ancient Persian Empire came to an end in A.D. 650 when it was defeated by the Arab armies of Islam. Until the late twentieth century, various foreign powers or dynasties ruled Iran. Iranian rulers, who were called shahs, wielded absolute power in 1906, when the country adopted its first constitution. In 1908 the country discovered oil in the Persian Gulf area. The Pahlavi dynasty began in 1925 when Reza Khan, an army officer, seized the throne. In 1941 he was forced to abdicate, and his son, Mohammad Reza Pahlavi, became the last shah of Iran.

The shah initiated a massive modernization program in 1961, but development brought an influx of foreign workers with new, Western ideas. A nationalist uprising began to develop in 1977, and by January 1979, the situation was so serious that the shah fled the country, which opened the door for the Ayatollah Ruhollah Khomeini, a radical religious leader.

Lebanon: Middle East Battleground

Perspective

1943	November 22. *Lebanon gains independence from France.*
1975	April. *Fighting between Christians and Palestinian guerrillas erupts.*
1976	April. *Syria invades Lebanon.*
1978	March 15. *Israel invades Lebanon; United Nations peacekeeping forces are deployed.*
1982	June 6. *Israel invades Lebanon.*
1985	June 6. *Israeli troops withdraw, but establish a "security zone" in southern Lebanon.*
1986	April 7. *Israelis bomb Palestinian refugee camps.*
1989	October 22. *Taif Accord is reached.*
1990	December 3. *Private militia withdraw from Beirut.*
1991	April 29. *Most militia surrender arms to the Lebanese army.* July. *Palestine Liberation Organization is defeated.*
1993	July 25. *Israelis launch "Operation Accountability" to drive civilians from southern Lebanon.*
1994	August 4. *Israel apologizes after accidentally killing 10 civilians in the security zone.*

After serving for years as the central battleground in Lebanon's civil war, the city of Beirut has begun the long process of rebuilding, both physically and economically. With the advent of relative tranquility in northern Lebanon and continuing progress in peace talks between Israel and its Arab neighbors, it is perhaps true that the worst is over for war-torn Lebanon. However, inhabitants of southern Lebanon continue to suffer from an ongoing war that involves Israel, Lebanon, Syria, and Iran.

Issues and Events

Peace came to northern Lebanon with the implementation of the Taif peace accord, a result of negotiations sponsored by Saudi Arabia. After Lebanese Christians were defeated in an all-out attempt to drive Syria from Lebanon, the provisions of the accord went into effect and all private militia evacuated Beirut for the first time in the history of the war. By mid-1991 almost all of the militia had surrendered their arms, and in July the Palestine Liberation Organization was forced to surrender its twenty-year reign over southern Lebanon.

Not all of the militia were disarmed. The Iranian-backed Hizbullah, or Party of God, has continued to fight against Israel's occupation of a six-mile-wide "security zone" along the southern Lebanese border. Another group that has not surrendered its arms is the Southern Lebanon Army, which is allied with Israel and opposes the Syrian occupation of Lebanon. The Hizbullah have the implicit approval of both the Syrians and the Lebanese government, who hope that the Hizbullah's ongoing artillery attacks can eventually drive the Israelis out of Lebanon.

Israel's "Operation Accountability" in 1993 was one of the most violent confrontations in the security zone. This offensive amounted to a full-scale air and artillery attack against 70 impoverished villages, in an attempt to drive civilians out of the zone and into Beirut. The Israeli government hoped to capture the attention of the Lebanese government and force them to disarm the Hizbullah. The week-long raid accomplished little politically, but resulted in 130 civilian deaths, 500 injuries, and massive property destruction.

The Israeli government refuses to leave until Lebanon disarms the Hizbullah and makes an effort to defend its southern border. Israel also demands that the Lebanese grant immunity to their allies, the Southern Lebanon Army.

Lebanon will remain a battleground for the Middle East conflict until there is a peace agreement between Syria and Israel, which are at odds about the fate of the Israeli-occupied Golan Heights. Meanwhile, fighting in the security zone continues to escalate.

Background

The Lebanese government established by the French in 1943 provided for fixed representation for various religious groups according to the 1932 census. The Christian community, which comprised 51 percent of the population at that time, was provided with a dominant role in government. The situation was complicated by a huge influx of Palestinian refugees, who were Muslim. By the 1970s, the Palestinians had established their headquarters in Beirut and the Muslim population outnumbered the Christians. When Muslims were unable to gain a more dominant role commensurate with their numbers, sectarian tensions erupted into civil war in 1975.

By the 1980s, Lebanon had fractured into various groups, each with its own small army. What started as a struggle between Christians and Palestinians ultimately developed into dozens of conflicts among virtually every special interest group imaginable. Christians made war against other Christians, and Muslims against other Muslims. More than 150,000 were killed during the 15 years of fighting, and much of Beirut was destroyed.

The Syrians, who entered the war in 1976, control most of the country and are allied by treaty with the Lebanese government. About 1,000 Israeli troops have occupied the security zone since 1985 in response to Arab attacks against northern Israel. About 5,000 United Nations peacekeeping forces are also stationed in southern Lebanon.

Egypt: Fundamentalist Terrorism

Perspective

1922	**February 28.** *Britain abolishes protectorate and recognizes Egyptian independence.*
1923	*Constitutional monarchy established.*
1952	**July 23.** *King Farouk overthrown by military junta.*
1953	**June 18.** *Egypt declared a republic.*
1967	**June.** *Israel wins six-day war, occupies Gaza Strip and Sinai.*
1970	*Prime Minister Gamal Abdel Nasser dies, succeeded by Anwar el-Sadat.*
1973	**October 6.** *Egypt and Syria attack Israel.*
1976	*Sadat cancels friendship treaty with Soviet Union.*
1979	**March 26.** *Camp David peace accords between Egypt and Israel signed.*
1981	**October 6.** *Sadat assassinated by Muslim extremists; succeeded by Hosni Mubarak.*
1986	*Security police in Cairo mutiny.*
1992	**Spring.** *Upsurge begins in Islamic militant violence.*
1993	**February 26.** *Egyptian radicals are involved in the bombing of the World Trade Center in New York.*

S eeking to overthrow the secular Mubarak government, Islamic militants have waged a campaign of terrorism which has targeted both government officials and Egypt's $3 billion-a-year tourism industry. A handful of foreign visitors have been killed, and reports of bullet-riddled tour busses, boats and trains have received extensive coverage worldwide. The impact on both tourism and foreign investment has been devastating. In response, the government has executed dozens of suspected terrorists and jailed thousands more. Such harsh measures have sparked protests over human rights abuses and have further inflamed fundamentalist passions.

Issues and Events
Since 1992, more than 400 government officials, police, informants, Christians and innocent bystanders have been killed in attacks ranging from Cairo to the impoverished south where some villages have become armed camps.

The militants are rooted in Egypt's vast slums, where, despite economic reforms, the gap between the nation's rich and poor continues to grow.

Egypt's population, currently at 57 million, is expected to reach 65 million by the year 2000. Half of the people are illiterate, and unemployment is a serious problem. Corruption among government officials is widespread, with new scandals being reported daily. In these conditions, the militants have found many people sympathetic to their cause.

Made up of loosely collaborating groups of Islamic fundamentalists, the rebels resisted early efforts of accommodation by the government because their goal allows for little negotiation: the replacement of the secular government with a strict Islamic state. By targeting foreigners, they have crippled tourism, Egypt's main source of outside income. They hope this will cause the Mubarak government to turn to the military to restore order, which would undermine its democratic legitimacy.

Although the Islamic fundamentalists have drawn thousands to their cause, they do not enjoy the support of most Egyptians. Long-established moderate Islamic groups have shunned them. The terrorist attacks, which have injured scores of innocent civilians, have turned public opinion against the radicals. Many Egyptians fear the strict Islamic society the rebels advocate, with its rule by religious, rather than democratic, dictate. Among the fundamentalists' stated goals is the destruction of pagan shrines, which include ancient Egyptian monuments, such as the pyramids.

The Islamic Group, which has claimed responsibility for much of the violence, has links to four men convicted for the 1993 bombing of the World Trade Center in New York. The Islamic Jihad is another radical organization that advocates terrorism as a means of achieving political change. It calls Sheik Omar Abdel Rahman—who has also been charged with the New York bombing—its spiritual leader.

Background
With its diverse religions, democratic traditions, arts, and close Western ties, Egypt has been among the most liberal of Arab states. After engineering a 1952 coup, Nasser boosted nationalist pride by thumbing his nose at Egypt's colonial past. He began grand projects, such as the Aswan dam, and played the superpowers against each other by courting the Soviet Union. After the disastrous losses from the 1973 war with Israel, Anwar el-Sadat gradually shifted Egypt's allegiance to the West and signed the historic peace treaty with Israel in 1979. The 1980s saw Egypt receiving massive amounts of aid from the United States. However, neither the policies of Sadat nor those of his successor Mubarak could cope with a rapidly expanding population that is no longer self-sufficient in food production.

After Iran's Islamic revolution, radical Islam spread throughout the Arab world. Based on strict religious interpretations, the movement decries liberal Western influences and has found willing believers among the poor who have little to show as a consequence of the foreign aid.

Sudan: A Clash of Cultures

Perspective

1898	*British and Egyptian forces conquer Sudan and administer it as two territories.*
1946	*Northern and southern territories are united.*
1955	*Fighting breaks out between the north and south.*
1956	*Sudan gains independence.*
1962	*Fighting escalates to civil war.*
1969	*Military coup places Gaafar Nimeiry in power.*
1972	*Government and rebels sign Addis Ababa peace accord.*
1983	*Sharia (Islamic law) is imposed, causing renewed fighting.*
1985	**April 6.** *Military coup overthrows Nimeiry.*
1986	**April 11.** *Elections are held in the north only. Sadiq Mahdi becomes prime minister.*
1988	*About 250,000 die from famine.*
1989	**April 1.** *Operation Lifeline-Sudan prevents mass starvation.* **June 30.** *Military coup ousts Mahdi. Islamic fundamentalists take over.*
1992	**February.** *Government attacks rebel outposts.* **September 30.** *United Nations suspends food aid.*
1994	**March.** *Peace talks begin.*

Sudan is the largest country in Africa—too large, perhaps, to accommodate the diversity of its peoples. Differences in their religions, languages, and cultures have polarized the two groups and threaten to tear the nation apart. Nine years after the country was united in 1946, fighting erupted between the northern Islamic Arabs and the southern Christian and Animist blacks. The most recent round of violence began in 1983 when the Muslim-controlled government attempted to impose the *sharia*, a severe code of traditional Islamic law on the south, where most people do not practice Islam.

Issues and Events

The coup that overthrew the government of Sadiq Mahdi in June 1989 sparked hopes for an end to the six-year conflict that had claimed more than ten thousand lives. The military had overthrown Mahdi because of his inability to bring peace to Sudan. Six years later, there is even less hope than before. The ruling government is accused of torture and other human rights abuses.

The government began 1992 with a major offensive and succeeded in capturing most of the rebel bases in the south, but this has not brought peace. When the southerners are not fighting each other, they launch attacks on the government from the vast hinterlands which they still control. About four million people have been displaced by the fighting, and starvation has become a chronic problem. An estimated one million Sudanese have died as a result of the war and its effects on crop production and food distribution. Relief agencies and all other foreigners have been evicted from the war zone, so there has been little or no world media attention to the tragedy which is occurring in southern Sudan.

Increasingly isolated because of its close ties to Iran, the Sudanese government is under mounting international pressure to make peace with the rebels. Although Sudan has been accused of sponsoring and supporting international terrorism, there has been little hard evidence presented to support this claim.

Several rounds of government-initiated peace talks, which began in 1994, have been unproductive. The government continues to insist that Islamic law must prevail in the south, while the rebels demand the right to determine their own future and practice their own religions.

Background

In 1898, British and Egyptian forces conquered Sudan. The region was administered as two territories until 1946. In 1952 preparations began for Sudanese independence. The southern Sudanese feared domination by the northern Muslims and started a revolt that still continues. Nevertheless, Sudan attained its independence in 1956.

In 1957 Christian mission schools in the south were forced to close, and all foreign missionaries were expelled in 1964. The southern Sudanese refused to allow the north to impose their religion and culture upon them and responded with military resistance.

Colonel Gaafar Nimeiry seized control of the government in a military coup in 1969. In 1972 he signed the Addis Ababa pact with the southern Sudanese, granting them some autonomy and temporarily halting the civil war. Renewed fighting resulted in 1983 when Nimeiry imposed Islamic law—a controversial legal code which prescribes punishments such as flogging, amputations, and stoning, which is used throughout the Arab world.

Widespread famine, economic instability, and the ongoing war led to Nimeiry's downfall in a 1985 military coup. In 1986 Sudan held its first democratic election in eighteen years, but the south protested the *sharia* laws by refusing to participate.

Libya: The Enigmatic Qadhafi

Perspective

1951	*Libya gains its independence.*
1959	*Oil is discovered.*
1969	**September.** *Qadhafi leads a coup that overthrows the king.*
1973	*Libya nationalizes United States' oil interests.*
1979	*Qadhafi gives up public office.*
1981	**August.** *U.S. and Libyan air forces clash over Gulf of Sidra.*
1986	**January.** *U.S. freezes Libyan assets.* **April 5.** *West Berlin discotheque bombing is linked to Libya.* **April 15.** *U.S. bombs Libya.*
1989	**January 4.** *U.S. shoots down two Libyan military aircraft.*
1992	**January 21.** *United Nations demands that Libya extradite two suspected terrorists.* **March 31.** *U.N. imposes sanctions against Libya.*
1993	**December 1.** *U.N. toughens sanctions.*
1994	**November 30.** *U.N. extends sanctions.*

Colonel Mu'ammar al-Qadhafi, the charismatic and eccentric leader of Libya, is a favorite villain in the Western press. Relations between Libya and the West, notably the United States, have been especially bitter. The United States, and most of the other Western powers, have objected in particular to Qadhafi's support, financial and otherwise, of international terrorist organizations. He has been the chief supporter of the Palestine Liberation Organization (PLO), and his denunciations of Israel have been particularly virulent. He has also angered other African leaders by his territorial ambitions, notably in Chad and Sudan, which have had a disruptive influence on African political affairs. Qadhafi's power is a direct result of the petroleum revenues that have been at his disposal since the mid-1970s, when the Arab oil boycotts caused the world price of oil to escalate dramatically.

Issues and Events

Relations between the United States and Libya reached an all-time low on April 15, 1986, when the United States Air Force hit five military targets in Libya in retaliation for the bombing of a West Berlin discotheque frequented by United States military personnel. It is believed that over one hundred Libyans died during the bombings, including Qadhafi's adopted infant daughter.

Relations between the United States and Libya were again strained in late 1991 when the United States accused two Libyans of the 1988 bombing of Pan Am flight 103 over Lockerbie, Scotland, that killed 270 people. The French also demanded justice for presumed Libyan involvement in the downing of a French airliner in 1989. In early 1992 the United Nations passed a resolution calling for extradition of those suspected in the bombings. Libya refused, although it claimed that it was conducting its own investigation into the matter. In March the United Nations voted to impose limited sanctions against Libya. The sanctions included air traffic and arms sales embargoes, but did not include trade or oil embargoes. In late 1993, the United Nations reacted to Qadhafi's intransigence by toughening the sanctions to include a freezing of Libyan assets abroad. Although the continuing sanctions do not affect oil revenues, there have been signs that support for Qadhafi and his policies has begun to wane, including reports of an unsuccessful uprising by members of the armed forces in October 1993. The United States has called for severer penalties, including the imposition of an international oil embargo. Against this, Qadhafi maintains his preoccupation with international affairs and continues to support foreign terrorist groups.

Oil-rich Libya will undoubtedly remain an important force in the Arab world. Many Western countries see in Libya vast economic opportunities. Many poor African countries have received large sums of aid and therefore see Libya as a great benefactor, while others fear Qadhafi's territorial ambitions. Most Arab leaders regard Qadhafi with suspicion, despite his continual diplomatic overtures and professed dedication to all Arab people.

Background

Following Libya's independence from Italian colonial rule after World War II, the country was ruled by King Idris, beginning in 1951. King Idris was overthrown by an army force led by 27-year-old Lt. Mu'ammar al-Qadhafi, who then instituted massive economic and religious reforms. Qadhafi also launched a cultural revolution to free Libya from foreign influences. Although he resigned from public office in 1979, Qadhafi has continued to rule despite the lack of a formal title.

Diplomatic ties between the United States and Libya were severed in 1981 after several incidents linking Libya to international terrorist attacks. Qadhafi has unfailingly denied any involvement but he has been an outspoken advocate of Palestinian rights. He has been accused of helping train and shelter radical terrorists such as Abu Nidal's group, although he denounces acts of violence against innocent civilians. The United States has stated that Libya must end its support for terrorism before normal diplomatic ties can be reestablished.

Algeria: Battling Militant Islam

Perspective

1830	*French colonial rule in Algeria begins.*
1954	**November.** *National Liberation Front (NLF) is formed. War against France ensues.*
1962	**July 3.** *Algeria achieves independence under NLF leadership.*
1988	**October.** *Food shortages prompt widespread rioting.*
1989	**February.** *A new constitution allows for multiparty elections.*
1990	**June 13.** *The Islamic Salvation Front (ISF) wins local elections.*
1991	**December 26.** *ISF wins the first round of national elections.*
1992	**January 11.** *Military government seizes power.* **February.** *Riots break out; emergency rule is imposed.* **June 29.** *Algerian president is assassinated.*
1994	**December 24.** *Islamic terrorists hijack a French airliner.*
1995	**January 30.** *Car bomb kills 42 people.*

The 1970s were a time of peace and prosperity in oil-rich Algeria. Its secular, one-party socialist government served as a model for many other African nations. In 1990 this once-model government was swept away as democracy opened the door to the specter of Islamic fundamentalism not unlike that which transformed Iran.

Issues and Events

When a deteriorating economy forced the implementation of a more democratic constitution in 1989, the ruling National Liberation Front (NLF) was sure that it could win in the country's first free elections in 1990. Shock waves rippled through the Arab world when local elections were won by the newly-formed Islamic Salvation Front (ISF), a fundamentalist religious group.

The ISF promoted a return to traditional Islamic values and practices. It advocated a strictly limited role for women in the society, the segregation of men and women in public places, and the abolition of alcoholic beverages. Another important platform was the adoption of the *sharia*, or Islamic law, which imposes severe penalties for infractions, such as amputating the hands of thieves and stoning adulterers.

In 1991, the ISF scored a major victory in the elections, and was virtually assured of a majority in the national government, but the military took over and set up a military council to govern the country. Violence flared, and a state of emergency was imposed. All constitutional rights were suspended and thousands of people were arrested, including the ISF leadership. Public outrage ensued, and the head of the ruling council was assassinated in June 1992. Terrorism has become widespread—an estimated 3,700 people have been killed since January 1992.

Since 1992, rebels have mounted a terrorist campaign against intellectuals, feminist leaders, entertainers, politicians, journalists, and foreigners. In late 1994, terrorists hijacked a French airliner, and in 1995 car bombs inflicted horrifying damage. The government has responded with its own crusade of terror by jailing moderate ISF leaders and their families, handing out hundreds of death sentences, and allegedly using torture and unfair legal practices. The number of fatalities in the conflict is somewhere between 10,000 and 30,000.

Western diplomats urge restraint on both sides, but negotiations have been unproductive. Algeria's military rulers seem disinclined to give the ISF any role in future government. Because most of the moderate ISF leadership has been killed and imprisoned, new organizations have formed to take their place. These new groups, of which the Armed Islamic Group (GIA) is the most notorious, are far more radical and ruthless in their tactics.

It has been suggested that Algeria's military takeover was an overreaction to the outcome of the 1991 elections, because many voters who disapproved of the ISF's policies voted for them only because they gambled that the ISF had the best chance of defeating the NLF. Also, the ISF had no clear plan for improving the economy and would probably have been ousted from power in the next elections, had democratic institutions remained intact. Instead, the violence that has resulted threatens to explode into guerrilla war which could eventually spread to neighboring Tunisia, Morocco and all of northern Africa.

Background

Arabs brought Islam to Algeria in the eighth century. The people have remained devoutly Muslim ever since. The French began to establish colonies and exert control over the area in 1830. In 1954 the Algerians formed a group called the National Liberation Front (NLF), which waged war against the French. More than 500,000 people were killed before independence was achieved in 1962. The NLF established itself as the sole political party. Under its leadership, Algeria flourished in the 1970s when its vast oil resources commanded high prices on the world market. By the 1980s, oil prices fell, as did the Algerian economy. Food shortages prompted riots among the population, one-quarter of which was unemployed. Inefficient centralized planning for agriculture also took its toll on the Algerian economy. Once self-sufficient in food production, today Algeria must import most of its food. Ultimately the NLF was forced to abandon its socialist policies and allow for the participation of rival political parties.

South Asia

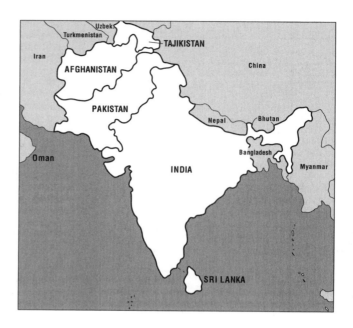

The major sources of conflict in South Asia are modern examples of ancient problems. In India, the Sikhs have been fighting for their own nation since Sikhism was founded in the fifteenth century. In Sri Lanka, the tribal wars between the majority Sinhalese and the minority Tamils can be traced as far back as the early centuries A.D., when the ancestors of the modern Tamils began migrating south from India. Afghanistan, strategically located between such great powers as Russia, Iran, and India, has historically been viewed as a buffer state by its powerful neighbors and fought over on that account. The invasion of Afghanistan by the Soviet Union in 1979 is only the modern manifestation of the traditional desire of Russia to extend its power to the south—with the goal of Russian access to the Indian Ocean.

Despite the cessation of aid from the United States and Russia, Afghanistan faces a continuing civil war among various factions of the fiercely independent guerrillas, known as *mujahidin.* The conflict is worsened by struggles between radical and moderate elements of Islam.

Religious and tribal antagonisms and rivalries continue to abound throughout South Asia. The seemingly irreconcilable differences between the Hindus and Muslims in India have cost the lives of millions of Indians in the twentieth century. Hindu-Muslim violence has also sporadically erupted into wars between India and Pakistan. Though brief, these fierce battles have claimed the lives of tens of thousands of people since the Hindu Indians and the Muslim Pakistanis gained independence in 1947.

Many minority ethnic groups in India have been agitating for independence since the founding of the nation in 1947. The Muslim people of Jammu and Kashmir held out for independence rather than union with Pakistan, but instead found themselves under Indian occupation. Sikhs have long sought their own homeland in the Punjab region and thousands have been killed in their struggle for independence. Violence has also flared in Assam, where Bodo tribesman demand their own land, and also in Nagaland, where the Naga people have rebelled against Indian rule.

Neighboring Pakistan is also racked with violence as a result of the partition of India in 1947. Many Indian Muslims moved to Pakistan at the time of India's independence, and this upset the ethnic balance in urban centers such as Karachi. Today Karachi is plagued by ethnic and religious strife that has made it one of the most dangerous cities in the world. The nation is also being torn by various radical factions of Islam.

To the south, Sri Lanka has been in the grips of an ethnic war between the nation's Tamil and Sinhalese populations. The conflict has also enraged Tamils living in India.

Political violence is common throughout the region, and many of India's leaders have met violent ends. Mahatma Gandhi, architect of Indian independence from Britain, was killed by a Hindu radical. Prime Minister Indira Gandhi was killed by Sikh separatists, and her son Rajiv was also assassinated, allegedly by Tamil terrorists.

India and Pakistan: Cold War on the Subcontinent

Perspective

1947	**August 15.** *India and Pakistan gain independence from Britain.* **October.** *War between India and Pakistan begins.*
1949	**January 1.** *War ends. United Nations mandates plebiscite.*
1965	**August.** *Armed Azad Kashmir troops invade India from Pakistan.*
1971	**December 3.** *War breaks out in Kashmir over Indian support for Bangladesh.*
1988	*Kashmiri dissidents begin an armed insurrection.*
1990	**February 11.** *India and Pakistan exchange gunfire.*
1991	**May.** *Indian troops kill 66 militants during one week of fighting.* **August.** *India and Pakistan exchange artillery fire.*
1992	**February 12.** *Pakistani troops shoot Azad Kashmiri dissidents.*
1993	**October 22.** *Twenty-nine people are killed following India's month-long siege of a Kashmiri mosque.*

Nestled high in the remote Himalayas, the Vale of Kashmir is world renowned for its legendary beauty. Part of the region known as Jammu and Kashmir, this picturesque and densely populated valley is the setting for a decades-old standoff between Pakistan and India that has produced three wars and threatens to provide the spark for nuclear war between the two regional powers.

Issues and Events

Relations between India and Pakistan were already strained when Kashmiri separatists in India began to wage a major terrorism campaign in 1988. The unceasing bombings, kidnappings, and strikes prompted the Indian government to send troops to the area in December 1989. Massive demonstrations ensued and Pakistan accused Indian troops of indiscriminate burnings, shootings, abductions, and torture against innocent Muslim Kashmiris. India accused Pakistan of arming and training Kashmiri rebels in camps on the Pakistani side of the border, known as Azad Kashmir. Pakistan denied training the rebels, but continued to champion their cause and provide them with arms.

Kashmiris on both sides of the border are divided on the future of the region. Some favor union with Pakistan while others want complete independence. The Pakistani government calls for India to allow the Kashmiris to decide their own future. India maintains that Jammu and Kashmir are integral parts of India. Several rounds of talks aimed at resolving the crisis have made little progress.

Tensions remain high and thousands are believed to be killed each year. In 1992 war was narrowly averted when Pakistani radicals tried to march across the border into India. They were stopped only after Pakistani troops opened fire on the group. In late 1993 violence erupted when Indian police laid siege to a mosque where Kashmiri rebels were believed to be hiding. Pakistanis were outraged at what they claimed to be sacrilege. Although these incidents were resolved without disaster, the threat of nuclear war looms large.

India first tested nuclear weapons in 1974, while Pakistan claims to have all of the necessary components. Both countries fear the other's nuclear capabilities and have stated that any nuclear attack would be reciprocated. Efforts by the United States to start negotiations aimed at denuclearizing both powers face numerous obstacles. Neither nation wants to limit its nuclear program unless the other does so first, and India says that it must retain its nuclear capabilities to guard against aggression from China.

Background

Home to both Hindus and Muslims, Jammu and Kashmir have served as a battleground for the animosities that divide them. Trouble began when Britain implemented its plan to create two independent nations in the region. Pakistan was envisioned as a Muslim homeland, and India, although predominately Hindu, was established as a secular nation. The Jammu and Kashmir region was given the opportunity to join either India or Pakistan, but it held out for independence.

In October 1947 Pakistani-backed Kashmiri militants demanding independence led an armed revolt. The Kashmiri government enlisted the aid of India to stop the violence, leading to the first war between India and Pakistan. According to the terms of a truce in 1949, the Kashmiri people were to be allowed to determine their future by means of a plebiscite, or referendum.

War broke out again in 1965 when armed Azad Kashmir troops from Pakistan once again invaded India. More than twenty-thousand were killed in the month of fighting that ensued. The next crisis began in 1971, when Pakistan accused India of aiding East Pakistan (now Bangladesh) in its quest for independence. In retaliation Pakistan invaded Jammu and Kashmir, but was defeated. The fighting lasted only two weeks but left eleven thousand dead.

India: Sectarian Politics in a Secular State

Perspective

1528	*The Babri mosque is built on the site of a Hindu temple.*
1850s	*British gain control over almost all of India.*
1855	*Indians try to destroy the Babri mosque.*
1947	**August 15.** *India gains its independence but is partitioned to form a Muslim homeland called Pakistan. Unprecedented violence erupts between Hindus and Muslims.*
1948	**January 30.** *Indian leader Mahatma Gandhi is killed by a Hindu radical.*
1949	*The Babri mosque is ordered closed.*
1980	*Bharatiya Janata Party (BJP) formed.*
1984	*Hindu fundamentalists launch a campaign to destroy the Babri mosque.*
1989	**November.** *BJP gains support in national elections by supporting Hindu fundamentalists.*
1990	**September.** *BJP stirs up violence when it sponsors a march to protest the Babri mosque.* **October 30.** *Thousands gather to try to destroy the mosque.* **November 7.** *India's prime minister is forced to resign; rioting continues.*
1991	**June.** *BJP becomes the major opposition party in national elections.*
1992	**January 26.** *BJP marches to protest separatist movements in Kashmir and the Punjab. Thirty are killed.* **December 6.** *The Babri mosque is razed during a BJP rally. Rioting breaks out throughout the country.* **December 15.** *Federal government ousts all BJP-controlled state governments.*
1993	**January 6.** *Serious rioting erupts in Bombay when Hindus attack Muslims.* **March 12.** *Thirteen bombs detonated in Bombay kill 260 people.*
1995	**March.** *BJP gains strength in state elections.*

When India gained its independence in 1947, its survival was imperiled when tensions between Hindus and Muslims exploded and one million people were left dead in the wake of the catastrophe. Although the government eventually established order, the resentment between Hindus and Muslims continues to smolder. In the early 1990s, a Hindu nationalist movement threatened to again plunge the nation of almost 900 million into religious violence. The danger receded in 1993 after voters firmly rejected the Hindu nationalists in state elections, but Hindu extremists remain a powerful and explosive force.

Issues and Events

At the center of the most recent conflict between the Hindus and the Muslims is the 16th century Babri mosque in the city of Ayodhya. For Hindu fundamentalists who seek to establish Hinduism as India's state religion, the Babri mosque has long been a symbol of Hindu subjugation to foreign rule. The mosque is believed to have replaced a Hindu temple to the god Rama in 1528. It was locked up in 1949 to prevent any further quarreling about the site.

Trouble began again in 1984 when Hindus launched a campaign to destroy the Babri mosque and rebuild a Hindu temple on the site. In 1986 the government tried to placate the Hindus by permitting them to worship on the grounds of the Muslim shrine. This action only encouraged the fundamentalists in their drive to take over the land, and in 1989 they began collecting holy bricks to be used to construct their temple. This action sparked rioting by Muslims throughout all of India.

The Babri mosque issue took on political overtones when the cause was embraced by the Bharatiya Janata Party (BJP), one of India's many minor political parties. Backing from the Hindu fundamentalists gave the BJP a new base of support, and they did well in elections held in 1989. The BJP then began to actively campaign for the destruction of the mosque, and in September 1990 they sponsored a march that once again stirred up communal violence between Hindus and Muslims. The following month thousands of militants gathered at the site and began to try to destroy the mosque. Once again rioting broke out and one thousand people were killed in clashes across India. This incident ultimately led to the downfall of India's Prime Minister V.P. Singh and served notice that the BJP's power was increasing dramatically.

In 1991 the BJP's success in stirring up Hindu nationalist sentiments was reflected in Indian elections. The BJP became the leading opposition party in India, second only to the Congress party which has ruled India since its independence. Several months later the BJP-controlled government of the state in which the mosque is located took possession of the land, but the Indian Supreme Court took quick action and ordered the state not to alter the site.

Despite ongoing negotiations between the Indian government and the BJP, the situation finally exploded in December 1992 when a BJP demonstration turned ugly and Hindu radicals reduced the mosque to rubble. Muslims throughout India and neighboring countries were infuriated by the gesture and well over one thousand people were killed in the ensuing riots that gripped the country for days.

The Indian government responded by outlawing all four BJP-controlled state governments, arguing that because they had supported radical Hindu groups banned by the Indian government, they had failed to maintain the separation of church and state.

In January 1993 an international incident was avoided when Bangladesh police turned back 150,000 people who were threatening to invade India and rebuild the mosque. Two days later severe rioting broke out in Bombay, India's commercial and financial capital, when Hindu radicals began targeting Muslim homes and businesses. Hundreds of Muslims were killed, many of them burned alive. Almost 100,000 Muslims evacuated the city. The government was accused of inaction, and the police were charged with complicity in the massacre.

In February the government tried to prevent any further violence by barring the BJP from staging a massive demonstration in the capital of New Delhi to demand fresh elections, hoping that they would be catapulted to power by the momentum of the growing Hindu nationalist movement. Although the government contained the BJP by arresting tens of thousands and assaulting demonstrators with tear gas, water cannons, and rubber bullets, the reputation of the BJP as a force to be reckoned with was enhanced.

Just as Bombay was recovering from the riots in January, the city was terrorized in March by a series of bombings that left several buildings in ruins and killed more than 250 people. It is widely believed that the bombings, which were carried out by organized crime figures, were in retaliation for the January riots. The leader of the BJP risked creating an international incident by accusing Pakistan of masterminding the attack, despite lack of proof to back up the theory.

In the wake of the violence in Bombay, the BJP tried to tone down its anti-Muslim rhetoric in preparation for state elections. This tactic resulted in the defeat of the party throughout India in 1993 and 1994. By 1995 the party seemed to have recovered, as indicated by its victories in state elections. On the national level, the party holds 119 out of 545 seats and remains an explosive force in Indian politics.

The BJP maintains its popularity by playing on Hindu prejudices and fears about Muslims and other minority groups. While the party's supporters applaud its honesty and efficiency in India's normally corrupt government, opponents accuse it of using fascist tactics. It is almost certain that a BJP victory in 1996 national elections will lead to a Muslim backlash, and terrorist acts like the bombing of Bombay will certainly become more commonplace. India is torn by the same kinds of divisions that ultimately led to the disintegration of the former Soviet Union and to the war in Yugoslavia. If these fissures continue to grow, a similar fate may await India.

Background

Civilization in India began around 2500 B.C. in the Indus River valley, and Hinduism is the traditional religion that developed along with the Indian culture. Islam is a relative newcomer to the region, having arrived in India with Turkish and Afghan invaders in the 10th and 11th centuries.

In 1525 India was conquered by Babur, a descendant of Genghis Khan, who established the Mogul Dynasty in India. Three years later the Muslim invaders reputedly tore down a Hindu temple in Ayodhya and built in its place the Babri mosque in Babur's honor.

The British gained their first foothold in India in 1619, and by 1850 they were in control of almost all of India. As the increasingly restive Indian population began to protest against British rule, the mosque at Ayodhya became one of the targets of their frustration about foreign rule. The first demonstration at Ayodhya took place in 1855.

In 1920 Mahatma Gandhi initiated a popular movement against the British colonialists which eventually led to Indian independence in 1947. On the eve of independence the British tried to solve the problem of rising tensions between Indians and Muslims by partitioning India into Hindu and Muslim homelands. The Hindu part became the secular republic of India, which stressed tolerance and respect for all religions. The predominately Muslim areas east and west of India were called Pakistan, but the eastern part ultimately broke away from Pakistan and named itself Bangladesh.

The partition of India created disaster when violence between Hindus and Muslims erupted and as many as one million people were killed. More than ten million people fled to their new homelands to avoid being targeted by mobs who sought to wipe out any minorities in their midst. The violence subsided only after Mahatma Gandhi was assassinated by a Hindu radical.

Since that time, the specter of Hindu-Muslim violence has loomed large in India, where Muslims still constitute more than ten percent of the population. The Indian government has continually sought to placate the Muslims and other minorities, but their efforts have not always been fruitful. Muslims in Jammu and Kashmir began an armed insurrection against the Indian government in 1988, and Sikh militants in the Punjab region of India were responsible for the assassination of Prime Minister Indira Gandhi in 1984. The Indians have a reputation for ruthlessness in these conflicts, and thousands have been killed in recent years.

Tajikistan: Communism Prevails

Perspective

1825	*Russians invade Central Asia.*
1929	*Tajik Soviet Socialist Republic is formed.*
1991	**September 9.** *Tajikistan declares its independence.* **November.** *Rakhmon Nabiyev is elected president.*
1992	**March.** *Violent demonstrations begin.* **May 11.** *A coalition government is installed.* **June.** *Fighting erupts between supporters and opponents of the new government.* **September 7.** *Opposition forces seize the capital and force Nabiyev to resign.* **December 10.** *Communists regain power.*
1993	**March 3.** *Russian peacekeeping forces arrive in Tajikistan.* **July 13.** *After 25 peacekeepers are killed, Russia sends reinforcements.*

The demise of the Soviet Union has resulted in the implementation of reforms and democracy in many former Soviet republics. The pattern has been different in most of Central Asia, where communists have remained in command. Throughout the region there are fears that democracy will pave the way for radical Islamic rule and the communists play on these fears by asserting that only they can guarantee peace and stability. In Tajikistan the communists were briefly usurped by reformers, but they managed to regain power by launching a bitter civil war in which tens of thousands were killed. Communist rule was strengthened by the introduction of Russian peacekeeping forces to keep the rebels at bay.

Issues and Events

The first serious threat to communist leadership took place in March 1992 when a series of violent demonstrations was launched by a coalition of opposition forces. One of the main groups, known as the Democratic Party of Tajikistan, was founded by intellectuals who promoted market reforms and increased political freedom. The other group, called the Islamic Party of Revival, advocated greater emphasis on traditional religious values. Despite the fact that Tajikistan's Muslims are of the moderate Sunni sect and have expressed no desire to establish an Iranian-style autocracy, the Islamic Party was labeled as a radical Islamic fundamentalist group by the communists.

Continuing pressure forced the government, under the leadership of former communist party boss Rakhmon Nabiyev, to allow these groups a limited role in the government, but this failed to appease opponents of the communists. Fighting broke out, fueled by arms which began pouring into Tajikistan from neighboring Afghanistan. In September Nabiyev was forced to resign, and in October the communists were ousted from the capital city of Dushanbe.

The reformers failed to consolidate their rule, and two months later the communists, under the leadership of a former convict and troublemaker named Sangak Safarov, managed to retake the capital. Another communist party official was installed as president. The communists immediately implemented a Stalin-like purge, and hundreds of thousands of villagers were forced to negotiate Tajikistan's rugged landscape and seek shelter in neighboring Afghanistan.

The situation remains highly volatile. Rebels reputedly armed by Afghanistan hide in the mountains and launch sporadic attacks against government troops and Russian peacekeepers. Although Tajikistan's Muslims are moderate, government persecution and repression are creating conditions that are ripe for the development of radicalized Islam. These same conditions are also tempting intervention by Takjikistan's radical neighbors in Afghanistan and Iran.

Background.

Iranian people settled in the region around the first century B.C., and the area was subsequently invaded by many different groups through the centuries. From marauding Persians the Tajiks inherited their language, and from the Arabs Tajikistan received its Islamic heritage. In 1895 Russia conquered Tajikistan along with the rest of Central Asia. Most Tajiks were opposed to Russian rule and fought against the Bolsheviks for several years before they were finally subdued in 1925. Violence continued as the Soviets seized all farmland and tried to force the people to abandon Islam.

The Russians remained suspicious of the Tajiks, and thus the Tajiks were ignored when the Soviets initially carved the region into republics. Tajikistan was not recognized as a separate state until 1929. The Soviets did little to establish industry in Tajikistan and economic activity was mainly confined to growing cotton. Despite an unrelenting campaign against religion throughout the Soviet period, Islam remained an important part of Tajik culture. Most Tajiks lived quiet lives until glasnost and the breakup of the Soviet Union heralded a new era of war and unrest.

Sri Lanka: A Possible Breakthrough

Perspective

1948	**February 4.** *Sri Lanka (Ceylon) gains independence.*
1983	**July.** *Rioting sparks civil war between the Sinhalese and Tamils.*
1987	**July 29.** *Indian troops are sent to Sri Lanka.*
1989	**June.** *Tamil Tigers and government agree to a cease-fire.*
1990	**March 24.** *Indian troops are withdrawn.* **June.** *Renewed fighting breaks out; government declares war against Tamils.*
1991	**May 21.** *Rajiv Gandhi, India's prime minister, is assassinated.*
1992	**May 20.** *India formally charges the Tamil Tigers with Gandhi's death.*
1993	**May 1.** *Sri Lanka's president is assassinated.*
1994	**November 9.** *New president is elected.*
1995	**January 8.** *Cease fire takes effect.* **April 18.** *Tamil attack against a government naval base breaks the cease-fire agreement.*

Sri Lanka, formerly Ceylon, a teardrop-shaped island off the southern tip of India, has been plagued by violence between factions of the majority Sinhalese and the minority Tamils. The Sinhalese, who compose three-quarters of the population, are primarily Buddhist, while the Tamils are primarily Hindu and speak the language of the fifty million Tamils in India. The Tamils live mainly in northern and eastern Sri Lanka, which is generally less prosperous than the south and west. In 1994 hopes for an end to the war rose when the nation elected a new president who promised to bring peace to this war-torn land.

Issues and Events
Traditional rivalries exploded into violence in 1983 when the Tamil Tigers, a radical separatist guerrilla group, killed thirteen Sinhalese soldiers. In response to what they claim is centuries of discrimination and mistreatment by the ruling Sinhalese, the Tamil Tigers aspire to establish an independent Tamil nation called Ealan in northern Sri Lanka.

Since the fighting began, the sporadic war has escalated, with more than 30,000 Sri Lankans killed. The Tamils have been accused of ethnic cleansing in areas under their control, and the government has repeatedly been criticized for torture and other abuses against the Tamils. Neighboring India, which also has a large Tamil population, entered into negotiations with Sri Lanka in an attempt to stop the violence.

On July 29, 1987, the Indian and Sri Lankan governments signed an accord that included several concessions to the Tamils, including increased political autonomy, citizenship for some Tamils, and acceptance of Tamil as an official language. In return, the Tamils were to abandon their campaign for an independent homeland. Three thousand Indian troops were sent to Sri Lanka to monitor the negotiated settlement and enforce a declared cease-fire. The Tamil Tigers, as well as other Sri Lankans, resented the presence of the Indian troops. The level of violence quickly escalated.

The withdrawal of Indian troops in March 1990 did nothing to improve the situation. Fighting intensified only three months later as the Tamils and Sinhalese abandoned their search for a negotiated settlement and resumed their struggle for a decisive victory.

The violence spilled over into India when an organizer of the Tamil Tigers was accused of masterminding the 1991 assassination of India's former prime minister, Rajiv Gandhi. The Tamil rebels denied involvement in the crime, but it was a Tamil woman who carried the suicide bomb that killed Gandhi. Sri Lanka's own president was assassinated in 1993.

In late 1994, Sri Lankans handed presidential candidate Candrika Kumaratunga a decisive victory. Kumaratunga had campaigned that she would bring peace to the nation, and after her election she quickly began negotiating with the Tamil Tigers. By January 1995 a cease-fire agreement was reached, only to be broken three months later by an attack against a government naval base.

Many problems remain. The government still refuses to dismantle an important military base in Tamil territory. Also, many Tamils feel that the government has not kept its promises to rebuild some of the areas destroyed by war, and also to lift fully an economic embargo that had been imposed on northern Sri Lanka.

Although fighting resumed four months later, it seems that most Sri Lankans on both sides of the cultural barrier are tired of war and ready to seek out some kind of agreement that will bring lasting peace.

Background
The Sinhalese have been established on the island of Sri Lanka since the sixth century B.C., but the Tamils did not appear in substantial numbers in Ceylon until the tenth century. Controlled first by India, then by the Portuguese, the Dutch, and finally, the British, Ceylon achieved independence on February 4, 1948. The country adopted a new constitution on May 22, 1972, which changed the island's name from Ceylon to the Republic of Sri Lanka.

Afghanistan: Cold War Casualty

Perspective

1919	**August 19.** *Afghanistan gains independence from Britain.*
1973	**July 17.** *Mohammad Daoud seizes power and abolishes constitution.*
1978	**April.** *People's Democratic Party of Afghanistan (PDPA) stages Marxist coup and establishes Nur Mohammad Taraki as president.* **December.** *Soviet Union and Afghanistan sign Treaty of Friendship, Good Neighborliness, and Cooperation.*
1979	**September.** *Internal rivalry splits PDPA; Hafizullah Amin kills Taraki and seizes power.* **December.** *Soviet Union invades. Soviet troops kill Amin and establish Babrak Karmal as head of new government.*
1986	**May 4.** *Karmal resigns and is replaced by former secret police chief Najibullah.*
1989	**February 15.** *Soviets withdraw remaining troops.* **February 23.** *Mujahidin establish government-in-exile.*
1992	**January 1.** *The United States and Russia agree to stop arms shipments.* **April 16.** *Najibullah resigns.* **April 25.** *Rebel troops invade Kabul.* **April 28.** *A moderate Islamic government is established.* **May 5.** *Islamic fundamentalists begin bombing Kabul.*
1994	**January.** *Fierce fighting is renewed among rival factions.*
1995	**February 23.** *United Nations presents a new peace plan.* **March 11.** *Taliban suffers its first defeat.*

The invasion of Afghanistan by the Soviet Union in 1979 precipitated a serious crisis during the Cold War between the United States and the Soviet Union. When the Soviet Union withdrew its troops from Afghanistan in 1989, Western analysts predicted that the Marxist government in Kabul, lacking popular support, would collapse within a few months. Months turned to years as the fighting dragged on until 1992, when a coalition of rebel forces seized control of the government. So far the revolution has failed to bring peace to Afghanistan, which has already suf-

fered two million deaths since the war began in 1979. Previously a pawn in the game of Soviet expansionism, Afghanistan is now in the grips of the regional conflict between moderate and fundamentalist Muslims.

Issues and Events

For many years after the Soviet troop withdrawal, the wily President Najibullah managed to cling to power against all odds. He tried to cultivate an image as a moderate, reasonable, competent leader while the mujahidin, who refused to negotiate, were portrayed as fanatical extremists who were concerned only with their own narrow self-interests. The Soviet Union continued to provide billions of dollars in aid to the Najibullah government, as well as millions in arms shipments.

In 1991 vital foreign aid began to dry up as the Soviet Union collapsed and Russia found itself unable to meet its financial commitments. Beginning in 1992, the United States and Russia expressed their changing priorities by implementing an agreement to halt all arms shipments to competing factions in an effort to end the war. Najibullah was arrested in April 1992 as he attempted to flee the country. Rebel forces seized control of the capital later that month.

A new, moderate Islamic government controlled by the Tajiks and Uzbeks was established. Burhanuddin Rabbani, a reclusive Islamic scholar, became president. Control of the military was given to Ahmad Masoud, the ruthless leader of the most successful resistance group. Just weeks after the new ruling coalition assumed power, fighting broke out when Islamic fundamentalists protested that they were being denied a significant role in the new government. In the next few years much of the city of Kabul, which was virtually untouched during the Soviet occupation, was reduced to rubble. Fierce fighting has left thousands dead.

The most powerful fundamentalist group, known as Hezb-i-Islami, is led by Gulbuddin Hekmatyar and consists primarily of Pathans, the ethnic group that has traditionally controlled the government. Hekmatyar, who receives aid from Pakistan, is allied to the Hezb-i-Wahadat, a Shiite fundamentalist group that is backed by Iran.

Another force that threatens Afghan unity is represented by General Abdul Rashid Doestam, who controls most of northeast Afghanistan. A former Communist and Islamic liberal, he receives military aid from neighboring Uzbekistan.

When Hekmatyar and Doestam combined forces to launch a major campaign against Masoud and the government in 1994, the United Nations became serious about developing a peace plan. In February 1995 the U.N. came up with a proposal that called for President Rabbani to relinquish power to a council of prominent Afghans. Unfortunately, the plan did not meet with the approval of a powerful new combatant in the ongoing war, the *Taliban*. This group of religious students emerged in

1994 and quickly gained popular support by advocating a government based strictly on Islamic law and condemning all the other groups fighting for power as corrupt and power-hungry. The Taliban achieved considerable military success in 1994 because most of their opponents, including the powerful Hekmatyar, refused to fight against them. By 1995 they had conquered more than one-third of the country, but they met with fierce resistance from Masoud when they attempted to take over Kabul. Although they may not be able to attain a military takeover, the Taliban's popularity makes their approval vital to the success of any peace plan.

The forces fighting in Kabul—while the most powerful and heavily armed—are but a few of the many factions that still hold sway throughout Afghanistan. Outside of Kabul, various tribal leaders are still heavily armed and fiercely protective of their territories. Allegiances shift frequently, and many factions continue to try to settle old scores that cropped up during the years of Soviet occupation.

Once of strategic importance in the cold war between the United States and the Soviet Union, Afghanistan was torn apart in a vicious struggle between the superpowers. Unfortunately, the country is still in the front lines, this time in the growing conflict between the moderate and radical Islamic republics of Asia, Saudi Arabia, Iran, and Pakistan. Fundamentalists in Iran are hopeful that their religious movement will eventually spread through Afghanistan into the heart of central Asia and beyond. Other Islamic nations, like Saudi Arabia, are providing military aid to moderate Muslims in their struggle to establish a stable government and prevent the spread of Iran's radical Islamic movement throughout the region.

Background

Turbulence has been the only constant in the region now called Afghanistan, located in the path of major trade and invasion routes from central Asia into the Middle East and India. Starting in 328 B.C. with the invasion by Alexander the Great, a succession of conquerors swept across Afghanistan. One result of the numerous invasions was great ethnic diversity, and society developed as a complex network of tribal interrelationships based on ancestry, ethnicity, and language. The arrival of Islam in A.D. 642 provided a common bond among people of various ethnic groups. Afghanistan's many tribes united to form an independent nation in 1747, when Ahmad Shah Durrani was elected king by tribal leaders.

Another result of Afghanistan's history as a major crossroads is a decided hatred of foreign intervention in its affairs. The British experienced the brunt of this animosity when they sought to halt Russian expansionism by establishing a presence in Afghanistan in 1839. This ignited the first of three wars between Great Britain and Afghanistan. By the third war in 1919, an exhausted Great Britain,

which had maintained control over Afghanistan's foreign affairs, gave in to Afghanistan's demands for total independence. Even after independence, real power was in many cases still vested in tribal leaders.

The throne continued to change hands until 1964, when parliamentary rule was put into effect with a new constitution. Extremists on both sides, however, grew increasingly vocal. Amid charges of corruption and the problems of a drought-ridden economy, former prime minister Mohammad Daoud staged a bloodless coup on July 17, 1973. Daoud declared Afghanistan a republic, which it remained until the People's Democratic Party of Afghanistan (PDPA), a newly formed coalition of two rival Marxist parties, killed Daoud and his family in 1978.

The Marxists attempted rapid social change by enacting radical decrees, including land reform, the emancipation of women, and programs to fight illiteracy. Violent opposition, mostly based on Islamic beliefs conflicting with the PDPA's policies, developed immediately and grew into a nationwide insurgency. After the original Marxist coup in April 1978, the Soviet Union signed a treaty with the new regime. As the insurgency movement grew, Russian advisers and equipment became critical to the survival of the Marxists.

A succession of bloody coups resulted in the eventual installation of Babrak Karmal, whom the Soviets immediately supported with an invasion of fifty thousand troops. The Soviet invasion prompted the rise of the mujahidin, or "holy warriors," who vowed to fight to the death to expel the invaders and protect their Islamic way of life.

When Mikhail Gorbachev came to power in 1985, the Afghanistan war had become one of the Soviet Union's most pressing problems. Gorbachev replaced Karmal with the ruthless former secret police chief Najibullah in an attempt to gain a military victory. But still the rebellious mujahidin could not be subdued and the war continued to escalate. By 1988, the Soviets disclosed that 13,000 of their soldiers had been killed, 35,000 were wounded, and 300 were missing. The war cost the Soviets over $1 billion a year and severely damaged the Soviet Union's relations with most of the Islamic world, as well as with the United States. The Soviets finally withdrew their troops in 1989.

Throughout their war against the Soviets, the mujahidin enjoyed overwhelming national and international support for their cause. Substantial amounts of money and arms from all over the world were funneled to the mujahidin through Pakistan. The Soviets, on the other hand, experienced nothing but condemnation for the invasion. The United Nations annually passed resolutions calling for Soviet troop withdrawal, and the Soviets' futile involvement in the war has been likened to the United States' intervention in Vietnam.

East Asia and the Pacific

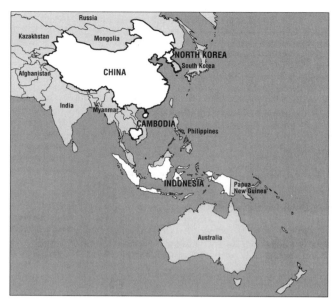

The next century is expected to be the Age of the Pacific. For East Asia the last 20 years have been a time of economic growth and prosperity. Japan has risen to become the world's second largest economic power. Although China lagged behind under communism, it has experienced impressive economic growth over the last few years as its leaders attempted to implement economic reforms without creating political instability.

But both China and Japan, with their long histories and rich cultures, face challenges as they adjust to their new roles as world leaders. Intense nationalism bordering on xenophobia threatens to keep both nations from realizing the benefits of full integration into the world community. In China, the long tradition of farming is rapidly being supplanted by fast-growing urbanism. The government is struggling to rein in the runaway economies of the coastal cities which threaten its own authority. In Japan, the once-omnipotent government has been destabilized as decades of corruption are exposed and a restive populace turns to opposition parties for leadership.

Conflicts that resulted from the Cold War between the United States and the Soviet Union plagued the region for decades. Korea was split into two parts after communists failed to take over the country in 1950. Vietnamese communists were more successful, and after a devastating war with the United States they managed to gain control of South Vietnam. Cambodia was unwillingly drawn into the Vietnam War and was later invaded by Vietnam. Taiwan and the People's Republic of China have maintained an uneasy standoff since China's communist revolution, each government claiming to be the one true China.

Today these conflicts have less international significance, and regional peace is close at hand.

Relations between the two Koreas and the two Chinas have thawed considerably, and both are discussing reunification. Vietnam has begun to recover economically and politically from the war.

Despite improved relations among the countries in the region, there are still threats to long-term stability. North Korea's nuclear program and the country's refusal to allow full international inspection of its nuclear facilities have raised tensions considerably. The death of long-time dictator Kim Il Sung only further increases worry about what direction the small but militarily powerful nation will take. In Cambodia, the Khmer Rouge continue to deny the long-suffering people the peace they desire.

International attention has also been focused on Asia's booming nations where political reform has not kept pace with fast-growing economies. Singapore, Indonesia and Thailand, among others, have all been accused of denying their citizens basic human rights taken for granted in the West. Whether the newly enriched populations will demand greater political freedom remains to be seen.

In the Pacific, competing ethnic groups continue to struggle to create a common vision for the future. Tensions between ethnic Fijians and Indians sparked a military takeover in that island nation. The people of East Timor have long protested the illegal occupation of their territory by the Indonesians. In Papua New Guinea, the inhabitants of Bougainville have declared their independence from the unstable central government and continue to struggle for control of their land. Native Kanaks in New Caledonia have been battling for independence from France, despite the objections of those of European descent.

North Korea: Nuclear Blackmail

Perspective

1910	**August 22.** *Japan annexes Korea.*
1945	*Following World War II, Korea is divided into Soviet and U.S. zones.*
1949	*North and South Korea set up separate governments.*
1950	**June 25.** *North Korea invades South Korea; United States sends troops to repel the invasion.*
1953	**July 27.** *Armistice is signed.*
1968	*North Koreans attempt to assassinate South Korea's president.*
1990	**September.** *Peace talks begin.*
1992	**April 9.** *North Korea agrees to allow limited nuclear inspections.*
1993	**March 12.** *North Korea withdraws from the Nuclear Non-Proliferation Treaty.* **November 1.** *U.N. passes resolution calling for North Korea to "cooperate immediately" with nuclear inspectors.*
1994	**March 1.** *North Korea obstructs nuclear inspectors.* **July 8.** *President Kim Il Sung dies.* **October 21.** *North Korea agrees to curtail its nuclear program.*

Nuclear proliferation became a focus of world attention after the Persian Gulf war when Iraq's nuclear capabilities came to light. Rumors that the North Koreans were producing large amounts of weapons-grade plutonium at its Yongbyon nuclear facility led to increased pressure by the international community for North Korea to disclose details about its nuclear weapons program. After years of haggling, an agreement was reached in 1994 and North Korea finally submitted to nuclear inspections. Although it has never been proven that North Korea has actually built any atomic weapons, the nation was able to secure billions of dollars' worth of concessions in exchange for freezing its nuclear program. Some claim that this amounts to nuclear blackmail.

Issues and Events

When North and South Korea began a series of peace talks in 1990, South Korea insisted that the North disclose information about its nuclear capabilities. The possibility of nuclear weapons in North Korea is of major concern not only to South Korea, but to Japan as well. It is known that North Korea has missiles which could deliver nuclear weapons to Japan. Some fear that this threat could upset the balance of power in the entire region and provide Japan with an incentive to develop its own nuclear program.

Under mounting pressure from the U.S., the North Koreans agreed to sign the Nuclear Non-Proliferation Treaty and allow International Atomic Energy Agency inspectors to examine its nuclear sites. North Korea allowed several inspections in 1992, but experts were denied full access to the Yongbyon facility, which the Koreans stated was used solely for electrical production. When the experts demanded special access to two more sites, North Korea angrily withdrew from the Nuclear Non-Proliferation Treaty.

Twice in 1994 the North Koreans agreed to allow inspections and subsequently denied the inspectors access to important facilities. After receiving a stern warning from the United Nations, North Korea returned to the bargaining table and in October an agreement with the U.S. was reached. North Korea agreed to dismantle its nuclear weapons program and submit to unlimited inspections. In exchange, the U.S. and its allies agreed to provide North Korea with two new reactors that produce less plutonium. They also agreed to provide North Korea with a five-year supply of oil. Furthermore, the U.S. agreed to begin the process of offering diplomatic recognition to North Korea.

Because the North Koreans failed to honor the terms of earlier agreements, it is questionable whether they will live up to the terms of this one. By February 1995 the North Koreans were already objecting to the fact that the new reactors were to be built by South Korea, even though this was part of the original agreement. Critics argue that the terms of the agreement were far too generous given that the Koreans may not even have the capability of building nuclear weapons. They fear that the North Koreans are bluffing, and that this is the first of an endless succession of demands.

Background

The neighboring Japanese, Chinese, and Russians have long fought over Korea. Japan gained control of Korea in 1910 and held the peninsula until the Soviets and Americans divided it following World War II. In 1949 rival governments were established in North and South Korea. Two years later, North Korea, supported by the Soviet Union and China, invaded the South but was repelled by the United States. The war lasted three years and resulted in three million casualties. Because no real peace treaty was ever signed, North and South Korea remain technically in a state of war.

North Korea has been involved in numerous acts of terrorism against the South Koreans, including an assassination attempt against South Korea's president in 1968 and the bombing of a South Korean airliner in 1987.

Kim Il Sung ruled North Korea with an iron fist for forty-eight years until his death in 1994. With its Soviet-style economy and dictatorship, North Korea has remained internationally isolated. Its economy has been in a downward spiral for several years and there are reports of food shortages. In stark contrast, South Korea has a thriving economy and enviable productivity, despite recurrent protests against government repression.

China: Economic Growth Outpaces Reform

Perspective

1949	*People's Republic of China is founded after four years of civil war.*
1950	*Land-reform law is adopted.*
1956	*Mao Zedong initiates "hundred flowers" campaign.*
1958	*Mao Zedong inaugurates Great Leap Forward.*
1966	*Cultural Revolution begins.*
1976	*Mao Zedong dies.*
1978	*Deng Xiaoping announces economic reforms.*
1986	**December.** *Student unrest leads to downfall of Hu Yaobang, head of the Communist party.*
1989	**April 15.** *Hu Yaobang's death prompts renewed student protests.* **April 27.** *Approximately 150,000 students gather in Beijing's Tiananmen Square.* **May 20.** *Martial law is imposed.* **May 22.** *Millions gather to deter military convoys.* **June 4.** *Chinese Army opens fire on demonstrators.*
1992	*Chinese economic growth tops 10 percent.*
1993	**June.** *Serious rioting occurs in Sichuan province in central China.*
1994	**May 26.** *United States renews China's favorable trade status.*

After the initiation of economic reforms in China resulted in the Beijing riots of 1989, many predicted that China would call its plan a failure and return to socialism. Although the turmoil marked the end of political reform in China, it also hailed the beginning of an accelerated transition from socialism to capitalism. State farms have been broken up, new businesses and cooperatives have been blossoming everywhere, and China has opened its doors to foreign trade and investment. While economic reform has done much to improve the lives of many Chinese, others continue to suffer under China's repressive political system.

Issues and Events
Economic reforms have been underway since 1978 when Deng Xiaoping launched a new program to modernize and expand China's economy. The new program represented a departure from the dogmatic conservatism of the 1960s and 1970s. For the first time, productivity was emphasized over politics. Workers were offered financial incentives for increased output, and decision-making by individuals rather than groups was encouraged. Intellectuals were elevated back to their pre-revolutionary status.

Chinese leaders were quick to deny that this was a return to capitalism, calling it a plan to "build socialism with Chinese characteristics." They tried to develop a unique and pragmatic program that would synthesize the benefits of capitalism into their socialist structure without suffering from its disadvantages.

By 1986, reform's negative effects began to cause concern. Limited government intervention resulted in a rising budget deficit, mounting inflation, and increased corruption in business. The country reported a $20 million trade deficit at the end of 1986. Many individuals felt they were unable to make the kinds of decisions expected of them after years of only group planning.

The reform program also manifested itself in growing student unrest. The first round of student demonstrations for more democracy and freedom of the press began in December 1986 in the city of Hefei and quickly spread to Shanghai and Beijing. Hu Yaobang, then leader of the Communist party, expressed sympathy for the students and was subsequently replaced by Zhao Ziyang.

Renewed cries for democracy and an end to corruption began in April 1989, following Hu Yaobang's death. Tiananmen Square became the rallying point for students from Beijing University, where the protests were centered. Student marches and demonstrations continued, and a thousand students launched a hunger strike days before the arrival of the Soviet Union's reform-minded leader Mikhail Gorbachev. During Gorbachev's visit, the crowds calling for reform grew to more than a million. Within weeks, the government imposed martial law and threatened to use force to stop the unrest.

Unmindful of the warnings, a million Beijing students and workers banded together to block incoming military convoys and urge the soldiers to defect to their side. For a while it seemed like the power of the people was invincible as the immense crowds marched through the streets calling for the government's resignation. But as troops continued to assemble in Beijing, it became clear that some kind of military action was imminent. Days later, when the troops moved into the city center, ten thousand people still remained. Violence broke out as students attacked the soldiers, who fought back with tear gas and cattle prods. By June 4 the army was given permission to open fire on anyone still in the streets.

According to Chinese authorities, three hundred people were killed, including twenty-three students. Western reporters claim the number was closer to two or three thousand. Thousands more were arrested, and reports circulated of torture and executions.

The Tiananmen Square incident prompted international outcry, and many Western nations flirted with the idea of imposing sanctions against China. The Chinese hotly contested that foreign governments had no right to interfere in China's internal affairs. China claimed that it respects human rights by providing all of its citizens with a "right to subsistence" because no one in China lacks food, shelter, and clothing. They pointed to homelessness and poverty in the United States and other countries and accused the West of hypocrisy in its criticism of China's human rights record. Despite continuing complaints about Chinese human rights abuses, most countries backed down and opted not to do anything that might interrupt their trade relations with China. By 1994, the United States completely abandoned its policy of linking human rights and trade issues and renewed China's Most Favored Nation (MFN) status.

Despite the political crisis, China continued on the road to prosperity. Because affluence is a powerful incentive for people to maintain the status quo, the Chinese government redoubled its efforts to expand its markets and provide its people with more consumer goods and economic opportunities. Unlike other former communist states, where the transition from planned to capitalist economies has resulted in hardship, economic reform has brought burgeoning prosperity to China. Private businesses have opened up throughout the country, and foreign investors have been scrambling to take advantage of China's cheap labor and huge market.

As a result of these policies, China has experienced rapid economic growth—at least ten percent annually since 1992. Economists predict that the economic expansion over the next decade could be explosive. Although it has brought prosperity to some, the rapidly expanding Chinese economy threatens to overwhelm government efforts to control it. With this spectacular economic growth has come an inflation rate of at least 15% per year. This surge in prices is ruinous to China's rural poor, who have not enjoyed the benefits of economic growth to offset the inflation. In 1993, riots broke out in Sichuan province in response to inflation and tax increases. Police fought for three days to disperse over 10,000 angry peasants.

Serious as this may be, the most daunting challenge facing Chinese leadership is whether it is possible to achieve true prosperity without allowing personal freedom. In China's rapidly growing cities, the residents are showing signs of restiveness with China's repressive political system. The nation's newfound riches are making the population increasingly independent in attitude. In China's new "special economic zones," the people enjoy personal freedoms unthinkable just a few years ago. The government has tried to suppress democracy movements through mass arrests and other repressive actions, but rumbles of discontent are ever-present.

Deng continues to cling to the notion that capitalism can be implemented without democracy. Despite growing prosperity, the political climate remains oppressive as Chinese leaders continue their unending battle to promote stability by maintaining tight control over the activities of China's vast population. Deng claims that regardless of what has transpired in Russia and the rest of the communist world, the system has

worked well for China. The Chinese are far more prosperous than they were before the revolution, and Deng claims that they are not plagued by the shortages and inefficiency that plagued the European socialist nations.

For now, those who do not agree with Deng seem content to wait patiently for the octogenarian's reign to end, as it inevitably must. So far the Chinese government has had to rely on force to maintain control over the people, and this trend will continue as long as there is no mechanism for pluralism in Chinese politics. The Chinese dissidents who launched the 1989 rebellion have not abandoned their cause for the rights of the individual and toleration of divergent opinions. Their anger remains a potentially explosive force in Chinese politics.

Background

Change never seems to come to China without bloodshed. Between 1937 and 1950, the Chinese suffered five million casualties as the result of the Japanese invasion, World War II, and the Communist Revolution. When Mao took over in 1949, the economy was in a shambles. Wars, floods, and famines had brought agriculture and industry to a virtual standstill. In the years immediately following the war, China's quick recovery was hailed as an economic miracle. During this period China also began a land reform program. About half of the arable land was wrested from wealthy landowners and redistributed to landless peasants. The Socialist transformation also had a dark side—another one million people were killed in the process.

A period of liberalization began in 1956 with the slogan, "Let a hundred flowers bloom, let a hundred schools of thought contend." This program backfired, however, when dissidents used the campaign to denounce the new government, and it was subsequently rescinded.

The Great Leap Forward was initiated by Mao in 1958 to raise agricultural and industrial output. The government encouraged the development of backyard factories, established huge agricultural communes, and stressed the merits of labor-intensive means of production. By 1960 the disillusioned and exhausted population suffered from food shortages and famine for the first time since the revolution. Industrial products of inferior quality flooded the country. The program was a disaster that came close to toppling Mao from power.

By 1966, Mao again took control by launching the Cultural Revolution, an attempt to revive revolutionary zeal among the people and destroy all remaining capitalist forces within the society. During this period, students were taken from their homes and forced to perform hard manual labor. Intellectuals and professionals were persecuted, and the Red Guard, a radical-left "army" of teenagers mandated to eliminate enemies of the state, was formed. What ensued was a "witch hunt" in which fifty thousand people, many of whom were innocent, were killed in vigilante-like purges. The cultural revolution finally ground to a halt in the early 1970s. After Mao's death in 1976, the government launched its new economic reform plan.

Cambodia:
Khmer Rouge Terrorism

Perspective

1941	*Prince Norodom Sihanouk is crowned king of Cambodia.*
1953	*Cambodia gains independence.*
1969	*United States bombs Cambodia.*
1970	*Lon Nol unseats Sihanouk with the help of the United States.*
1975	*United States withdraws from Vietnam; Cambodia falls to the Khmer Rouge under Pol Pot.*
1978	*Vietnam invades Cambodia.*
1979	*Vietnam overthrows Pol Pot.*
1989	**September 26.** *Vietnamese troops leave Cambodia.*
1991	**October 23.** *Peace treaty is signed.*
1992	**March 11.** *United Nations peacekeepers arrive in Cambodia.*
1993	**May 23-28.** *Sihanouk's royalist party wins elections.* **September 24.** *Sihanouk becomes King for second time in 50 years.*
1994	**July 7.** *Government bans Khmer Rouge.* **November 15.** *Khmer Rouge admits to killing five Western hostages.*

One of the worst cases of genocide in the twentieth century occurred in Cambodia during the regime of the Khmer Rouge, a communist organization which ruled the country between 1975 and 1978. Led by Pol Pot, the Khmer Rouge implemented a reform program that resulted in the death of almost one-sixth of the population and the total collapse of the country's economic and social structures. Although the United Nations spent almost $3 billion to bring peace and democracy to Cambodia, the Khmer Rouge continues to wage a campaign of terror against the Cambodian people.

Issues and Events

After decades of civil war, a negotiated settlement was reached in 1991 when various factions, including the Khmer Rouge, signed a cease-fire agreement. The treaty called for disarmament of warring groups and United Nations-supervised elections in May 1993. Despite their original compliance with the agreement, the Khmer Rouge failed to surrender its weapons to United Nations peacekeepers, refrained from participating in the elections, and refused to recognize the elected government.

The winner of the elections was one of the world's most enduring politicians, Norodom Si-

hanouk. As king of Cambodia, Sihanouk ruled the country from 1941 until he was forced from office by Lon Nol in 1970. Sihanouk was reinstated as a figurehead when the Khmer Rouge took over in 1975, but he had no real power. A new constitution passed in 1993 reinstated Sihanouk as king.

Unfortunately Sihanouk's government has failed to bring peace to Cambodia. By early 1994 there were rumors of fierce fighting between government forces and Khmer Rouge guerrillas in northern Cambodia. Peace talks in May and June were unproductive, and the government closed the door to further negotiations by outlawing the Khmer Rouge in July 1994. The Khmer Rouge stepped up its campaign of terror by kidnapping thousands of civilians and either killing them or holding them in concentration camps. Fear has returned to the Cambodian countryside, and as many as 80,000 villagers have reportedly fled their homes.

Growing instability has hurt the new government's attempts to bring in foreign investment. Even more important, the nation's potentially lucrative tourist industry has been crippled because most of the nation's important historic ruins are located in areas controlled by the Khmer Rouge. Five foreign tourists were slain by the Khmer Rouge during 1994 just as tourism had begun to increase. Another problem is that Sihanouk's government is becoming increasingly corrupt and repressive as it steps up its campaign to quell the incessant terrorism.

Few people believe that the Khmer Rouge will ever gain enough momentum to take over Cambodia; nevertheless, it continues to plague the growth and development of this fragile nation which has already known too much violence and hardship.

Background

Cambodia broke away from French rule in 1953, under the leadership of King Norodom Sihanouk. Sihanouk's attempts to maintain neutrality in the Vietnam War were doomed to failure, and in 1969 the United States began bombing North Vietnamese bases and supply routes within Cambodia. A United States-backed General—Lon Nol—came to power by overthrowing Sihanouk. Continued bombing by the United States military fostered a hatred of Lon Nol's regime that led to a bloody civil war and the rise of the Khmer Rouge. In 1975, as the Vietnam War was drawing to a close, the Khmer Rouge became strong enough to overthrow Lon Nol.

The Khmer Rouge sought to establish the rule of the peasant, an idea which still appeals to many of the rural poor in northern Cambodia. Under the leadership of Pol Pot, the Khmer Rouge began a genocidal reign of terror. Urban residents of all ages were placed in work camps in an attempt to create farmland out of the jungle, and anyone with an education was murdered. Between the political exterminations and those who succumbed to the famine and rigors of the work camps, it has been estimated that at least one million of Cambodia's six million people died. The Khmer Rouge was forced into exile by the Vietnamese, who ruled the country from 1979 to 1989.

Indonesia:
Repression in East Timor

Perspective

1520	*Portuguese settlers arrive in East Timor.*
1859	*Portugal and the Netherlands divide Timor.*
1949	*West Timor joins Indonesia.*
1974	*Portugal begins decolonization of East Timor.*
1975	**August 10.** *Civil war breaks out.* **September 8.** *Revolutionary Front for an Independent Timor (Fretilin) wins the war and sets up a provisional government.* **November 25.** *East Timor declares its independence from Portugal.* **December 7.** *Indonesia invades East Timor.*
1976	**July 15.** *East Timor is annexed by Indonesia.*
1989	**January 1.** *Indonesia opens up East Timor to travel and tourism.*
1991	**November 12.** *Indonesian troops open fire on protesters.*
1992	**November 20.** *Rebel leader Jose "Xanana" Gusmao is captured.*
1994	**November 11.** *Riots break out in East Timor's main city.*

A tropical paradise located just north of Australia, East Timor has suffered a turbulent past. In the aftermath of Indonesia's invasion of East Timor in 1975, it is believed that at least one in six of the people living there died. Some were killed in military action, but many more were killed by starvation and disease. Both the Timorese and the rest of the world seemed to eventually resign themselves to Indonesian rule, but what was described by witnesses as a massacre against unarmed civilians in 1991 turned world attention to this remote corner of the world.

Issues and Events

Fifteen years after Indonesia's invasion of East Timor, it seemed to most observers that the Timorese people's aspirations for independence had faded. It was therefore a surprise in 1991 when the funeral service for a young Timorese who had been killed by Indonesian security forces erupted into a demonstration. Tragedy ensued when police opened fire on the crowd, killing as many as 200 unarmed people.

The event marked the beginning of an era of renewed unrest, repression and arrests. At least 300 were arrested in the wake of the violence, including Xanana Gusmao, the leader of the remnants of the rebel forces. When Gusmao was sentenced to life imprisonment, international outcry prompted Indonesia to reduce his sentence to 20 years.

Indonesia claims that East Timor's problems should be blamed on Portugal, which irresponsibly abandoned the territory and left it vulnerable to a communist takeover. It asserts that the casualty figures cited for the period following Indonesia's invasion are grossly exaggerated and that Indonesia has improved the lives of the Timorese by spending millions of dollars on roads, schools, hospitals, and other infrastructure. The recent outbreaks of rioting are blamed on the presence of the western press and its tendency to encourage radical fringe groups and ignore the sentiments of average citizens.

Despite massive aid, most Timorese remain poor. Since the ban on travel to Timor was lifted in 1989 there has been massive immigration of Indonesians from other islands to Timor. The Timorese complain that Indonesians grab the best land and jobs for themselves. Right wing death squads known as "ninjas" roam the streets at night and attack those who are rumored to support Timorese independence. The biggest problem for most Timorese, however, is the pervasive fear of a government that has one of the world's worst human rights records and routinely engages in illegal torture and executions.

The United Nations continues to regard Portugal as the legal administrator of East Timor. Each episode of unrest and violence prompts renewed calls by Portugal and other nations for Indonesia to relinquish its claims to East Timor and allow the people to vote on the future of their nation. Surprisingly, international pressure is limited in its impact. Indonesia is a large, powerful nation with massive oil reserves and most of its trade partners are reluctant to do anything that might damage their relations with Indonesia.

Background

Timor was originally populated by Melanesians and Malay people. The Portuguese settled on Timor as early as 1520, and the Dutch arrived in 1613. The island was officially divided between the two countries in 1859. In 1945, Indonesia gained independence from the Netherlands, and West Timor joined Indonesia four years later.

Political unrest at home prompted Portugal to begin to divest itself of its foreign colonies in the mid-1970s. At this time, Portugal suggested that the Timorese should decide their own future. Instead, civil war broke out in East Timor and a leftist group known as the Revolutionary Front for an Independent Timor (Fretilin) gained control of the government. Fretilin soon declared its independence from both Portugal and Indonesia. Fearing the spread of communism, Indonesia invaded East Timor two weeks later. Indonesia annexed East Timor in 1976, and has maintained a military presence in there ever since.

Sub-Saharan Africa

As the twentieth century draws to a close, Africa—especially that part south of the Sahara—is beset by problems already solved or alleviated to a large degree in the rest of the world. Widespread famine is the most serious issue, and it is accompanied by the related problem of ongoing civil wars. Although South Africa has made tremendous political progress, the rest of southern Africa is still torn by conflicts arising from colonial policies of the past, including land distribution, racial and ethnic rivalries, and religious divisions.

Since the early 1980s, widespread and long-lasting drought has struck Africa. Its effects have been felt most by the already poverty-stricken nomadic and seminomadic peoples. Accustomed to living just above the starvation level in even the best years, these peoples have died by the hundreds of thousands. Worldwide efforts to rush relief to the famine victims have resulted in vast amounts of food finding its way to Africa, but ongoing civil wars and inefficient government agencies have slowed food distribution. Worse yet, some regimes have used food as a weapon to starve their enemies. Experts agree that the real cure for the seemingly endless cycle of famine is peace.

Democracy has proven as fragile as Africa's food supply. Dictators continue to rule throughout much of the continent, and many countries are under the control of a single political party. As a consequence, violent internal protests are common. This unrest has caused much misery and further weakens already troubled economies. In Liberia, Ethiopia, and Somalia violent uprisings against repressive military governments have resulted in chaos and economic collapse.

In Sudan, Rwanda, and Burundi, the civil wars that have contributed so heavily to famine and suffering are based on long-standing ethnic rivalries. The exodus of two million refugees from Rwanda in 1994 was one of the largest in world history and was accompanied by unimaginable suffering. In other conflicts, ethnicity and race play little or no role in wars that are strictly political in origin. The former Portuguese colony of Angola has not known peace since it gained independence in the 1970s. Angola's socialist government has had to wage continuous battles against opposition groups to the detriment of its economic development.

All of these wars compound regional problems as millions of refugees flood neighboring countries and strain scarce resources. More than five million Africans have been forced to leave their countries, and many millions more are internal refugees who have fled or have been evicted from their homes.

One bright spot on the continent has been South Africa. In 1994, decades of the brutal discrimination known as apartheid came to an end when the first all-inclusive elections were held. Nelson Mandela, who had spent much of his life in South African jails, and his once-banned African National Congress took a majority of the votes. It was a dramatic climax to the long struggle of blacks who had fought for political representation and the end of enforced racial segregation.

Liberia: Descent into Anarchy

Perspective

1822	*Freed American slaves colonize Liberia.*
1847	*Liberia becomes Africa's first independent republic.*
1980	*General Samuel Doe stages a coup.*
1989	**December 24.** *Rebel troops led by Charles Taylor and the National Patriotic Front of Liberia (NPFL) invade Liberia.*
1990	**August 25.** *West African peacekeeping forces arrive in Liberia.* **September 10.** *President Doe is killed by a NPFL splinter group.*
1991	**June.** *Former Doe supporters form ULIMO (United Liberation Movement of Liberia for Democracy).* **September 7.** *ULIMO attacks West African forces.* **October 31.** *Yamoussoukro agreement is signed by two factions.*
1993	**July 25.** *Three main warring factions sign a peace treaty in Cotonou, Benin.*
1994	**March 7.** *Interim government is inaugurated.* **September 12.** *Akosombo peace treaty is signed, but it collapses five days later.* **December 19.** *Rioters protest lack of political progress.* **December 22.** *Another peace agreement is reached.*

When Charles Taylor's National Patriotic Front of Liberia (NPFL) made its move to take over the country in 1989, it marked the beginning of the darkest period to date in Liberian history. During the next four years, 150,000 people died from the fighting and from starvation, and more than half the nation's population was forced from their homes.

Since then there has been a long succession of failed peace agreements. On December 19, 1994 the long-suffering people of Liberia demonstrated their growing anger and frustration by rioting in the streets of Liberia's capital to protest the ongoing violence. The warring factions got the message and passed yet another treaty four days later, but given Liberia's recent history of failed accords there is little cause for optimism.

Issues and Events

When Taylor and the NPFL invaded Liberia from neighboring Sierra Leone in 1989, the nation was being run by General Samuel Doe, who had himself gained power in a coup nine years earlier.

Fierce fighting continued into 1990, when neighboring West African countries joined together to create a peacekeeping force to defend the capital of Liberia from the NPFL.

The West African force, dominated by Nigeria, became embroiled in the conflict despite its mandate to restore peace to Liberia. Although the NPFL gained control over most of the Liberian countryside, the West Africans prevented the NPFL from achieving a total takeover.

In 1990 Doe was killed by an NPFL splinter group, but fighting continued among four main factions who hoped to take over the government. When all of these competing groups agreed to stop fighting in 1991, it appeared as though the war might be over. It was not to be. A new group called the United Liberation Movement of Liberia for Democracy (ULIMO), which was composed of former Doe supporters, launched a full-scale attack against the West Africans. ULIMO later began to wage war against the NPFL.

Taylor used ULIMO's presence as an excuse not to disarm his own troops in accordance with the Yamoussoukro peace agreement he signed in October 1991. ULIMO launched a second, more vicious attack in 1992 which prompted Taylor to make another unsuccessful assault on the capital city of Monrovia.

In July 1993 a peace treaty was signed by the Armed Forces of Liberia (the remnants of the former Government of Liberia army), the NPFL, and ULIMO. The agreement, which was brokered by neighboring African nations, began to be implemented seven months later when a new interim government was installed under the leadership of Amos Sawyer.

Unfortunately the treaty was doomed to failure, mainly because there had been no progress in getting contestants to surrender their weapons. Today these three groups continue to contend for power, but the situation is further complicated by the formation of an array of other groups which continue to spring up. Every time a new group forms, the peace process is further complicated. The Yamoussoukro agreement in 1991 was signed by only two groups and failed to include ULIMO. The Cotonou agreement in 1993 included ULIMO, but did not include other splinter groups. Despite the fact that the December 1994 treaty was signed by six groups, several other new factions were not included. Fighting continues unabated.

Background

Liberia was founded in 1822 by freed American slaves, and became Africa's first independent republic in 1847. The former Americans intimidated the local people, and their decendants maintained control of the government until 1980, when General Samuel Doe staged a bloody coup against the Liberians of American descent.

Charles Taylor procured a job in Doe's government. After being accused of embezzling almost one million dollars from the Liberian treasury, he left the country. It was in Libya that he received support for his plan to take over the country.

Somalia: Clan Warfare in the Horn of Africa

Perspective

1887	*British Somaliland is established in northern Somalia.*
1889	*Italians gain control of southern Somaliland.*
1950	*Italian Somaliland is placed under a United Nations trusteeship.*
1954	*United Nations awards Ogaden region to Ethiopia.*
1960	**July 1.** *Italian Somaliland and British Somaliland merge to form a new, independent Somalia.*
1969	**October 1.** *General Mohammed Siad Barre stages a coup.*
1977	*War with Ethiopia begins.*
1988	**April.** *Peace treaty with Ethiopia is signed.* **May.** *Civil war begins as rebels launch a military offensive.*
1989	**July 14.** *Government troops kill 400 demonstrators.*
1990	**October.** *Siad Barre approves multiparty elections.* **December 28.** *United rebel troop factions launch a coup against President Siad Barre.*
1991	**January 26.** *Siad Barre is forced to flee.* **May 18.** *Northeast Somalia secedes and forms the Somaliland Republic.*
1992	**July 27.** *U.N. approves emergency food aid.* **September 14.** *U.N. sends 500 soldiers to protect food shipments.* **December 9.** *United States sends 24,000 troops to Somalia.*
1993	**February 24.** *Ten people are killed in anti-American riots.* **May 4.** *U.N. takes over relief effort.* **June 5.** *Ambush kills 24 Pakistani troops.* **October 3.** *Eighteen American troops die in attempt to capture General Mohammed Farah Aidid.*
1994	**March 25.** *Most U.S. forces leave Somalia.*
1995	**March 3.** *U.N. soldiers withdraw from Somalia.*

They were the kind of nightmarish pictures that can move a world seemingly immune to any more nightmares. Hundreds of thousands of Somalis dead from hunger, with thousands more—mere walking skeletons—awaiting their own tragic fate. In 1992, the world collectively acted to stop the famine, a consequence of anarchy and clan fighting that had destroyed the small African nation's very fabric. Through the United Nations, countries from Europe, America, Africa and Asia came together for the most expensive U.N. relief effort ever. International military forces, led by 24,000 troops from the United States, landed in Somalia with one goal: restore order so that food could reach the people and end the starvation.

Today the foreign troops are gone, international aid is waning, and the same conditions that existed in 1992 are reasserting themselves. Power-hungry rival clans intent on defeating each other at any cost have erased many of the gains made during the three-year U.N. mission. And now there seems to be little chance of further outside intervention. The nations of the world failed in their attempt to bring peace and restore order to Somalia. It is now up to the Somalis to look after themselves.

Issues and Events

When Siad Barre fled Somalia in 1991 after 22 years of rule, it set off a chain of events that plunged the country into an ever steeper downward spiral. Siad Barre left a nation of clans consumed with hatred for each other. Old scores were settled and new ones were spawned. During the next year, as many as 10% of Somalia's six million people were uprooted as violence swept the land. Hundreds of thousands sought shelter in refugee camps. Others were killed in mass slaughters. Without a government or national forces to enforce the law, warring groups terrorized the people. Commerce, agriculture and transportation virtually came to a halt, and the year's harvest was a disaster. The result was famine.

When the U.N. began to try to deliver aid in May 1992, the situation had become all but hopeless. Aid convoys were routinely looted by clans under the leadership of warlords vying for power. Food destined for the starving in the refugee camps turned up for sale on the black market in the capital, Mogadishu. Relief agencies were forced to hire the very gangs who were stealing the food to protect it, but with usually futile results. Ports and airports were controlled by warlords who extorted ever-increasing protection payments from the humanitarian groups.

Meanwhile, the U.N. was in an impossible situation. The agency was very unpopular with the Somalis. Some thought it favored a return of the hated Siad Barre, while others accused it of incompetence. Some factions considered the U.N. an obstacle to their hoped-for dominance of the country. In the fall of 1992, the U.N. accepted a U.S. offer to send 24,000 troops into the country to restore order.

At first the arrival of the Americans was widely welcomed, but then the situation soured. Warlords, realizing that the U.S. might pose an even bigger threat to their empires than the U.N., orchestrated protests and attacks on the soldiers. When ten people were killed in anti-American riots in early 1993, esteem for the forces in Mogadishu plummeted. But in the countryside, it was another matter. The Americans were able to achieve many of their goals. Food convoys, protected by U.S. heavy weapons and helicopters, reached the refugee camps without incident. Many Somalis, feeling more confident about their future, began returning to their homes. Schools reopened and merchants began selling goods again.

The peace, however, was perilous, and many obstacles remained. The very aid which was saving the lives of the starving had shattered the market for food, driving prices down and causing many farmers to quit farming. Violence continued throughout the country, although not at the level of the year before. In Mogadishu, the situation was especially acute. One warlord, Gen. Mohammed Farah Aidid, had emerged as the strongest. He openly taunted the foreigners; his forces harassed the troops with snipers, mines and skirmishes.

In May 1993, the U.S. turned command of the mission over to the U.N. For the Americans the situation had become an imbroglio. They had succeeded in their initial objective of ending the famine, but now they were embroiled in a political fight with no obvious resolution.

Under U.N. leadership, the peace-keeping force became truly multinational. The Americans were joined by military units from India, Morocco, Egypt, Malaysia, Canada, Greece, Italy, Belgium and other countries. The forces, however, were not organized into a cohesive unit. Most, including the Americans, stayed close to their compounds, avoiding contact with hostile Somalis.

This situation ended on June 5 when Aidid's forces ambushed a Pakistani patrol, killing 24. The various U.N. contingents now had a clear objective: capture Aidid. They did not. Protected by his scores of supporters, Aidid easily hid in the sprawling and primitive back streets of Mogadishu. The futile efforts of the U.N. forces to find Aidid only bolstered his image among many Somalis. The situation peaked on October 3, when the Americans launched a raid to capture him at a Mogadishu hotel. The results were disastrous. Seventeen Americans were killed, another captured, and 77 wounded. Aidid escaped and images of jubilant Somalis abusing the body of a dead American helicopter pilot were broadcast to the world.

The U.S. responded to the incident by announcing that it would withdraw most of its troops by March 1994 and leave the peacekeeping operation in the hands of the United Nations. Ongoing violence continued to plague the mission, and the U.N. recalled its troops one year later.

The U.N.'s original goal was to relieve food shortages and help the starving Somali people. By this standard the Somalia mission was a great success. It is estimated that the food distribution program enacted by the foreign troops saved at least 100,000 lives. However, the peacekeepers failed to bring about a permanent solution to Somalia's food crisis by helping them create a stable government. The decision to target Aidid was a dismal failure, and attempts to negotiate a political settlement did not include all of the many clan leaders who currently are in control of various areas of the country. Neither Aidid's forces nor those of any of his rivals have the strength to win control of the country. In the continuing absence of government, anarchy and lawlessness prevail.

Background

The British were the first Europeans to make a serious claim for Somalia, establishing the north as a protectorate of Britain in 1887. The Italians later established Italian Somaliland in the southern part of the country. During World War II, the Italians invaded British Somaliland, but the British retaliated and reclaimed both their own territory as well as that of Italy.

Although the Somalis had resisted the British early in the century, relations were generally good with the European nations until 1948 when the Ogaden region was returned to Ethiopia by the British. The loss of the land with its traditional grazing ground for nomadic herders was deeply resented. Despite reparation payments to Ogaden clan chiefs, resentment towards Western nations grew. The region became destabilized, which led eventually to war with Ethiopia.

Modern Somalia was formed when the British and former Italian lands were merged to form an independent nation in 1960. For the next nine years, the nation enjoyed a thriving democracy, which ended with the assassination of the president. Frustrated with civilian rule, the army staged a coup, installing Gen. Mohammed Siad Barre as president. Politicians were arrested and rival parties were banned. Siad Barre set up a socialist state under the control of the Somali Revolutionary Socialist Party, the sole legal political party.

During the next two decades, Siad Barre was credited with improving Somalia's infrastructure and schools. However, human rights abuses grew worse over time. In 1989 government troops opened fire on demonstrators protesting the arrest of several Islamic leaders and the assassination of a Roman Catholic bishop. Four hundred people are believed to have been killed, and several others were later executed. Barre attempted to defuse the growing unrest by approving a new constitution which called for political pluralism, but most felt that he was offering too little, too late. The coup that unseated Siad Barre took place only two months later.

Even before the war, Somalia was one of the world's poorest nations. The country is largely undeveloped and nomadic herding is the principal occupation. Despite the fact that almost all Somalis share the same culture, language, and religion, clan rivalries abound among the Somalis. Siad Barre capitalized on these traditional rivalries and maintained his power by artfully playing one clan against another. The legacy of hatred engendered by this tactic is probably the most atrocious of Siad Barre's crimes against his people.

The northeast region of Somalia seceded from the rest of the country shortly after Siad Barre was overthrown. The Somaliland Republic, as it is known, has not received international recognition.

South Africa: Charting a New Course

Perspective

1899-1902	*Boer War is fought between British and Boers.*
1910	*Union of South Africa is created.*
1913	*African National Congress (ANC) is formed in response to Native Lands Act.*
1950s	*National party institutes apartheid.*
1960	**March 21.** *Police open fire on a peaceful demonstration at Sharpeville. ANC is subsequently banned.*
1962	*ANC leader Nelson Mandela is jailed.*
1976	*Riots occur at Soweto.*
1984	*New constitution is implemented.*
1985	**July.** *State of emergency is imposed.*
1986	**April.** *Pass laws are abandoned.* **May.** *Crossroads Riots erupt.*
1989	**August 14.** *F.W. de Klerk replaces P.W. Botha as president.*
1990	**February 2.** *Ban on African National Congress (ANC) is lifted.* **February 11.** *Nelson Mandela is freed from prison.* **May 2.** *Government begins formal talks with ANC.* **June 7.** *National state of emergency is lifted.*
1991	**June.** *Remaining apartheid legislation is repealed.*
1992	**June 17.** *Boipatong massacre claims at least 40 lives.*
1993	**April 10.** *Rioting breaks out after the assassination of Chris Hani.* **July 25.** *Twelve die and 50 are injured in an attack on a white South African church.* **December 31.** *Black radicals open fire on a white South African pub.*
1994	**April 26–29.** *ANC wins landslide victory in first non-racial democratic elections.* **May 10.** *Mandela takes office as President with great ceremony.*

In 1962, Nelson Mandela was jailed for opposing apartheid, the system whereby the white minority had complete domination of South Africa and its black majority. When Mandela was released after 28 years, he found a country that was in the throes of change. South Africa was the object of world condemnation and sanctions. The president, F.W. de Klerk, had begun the process of tearing down the foundations of the white supremacist society, and the situation was volatile. Black groups began competing for power, and waves of factional bloodshed swept the country. Eventually all sides met at the negotiating table and South Africa's first non-racial democratic elections were held in April 1994. Mandela and his African National Congress party scored big and he took office as president the following month, 32 years after he had been jailed. Mandela now faces the enormous challenge of guiding South Africa through the minefield of conflicting interests and on to political stability.

Issues and Events

Apartheid, which is Afrikaans for "apartness," was used to separate the races in all aspects of life, but by the early 1980s, the normally intransigent ruling National Party recognized the fact that change was inevitable. President P.W. Botha then set into motion the dismantling of the apartheid laws. These reforms, which included the passage of a more liberal constitution and the repeal of several apartheid laws, prompted unrest among both blacks and whites. Rising black protests led to the declaration of a state of emergency, and white anger erupted in the "Crossroads Riots," which left 69 dead and 60,000 blacks homeless. The state of emergency, which began in 1985, remained in effect most of the time until 1990. More than 4,000 people were killed during this violent chapter in South African history.

F.W. de Klerk replaced P.W. Botha as president in 1990. He began 1990 by lifting a thirty-year ban on the powerful African National Congress (ANC) and releasing political activist Nelson Mandela from prison. Mandela emerged as a leader of the ANC, and in his new role as statesman took part in negotiations with de Klerk. By 1991 all of the remaining apartheid laws had been repealed, and late in the year negotiations about the nation's future began.

While the negotiations brought hope for political progress, they also led to a terrifying outbreak of factional violence between the ANC and Inkatha, an organization led by Zulu chief Mangosuthu Buthelezi. The ANC and Inkatha have been long-time rivals for political influence in the black community. In the 1980s the ANC advocated armed struggle and international sanctions against the whites, while Inkatha argued that it was impossible to defeat the whites militarily and that sanctions hurt the blacks more than the whites. As a result of its more moderate policies, Inkatha received support from the government, while the ANC was banned for its radical stance.

With the initiation of reforms and the release of Mandela, the government began negotiations exclusively with the ANC. This tactic infuriated Inkatha supporters, who claimed that the ANC sought to establish itself as the head of a dictatorship. Violence between the ANC and Inkatha resulted in thousands of deaths after Mandela's release, and attempts by both Mandela and Buthelezi to stop the violence met with little success.

One of the most violent incidents in recent history was the Boipatong massacre, in which an Inkatha attack on ANC supporters resulted in at least 40 deaths. The attackers were residents of one of South Africa's many company-run hostels where black men are forced to live without their families in deplorable conditions. As in many other cases, the police were accused of passively observing the attack and failing to intervene.

Racially-motivated violence also rose dramatically. Both blacks and whites engaged in terrorism aimed at derailing South Africa's shift to a free society. In April, 1993 rioting broke out across South Africa after Chris Hani, the charismatic black leader of the South African Communist Party, was assassinated by white racists. Black extremists also took up arms. In December two radical groups took responsibility for a brutal attack against whites at a South African pub. Other acts of terrorism were engineered to create fear and suspicion on all sides, as when a group of mixed blacks and whites led an attack against a white church which resulted in the deaths of a dozen people and the wounding of fifty others.

Amidst the growing violence, multiparty constitutional talks were held in 1993. It was a comprehensive gathering with delegates from 265 parties, including the government, the ANC, Inkatha, the white Conservative Party, and the black Pan-Africanist Congress. In the months that followed, political wrangling continued as various factions tried to secure concessions. The outcome was historic elections in which more than 22 million South Africans voted. As expected, the ANC won in a sweeping victory.

Transformed from outcast to statesman, Mandela began a policy of inclusion when he took office as president on May 10. He appointed de Klerk his second deputy and went to great lengths to include whites and rival blacks in his first government. His first budget called for aid to impoverished blacks, but he avoided the huge tax increase that had been feared by many middle class whites.

Although the violence that surrounded the transition to democracy has died down, Mandela and his government face many challenges. Mandela must determine how to redistribute land from white owners to 40,000 blacks who were denied land ownership under apartheid. Black communities need clinics, water, sanitation, and housing. Tribal leaders protest upcoming local elections as an infringement of their authority. A growing rift in Zulu leadership threatens to explode into violence. Although international sanctions have been lifted, outside investment in South Africa has not been as brisk as expected. Finally, the country has been plagued by labor strikes as blacks complain that Mandela has not done enough to improve their quality of life.

Navigating through these and a myriad of other controversies and issues will not be easy for Mandela and the government. But if South Africa is to have a future as a peaceful democracy where every person enjoys equal rights, they will have to succeed.

Background

Race has been the central cause of problems in South Africa since the arrival of the first Dutch settlers, called Boers, in the 1650s. When the British took over the Cape Colony in 1803, four major groups inhabited the territory, including the Boers, or Afrikaners; slaves of African-Malay descent, who would be the basis of the country's colored population; the nomadic Hottentots, who were badly treated by the Boers; and the black Bantu peoples, who lived beyond the frontiers and were in constant conflict with the expanding settlements.

British attempts to integrate these groups led to an exodus of the Boers in 1836, known as the Great Trek. More than twelve thousand Boers left the southern Cape province for Natal and Transvaal to the northeast, where they created their own states and laws. After the discovery of diamonds and gold in the Transvaal, the British asserted rule in the region and the Boer War ensued. The Boers lost, and the Union of South Africa was created under British auspices in 1910.

The country passed the Native Lands Act in 1913, establishing Bantu areas and forbidding black ownership of land within designated white areas, which comprised over 87 percent of the total area. When the predominantly white Afrikaner National Party came to power in 1948, the concept of "separate development," or apartheid, came to fruition.

In 1949 the Mixed Marriages Act made interracial marriage a crime. In 1950 the Population Registration Act required all citizens to be registered by race, while the Group Areas Act of 1950 allocated specific residential areas to various racial groups. The Reservation of Separate Amenities Act and Black Education Act resembled segregation laws of the American South before the 1950s.

The African National Congress (ANC) was formed in 1913 in response to the Native Lands Act. This predominantly black organization waged a political war against the white government and its racist laws until it was banned in 1960, following a police attack against peaceful demonstrators at Sharpeville. The ANC and many of its leaders, including Nelson Mandela, subsequently began advocating violence as a means of overthrowing the government. The organization was not endorsed by many blacks, who were alienated by the ANC membership because they were richer and better-educated than most.

Student protests erupted into full-scale rioting in 1976 in Soweto, a black section of Johannesburg, resulting in hundreds of deaths and thousands of injuries. The riots marked the awakening of true black political consciousness in South Africa and the beginning of a growing protest movement among many ordinary black people.

An important part of apartheid was the creation of "homelands" for the native black population. The homelands were to be organized along ethnic lines and given what the South African government called "full independence." Homelands residents were forced to renounce South African citizenship, a ploy by the government to create a white majority of South African citizens. Neither the United Nations nor any foreign government recognized Transkei, Bophuthatswana, Venda, or Ciskei as sovereign countries. The homelands were abolished in 1994.

Angola: A Tentative Peace

Perspective

1961	*War for independence begins.*
1975	**November 11.** *Angola gains independence; civil war ensues; Cuban troops arrive.*
1976	*Popular Movement for the Liberation of Angola (MPLA) gains control of the government. National Union for the Total Independence of Angola (UNITA) continues to wage war.*
1988	**December 22.** *Regional accord is reached, but fighting continues.*
1991	**May 1.** *Peace accord is reached.* **May 25.** *Cuban troops leave Angola.*
1992	**September 29.** *UNITA refuses to accept defeat in Angola's first multiparty elections.* **October 17.** *Fighting resumes.*
1994	**June 14.** *United Nations cancels food aid to Angola.* **November 20.** *Another peace treaty is signed.*
1995	**February 8.** *United Nations votes to send peacekeeping forces to Angola.*

When Angolans went to the polls in 1992 for their country's first multiparty elections, they were confident that peace had finally come after sixteen years of civil war. However, hopes that democracy would bring stability and prosperity were shattered when the results of the elections sparked renewed fighting. In 1994 another peace treaty was signed, but war-weary Angolans are more cautious than before. While everyone hopes that this time peace will last, they also know that it could be just another interlude in the ongoing dispute.

Issues and Events

After a war for independence that lasted thirteen years, the Portuguese finally relinquished Angola in 1974. When fighting broke out in 1975 foreign intervention swiftly followed. Cuban troops moved in that same year to aid the Popular Movement for the Liberation of Angola (MPLA), while the South Africans came to the aid of their opposition, a coalition of the National Union for the Total Independence of Angola (UNITA).

By 1976 the MPLA had gained control of the government, but the fighting between the rival groups continued. The MPLA evolved into a single-party Marxist-Leninist state and received assistance from the Soviet Union. UNITA enjoyed the support of those nations which opposed the spread of communism in Africa, including the United States.

The end of the cold war heralded an era of cooperation between the Soviet Union and the United States, and the two superpowers mediated a negotiated settlement in 1988, but the war raged on until a true peace accord was reached in May 1991 which called for a cease-fire and multiparty elections monitored by the United Nations.

The elections, which were held in the following year, resulted in a sound victory for the MPLA. Despite claims by independent observers that the elections were fair, UNITA refused to recognize the results and conflict resumed one month later. Mass migration from the war-torn countryside brought agricultural production to a standstill and massive starvation ensued.

Each side has been accused of indiscriminately killing civilians suspected of supporting the opposing side. The MPLA is accused of corruption and repression, while UNITA is blamed for countless massacres and atrocities.

Escalated fighting in 1994 caused the interruption of food aid to starving people and resulted in tens of thousands of deaths. By late in the year, UNITA was severely weakened and agreed to sign another peace treaty.

The new treaty is an improvement over the old one because it guarantees some power to UNITA, and also because the truce will be enforced by 7,000 United Nations peace-keeping forces. UNITA's continuing decline seems assured unless it can come up with new foreign support. Not only has funding from foreign sources like the United States and South Africa dried up, but it has also lost control of the diamond mines that it used for financing the war.

However, peace is by no means assured. Neither UNITA nor the MPLA seems to be ready for true power-sharing and no provisions have been made for disarming opposing factions. It is possible that UNITA signed the agreement only to give itself time to rebuild its depleted army. Meanwhile, economic problems and a shattered infrastructure plague the nation. Hunger, disease, and leftover land mines continue to take their toll on the devastated populace.

Background

The Portuguese began colonizing Angola in the 15th century and used it primarily as a source for slave labor for Brazil. After slavery was abolished in Angola in 1858, Portugal concentrated on exploiting Angola's rich agricultural and mineral resources. When the Portuguese finally relinquished sovereignty in 1974, they failed to make provisions for a smooth transition of power and civil war erupted the following year when Angolan independence was complete. Oil-rich Angola could be one of Africa's most prosperous nations if political stability could be achieved.

Rwanda: Tribal Holocaust

Perspective

1400s	*The Tutsi establish a monarchy in the Rwandan area.*
1916	*Belgium gains control of Rwanda.*
1959	*Rwandan war for independence ends with Hutu in power.*
1962	*160,000 Tutsi refugees flee the country.*
1973	**July 5.** *A military coup is launched by General Juvenal Habyarimana.*
1978	*Habyarimana is elected President.*
1990	*Tutsi soldiers known as the Rwandan Patriotic Front (RPF) attempt to take over Rwanda.*
1993	**August.** *Peace treaty between the government and RPF is signed.*
1994	**April 6.** *Habyarimana is killed in a suspicious plane crash. Hutu militia begin slaughtering Tutsi.* **July 18.** *RPF invades and declares victory over the Hutu government. One million Hutu flee to Zaire.*
1995	**April 22.** *Thousands of refugees are killed by government troops.*

For centuries the cattle-rearing Tutsi and the agrarian Hutu lived together relatively peacefully in the area now known as Rwanda. First Germany, then Belgium, set up regimes that insidiously played the two tribes against each other. The minority Tutsi were given preferential treatment, which raised the ire of the majority Hutu.

Ethnic and political tensions exploded in 1994 and the world witnessed one of the most tragic examples of genocide ever enacted. Hutu military units began a systematic killing spree in which at least 500,000 people—mainly Tutsi—were killed.

Issues and Events

The violence began when the president of the Hutu-dominated government was killed in a mysterious plane crash. Because the massacre of Tutsi began nation-wide only hours after the crash, many suspect that the crash was engineered by radical Hutu who opposed the increasingly liberal government of President Habyarimana. Besides killing Tutsi, Hutu militia and government troops also executed moderate Hutu who had favored political empowerment for the Tutsi.

The reports that made it out to the rest of the world were horrific. Tutsi hiding in churches were locked inside while the buildings were set on fire. People were buried alive. Refugees were bombed. Entire villages were wiped out. Red Cross workers and the orphans they were guarding were killed.

The insanity ended in July when the Tutsi-dominated Rwandan Patriotic Front (RPF) defeated the Hutu government. The RPF had been at war with the government since 1973. Despite being outnumbered, the Tutsi were able to defeat the Hutu with their superior military skills and rigid discipline. Most of the members of the RPF had been refugees since the war for independence in the early 1960s and had served in the Ugandan army.

Fearing retaliation, between one and two million Hutu refugees fled Rwanda and were packed into refugee camps where starvation, exhaustion, cholera, and dysentery claimed thousands of lives. Today most of these people are still refugees, many of them virtual hostages of former Hutu militia who terrorize them with tales of Tutsi retribution. The Hutu's fears were realized when thousands were killed during the attempted closure of one of the camps. Government troops surrounded the camp and herded 50,000 refugees to a nearby hillside, where they were held without adequate food and water. Armed Hutu militia within the camp incited the refugees to try to break away from the soldiers. In the ensuing panic, thousands of unarmed people were either shot or trampled to death.

The Tutsi government claims that reports of thousands of deaths are greatly exaggerated and that the Hutu militia provoked the incident. The President of Rwanda expressed his regrets, and denied that it was an example of Tutsi revenge against the Hutu. The Tutsi government's official position is that it is trying to form a coalition government by placing many Hutu in high government offices.

National reconciliation is imperative to Rwanda's future. Until the government can lure the refugees back, the prospects for the future are grim. Ongoing attacks launched from Hutu refugee camps are inevitable. Perhaps even more serious is the effect on the economy. Although many Tutsi who had been refugees since the 1960s are returning to Rwanda, their numbers are not enough to stimulate economic activity and produce enough food for the country. It is estimated that about half of the population of Rwanda faces food shortages during 1995.

Background

Tutsi kings ruled Rwanda for hundreds of years before the arrival of Europeans. Germany colonized Rwanda for a short time, but Belgium soon gained control. The nation was born out of a civil war in which the majority Hutu tribe was victorious. A military coup in 1973 resulted in a government still dominated by Hutu.

Rwanda is a poor country which suffers from severe overpopulation. Observers fear that the violence in Rwanda could be the first of many "population wars" and that the real reason for the war was Rwanda's scarcity of land and other resources. The war in Rwanda is of special concern to neighboring Burundi, which is also trying to control growing violence between the Hutu and Tutsi tribes and suffers from similar overcrowding.

South America

The South American republics have often been characterized by political instability. The military plays an important part in their political life, and civilian governments frequently rule only with military approval. Popularly elected democratic governments are often overthrown and replaced by military juntas. Human rights abuses become commonplace as these governments cling to the reins of power despite a lack of popular support.

Recent political reforms throughout the region have left the causes of unrest unchanged. In most South American countries there is dramatic economic polarity: a political and economic elite which enjoys luxury and privilege, contrasted with oppressed masses who survive in the most dire poverty. This large, underprivileged majority has often been systematically exploited by a succession of rulers interested only in personal wealth and power.

The patterns of inequity in South America's wealth distribution were set down hundreds of years ago during the region's colonial period, and the situation in modern South America is partly a result of European colonial influences upon an indigenous population.

The dominant colonial power in South America was Spain, although Portugal, the Netherlands, Britain, and France also acquired possessions in the area. Portugal's influence is evidenced in Brazil, where Portuguese is the predominant language.

Prior to the arrival of the Europeans around the sixteenth century, various Indian peoples inhabited the region. Among these were the Incas, whose sophisticated civilization flourished in the areas of present-day Ecuador, Peru, and Bolivia.

The first major wave of European settlement occurred in the 1500s with the arrival of the Spanish conquistadors. The resistance offered by most Indian groups was ineffectual, and Indian lands quickly fell to the invaders.

Many of the early settlers were drawn to South America by the promise of wealth. As word of the continent's natural riches spread back to Europe, fortune-seeking colonists flocked to the region. Oftentimes the promise of gold and silver remained unfulfilled, but most settlers stayed on, establishing large plantations that laid the basis for much of South America's present economy. The colonists took the conquered Indians as slaves to work their farmlands, and soon a thriving agriculture was established.

Much of the indigenous population disappeared during the colonial period. Wars with the settlers, labor-intensive plantations, and exposure to European diseases claimed thousands of Indian lives. In addition, many of the Indians who managed to survive intermarried with the Europeans. Modern South America's large mestizo population, of mixed Spanish and Indian blood, is a result of these relationships.

As the Indians were decimated by colonial rule, blacks were brought from Africa to continue slave labor on the plantations. Development increased, and the descendants of the early settlers soon established a unique South American culture, combining influences of their ancestors into a lifestyle evolved from the plantation economy.

Prosperity continued, and in time the large-estate holders, many of them mestizos, found themselves wielding economic influence but enjoying few of the benefits of their profits. Native-born South Americans of Spanish descent were equally dissatisfied with colonial status. Political power remained in the hands of the mother country, whose people and government now had little in common with South American life. Resentment toward the ruling powers grew, along with the colonies' demands for a voice in their government.

The region remained politically unstable following independence. It was a class that already possessed a certain amount of influence that won the fight for self-rule during the 1800s, and the change in government only shifted power from the European rulers to South American elite. Thus the change in leadership did not bring beneficial reforms to the many people outside the small circle of those with economic influence. Subsequent economic development concentrated wealth more solidly in the hands of the rich. Land ownership is a critical issue throughout South America, where most of the arable land is held by a few, while most of the rural population holds none.

Great inequities in the distribution of wealth led to the emergence of left-wing guerrilla groups such as the Shining Path in Peru and the National Liberation Army in Colombia. The rich, having a vested interest in maintaining the status quo, supported the rise of military governments and right-wing vigilante groups throughout the region to fight these leftist movements. The governments developed ruthless tactics to stay in power, such as the use of "disappearances," or kidnappings followed by secret executions. Military governments also terrorized the populace by using "death squads," or government-sanctioned vigilante groups, to eliminate their opposition. The emergence of elected governments throughout South America has reduced but not ended the struggle between right-wing terrorists and various Marxist groups. However, there is no doubt that if democratically elected governments fail to bring reform and economic prosperity, they may once again fall prey to dictatorships or military regimes. In Peru, democracy and freedom of the press have been all but eliminated by President Fujimori in his attempt to thwart a terrorist takeover. Chile's tenuous democracy is also threatened by growing friction between the government and the country's powerful military about human rights issues.

Political problems have been compounded by growing economic instability in the region. During the 1960s South American countries began taking out loans from foreign banks and governments to finance major development programs, such as roads, airports, and hydroelectric projects. Much of the money was wasted through mismanagement and corruption, and, by the early 1980s, many of the countries were unable to keep up their payments on the loans. Suddenly the flow of foreign capital dried up and the region began a period of runaway inflation, rising poverty, unemployment, and severe economic recession. This economic failure and growing concern for human rights led to the establishment of civilian governments in most nations by the end of the decade, but the problems created by the previous governments endure.

Political stability in the region will largely depend upon whether the civilian governments will be able to improve the overall standard of living. Argentina is a prime example of a country that was governed by a series of military or civilian dictatorships until 1983, when the junta fell to a democratically elected government. In an attempt to reduce triple-digit inflation and to amass capital to keep up its debt payments, the government was forced to implement a severe austerity program. The result was recession, unemployment, and a drastic reduction in social services. By 1993, however, the economy was showing some hopeful signs. Inflation for the year was four percent and progress was made on reducing foreign debt. Major elections have proceeded as planned and it is hoped that the Argentinean government is now on firm footing. Other nations in the region are looking to mimic the Argentinean model.

South America's economic malaise has been a boon for the lucrative drug trafficking industry. Cocaine is the main source of income for thousands of peasant farmers in Peru, Bolivia and neighboring nations. Colombia's mammoth cocaine processing industry has resulted in economic vitality, but the cocaine trade generates such huge profits that corruption and violence are the law of the land in some areas where governmental authority is widely flaunted. The United States, the major market for the illicit drug, has tried to pressure the South American countries to stop the production and exportation of cocaine, without much success.

Perhaps the most far-reaching consequence of the South American debt crisis is the over-exploitation of the area's resources, such as the rain forest. Throughout the region, vast tracts of virgin forest have fallen prey to those who would put the land to alternative uses. In Brazil, poverty and the largest foreign debt in South America led to a drive to convert the Amazonian rain forest to agricultural and other uses with disastrous results. International outcry has subsequently forced the government to come up with a rational plan to develop and exploit the rain forest without destroying it. But Brazil's own problems with widespread corruption have hampered these efforts.

Peru: Democracy Fails

Perspective

1542	*Spanish conquistadors defeat Peruvian Incas.*
1824	*Peru gains independence from Spain.*
1968	*Military government adopts the socialist Inca Plan.*
1979	*A new constitution brings back democracy and private ownership.*
1980	*Abimael Guzman founds the Shining Path.*
1982	*The Shining Path frees 250 prisoners from jail; a state of emergency is declared.*
1984	*The Tupac Amaru Revolutionary Movement is formed.*
1989	**March 23.** *The Shining Path disrupts mining operations.*
1990	**June 10.** *Reform candidate Alberto Fujimori is elected president.* **August.** *Fujimori implements economic austerity measures.* **September.** *Seventy people are killed during clashes between the Shining Path and the army.*
1991	**April 5.** *The Shining Path launches a campaign of urban terrorism with a series of bombings in several Peruvian cities.*
1992	**April 6.** *Fujimori dissolves the government and suspends the constitution.* **September 12.** *Guzman is arrested.*
1993	**August 19.** *Shining Path guerrillas are accused of killing over 60 Indian villagers.* **October 31.** *Voters approve a new constitution strengthening Fujimori's powers.*
1994	**April 5.** *Government offensive against terrorists draws protests from human rights advocates.*
1995	**January.** *War with Ecuador begins.* **March 1.** *Cease-fire agreement is signed.* **April 9.** *Fujimori is reelected as president.*

Despite its rich resources, Peru remains a poor country. Like many other South American countries, it has been unable to free itself from the legacy of its colonial past and heritage of political repression. Over 80 percent of the people are either native American or mestizo, but the country remains in the hands of a very small, wealthy, white ruling class which controls the government and the economy. This racially divided country has had little experience with democracy, and the ever-expanding chasm between the rich and the poor has made it an ideal breeding ground for the development of radical terrorist groups who find sympathy among the poor. Terrorism was one of many factors that led to the suspension of Peru's fragile democracy by President Alberto Fujimori in 1992. Although he has indicated that he is willing to share power with a new government, many wonder whether he will succumb to the temptation to retain power for himself and become another in the long list of South American dictators.

Issues and Events

At the time of Fujimori's election in 1989, the Peruvian economy was in a shambles as a result of thirty years of corruption and mismanagement. Hyperinflation had devastated the economy and real wages had fallen by more than 60 percent between 1987 and 1989. Extreme poverty was widespread, and desperation fueled the growth of terrorist groups such as the Shining Path and the Tupac Amaru Revolutionary Movement, who were waging a campaign that came perilously close to plunging the country into anarchy.

The Shining Path vowed to defeat the government by the year 2000, and it seemed as though this goal might be within reach. After years of terrorizing the countryside, the Shining Path struck at the heart of the Peruvian economy in 1989 when it directed a series of attacks against the nation's lucrative mining industry. In 1991 it moved its campaign of terror from the countryside to the nation's urban areas. In a single day in April, it bombed several embassies and banks and knocked out electrical power in several Peruvian cities, including Lima. The Tupac Amaru Revolutionary Movement caused havoc later in the year with twelve more bank bombings and a grenade attack against the presidential palace. By 1992 terrorism by all groups had claimed more than 25,000 lives.

The growth of the Shining Path was paralleled by increased abuses by the Peruvian security forces. Since the government began cracking down on terrorism, more than 3,700 people "disappeared," probably kidnapped and secretly killed by the military, making Peru's human rights records one of the worst in the world. The army was also accused of raiding villages and killing innocent people rumored to be in league with the Shining Path. By far the largest number of casualties in the war between the Shining Path and security forces were innocent civilians caught in the crossfire.

Although Fujimori managed to bring inflation under control with severe economic austerity measures, he argued that political and economic reform could not be accomplished until the terrorist insurgency was defeated. Frustration with congressional opposition to measures designed to end terrorism was the official reason given by Fujimori for dismissing the government in April 1992 and assuming dictatorial powers.

The abandonment of democracy by Fujimori was not well received by the international community and resulted in diplomatic isolation for Peru. A measure of Peruvian disillusionment with democracy is that the people of Peru remained supportive of Fujimori and any action that might bring an end to mounting terrorism.

Five months later Fujimori was vindicated when security forces managed to capture the Shining Path's leader, Abimael Guzman. Even though it was rumored that the operation was conceived and executed without Fujimori's knowledge, Guzman's arrest and imprisonment was a profound psychological victory for Fujimori and it served to greatly reduce public fear of a Shining Path takeover. In the months that followed, hundreds of other Shining Path leaders and followers were jailed, as were members of other terrorist groups.

Fujimori's popularity soared in 1995 in the aftermath of a short-lived war between Ecuador and Peru regarding a longstanding territorial dispute. Even though Peru, with its superior numbers and resources, was unable to defeat Ecuador, the war aroused nationalist sentiments in both countries. The war also served to eclipse other problems, such as ongoing accusations of human rights violations and corruption. As a result, Fujimori won a landslide victory in presidential elections that were held in April, only one month after a cease-fire agreement was reached.

Peruvians persist in their support of Fujimori because they feel that he is leading the country to peace and prosperity. The economy continues to improve, foreign debt has been reduced, and the budget is being balanced. While these accomplishments have been applauded by foreign observers and investors, the plight of the poor has not improved. Only one-third of all Peruvians are adequately employed, and almost all of the wealth remains in the hands of the aristocracy. Sporadic terrorist attacks are still common, and many areas remain under a state of emergency.

Although he has accomplished much, Fujimori himself is perhaps the greatest threat to Peru's long-term stability. His assumption of almost absolute power has improved economic conditions and at least temporarily derailed the existing terrorist movements, but these accomplishments will be short-lived if he cannot steer the country back toward democracy. In 1992 he instituted a new congress heavily stacked with his allies, and in 1993 he substantially increased his powers by introducing a new constitution that gave him increased powers over the courts, legislature, and the military. It also contained a clause that could allow Fujimori to remain in office until the year 2005.

Fujimori is likely to remain a volatile force in South American politics for years to come. Peace and stability cannot be achieved as long as the conditions that brought Peru to the brink of disaster in the 1980s still exist. Fujimori has not yet faced off with the Peruvian aristocracy by making any serious attempts to redistribute Peru's wealth. Until economic justice is achieved, the nation will continue to teeter on the brink of chaos.

Background

Indian civilization flourished in Peru for more than a thousand years before the invasion of the Spanish. In the thirteenth century the Incas established a great empire which included almost all of Peru and much of Chile. The Incas had a sophisticated system of government, and were also known for their lavish art and monumental architecture.

Weakened by a civil war, the Incas were easily defeated after they were first encountered by Francisco Pizarro in 1531. The Spanish gained complete control of the former Inca empire by 1542 and established Peru as their colony. The land was rich in gold and silver, and the treasures of Peru made Spain one of the world's richest nations. During the period of colonial rule, the Indians were ruthlessly exploited and all wealth was concentrated in the hands of the Spanish aristocracy who lived in Lima, the capital. Despite several attempted Indian uprisings, the Spanish aristocracy managed to hold on to power, and the patterns of wealth have remained largely intact for centuries.

Peru might have remained a colony of Spain had it not been for independence movements in other countries that sought to drive Spain from the Western Hemisphere. Spanish influence ended in 1824, and Peru's history has since been dominated by dictators and military governments. The most recent military government took over in 1968 and instituted the Inca Plan, which advocated socialism and land reform. Despite its lofty goals, the plan suffered from mismanagement and ultimately failed to bring prosperity to the people. A new constitution was passed in 1979 and elections were held in 1980, but the legacy of economic mismanagement and social inequity continues to plague the Peruvian people.

Both the Shining Path and the Tupac Amaru Revolutionary Movement were formed in the early 1980s as a protest to the democratic government's abandonment of socialist programs and the subsequent return to capitalism. The Tupac Amaru Revolutionary Movement advocates a Cuban-style revolution. It wages its war primarily against foreigners and government institutions. The Sendero Luminoso, or Shining Path, was founded by Abimael Guzman, a former professor of philosophy who advocated an all-out war against capitalism.

Colombia: Cocaine, Corruption, and Chaos

Perspective

1899–1902	*Bloody civil war casts Colombia into series of bitter class struggles.*
1948–66	La Violencia *rages for two decades.*
1979	*Colombia and United States sign extradition treaty.*
1984	**March 10.** *Colombian narcotics squads raid Tranquilandia.* **April 30.** *Minister of Justice is assassinated.* **May 1.** *National state of emergency is declared; extradition of narcotics traffickers to United States begins.*
1985	**November.** *Guerrillas seize the Palace of Justice; 106 people die.*
1987	**February 4.** *Carlos Lehder is extradited to the United States.* **June.** *Extradition treaty is declared unconstitutional.*
1988	**January.** *Attorney General Carlos Mauro Hoyos is assassinated.*
1989	**August 18.** *Presidential front-runner Luís Carlos Galán is assassinated.* **December 15.** *Gonzalo Gacha is killed in shoot-out with Colombian authorities.*
1990	**September.** *Government waives extradition of drug traffickers.* **December 18.** *Fabio Ochoa Jr. surrenders.*
1991	**January 15.** *Jorge Ochoa surrenders.* **June 19.** *Pablo Escobar surrenders.*
1992	**July 22.** *Escobar breaks out of jail.*
1993	**December 2.** *Escobar is killed by federal squad.*
1994	**August 7.** *Ernesto Samper is sworn in as President despite possible ties to the Cali cartel.* **December 22.** *Peasant farmers protest cocaine eradication program.*

Colombians had reason for optimism as 1993 ended with the death of Pablo Escobar, the ruthless leader of the infamous Medellín cocaine cartel. Escobar was the last of the Medellín drug lords; all of the others had been arrested or killed. For more than a decade, the cartel had engaged in the illegal processing and sale of cocaine, and its leaders had amassed tremendous fortunes. By means of extortion and terrorism, the Medellín cartel held a stranglehold on the Colombian government and judicial system.

However, the demise of the Medellín cartel has had virtually no effect on the flow of illegal drugs out of Colombia and into the United States. A rival narcotics cartel based in the city of Cali has profited from the collapse of the Medellín cartel and has taken over the Colombian drug trade. Although its tactics are different, its control over the Colombian government is just as strong.

Issues and Events

Cocaine has had a tremendous effect on the Colombian economy. The profits are enormous. A kilogram of cocaine can be purchased in Colombia for $2,000 and resold in the United States for as much as $20,000. It is believed that revenue from illegal exports of cocaine exceeds that of coffee, Colombia's leading legitimate export crop. For farmers, coca has become the crop of choice because it is about six times more profitable than any of the legitimate alternatives. It is estimated that as many as 300,000 people are currently engaged in growing coca in Colombia.

Thousands are employed as processors, pilots, distributors, lawyers, and killers. Billions of cocaine dollars are invested in Colombia each year. While the effect on the economy has been positive, Colombia has paid a high price for its prosperity. The country experiences an unparalleled level of peacetime violence, much of it drug-related. The homicide rate in Colombia is six times higher than in the United States, and paid assassins can be bought for as little as $10.

The Medellín cartel instilled fear throughout the government. Escobar was particularly vicious in his war against all who opposed him, and was believed to be responsible for hundreds of deaths. Among the many victims were a presidential candidate, a justice minister, and an airliner full of passengers.

The judicial system was hit the hardest. Judges learned to live with continual threats of violence against themselves and their families. More than 200 judges and judicial employees were assassinated by the drug lords. In 1985, guerrillas enticed by drug money seized the Palace of Justice and killed eleven Supreme Court justices. Most drug-related crimes went unpunished because judges feared the wrath of the cartel. On several occasions, judiciary officials went on strike to protest the lack of protection afforded them by the government, and thousands have resigned in recent years.

Unlike the Medellín cartel, the Cali cooperative relies less on violence and more on greed. Rather than trying to intimidate officials with assassinations and bombings, the Cali cartel has achieved success by buying off Colombia's police, armed forces, politicians, customs agents, airport authorities, and judges. Corruption is a growing problem at all levels of government. In an ongoing scandal, Colombia's new president Ernesto Samper has been accused of accepting huge campaign contributions from the Cali cartel. The Cali cartel is believed to control more than 75 percent of the world's cocaine trade, and a growing percentage of the heroin trade.

Over the years Colombia has faced mounting pressure to control its outflow of illegal drugs to the United States. In 1979 the two countries signed an extradition treaty which provided for drug dealers to be sent to the United States to face trial. Extradition has been a powerful weapon against the Colombian drug lords, whose power and influence do not extend to the United States. Also, the U.S. penalties for drug smuggling are far more severe than those meted out in Columbia. In addition, the United States has assisted the Colombian government by providing $100 million for narcotics control and furnishing technical advice to Colombia on law enforcement techniques and crop eradication methods.

The U.S. is less than satisfied with Colombia's drug enforcement efforts. In 1995 the State Department issued a statement that Colombia's weak legislation, corruption and inefficiency have hampered its efforts to bring narcotics traffickers to justice. They argue that there were no major drug prosecutions and that coca production increased by over 10 percent during 1994.

Without U.S. intervention, it is doubtful that the Colombians would do much to reduce the drug trafficking. It is enormously profitable, and the Colombians do not consider it a moral issue. They resent the continual interference by the United States and argue that the US should do more to curb its appetite for illegal drugs. In 1994 Colombia legalized personal drug use, and many people, including Colombia's Prosecutor General, believe that the only way to defeat the drug lords is to legalize all drug sales and place it under government control.

Farmers are increasingly angry about the government's crop eradication program, which involves spraying coca fields with herbicides that also ruin the farmers' food supplies. In December 1994 thousands of peasant farmers banded together and stopped the flow of oil in a major oil pipeline until the government agreed to stop spraying smaller fields. The government fears that if it continues to try to get the farmers to quit growing coca, they will be playing into the hands of the many left-wing guerrilla movements that plague the nation.

Background

Ever since the constitutions of 1853 and 1858 were instituted, Colombia has been held up as a model republic—one of Latin America's few enduring democracies. It has, however, had more than its share of violence. Between 1899 and 1902, it underwent a horrendous civil war during which nearly 150,000 people were killed. Two more decades of unabated violence terrorized the country between 1948 and 1968, following the assassination of Jorge Eliécer Gaitán—hero of the underprivileged classes. During this era, known as La Violencia, 300,000 people were murdered as city streets became battlegrounds and the countryside was drowned in anarchy.

The greatest cause of so much unrest in Colombia's history has been the gross inequities of land and wealth distribution. The economy typically has had to rely on bonanza crops of one sort or another, rather than on steady growth.

Cocaine, the latest bonanza crop, is not native to Colombia. The Colombian drug lords, known as narcos, make their money purchasing coca leaves and paste from Peru and Bolivia, refining the raw coca in Colombia, then overseeing its distribution in the United States. By handling all aspects of the cocaine's manufacture and sale, the narcos are able to reap fantastic profits.

Medellín's most famous cartel member was Pablo Escobar Gaviria, known by many as "Don Pablo the Good" for his many philanthropic works. Medellín boasts a large zoo built by Escobar, as well as rows of housing for the poor. Carlos Lehder was one of the masterminds of the cartel. Other drug lords included Fabio Ochoa and his sons Jorge, Juan, and Fabio, Jr. Gonzalo Rodriguez Gacha rose to prominence during 1988 after the arrest of Carlos Lehder. Known as "El Mexicano" for his love of Mexico, he once gave a sombrero to every resident of his home town. Colombia's war against the narcos heated up in 1984 when the government forces raided a major drug operation called Tranquilandia ("Land of Tranquillity"), located deep in the jungle, and seized more than a billion dollars' worth of cocaine. The narcos fought back by assassinating the country's Minister of Justice.

In 1987, Carlos Lehder was the first member of the Medellín cartel to face extradition to the United States. U.S. courts sentenced 39-year-old Lehder to life plus 150 years at a high-security facility in Illinois. Lehder's extradition angered many Colombians, and the Colombian supreme court declared the treaty unconstitutional.

The treaty was reinstated in 1989 after the Medellín cartel was accused of assassinating a presidential hopeful during a political rally. The killing outraged the public, and the government launched another serious assault against the narcotics traffickers. They seized more than $200 million in property, made more than 11,000 arrests, and offered special protection for judicial officials. They also sought out Medellín cartel leader Gonzalo Gacha, who was killed in a shoot-out with Colombian authorities. Despite increased extraditions and arrests, the number of bombings and murders escalated throughout 1990, resulting in thousands of deaths and millions of dollars in property damage.

Mounting violence prompted the government to relent and waive extradition for any drug dealers who surrendered and confessed. Following the announcement, cartel leaders Fabio Ochoa, Jorge Ochoa, and Carlos Escobar surrendered. For more than a year Escobar ran the cartel from a luxurious new jail built especially for him. When Escobar tired of captivity in 1992, he was rescued by his own soldiers, who stormed the prison. During the next few months Escobar conducted his own war against the Medellín police, and launched a bombing campaign in the Colombian capital of Bogota. With the help of information provided by the Cali cartel, the government mounted an intense search that ended in 1993 with the death of Colombia's most infamous drug lord.

Brazil: The Imperiled Rain Forest

Perspective

1960	*Capital of Brazil is moved from Rio de Janeiro to Brasília.*
1973	*Trans-Amazon highway is completed.*
1979	*Gold at Serra Pelada draws miners to Amazonia.*
1987	*Roraima gold rush begins.*
1988	**October 13.** *Government halts incentives for Amazon development.* **December 22.** *Chico Mendes is murdered.*
1989	**April 6.** *Our Nature program is launched.*
1990	**January.** *Miners are barred from Yanomami homeland.* **March.** *Government orders bombing of miners' airstrips.*
1991	**February.** *The first of several environmentalists is killed.* **June 24.** *Brazil agrees to debt-for-nature swaps.* **November.** *Government creates several huge Indian reserves.*
1992	**June 3.** *Earth summit convenes in Rio de Janeiro.*
1993	**August.** *Reports surface about a massacre of Yanomami Indians by gold miners.*
1994	**December.** *Farmers protest creation of a new Indian reservation.*

Chico Mendes would have been happy to know that in 1992 Brazil was the site of the earth summit, the largest gathering of world leaders ever assembled. Their purpose was to discuss ways to save the environment from further damage due to industrialization and uncontrolled development. As the head of Brazil's rubber tappers' union, Mendes had worked to preserve the great Amazonian rain forest long before it was fashionable. This goal put Mendes on a collision course with the region's cattle ranchers, who along with miners are responsible for the large-scale destruction of the rain forest in recent years. Cattle ranchers assassinated Mendes in 1988, but his legacy is preserved by others who carry on the fight.

Issues and Events

The great rain forests of the world cover only about seven percent of the earth's surface, yet they contain about 80 percent of all vegetation. About one-third of the world's rain forests is located in Brazil. Scientists have long warned that the destruction of the rain forest could cause a global warming trend called the "greenhouse effect" that could ultimately render the planet uninhabitable.

In an unprecedented move, the government of Brazil admitted in 1988 that development of the rain forest had gotten out of hand after more than 6,000 man-made fires were reported in a single day in Rondonia along one of Brazil's new roads through Amazonia. This startling information inspired the wrath of environmentalists throughout the world, and Brazil was subjected to mounting international criticism regarding its environmental policies at a time when its economy was lagging and foreign investment was critically needed.

Among the principal culprits responsible for large-scale destruction of the rain forest in Brazil are cattle ranchers, who burn huge tracts of forest to allow grasses to grow as range for livestock herds. Unfortunately, rain forest soils are very poor because the heavy rains leach out the valuable nutrients. Without the protection of the forest canopy, what remains of the soil is washed away. Virtually all of the cattle ranches that existed in 1978 have been destroyed in this manner and subsequently abandoned.

The government tried to subdue international criticism by enacting legislation to control—but not curtail—Amazonian development. Government efforts to curb the destruction of the rain forest included the discontinuation of subsidies for cattle ranchers, miners, and lumbering concerns in the region. The first comprehensive Amazonian forest management program was launched the following year. The plan, called "Our Nature," included 49 new environmental laws concerning zoning, nature reserves, and mandatory burning permits. These measures, although conservative, met with violent resistance. Several of the government's enforcement agents were assassinated, as well as many Brazilian environmental leaders.

No group has suffered more from Amazonian development than the region's Indian populations, which have in some cases been devastated. Reports of Indians being slaughtered at the hands of cattle ranchers and gold miners have filtered out of the jungle for decades. Proposals by the Brazilian government to set aside large portions of the Amazon exclusively for the Indians have met with particularly vehement resistance by state governments and developers.

In 1990, international attention turned to the plight of the Yanomami Indians, one of the world's last isolated tribes. In 1987, some 45,000 gold miners began pouring into the Yanomami's homelands in Roraima state. More than 10 percent of the Yanomami have subsequently perished as a result of the invasion. The government tried to bar miners from the area, but when this proved ineffective, they bombed the miners' airstrips to cut off their supply lines. Meanwhile, the Yanomami are threatened with extinction from the white men's diseases, such as measles, malaria, and venereal disease. They also suffer from malnutrition due to increased pressure on the region's food supply, and mercury poisoning from the miners' gold recovery process.

In 1991 the Brazilian government stepped up its conservation efforts by agreeing to a "debt-for-nature" swap, whereby a portion of Brazil's massive foreign debt would be forgiven if Brazil used the money for environmental protection. Also, a huge reserve the size of Indiana was created for the Yanomami. This was one of more than seventy reserves created during the year. In addition, Brazil began encouraging environmental tourism and marketing rain forest products to help the region's fragile economy.

These measures have further angered the region's miners, farmers, and loggers. Tensions between the government and developers remain high. In 1994, some 10,000 angry farmers gathered to protest the decision to create a new Indian reservation in northern Brazil. Three police who had been assigned to protect surveyors in the area were captured and held hostage.

In Brazil, concerns about the fate of the Amazonian rain forest are tempered by more immediate concerns, such as politics, the economy and individual rights. Because Brazil has a 41 percent poverty rate, the pressures for development are enormous. Some, like early pioneers in the United States, believe that the wilderness is somehow too vast to be destroyed. Others argue that foreigners should not preach about the fate of the Amazon, given the environmental crimes committed by other nations in their quests for wealth. Also, many Brazilians think that international pressure to preserve the rain forest is just a ruse to allow other nations, such as the United States, to develop the land themselves. Many generals in the army have publicly stated that the U.S. and other nations are looking for an excuse to invade the Amazon and challenge Brazil's sovereignty. While there is no evidence to back up these claims, they strike a resonant chord with the people.

About 12 percent of the total rain forest has been lost. If development must continue, Brazil will have to find new and innovative means of using the forest without destroying it. Chico Mendes proposed the establishment of "extractive reserves" to be protected and managed for ongoing forest industries such as rubber, nuts, and resins. Traditional farming and cattle ranching techniques are devastating, but native Brazilians have long practiced a type of slash and burn agriculture that has a very low environmental impact. Modern lumbering techniques such as selective cutting need to be employed instead of the cheaper, clear-cutting approach. The country's many parks and reserves need to be protected against illegal encroachment. The world can only hope that Brazil will begin to comprehend the global importance of its rich forest resources and make an even stronger commitment to manage them in a more responsible manner.

Background

Brazil was colonized during the early 1500s by Portuguese settlers, most of whom grew sugar along the northeast coast. The discovery of gold in 1693 started a gold rush to the central highlands in the present-day state of Minas Gerais. By the mid-1800s, coffee had become the country's leading export as people flocked to the São Paulo region to work on the new plantations. During the late 1800s, the rubber boom prompted limited migration to the Amazonian region. Each of these economic booms resulted in the establishment of large new plantations controlled by a few wealthy landowners. Land ownership patterns have changed very little over the years: over 60 percent of the arable land in Brazil is still owned by less than 2 percent of the population, and 70 percent of all rural families have no land at all.

After World War II Amazonia was hailed as the land of opportunity for landless Brazilians, and in 1960 the nation officially moved its capital from Rio de Janeiro to the futuristic new city of Brasília to serve as a base for the development of Amazonia. The Trans-Amazon Highway opened up the area to ranching, farming, forestry, and mining. Peasants were lured to the wilderness by offers of free land, and the rich made even bigger fortunes by exploiting the free land. The government hoped to relocate 100,000 landless families to Amazonia by 1974, but poor farming conditions and a lack of facilities hindered development. By 1977, only about 7,000 families had been established along the highway, which is rendered impassable for six months of the year by seasonal rains.

In 1979, thousands of impoverished peasants flocked to Amazonia to find gold at Serra Pelada. In a few short years, over 60,000 prospectors using crude hand tools dug a crater 250 feet deep in search of instant wealth. Tremendous quantities of gold, iron ore, bauxite, and manganese are all currently being mined at various locations in Amazonia. The forest is incredibly rich.

More than one-third of all pharmaceuticals have been developed from compounds found in nature. For scientists, the Amazon, with its incredible diversity of plant and animal life, is like a big drug store whose contents are waiting to be discovered. A common argument used by environmentalists is that a plant with a cure for cancer could be growing right now in the rain forest. Given past events, they may be right.

Scientists also fear that global warming will be accelerated by destruction of the Amazon, which many call the "lungs of the Earth." Its vast area of vegetation is a major source of oxygen in the atmosphere. Ironically, the most common tool for clearing the rain forest is fire, which produces enormous amounts of smoke and carbon dioxide. In death, the Amazon contributes to the problem it solved in life.

North America

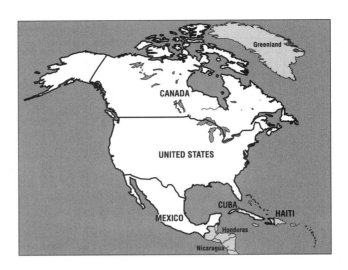

Since the mid-1800s, the United States has played a dominant role in shaping the political and economic landscape of the North American continent. Although the North American Free Trade Agreement (NAFTA) binds the United States, Canada and Mexico closer than ever, the United States remains overwhelmingly the dominant force not just in North America but elsewhere in the hemisphere as well. Although the nations of Central America are linked to their neighbors in the Southern Hemisphere by culture, language, and history, the United States has had a profound effect on their development, and has long considered Central America to be within its sphere of influence.

The policy of United States intervention in Central American affairs had its genesis with the Monroe Doctrine of 1823, when President James Monroe stated that no further European colonization or intervention in the New World would be tolerated. The statement was made primarily to warn Spain not to try to recapture any of its newly independent colonies and also to ward off further Russian expansion in Alaska.

The United States' first military action in Central America took place in 1846 during the Mexican-American War over the territory of Texas. Over twenty-one thousand were killed in the fighting, which resulted in an American victory and Mexico's loss of nearly half its territory. By 1860 the United States had entered a period of isolationism that lasted until 1889. During this year, the United States announced a new "good neighbor" policy, calling for political and military alliance among all of the nations in the Western Hemisphere.

The year 1898 saw the beginning of the Spanish-American War and the transfer of Puerto Rico to American sovereignty. In 1899 an American entrepreneur founded the United Fruit Company, initiating an era of economic domination of Central America by United States interests. Within a short time, the company had acquired vast tracts of land for its banana plantations. Although the host countries initially benefited from the construction of new railroads and shipping facilities, the profits of these operations went to stockholders in the United States and proved to be a drain on the local economies.

In 1903 an agreement was reached to build the Panama Canal, which opened in 1914. Growing American interests in the area prompted the adoption of the Roosevelt Corollary of the Monroe Doctrine, stating United States intentions to exercise international police power in Latin America and effectively placing the entire region under United States military authority. Between 1904 and 1933, the United States repeatedly sent troops to the Dominican Republic, Cuba, Honduras, Nicaragua, and Haiti. Troops were sent to Mexico in 1914 after the Mexican Revolution and again in 1916 to try to capture Pancho Villa.

By the 1930s, the countries of Central America began to resent the United States intervention in their internal affairs, and America renounced the Roosevelt Corollary. After World War II, the "good neighbor" policy was reintroduced and prompted the founding of the Organization of American States (OAS), designed to establish cooperation and create a defensive alliance. Throughout the 1950s and 1960s, the United Fruit Company experienced decline as more and more of its land was nationalized by host governments. In 1959 Cuba nationalized American sugar interests, which led to an embargo and break in diplomatic relations in 1960. In 1961 Castro's Communist government came to power. Cuba turned to the Soviet Union for economic assistance, a move that further infuriated the United States and led to the Cuban missile crisis of 1962. Since then, the United States has done everything in its power to isolate Cuba economically, which has been especially effective since the island nation lost its flow of Soviet aid. In addition, the United States has generally welcomed Cuban refugees who tend to be from the Cuban upper classes. It has not extended these rights to other Latin American refugees, who tend to be much poorer.

After the Cuban revolution, the United States generally tried to back right-wing or military governments in an effort to prevent any further Communist takeovers. During the years of the Reagan administration, intervention in Central America increased as leftist factions in Nicaragua and El Salvador gained strength. In Nicaragua, Daniel Ortega's leftist government was voted out in free elections in favor of United States-backed Violeta Chamorro. In El Salvador, the civil war raged on until the two sides negotiated a shaky peace in 1992. Elsewhere, the United States invaded the tiny island nation of Grenada in 1983 to oust a Marxist government. In late 1989, an invasion of Panama resulted in the arrest of the country's dictator, Manuel Noriega, for his involvement in international drug smuggling. The military government in Haiti also drew the ire of the United States, which threatened an invasion to restore the elected government.

Relations between Mexico and the United States have been strained repeatedly over the issues of drug traffic, the environment, and trade. Despite this, the two countries enjoy substantial foreign exchange, and tourists from the United States provide Mexico with additional revenues.

The biggest problem facing the United States and Mexico has been the issue of illegal immigration to the United States. Several million Mexicans live illegally in the United States, where the federal government claims they steal jobs from American workers and place a strain on social services, especially education. In their defense, many argue that Mexican workers perform the low-level jobs many Americans do not want. In 1986 the United States passed the Immigration Reform and Control Act, which threatened United States employers with fines for employing illegals and offered amnesty to three million illegals who could prove that they had been in the United States since 1981. The Mexican government denounced the passage of the act as racist and repressive although, in fact, Mexican leaders were probably more concerned that a crackdown on illegals would result in a loss of foreign exchange. Many illegals send back most of their wages to Mexico, and the country can ill afford to lose any of its revenues in this time of economic crisis. Enforcement of the law has been difficult, as illegals have become an integral part of many sectors of the American economy.

The adoption of NAFTA has raised fears that Mexicans will no longer have to come to the United States for jobs, because instead the jobs will go to them at the expense of the American workers who once did them. It will take time to see if these dire predictions are true. It will also take time to see if NAFTA results in Mexicans buying more American goods as the trade agreement's supporters assert. In the meantime, the future of Mexican-American relations may be found in cross-border urban areas such as El Paso and Ciudad Juárez where thousands of workers and tons of goods cross the borders each day while the two cities work to solve regional issues such as human services and pollution.

While the United States' relations with Canada have been more peaceful than those with nations to the south, the Canadians still are wary of their American neighbors. Canada has enjoyed a shared history with the United States, but despite a long and fruitful trade relationship, many Canadians regard Americans with suspicion. Many Canadians worry that America's economic strength will overwhelm the Canadian market. The fear of economic and cultural domination prompted a nationalist movement among Canadians. These concerns surfaced when the two nations signed a trade agreement in 1989 and then again during NAFTA negotiations. Canadians are also concerned about agricultural subsidies and whether their government will still be able to enforce policies that required American firms doing business in Canada to also invest there.

A more pressing concern for most Canadians is their own nation's future, given the renewed vigor shown by separatists in Quebec. Should the nation split, there are fears that the individual parts will be even more prone to American dominance than the whole.

The United States: Debate Over Guns

Perspective

1623	*Virginia orders colonists to own guns.*
1644	*Massachusetts fines unarmed citizens.*
1791	*Second Amendment guaranteeing the right to bear arms added to United States Constitution.*
1813	*Carrying concealed weapons is outlawed in Kentucky.*
1871	*National Rifle Association (NRA) is founded.*
1934	*Heavy federal taxes placed on sales of machine guns and sawed-off shotguns.*
1938	*Firearms businesses required to register with the federal government, and the sale of guns to known criminals is prohibited.*
1968	*Interstate firearms sales banned, gun ownership restrictions increased and some imports prohibited.*
1981	**June.** *Morton Grove, Illinois bans sale and possession of all handguns.*
1986	*Numerous federal restrictions on gun sales loosened.*
1987	**October.** *Florida makes it legal to carry concealed weapons.*
1988	*Maryland bans "Saturday Night Specials."*
1993	**February 28.** *Four federal agents are killed in Branch Davidian headquarters in Waco, Texas.* **April 19.** *Waco siege ends in fire; 80 are killed.* **November 30.** *"Brady Bill" calling for restrictions on gun sales signed into law.*
1994	**August 25.** *Assault weapons ban is enacted.* **November 8.** *Republicans gain control of Congress.*
1995	**April 19.** *Oklahoma City bombing kills more than 160 people. Members of private militia are implicated.*

In 1992 handguns killed 13,220 people in the United States. Across the border in Canada they killed only 128 people. The gun murder rate for Wichita, Kansas—a relatively peaceful Midwestern town—is three times that of Belfast, Northern Ireland—a town known the world over for its violence. Both cities have similar populations. Americans' increasing fear of crime and violence has led to an outcry for an end to the bloodshed. Some believe that limiting the manufacture and sale of guns would make the country a safer place to live, while other argue that such measures would rob people of the means to protect themselves.

One sure thing is that America is awash in guns. From tiny "Saturday Night Specials" to formidable .357 Magnums, from precision hunting rifles to crude rapid-fire assault weapons, there is a gun for every taste and budget.

Like abortion, gun control is a polarizing issue in the United States. Passions run high on both sides. Gun advocates claim that restrictions on gun ownership violate the Constitution's Second Amendment which provides for the right to bear arms. They feel that any form of gun control is an assault on a basic right and may be a precursor to an assault on the rest of the Bill of Rights. The gun lobby argues that people have the right to defend themselves from bodily harm and home invasion, just as they have the right to hunt or engage in target practice.

Those favoring restrictions, if not outright bans, on gun ownership say that the Second Amendment was never intended to allow every citizen to carry a gun, and that regardless of this issue, guns are largely to blame for the wave of crime sweeping America. Easy access to firearms, they say, allows criminals to easily engage in mayhem. They cite horrific statistics of the number of Americans killed by guns each year, and point to well-publicized cases where a person was able to purchase a gun and then go on a rampage of killing.

Issues and Events

Efforts at controlling the sale and manufacture of guns still more are fraught with peril for any politician who tries to do so. The NRA is one of the richest lobbying organizations in America. Each year it dispenses millions of dollars to favored politicians. But more effectively, it also uses its money to target politicians. If a politician votes against the NRA, his or her opponent in the next election is likely to receive substantial contributions from the organization's political arm.

By contrast, gun control advocates have far less money to work with. They don't enjoy huge contributions from gun and ammunition manufacturers nor the largess of rich gun dealers and owners. They are more populist and rely on forming alliances with groups such as police chiefs and trauma surgeons to get their message across.

It is this disparity of money that is responsible for Congress' history of stone-walling on gun control despite a myriad of polls indicating that the public by a wide margin favors such restrictions. For a long time, it has been standard congressional dogma that a vote against the NRA was the same as setting one foot out of office.

However, the tide is turning. Gun advocates have been helped by both rising crime and a barrage of well-publicized murders and assaults. In 1993, the Brady Bill was finally passed by Congress six years after it was first introduced. Named after its sponsor, James Brady, who was severely injured during the 1981 attempt on the life of President Reagan, the bill has modest goals: a five-day waiting period for the purchase of a gun, accompanied by a police background check. Although some states already have their own versions of the Brady Bill, there is as yet little statistical evidence to validate its effectiveness. Nevertheless, it has received enthusiastic public support.

In August 1994, gun control advocates celebrated another Congressional victory when they passed a bill banning certain types of assault weapons. Again the NRA had bitterly fought the ban, only to lose after politicians emboldened by the group's other losses voted against it.

When Republicans gained control of both chambers of Congress in 1994, one of the first things they promised to do was rescind the assault weapons ban. However, momentum to repeal the ban was lost in the aftermath of the April 1995 Oklahoma City bombing, the worst terrorist attack in the history of the United States. More than 160 people were killed and 300 buildings were damaged or destroyed.

The perpetrators of the bombing are believed to be associated with the Michigan Militia, one of a number of right-wing extremist groups throughout the United States which actively campaign against any form of gun control and accuse the federal government of conspiring to take away their freedom. In addition to conducting maneuvers, these groups also collect weapons and information on guerrilla warfare and terrorism tactics.

The attack took place on the second anniversary of a tragic event in Waco, Texas in which the Federal government stormed the headquarters of the Branch Davidian religious cult, with disastrous results. The group, which had been accused of stockpiling massive amounts of weapons at its headquarters, was responsible for killing four Federal agents in an earlier attempt by the government to raid the compound. When government forces launched a second assault on the group, a massive fire engulfed the building and 80 people, including many women and children, were killed.

In a blow to opponents of gun control, media attention after the Oklahoma City bombing turned not only to the private militia, but also to the NRA, which often uses the same anti-government rhetoric as the militia. Both of these groups blasted the government for its treatment of the Waco affair and upheld the constitutional right of the Branch Davidians to have as many weapons as they wanted. The NRA also received negative publicity when one of its fund-raising letters referred to federal agents as "jack-booted thugs" and prompted former president George Bush to renounce his membership in the organization. The NRA denies all responsibility—direct and indirect—for the Oklahoma bombing and insists that it is not a gun issue. Nevertheless the perception of the NRA as an increasingly radical right-wing political group was heightened.

Background

The traditions of gun ownership in America began with the early colonists who were urged to own guns so they could defend themselves against Indians, dangerous animals, and other colonists. During the Revolutionary War, most of the fighting against the British was done by colonists using their own weapons. The colonists would serve in the militia for a few months and then return home to tend to their crops.

When the Constitution was framed, it was decided that a right to bear arms should be guaranteed to all Americans, and thus the Second Amendment in the Bill of Rights was born. Gun ownership continued to be encouraged into the 20th Century, although some states banned carrying concealed weapons.

In the 1930s, however, Prohibition and gangs brought a lawlessness that had not been previously seen in the U.S. In 1934, the first federal laws aimed at restricting guns were passed. In 1938, another bill was passed, but this time it was the work of the NRA, which, fearing a tougher gun control law, promoted its own watered-down version.

Ownership of all types of weapons grew during and after World War II. In 1968, the murders of Robert Kennedy and Martin Luther King in quick succession with guns sparked a flurry of activity in Congress. The resulting law greatly expanded federal regulations. Interstate gun sales were prohibited so that communities could set their own regulations. A large number of people, including felons, minors, and illegal aliens, were denied the right to own guns. The resulting permit process was bitterly opposed by the NRA. The final provision of the act put greater restrictions on imported guns, such as cheap "Saturday Night Specials" which are useful for little more than shooting another person.

In 1986, the NRA, with strong backing from the Reagan Administration, succeeded in getting passage of the Firearms Owners Protection Act. The law did away with "unreasonable curbs" and made it easier to both purchase and sell guns.

Some of the hottest debate over firearms has occurred in states and local communities where a panoply of laws has been passed. They range from Morton Grove, Illinois, which banned handgun ownership in 1981, to Florida, which in 1987 made it legal to carry a concealed weapon.

Founded after the Civil War as an organization dedicated to improving marksmanship throughout the country, most of the NRA's members are target shooters, gun collectors, hunters, gunsmiths, and policemen. After the 1968 ban on interstate firearms sales was enacted, the group became increasingly involved in politics and developed into a powerful Congressional lobby. The NRA has been criticized by some of its two-to-three million members for becoming too preoccupied with politics and losing touch with the needs and interests of ordinary gun owners.

Mexico: Dissent in Chiapas

Perspective

1521	*Spain overthrows Aztec Empire.*
1810	*Rebellion begins against Spain.*
1821	**September 27.** *Treaty of Cordoba signed granting Mexican independence.*
1848	**February 2.** *Mexico cedes vast territory to the United States.*
1867	**June 19.** *Benito Juarez executes Emperor Maximillian, ending French rule.*
1911	**May 25.** *Porfirio Diaz resigns in the face of revolution, ending 30 years of rule.*
1917	**February 5.** *New Constitution adopted.*
1934	*Lazaro Cardenas elected President, begins vigorous modernization plan, including land reforms.*
1976	**July 4.** *José Lopez Portillo elected President, oversees rapid economic expansion fueled by oil boom.*
1988	**July 6.** *Carlos Salinas de Gortari elected with a bare 50.39 percent of the vote, a record low for the entrenched Institutional Revolutionary Party (PRI). Other parties immediately claim widespread fraud.*
1991	**August 18.** *PRI nearly sweeps legislative and gubernatorial elections. Widespread voting irregularities reported.*
1992	*Mexico approves North American Free Trade Agreement with Canada and the United States.*
1994	**January 1.** *NAFTA Treaty takes effect. Indians in southern state of Chiapas stage armed rebellion.*
1995	**January 10.** *Economic instability leads to financial panic.* **February 9.** *Government launches major offensive against rebel strongholds.*

After a year of optimism fueled by the NAFTA Treaty and its promised closer links with the economically powerful United States and Canada, the first three months of 1994 brought a series of events that shook Mexico as at no time since the 1910 revolution.

On January 1, the nation planned to celebrate the implementation of the NAFTA accords; instead, armed rebellion broke out in the impoverished southern state of Chiapas. Indians, after years of preparation, took control of several towns, ambushed army units trying to restore order, and became symbolic of the huge gulf that exists between Mexico's haves and have-nots. The violence spread to other parts of the country and did not begin to subside until the government promised sweeping reforms and massive new aid to poor regions.

However, the situation remains volatile as the rebels and the Mexican government continue to negotiate in an attempt to reach a permanent settlement.

Issues and Events

The flames that consumed the town hall in San Cristobal on January 1, 1994 were not sparked overnight. They were fueled by generations of Indians angry over perceived economic and political discrimination by Mexico's government. In the days that followed, as many as 2,000 guerrillas occupied six other towns in Mexico's southernmost state of Chiapas. They destroyed government offices, took wealthy landowners, police and politicians hostage, and found a worldwide audience for their grievances. When the Mexican army fought back, the rebels returned to their mountain hideouts, waging running battles with soldiers backed by airplanes. At least 140 people, and perhaps many more, died. There were widespread charges that the army had executed rebels in its custody and that it fired indiscriminately into groups of peaceful civilians.

The rebellion also tarnished the efforts of President Carlos Salinas de Gotari to portray Mexico as a nation on the verge of moving into the ranks of other industrialized nations. The rebels, calling themselves the Zapatista National Liberation Army, after Emiliano Zapata, a legendary hero of the 1910 revolution, claimed NAFTA would eliminate their culture and lead to economic ruin. They charged that the wealthy farmers in Chiapas, who have resisted the land reforms implemented elsewhere in the Mexico, would benefit from free trade of their high-value crops to the U.S. Meanwhile, the Zapatistas claimed, small farmers would lose government subsidies for staple crops like corn. Forced off their land by the resulting poverty, the farmers would end up living in vast shantytowns around already population-choked cities like Mexico City.

Late in January, Salinas ordered a unilateral cease-fire by the army and called for the rebels to come to the peace table. But the Zapatistas proved coy as the violence spread to other regions. Bombings in Mexico City and scores of bomb threats to airlines and businesses were blamed on other leftist groups seizing the moment. Tens of thousands of Indians in southern and western provinces went on strike, seized government offices, and declared that they wished to become official Zapatistas. With August elections drawing closer, the government tried to act quickly to appease the protests. Chiapas was given $250 million for improvements, while aid for social programs in neighboring Oaxaca was nearly tripled.

But such moves had little immediate effect on the Zapatistas. As a more detailed picture of their organization emerged, it became clear that the rebellion had been years in the making. Young Indians—descendants of the ancient Mayan Empire—were recruited early in a land where four out of five homes are mud huts with dirt floors. The recruitment pitch was simple: you have no future unless you fight for it.

In addition to demanding an end to economic disparity and the preservation of their culture, the Zapatistas also focused on the long-festering issue of political reform. The ruling PRI party rarely has close elections, and when it faces a real challenge, there have been numerous accusations of vote fraud. In the south, the situation has more closely resembled that of nearby Central American dictatorships, with PRI politicians staying in office for life while conspiring with wealthy landowners for mutual enrichment. The Zapatistas' call for fair elections and truly representative government brought increased attention to an issue that had already been in the national spotlight.

In March, the government and Zapatista representatives reached agreement on peace accords that would give Indians sweeping new political power. Among the provisions were a new criminal code and judges that respect human rights, mandatory education about Indian culture in all Mexican schools, new Indian-controlled political districts, and massive new aid to fund schools, roads and health care in poor areas. Many Indians were unmoved by the accords, however, and violence deepened in Chiapas as landowners began using force to remove squatters occupying their lands. Churches and clergy came under attack from conservatives who said that the Roman Catholic Church was encouraging the rebellious peasants.

Until Mexico can satisfy the demands of its poor there will be continuing political and economic instability. The rebels continue to wage a low-level war against the government, and this ongoing conflict was cited as one of the causes of a serious economic crisis in January 1995. Mexico was forced to implement harsh austerity measures that resulted in soaring inflation and unemployment, conditions which always impact the poor most severely, and in turn breathed new life into the rebel movement. The government retaliated by launching a military sweep of Chiapas and seizing dozens of villages which had been under rebel control. The guerrillas fled back to their jungle strongholds where they continue to plan their campaign to force the government to implement political and economic reforms.

Negotiations have been fruitless. The government demands that the rebels confine themselves to three designated areas and has offered to provide them with food, shelter, and safety while the talks continue. The rebels refuse to be confined to restricted areas, and have stated their demand that the government should relinquish the villages it captured during its 1995 offensive.

Background

Since Tenochtitlán fell to Hernán Cortés in 1521, marking the end of the great Aztec Empire, the land that became Mexico has seen much revolution and violence. New Spain grew rapidly in the 16th Century, eventually extending north through what are today Texas and California, and south through Central America. The Indians in these regions, whether descendants of the great civilizations like the Mayas or just simple agrarians, were exploited for their labor. Huge estates and vast mining empires were established that relied upon Indian slave labor for their economic success.

In 1765, Charles III, King of Spain, began a series of blunders that were to mirror those its colonial rival England committed with its own territory in the future United States. Charles instituted widespread new taxes and other burdens on New Spain. He also cracked down on the Catholic Church, which he saw as a rival for power and wealth. A series of repressive actions by the militia further angered the populace.

In late 1810, rebels led by Miguel Hidalgo y Costilla began an 11-year revolution for Mexican independence that would end up costing thousands of lives, including Hidalgo's. Gradually, rebel forces from the various provinces united, and on September 27, 1821, Mexico achieved independence through the Treaty of Córdoba. One of the first moves of the new provisional government was to name a new Emperor of Mexico. This went over poorly with the other revolutionaries and in 1823, Augustin I resigned and was replaced by a republic. A series of governments followed, where rule of succession was by violent coup, rather than by election.

Meanwhile, relations with the United States soured over the question of Texas. A move by the U.S. Congress in 1845 to annex the then-independent state of Texas touched off a war that ended in 1848 with Mexico losing California and the neighboring southwest. In 1855, a group of Mexican intellectuals that included Benito Juárez staged a coup. It was the Mexican equivalent of the French Revolution, and it brought about reform laws designed to guarantee civil liberties and curtail the power of the church. Instead, the reforms prompted a civil war that ended when France invaded the country seeking repayment of debts. French rule lasted until 1867, when Emperor Maximillian was executed. Elections were called, and Juárez took office as president. More political uncertainty followed until José de la Cruz Porfirio Díaz took control in 1876. Except for a four-year respite, he remained in power until 1911.

During this time, Mexico's land-holders increased their wealth and a new middle class was born. But much of this prosperity came at the expense of the Indians, who were often brutally repressed. In 1910, a liberal revolution began with widespread support. One of the most famous rebels was Emilio Zapata, who had a peasant background and who championed the cause of poor people whose land had been stolen by the wealthy.

Despite years of chaos as rival factions vied for power, a constitution was passed in 1917 that—although heavily modified—is the basis for the modern Mexico. General Plutaco Elias Calles came to power in 1928. He railed against the church and foreign investment and was also the founder of the predecessor to PRI, which continues to control Mexican politics to this day.

Canada: Quebec's Clash of Cultures

Perspective

1867	*British North America Act marks founding of Canadian confederation.*
1970	**October.** *Canadian government declares a state of emergency after Quebec separatists kill Canada's labor minister.*
1976	*Parti Québecois elected to power in Quebec.*
1977	*Quebec's French Language Charter restricts use of English in business and schools.*
1980	*Quebec voters reject referendum for independence.*
1987	*Meach Lake Accord modifies constitution to guarantee Quebec's status as a distinct society.*
1990	**June 23.** *Meach Lake Accord collapses. Quebec threatens to secede.*
1992	**October 26.** *Voters reject Charlottetown Constitutional Reforms.*
1993	**October 25.** *Separatist Bloc Québecois finishes second in national elections.*
1994	**September 12.** *Parti Québecois regains power in Quebec and promises to hold a referendum on independence.*

Most French-Canadians live in Quebec, Canada's largest province. The Quebecois see their province as a bastion of French-Canadian language and culture, and they have fought a vigorous political battle against cultural assimilation by Canada's English-speaking majority. Quebecois have been debating their future as part of Canada for several decades. Most Canadians are opposed to granting special treatment for Quebec within the Canadian federation, and this attitude has strengthened the Quebec independence movement. The issue is a highly emotional one, and the future of the Canadian union grows ever more uncertain.

Issues and Events

Growing nationalism began to change the political climate in Quebec in the 1960s. In 1970 a Quebecois extremist group assassinated Canada's labor minister, and forced the Canadian government to declare a state of emergency. A separatist political group called the Parti Québecois was elected to power in 1976 and a radical language bill was passed in 1977 that restricted the use of English in business and education, causing many English-speaking businesses and citizens to move out of Quebec. The weakening economy was in part responsible for the defeat of a 1980 referendum in

Quebec calling for independence from Canada. After this defeat, separatism seemed to die down as Canada turned its attention to drafting a new constitution in 1982. Quebec refused to endorse the document, until it was altered in 1987, as part of the Meach Lake Accord, to recognize Quebec's status as a "distinct society" within Canada. The area's earliest occupants—the Native Canadians—managed to derail the passage of the accord, which reignited separatist fires. The next agreement, called the Charlottetown Constitutional Reforms, included the right to self-government for native populations but suffered the same fate as Meach Lake.

The failure of the Quebec and Canadian governments to reach a viable solution regarding the future of Quebec has left many Canadians feeling disillusioned and bitter. The nation was stunned when a Quebec separatist party finished second in 1993 national elections, making it the official opposition party in Parliament. In 1994 the Parti Québecois scored a major victory in Quebec provincial elections, and the new government vowed to hold a referendum on Quebec independence by the end of 1995.

Although it might seem that independence is inevitable, polls persist in indicating that the majority of the people of Quebec do not favor independence. The sweeping election victories of the past two years are therefore interpreted as votes against the ruling party, rather than as a mandate for an independent Quebec.

Quebecois separatists advocate an economic union with Canada and predict that there would be a minimal effect on Quebec's economy should Quebec secede. Canada, however, has promised Quebec will suffer great economic losses if it secedes from Canada, and it will not guarantee any kind of economic union with a sovereign Quebec. That, Canada argues, would be allowing Quebec to receive the benefits of Canadian union without the responsibilities.

Also, Quebec's increasingly assertive native Canadians are adamantly opposed to Quebec independence and vow that their vast lands, which account for two-thirds of Quebec's land area, will remain part of Canada.

Background

The ethnic groups that are the focus of Canada's struggles today are a heritage of the original conflict among the Native Americans, the French, and the British over sovereignty of the area now known as Canada. The French ceded the territory to the British following their military defeat in 1759. When the nation of Canada was born in 1867 with the adoption of the British North America Act, the French-dominated province of Quebec was guaranteed linguistic freedom. The Native Americans weren't so lucky. Their reservations have always been considered Canadian territory and they are governed directly by Canadian law. In recent years the Native Canadians have become more assertive in their claims for the return of their tribal lands and also for political autonomy within the Canadian federation.

Cuba: Economic Hardship

Perspective

1898	*The United States takes possession of Cuba from Spain.*
1902	*Cuba gains its independence.*
1959	**January 1.** *Fidel Castro comes into power.*
1961	**January 3.** *The United States and Cuba break diplomatic relations.* **April.** *Bay of Pigs invasion fails.* **December 2.** *Castro embraces Marxist-Leninist policies.*
1962	**October.** *Cuban missile crisis brings the United States and the Soviet Union to the brink of nuclear war.*
1991	**September 11.** *Soviet Union announces troop withdrawal from Cuba.*
1992	**January 17.** *Russia revokes Cuba's special trade privileges.* **November 24.** *United Nations calls on the United States to repeal the Cuban trade embargo.*
1994	**August 5.** *Rioting erupts in Havana.* **August 11.** *Massive exodus of Cubans to the U.S. begins.* **September.** *U.S. and Cuba reach refugee accord.*

Separated by only about ninety miles (145 km), Cuba and the United States enjoyed close relations until 1960, when Cuba chose to assert its independence from its powerful neighbor to the north. Since that time, Cuba and the United States have been worlds apart.

Issues and Events

Not since the original imposition of the United States embargo in 1963 has Cuba faced such economic uncertainty. In the 1980s, Cuba relied on the Soviet Union and the nations of Eastern Europe for more than three-quarters of its international trade. With an economy based primarily on sugar and tobacco, Cuba is utterly dependent on foreign oil, foodstuffs, and consumer goods. Cuba's trade began to suffer with the collapse of communism in Europe, but the most devastating blow came with the unraveling of the Soviet Union.

With its strategic location, the Soviets prized their relationship with Cuba and rewarded Castro with extravagant subsidies. They bought Cuban sugar at prices far higher than those dictated by the world market, and sold oil to Cuba at drastically reduced prices. When the Soviet economy began to collapse in 1990, exports to Cuba began to decrease to a slow trickle and the new Russian government announced an end to the subsidies. To add further pain, the sugar harvest has been poor and storms have battered coffee and banana crops.

Ever resourceful, Castro has managed to compensate for the loss of most of Cuba's foreign trade. Food and electricity are rationed. Factories that produced non-essential items have been closed, and surplus labor is encouraged to help with agriculture or face drastic pay cuts. Massive numbers of bicycles have been imported from China to meet the nation's transportation needs. The tourism industry has been revived and foreign investors have announced plans for new hotels and resorts.

Cuba's economic problems could be alleviated if the United States would lift its trade embargo against Cuba, but instead the United States tightened the embargo in 1992 in an attempt to spark a popular uprising that might force Castro from office. This action brought world opinion to bear against the United States, as evidenced by the passage of United Nations resolutions calling on the United States to end the embargo.

The first anti-government riot since the beginning of Castro's reign broke out in Havana in August 1994. Castro tried to force the United States to lift the embargo by allowing more than 30,000 refugees to emigrate to the United States within a single month. These boat people were picked up by U.S. authorities and detained in Cuba at the U.S. military base at Guantanamo. Frustration among the refugees exploded into riots, and the United States was forced to negotiate a new refugee accord with Castro. Cuba agreed to stop illegal emigration and the U.S. promised allow more Cubans to enter legally.

Despite the ending of the Cold War and the erosion of the basis for animosity between the two nations, the ideological barrier remains formidable. Meanwhile many hundreds of Cubans bridge the gap between the two nations each year in wooden boats and rafts.

Background

The United States gained sovereignty over Cuba in 1898 following the Spanish American War. Although the United States set Cuba free in 1902, it continued to intervene in Cuban affairs. Under corrupt leadership, Cuba became a mecca for organized crime, gambling, drugs, and prostitution.

At first the United States supported the revolution led by Fidel Castro, who pledged to restore democracy and end corruption. However, Cubans resented the continuing United States involvement in their internal affairs. In 1961 the United States engineered the failed Bay of Pigs invasion by anti-Castro Cubans who had fled to the United States. Several months later, Castro announced Cuba's conversion to communism, and established a Soviet-style government and economy.

The United States was infuriated by Castro's actions, and the Soviets responded to Cuba's pleas for help by sending nuclear missiles to Cuba, an act which brought the United States and the Soviet Union to the brink of nuclear war. The Soviets eventually withdrew the missiles, but a United States embargo imposed shortly after the crisis remains in effect.

Haiti: Aristide Returns

Perspective

1804	*Independence from France is won.*
1957	*François "Papa Doc" Duvalier is elected president.*
1971	*Papa Doc dies; Jean-Claude "Baby Doc" Duvalier succeeds as president.*
1986	**February 7.** *Haitian President Jean-Claude Duvalier is overthrown and forced into exile; a junta, led by former Lt. General Henry Namphy, assumes power.*
1987	**November 29.** *Elections are canceled after thirty-four voters are killed.*
1988	**January 17.** *Leslie Manigat is elected president by less than 10 percent of the people.* **June 20.** *Namphy overthrows Manigat.* **September 18.** *Namphy is overthrown in another coup. General Prosper Avril assumes power.*
1990	**March.** *Growing civil unrest leads to Avril's resignation.* **December 16.** *Jean-Bertrand Aristide is elected president.*
1991	**September 30.** *Aristide is overthrown in a military coup.*
1994	**May 6.** *U.N. imposes near-total embargo.* **September 18.** *Haitian military government agrees to step down.* **September 19.** *United States peacekeepers arrive in Haiti.* **October 15.** *Aristide returns to Haiti*

Haiti has long been recognized as the most impoverished country in the Western Hemisphere. It was hoped that the fall of the Duvalier regime in 1986 would mark the beginning of a new era of peace and prosperity, but political instability and grinding poverty continue to plague this island nation.

Issues and Events

Despite unrelenting political unrest, the real struggle for most Haitians has been survival. A lack of natural resources, a devastated agricultural base, an uneducated work force, political repression, and rampant corruption fuel the cycle of poverty. Only a tiny fraction of Haiti's population owns more than one-half of the nation's wealth, and these elite, who control the military, are determined to maintain political and economic control.

As a result, democracy has failed to take root in Haiti. Elections in 1987 were canceled after dozens were killed, and the nation was then subjected to a series of military coups. In December 1990 hopes again were raised when Catholic priest Jean-Bertrand Aristide was chosen in fair and nonviolent presidential elections.

The charismatic Aristide was immensely popular with the poor because he promised to promote justice and redistribute Haiti's wealth. His fiery rhetoric alienated Haiti's wealthy class, who claimed that Aristide was an aspiring dictator, and less than one year after his election Aristide was deposed in a military coup and forced to flee the country.

The military government began a campaign of terror against supporters of Aristide, and the world responded by imposing a devastating embargo against Haiti. Conditions for the poor became so deplorable that thousands of Haitians risked drowning at sea to flee the nation in leaky boats in search of asylum in the United States.

In 1994 the United States responded to the growing flood of refugees by threatening to launch a military invasion and force the Haitian government from power. The day before the scheduled invasion, the military agreed to relinquish power and the United States military forces landed peacefully in Haiti to oversee Aristide's return in October. In March 1995 the United Nations took over the peacekeeping operation in anticipation of elections later in the year.

Although the embargo has been lifted and humanitarian aid to Haiti has resumed, the nation still faces enormous problems. The society is steeped in violence and corruption. About 75 percent of the people live in abject poverty, without access to safe drinking water, decent medical care, or sufficient food. The rich, in conjunction with the police and the military, conspire to perpetuate the plight of the poor and repress the development of democratic institutions in Haiti.

Background

Christopher Columbus landed on Hispaniola in 1492. In 1697 the island's western third, which was to become Haiti, was deeded to the French, while the eastern two-thirds would become the Dominican Republic. After a struggle for freedom by the slaves, who made up 90 percent of the population, Haiti gained its independence in 1804. A mulatto elite ruled the country for the next century. In 1957 François "Papa Doc" Duvalier was elected president and changed the constitution to extend the president's term to a lifetime.

Papa Doc's reign became synonymous with brutality and torture; dissenters were often murdered. His regime lasted until his death in 1971, when his 19-year-old son, Jean-Claude—known as "Baby Doc"—became president-for-life.

The military strength of the Duvalier government had been sufficient to control the Haitian people until 1986 when the Catholic church led thousands in demonstrations to protest the increasingly corrupt and repressive government.

WORLD GAZETTEER: PROFILES OF NATIONS & PLACES

Varanasi, India: Hindu faithful bathe in the waters of the Ganges River.

The following World Gazetteer presents an up-to-date overview of the world's independent countries and their possessions. Geographic, political, and population-related information is derived from the most current Rand McNally data available. Ethnic groups, religions, trade partners, exports, and imports are listed in order of decreasing size and/or importance. Languages are similarly organized, with official language(s) listed first. Political parties are cited alphabetically, as are membership entries, which represent member nations of the following organizations:

Arab League (AL)
Association of South East Asian Nations (ASEAN)
Commonwealth of Independent States (CIS)
Commonwealth of Nations (CW)
European Union (EU)
North Atlantic Treaty Organization (NATO)
Organization for Economic Cooperation and Development (OECD)
Organization of African Unity (OAU)
Organization of American States (OAS)
Organization of Petroleum Exporting Countries (OPEC)
United Nations (UN)

AFGHANISTAN

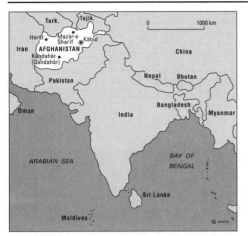

Official name Islamic State of Afghanistan
PEOPLE
Population 19,715,000. **Density** 78/mi² (30/km²).
Urban 18%. **Capital** Kabul, 1,424,400. **Ethnic groups** Pathan 38%, Tajik 25%, Hazara 19%, Uzbek 6%. **Languages** Dari, Pashto, Uzbek, Turkmen. **Religions** Sunni Muslim 84%, Shiite Muslim 15%. **Life expectancy** 44 female, 43 male. **Literacy** 29%.
POLITICS
Government Islamic republic. **Parties** Islamic, Islamic Revolutionary Movement, Islamic Society, Islamic Union, National Liberation Front, others. **Suffrage** None. **Memberships** UN. **Subdivisions** 30 provinces.
ECONOMY
GDP $3,000,000,000. **Per capita** $205. **Monetary unit** Afghani. **Trade partners** Exports: Former Soviet Republics, Pakistan, India. Imports: Former Soviet Republics, Japan, Singapore. **Exports** Natural gas, fruits and nuts, carpets, wool, cotton, hides, pelts. **Imports** Food, petroleum.
LAND
Description Southern Asia, landlocked. **Area** 251,826 mi² (652,225 km²). **Highest point** Nowshāk, 24,557 ft (7,485 m). **Lowest point** Along Amu Darya River, 850 ft (259 m).

People. Afghanistan shares borders with China, Iran, Pakistan, Tajikistan, Turkmenistan, and Uzbekistan. This crossroads position has created a population that is ethnically and linguistically diverse. Religion, however, plays a strong unifying role. Most Afghans are Muslim, and Islamic laws and customs determine lifestyles and beliefs, both religious and secular. The population is mainly rural, consisting primarily of farmers and a small nomadic group.

Economy and the Land. The main force behind Afghanistan's underdevelopment is agriculture and the recent civil war. Subsistence farming and animal husbandry account for much of the agricultural activity. Irrigation systems have aided crop production. A terrain of mountains and valleys, including the Hindu Kush, separates the desert region of the southwest from the more fertile north, an area of higher population density and the site of natural gas deposits. Increased development has made natural gas an important export. Winters are generally cold, and summers are hot and dry.

History and Politics. Once part of the Persian Empire, the area of present-day Afghanistan saw invasions by Persians, Macedonians, Greeks, Turks, Arabs, Mongols, and other peoples. An Arab invasion in A.D. 652 introduced Islam. In 1747 Afghan tribes led by Ahmad Shah Durrani united the area and established today's Afghanistan. Power remained with the Durrani tribe for more than two centuries. In the nineteenth and early twentieth centuries Britain controlled Afghanistan's foreign affairs. A Durrani tribe member and former prime minister led a military coup in 1973 and set up a republic, ending the country's monarchical tradition. The new government's failure to improve economic and social conditions led to a 1978 revolution that established a Marxist government and brought Soviet aid. Intraparty differences and citizenry dissent led to a Soviet invasion in 1979. Fighting erupted between government forces and the *mujahidin* (holy warrior) guerrillas. In 1988 the Soviets agreed to remove their military forces and in 1991 the United States and Russia stopped all military assistance to the warring factions. However, fighting continues. ∎

ALBANIA

Official name Republic of Albania
PEOPLE
Population 3,394,000. **Density** 306/mi² (118/km²). **Urban** 36%. **Capital** Tiranë, 238,100. **Ethnic groups** Albanian (Illyrian) 90%, Greek 8%. **Languages** Albanian, Greek. **Religions** Muslim 70%, Greek Orthodox 20%, Roman Catholic 10%. **Life expectancy** 77 female, 71 male. **Literacy** 72%.
POLITICS
Government Republic. **Parties** Democratic, Omonia, Republican, Socialist. **Suffrage**

Universal, over 18. **Memberships** NATO, UN.
Subdivisions 26 districts.
ECONOMY
GDP $3,300,000,000. **Per capita** $998. **Monetary unit** Lek. **Trade partners** Italy, Macedonia, Germany. **Exports** Asphalt, metals and metallic ores, electricity, crude oil, vegetables. **Imports** Machinery, consumer goods, grains.
LAND
Description Southeastern Europe. **Area** 11,100 mi^2 (28,748 km^2). **Highest point** Korabit Peak, 9,035 ft (2,754 m). **Lowest point** Sea level.

People. A homogeneous native population characterizes Albania, where Greeks are the main minority. Five centuries of Turkish rule shaped much of the culture and led many Albanians to adopt Islam. Since 1944 an increased emphasis on education has more than tripled the literacy rate. From 1967 until 1990 religious institutions were banned.

Economy and the Land. The poorest country in Europe, Albania has tried to shift its economy from agriculture to industry. Farms employ about 50 percent of the work force, a significant decrease from more than 80 percent before 1944. Agriculture has expanded since economic reforms resulted in the privatization of 90 percent of the farm land. Mineral resources make mining the chief industrial activity. The terrain consists of forested hills and mountains, and the climate is mild.

History and Politics. Early invaders and rulers included Greeks, Romans, Goths, and others. In 1468 the Ottoman Turks conquered the area, and it remained part of their empire until the First Balkan War in 1912. Albania was invaded by Italy and occupied by Germany during World War II. A communist government was established after the war. The failure of Soviet communism increased instability within Albania and in 1991 the communist government resigned. Elections in 1992 provided Albania with its first democratic president. Living conditions are poor but land has been privatized and the economy has begun to grow. Relations with Greece have been deteriorating. ∎

ALGERIA

Official name Democratic and Popular Republic of Algeria
PEOPLE
Population 27,965,000. **Density** 30/mi^2 (12/km^2). **Urban** 52%. **Capital** Algiers, 1,507,241. **Ethnic groups** Arab-Berber 99%. **Languages** Arabic, Berber dialects, French. **Religions** Sunni Muslim 99%, Christian and Jewish 1%. **Life expectancy** 67 female, 65 male. **Literacy** 57%.
POLITICS
Government Provisional military government.
Parties Islamic Salvation Front, National Liberation Front, Socialist Forces Front, others.
Suffrage Universal, over 18. **Memberships** AL, OAU, OPEC, UN. **Subdivisions** 48 departments.
ECONOMY
GDP $89,000,000,000. **Per capita** $3,305.

Monetary unit Dinar. **Trade partners** Exports: France, U.S., Italy. Imports: France, Germany, U.S. **Exports** Petroleum, natural gas. **Imports** Machinery, manufactures.
LAND
Description Northern Africa. **Area** 919,595 mi^2 (2,381,741 km^2). **Highest point** Tahat, 9,541 ft (2,908 m). **Lowest point** Chott Melrhir, -131 ft (-40 m).

People. Indigenous Berbers and invading Arabs shaped modern Algeria's culture, and today most of the population is Muslim and of Arab-Berber descent. European cultural influences, evidence of over a century of French control, exist in urban areas. Since independence in 1962, free medical care has been instituted and the educational system has been greatly improved.

Economy and the Land. A member of the Organization of Petroleum Exporting Countries (OPEC), Algeria produces oil and natural gas. Agriculture is divided between state and privately-owned farms. The government continues to emphasize gas production and exportation, while it maintains a socialistic economy and promotes development of private business. Algeria's terrain is varied. The Tell, Arabic for hill, is a narrow Mediterranean coastal region that contains the country's most fertile land and highest population. South of this lie high plateaus and the Atlas Mountains, which give way to the Sahara Desert. The climate is temperate along the coast and dry and cool in the plateau region.

History and Politics. In the eighth and eleventh centuries, invading Arabs brought their language and religion to the native Berbers. The Berbers and Arabs together became known as Moors, and conflicts between Moors, Turks, and Spaniards erupted periodically over several centuries. France began conquering Algeria in 1830, and by 1902 the entire country was under French control. The revolution against French rule began in 1954, but it was not until 1962 that the country was declared independent. Since a bloodless coup in 1965, the political situation has been relatively stable. A 1989 referendum approved a new constitution allowing multiparty elections. The first free national elections since independence were held in 1991. The fundamentalist Islamic Salvation Front (ISF) won in a landslide victory, prompting a military takeover. In 1992 the government banned ISF and jailed its leaders, but Muslim militants continue their opposition.   ■

AMERICAN SAMOA
See UNITED STATES.

ANDORRA

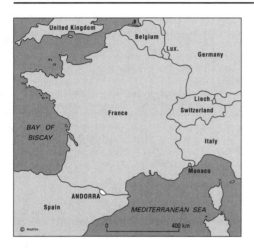

Official name Principality of Andorra
PEOPLE
Population 59,000. **Density** 337/mi^2 (130/km^2).
Urban 63%. **Capital** Andorra, 20,437. **Ethnic groups** Spanish 61%, Andorran 30%, French 6%.
Languages Catalan, Spanish (Castilian), French.
Religions Roman Catholic. **Life expectancy** 81 female, 75 male.
POLITICS
Government Parliamentary co-principality (Spanish and French protection). **Parties** Liberal Union, National Coalition, National Democratic Group, New Democracy, others. **Suffrage** Universal, over 18. **Memberships** UN.
Subdivisions 7 parishes.
ECONOMY
GDP $760,000,000. **Per capita** $14,074.
Monetary unit French franc, Spanish peseta.
Trade partners France, Spain. **Exports** Electricity, tobacco products, furniture. **Imports** Manufactures, food.
LAND
Description Southwestern Europe, landlocked.
Area 175 mi^2 (453 km^2). **Highest point** Pic de Coma Pedrosa, 9,665 ft (2,946 m). **Lowest point** Along Valira River, 2,756 ft (840 m).

People. Much of Andorran life and culture has been shaped by its mountainous terrain and governing countries, France and Spain. Population is concentrated in the valleys, and despite a tourism boom in past decades, the peaks and valleys of the Pyrenees have isolated the small country from many twentieth-century changes. Catalan is the official language, and cultural and historic ties exist with the Catalonian region of northern Spain. The majority of the population is Spanish; Andorran citizens are a minority.

Economy and the Land. The terrain has established Andorra's economy as well as its lifestyle. Improved transportation routes together with other factors have resulted in a thriving tourist industry—a dramatic shift from traditional sheepherding and tobacco growing. In addition, duty-free status has made the country a European shopping mecca. Tobacco is still the main agricultural product, though only about 4 percent of the land is arable. Climate varies with altitude; winters are cold and summers are cool and pleasant.

History and Politics. Tradition indicates that Charlemagne freed the area from the Moors in A.D. 806. A French count and the Spanish bishop of Seo de Urgel signed an agreement in the 1200s to act as co-princes of the country, establishing the political status and boundaries that exist today. The coprincipality is governed by the president of France and the bishop of Seo de Urgel. In 1994 Andorra adopted a new constitution, ending a system of government in effect since the 13th century.   ■

ANGOLA

Official name Republic of Angola
PEOPLE
Population 10,690,000. **Density** 22/mi^2 (8.6/km^2).
Urban 28%. **Capital** Luanda, 1,459,900. **Ethnic groups** Ovimbundu 37%, Mbundu 25%, Kongo 13%, mulatto 2%, European 1%. **Languages** Portuguese, indigenous. **Religions** Animist 47%, Roman Catholic 38%, Protestant 15%. **Life expectancy** 48 female, 45 male. **Literacy** 42%.
POLITICS
Government Republic. **Parties** National Union for the Total Independence of Angola, Popular

Movement for Liberation, others. **Suffrage** Universal, over 18. **Memberships** OAU, UN. **Subdivisions** 18 provinces.

ECONOMY

GDP $5,700,000,000. **Per capita** $531. **Monetary unit** Kwanza. **Trade partners** Exports: U.S., Bahamas. Imports: U.S., France, Brazil, Portugal. **Exports** Petroleum, diamonds, coffee, sisal, fish, lumber, cotton. **Imports** Machinery and electrical equipment, food, transportation equipment.

LAND

Description Southern Africa. **Area** 481,354 mi^2 (1,246,700 km^2). **Highest point** Serra do Môco, 8,596 ft (2,620 m). **Lowest point** Sea level.

People. Angola is made up mostly of various Bantu peoples—mainly Ovimbundu, Mbundu, Kongo, and others. Despite influences from a half-century of Portuguese rule, Angolan traditions remain strong, especially in rural areas. Each group has its own language, and although Portuguese is the official language, it is spoken by a minority. Many Angolans, retaining traditional indigenous beliefs, worship ancestral spirits.

Economy and the Land. A 1975 civil war, the resultant departure of skilled European labor, and continuing guerrilla activity have taken their toll on Angola's economy. The country has been working toward recovery, however, encouraging development of private industries and foreign trade. Although not a member of the Organization of Petroleum Exporting Countries (OPEC), Angola is a large oil producer. Cabinda, an enclave separated from the rest of the country by Zaire and the Zaire River, is the main site of oil production. Diamond mining remains an important activity, as does agriculture. Much of the land is forested, however, and is therefore not suited for commercial farming. The flat coastal area gives way to inland plateaus and uplands. The climate varies from tropical to subtropical.

History and Politics. Bantu groups settled in the area prior to the first century A.D. In 1483 a Portuguese explorer became the first European to arrive in Angola, and slave trade soon became a major activity. Portuguese control expanded and continued almost uninterrupted for several centuries. In the 1960s ignored demands for popular rule led to two wars for independence. Three nationalist groups emerged, each with its own ideology and supporters. In 1974 a coup in Portugal resulted in independence for all Portuguese territories in Africa, and Angola became independent in 1975. A civil war ensued, with the three groups fighting for power. By 1976, with the assistance of Cuban military personnel, the Popular Movement for the Liberation of Angola (PMLA) had established control. Angola, Cuba, and South Africa signed an accord in 1988 providing for Cuban troop withdrawals by July 1991. The country's first democratic elections were held in 1992 but were disputed. Fragile peace treaties and intermittent civil war have plagued the country since. ∎

ANGUILLA

See UNITED KINGDOM.

ANTARCTICA

Official name Antarctica

Capital None. **Memberships** None.

LAND

Description Continent in Southern Hemisphere. **Area** 5,400,000 mi^2 (14,000,000 km^2). **Highest point** Vinson Massif, 16,066 ft (4,897 m). **Lowest point** Deep Lake, -184 ft (-56 m).

People. Antarctica, which surrounds the South Pole, is the southernmost continent, the coldest place on earth, and one of the last frontiers. There are no native inhabitants, and its temporary population is made up mainly of scientists from various countries operating research stations.

Economy and the Land. Harsh climate and terrain have inhibited resource exploration and development. Antarctica's natural resources include coal, various ores, iron, offshore oil, and natural gas. Fishing for krill, a marine protein source, is another activity. Crossed by several ranges collectively known as the Transantarctic Mountains, Antarctica can be roughly divided into a mountainous western region and a larger eastern sector consisting of an icy plain rimmed by mountains. With its tip about 700 miles (1,127 km) from southern South America, the mountainous Antarctic Peninsula and its offshore islands jut northward. Nearly all Antarctica is ice covered, precipitation is minimal, and the continent is actually a desert.

History and Politics. In the 1770s Captain James Cook of Britain set out in search of the southernmost continent and sailed completely around Antarctica without sighting land. Explorations beginning in 1820 resulted in sightings of the mainland or offshore islands by the British, Russians, and Americans. British explorer Sir James C. Ross conducted the first extensive explorations. After a lull of several decades, interest in Antarctica was renewed in the late nineteenth and early twentieth centuries. Captain Robert F. Scott and Ernest Shackleton of Britain and Roald Amundsen of Norway led the renewed interest. Amundsen won the race to the South Pole in 1911. An Antarctic Treaty signed in 1959 permitted only peaceful scientific research to be conducted in the region. It also delayed settlement until 1989 of overlapping claims to the territory held by Norway, Australia, France, New Zealand, Chile, Britain, and Argentina. In 1988 several countries signed agreements to allow exploitation of Antarctica's natural resources. ∎

ANTIGUA AND BARBUDA

Official name Antigua and Barbuda

PEOPLE

Population 67,000. **Density** 392/mi^2 (152/km^2). **Urban** 32%. **Capital** St. John's, Antigua I., 24,359. **Ethnic groups** Black, British, Portuguese, Lebanese, Syrian. **Languages** English, local dialects. **Religions** Anglican, Protestant, Roman Catholic. **Life expectancy** 75 female, 71 male. **Literacy** 89%.

POLITICS
Government
Parliamentary state.
Parties Labour, United
Progressive. **Suffrage**
Universal, over 18.
Memberships CW,
OAS, UN.
Subdivisions 7
parishes.
ECONOMY
GDP $368,500,000.
Per capita $4,786.
Monetary unit East
Caribbean dollar.
Trade partners
Exports: U.S., U.K.,
Canada. Imports: U.S.,
U.K., Yugoslavia.
Exports Petroleum,
manufactures, food, machinery and transportation
equipment. **Imports** Food, machinery and trans-
portation equipment, manufactures, chemicals.
LAND
Description Caribbean islands. **Area** 171 mi^2 (442
km^2). **Highest point** Boggy Pk., 1,319 ft (402 m).
Lowest point Sea level.

People. Most Antiguans are descendants of black
African slaves brought by the British to work sugar-
cane plantations. The largest urban area is St. John's,
but most Antiguans live in rural areas. British rule has
left its imprint; most people are Protestant and speak
English.

Economy and the Land. The dry, tropical climate and
white-sand beaches attract many visitors, making tourism
the economic mainstay. Once dependent on sugar cultivation, the nation has shifted to a multicrop agriculture.
The country is composed of three islands: Antigua,
Barbuda, and uninhabited Redondo. Formed by volcanoes, the low-lying islands are flat.

History and Politics. The original inhabitants of
Antigua and Barbuda were the Carib Indians. Columbus
arrived at Antigua in 1493, and after unsuccessful
Spanish and French attempts at colonization, the British
began settlement in the 1600s. The country remained
a British colony until 1967, when it became an associated state of the United Kingdom. Antigua gained
independence in 1981. In March 1994, the Antigua
Labour Party was returned to power for the third
time, pledging a more open political system. ■

ARGENTINA

Official name Argentine Republic
PEOPLE
Population 34,083,000. **Density** 32/mi^2 (12/km^2).
Urban 86%. **Capital** Buenos Aires (de facto),
2,960,976; Viedma (future) 24,346. **Ethnic groups**
White 85%; mestizo, Amerindian, and others 15%.
Languages Spanish, English, Italian, German,
French. **Religions** Roman Catholic 90%, Jewish
2%, Protestant 2%. **Life expectancy** 75 female,
68 male. **Literacy** 95%.

POLITICS
Government Republic.
Parties Justicialist
(Peronista), Radical
Civic Union, Union of
the Democratic Center,
others. **Suffrage**
Universal, over 18.
Memberships OAS,
UN. **Subdivisions** 22
provinces, 1 district, 1
national territory.
ECONOMY
GDP
$185,000,000,000. **Per
capita** $5,615.
Monetary unit Peso.
Trade partners
Exports: U.S., Brazil,
Netherlands. Imports:
U.S., Brazil, Germany. **Exports** Meat, wheat, corn,
oilseed, hides, wool. **Imports** Machinery, chemi-
cals, metals, fuel.
LAND
Description Southern South America. **Area**
1,073,519 mi^2 (2,780,400 km^2). **Highest point**
Cerro Aconcagua, 22,831 ft (6,959 m). **Lowest
point** Salinas Chicas, -138 ft (-42 m).

People. An indigenous Indian population, Spanish
settlement, and a turn-of-the-century influx of immigrants have made Argentina an ethnically diverse
nation. Today, most Argentines are descendants
of Spanish and Italian immigrants. Other Europeans,
mestizos of mixed Indian-Spanish blood, Indians, Middle
Easterners, and Latin American immigrants diversify
the population further. Spanish influence is evident
in the major religion, Roman Catholicism; the official
language, Spanish; and many aspects of cultural life.

Economy and the Land. Political difficulties beginning in the 1930s have resulted in economic problems
and have kept this one-time economic giant from realizing its potential. The most valuable natural resource
is the rich soil of the pampas, fertile plains in the east-
central region. The greatest contributors to the economy, however, are manufacturing and services. The
second largest country in South America, Argentina
has a varied terrain, with northern lowlands, the
east-central pampas, the Andes Mountains in the west,
and the southern Patagonian steppe. The climate like-
wise varies, from subtropical in the north to subarctic in the south.

History and Politics. The earliest inhabitants of
the area were Indians. In the 1500s silver-seeking
Spaniards arrived, and by 1580 they had established a colony on the site of present-day Buenos Aires.
In 1816 Argentina officially announced its independence from Spain. A successful struggle for independence ensued, and in 1853 a constitution was
adopted and a president elected. Prosperity continued through the 1920s, and immigration and foreign
investment increased. Unsatisfactory power distribution and concern over foreign investment resulted
in a military coup in 1930. Thus began a series of civil
and military governments; coups; the election, overthrow, and reelection of Juan Perón; and controversial

human-rights violations. In 1982 Argentina lost a war with Britain over the Falkland Islands. Years of struggling with human rights transgressions followed. Since winning the election in 1989, the Perónistas have introduced austere economic reforms and rescheduled foreign debts. ∎

ARMENIA

Official name Republic of Armenia
PEOPLE
Population 3,794,000. **Density** 330/mi^2 (127/km^2). **Urban** 68%. **Capital** Yerevan, 1,199,000. **Ethnic groups** Armenian 93%, Azeri 3%, Russian 2%. **Languages** Armenian, Russian. **Religions** Armenian Orthodox 94%. **Life expectancy** 75 female, 68 male. **Literacy** 98%.
POLITICS
Government Republic. **Parties** Democratic, National Democratic Union, National Movement, Revolutionary Federation, others. **Suffrage** Universal, over 18. **Memberships** CIS, UN. **Subdivisions** None.
ECONOMY
GDP $7,100,000,000. **Per capita** $2,071. **Monetary unit** Dram. **Trade partners** Former Soviet republics. **Exports** Machinery and transportation equipment, metals, chemicals. **Imports** Machinery, energy, consumer goods.
LAND
Description Southwestern Asia, landlocked. **Area** 11,506 mi^2 (29,800 km^2). **Highest point** Mt. Aragats, 13,419 ft (4,090 m). **Lowest point** Along Debed River, 1,280 ft (390 m).

People. The Armenians are among Europe's oldest and most distinct ethnic groups, having inhabited the area east and south of the Black Sea since the seventh century B.C. Both the Armenian alphabet and the Armenian church date back to the fourth century and remain substantially unchanged today. Early Armenia left a legacy of many gifted artists, writers, and philosophers.

Economy and the Land. Most of Armenia is mountainous and dry. Despite fertile soils in some of the mountain valleys, agriculture is of little importance. Armenia's great rivers have provided hydroelectric power for an important machine-building industry. Armenia is subject to severe earthquakes, and it is still rebuilding from a 1988 earthquake that killed twenty-five thousand people and destroyed one-tenth of the nation's industrial capacity and housing. Transportation is not well developed and, in recent years, blockades imposed against Armenia by neighboring Azerbaijan have crippled the economy.

History and Politics. Armenia traces its beginnings to the first millennium B.C. when the Urartu empire fell to the Armens. Alexander the Great conquered Armenia around 300 B.C., but its independence was restored one hundred years later. By the early part of the first century A.D., Armenia encompassed parts of present-day Turkey, Syria, Iraq, Iran, and the former Soviet Union. Later, various groups invaded Armenia, including the Arabs, Turks, and Persians. The Russians gained control over the nation in 1828. Continued calls for independence led to the massacre of more than two hundred thousand Armenians by the Turks in the 1890s. Armenians tried to assert their independence in 1918, but the Soviets took full control in 1920. Protests by ethnic Armenians in the enclave of Nagorno-Karabakh within Azerbaijan led to escalating violence between Armenia and Azerbaijan. The struggle fueled rising Armenian nationalism, and Armenia first declared its independence from the Soviet Union in August 1990. The country did not achieve true sovereignty until the break-up of the Soviet Union in September 1991. The Nagorno-Karabakh problem remains unsolved, although a cease-fire was signed in May 1994. ∎

ARUBA
See NETHERLANDS.

ASCENSION
See UNITED KINGDOM.

AUSTRALIA

Official name Commonwealth of Australia
PEOPLE
Population 18,205,000. **Density** 6.1/mi^2 (2.4/km^2). **Urban** 85%. **Capital** Canberra, 276,162. **Ethnic groups** Caucasian 95%, Asian 4%, Aboriginal and other 1%. **Languages** English, indigenous. **Religions** Anglican 26%, Roman Catholic 26%, other Christian 24%. **Life expectancy** 80 female, 74 male. **Literacy** 100%.
POLITICS
Government Parliamentary state. **Parties** Labor, Liberal, National. **Suffrage** Universal, over 18. **Memberships** CW, OECD, UN. **Subdivisions** 6

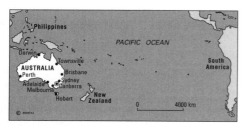

states, 2 territories.
ECONOMY
GDP $339,700,000,000. **Per capita** $20,024.
Monetary unit Dollar. **Trade partners** Exports: Japan, U.S., New Zealand, Korea. Imports: U.S., Japan, U.K. **Exports** Metals, minerals, coal, wool, grain, meat, manufactures. **Imports** Manufactures, machinery, consumer goods.
LAND
Description Continent between South Pacific and Indian oceans. **Area** 2,966,155 mi² (7,682,300 km²). **Highest point** Mt. Kosciusko, 7,310 ft (2,228 m). **Lowest point** Lake Eyre (North), -52 ft (-16 m).

People. Australia's culture reflects a unique combination of British, other European, and aboriginal influences. Settlement and rule by the United Kingdom gave the country a distinctly British flavor, and many Australians trace their roots to early British settlers. Planned immigration also played a major role in Australia's development, bringing more than three million Europeans since World War II. Refugees, most recently from Southeast Asia, make up another group of incoming peoples. The country is home to a small number of aborigines. The nation's size and a relatively dry terrain have resulted in uneven settlement patterns, with people concentrated in the rainier southeastern coastal area. The population is mainly urban, though overall population density remains low.

Economy and the Land. Australia's economy is similar to economies in other developed nations, and is characterized by a postwar shift from agriculture to industry and services, as well as inflation and unemployment. Wool is a major 'export, and livestock raising takes place on relatively flat, wide grazing lands surrounding an arid central region. Commercial crop raising is concentrated on a fertile southeastern plain. Plentiful mineral resources provide for a strong mining industry. Australia is the world's smallest continent but one of its largest countries. The climate is varied, and part of the country lies within the tropics. Because it is south of the equator, Australia has seasons the reverse of those in the Northern Hemisphere.

History and Politics. Aboriginal peoples probably arrived about forty thousand years ago and established a hunter-gatherer society. The Dutch explored the area in the seventeenth century, but no claims were made until the eighteenth century, when British Captain James Cook found his way to the fertile east and annexed the land to Britain. The first colony, New South Wales, was founded in 1788, and many of the early settlers were British convicts. During the 1800s, a squatter movement spread the population to other parts of the island, and the discovery of gold led to a population boom. Demands for self-government soon began, and by the 1890s all the colonies were self-governing, with Britain maintaining control of foreign affairs and defense. Nationalism continued to increase, and a new nation, the Commonwealth of Australia, was created in 1901. Participation in international affairs has expanded since World War II, with attention turned particularly to Asian countries. Currently a movement is underway to declare Australia a republic and thus loosen ties with Britain. ∎

AUSTRIA

Official name Republic of Austria
PEOPLE
Population 7,932,000. **Density** 245/mi² (95/km²). **Urban** 58%. **Capital** Vienna, 1,539,848. **Ethnic groups** German 99%. **Languages** German. **Religions** Roman Catholic 85%, Protestant 6%. **Life expectancy** 79 female, 73 male. **Literacy** 99%.
POLITICS
Government Republic. **Parties** Freedom,

Places and Possessions of AUSTRALIA

Entity	Status	Area	Population	Capital/Population
Ashmore and Cartier Islands (Indian Ocean; north of Australia)	External territory (Australia)	1.9 mi² (5.0 km²)	None	None
Christmas Island (Indian Ocean)	External territory (Australia)	52 mi² (135 km²)	1,000	The Settlement
Cocos (Keeling) Islands (Indian Ocean)	Territory (Australia)	5.4 mi² (14 km²)	600	West Island
Coral Sea Islands (South Pacific)	External territory (Australia)	1.0 mi² (2.6 km²)	None	None
Heard and McDonald Islands (Indian Ocean)	External territory (Australia)	154 mi² (400 km²)	None	None
Norfolk Island (South Pacific)	External territory (Australia)	14 mi² (36 km²)	2,700	Kingston
Tasmania (South Pacific island; south of Australia)	State (Australia)	26,178 mi² (67,800 km²)	492,000	Hobart, 47,106

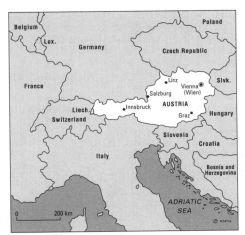

Hapsburg emperor was overthrown, Austria became a republic, and present-day boundaries were established. Political unrest and instability followed. In 1938 Adolf Hitler incorporated Austria into the German Reich. A period of occupation after World War II was followed by Austria's declaration of neutrality. Austria joined the European Union in June 1994. ■

AZERBAIJAN

Official name Azerbaijani Republic
PEOPLE
Population 7,491,000. **Density** 224/mi² (87/km²).
Urban 54%. **Capital** Baku, 1,080,500. **Ethnic groups** Azeri 83%, Armenian 6%, Russian 6%.
Languages Azeri, Russian, Armenian. **Religions** Muslim 87%, Russian Orthodox 6%, Armenian Orthodox 6%. **Life expectancy** 75 female, 67 male. **Literacy** 98%.
POLITICS
Government Republic. **Parties** Musavat, National Independence, Popular Front, Social Democratic, others. **Suffrage** Universal, over 18.
Memberships CIS, NATO, UN. **Subdivisions** 1 republic.
ECONOMY
GDP $15,500,000,000. **Per capita** $2,064.
Monetary unit Manat. **Trade partners** Former Soviet republics, European countries. **Exports** Oil and gas, chemicals, oil-field equipment, textiles, cotton. **Imports** Machinery and parts, consumer durables, food, textiles.
LAND
Description Southwestern Asia, landlocked. **Area** 33,436 mi² (86,600 km²). **Highest point** Mt. Bazardyuzyu, 14,652 ft (4,466 m). **Lowest point** Caspian Sea, -92 ft (-28 m).

People. The Azeris are Turkic people and account for more than 80 percent of the population. There are also small Armenian and Russian minorities. Most Azeris are Shiite Muslims, although the Armenians in the enclave of Nagorno-Karabakh are Christian. About one-half of the people live in urban areas.

People's, Social Democratic, others. **Suffrage** Universal, over 19. **Memberships** OECD, UN.
Subdivisions 9 states.
ECONOMY
GDP $134,400,000,000. **Per capita** $17,015.
Monetary unit Schilling. **Trade partners** Exports: Germany, Italy, Switzerland. Imports: Germany, Italy, Japan. **Exports** Machinery and equipment, iron and steel, wood, textiles. **Imports** Petroleum, food, machinery, transportation equipment, chemicals.
LAND
Description Central Europe, landlocked. **Area** 32,377 mi² (83,856 km²). **Highest point** Grossglockner, 12,457 ft (3,797 m). **Lowest point** Neusiedler See, 377 ft (115 m).

People. The majority of Austrians are native born, German speaking, and Roman Catholic, a homogeneity belying a history of invasions by diverse peoples. With a long cultural tradition, the country has contributed greatly to music and the arts. Vienna, the capital, is one of the great cultural centers of Europe.

Economy and the Land. Austria's economy is a blend of state and privately-owned industry. After World War II the government began nationalizing industries, returning many to the private sector as the economy stabilized. Unemployment is low, and the economy remains relatively strong. The economic mainstays are services and manufacturing. Agriculture is limited because of the overall mountainous terrain, with the Danube River basin in the east containing the most productive soils. In addition to the country's cultural heritage, the alpine landscape also attracts many tourists. The climate is generally moderate.

History and Politics. Early in its history, Austria was settled by Celts, ruled by Romans, and invaded by Germans, Slavs, Magyars, and others. Long rule by the Hapsburg family began in the thirteenth century, and in time Austria became the center of a vast empire. In 1867 Hungarian pressure resulted in the formation of the dual monarchy of Austria-Hungary. Nationalist movements against Austria culminated in the 1914 assassination of the heir to the throne, Archduke Francis Ferdinand, and set off the conflict that became World War I. In 1918 the war ended, the

Economy and the Land. Azerbaijan varies from the cool slopes of the Caucasus to flat, dry steppes. Cotton is produced in abundance. Sheep and cattle are also raised on the dry, grassy pasture of the steppes. The Lenkoran lowland in the extreme southeast part of the country is semitropical and produces many fruits and vegetables. The area around Baku is a major oil-producing and refining center, although production has been steadily declining.

History and Politics. Azerbaijan is part of a larger historical region of the same name, which includes parts of neighboring Iran. Arabs conquered the region and brought Islam in A.D. 642. Later, Mongols, Turks, and Persians invaded the region. Russian interest in the area began during the reign of Peter the Great and led to several wars with Persia. In 1828 Azerbaijan was formally divided between Russia and Persia (now Iran). The country enjoyed a brief period of independence from 1918 to 1920, when a Soviet invasion forced its incorporation into the Soviet Union. Fighting between Azerbaijan and neighboring Armenia over the Armenian enclave of Nagorno-Karabakh began in 1987, and prompted a renewed Soviet invasion of the capital city of Baku in early 1990. Azerbaijan declared its independence in August 1991. The country attained real independence after the dissolution of the Soviet Union at the end of 1991. Continuing strife with Armenia over the enclave of Nagorno-Karabakh has disrupted government functions. In June 1993, Azerbaijan's first elected president was overthrown. Political unrest continues, particularly in Nagorno-Karabakh. ■

AZORES
See PORTUGAL.

BAHAMAS

Official name Commonwealth of the Bahamas
PEOPLE
Population 275,000. **Density** 51/mi2 (20/km2).

Urban 64%. **Capital** Nassau, New Providence I., 141,000. **Ethnic groups** Black 85%, white 15%. **Languages** English, Creole. **Religions** Baptist 32%, Anglican 20%, Roman Catholic 19%, Methodist 6%. **Life expectancy** 76 female, 69 male. **Literacy** 90%.
POLITICS
Government Parliamentary state. **Parties** Free National Movement, Progressive Liberal. **Suffrage** Universal, over 18. **Memberships** CW, OAS, UN. **Subdivisions** 21 districts.
ECONOMY
GDP $4,400,000,000. **Per capita** $16,604.
Monetary unit Dollar. **Trade partners** Exports: U.S., U.K., Japan. Imports: Saudi Arabia, U.S., Nigeria. **Exports** Pharmaceuticals, cement, rum, crawfish. **Imports** Food, manufactures, fuel.
LAND
Description Caribbean islands. **Area** 5,382 mi2 (13,939 km2). **Highest point** Mt. Alvernia, 206 ft (63 m). **Lowest point** Sea level.

People. Only about 29 of the 700 Bahamian islands are inhabited, and most of the people live on Grand Bahama and New Providence. The majority blacks are mainly descendants of slaves routed through the area or brought by British Loyalists fleeing the American colonies during the revolutionary war.

Economy and the Land. Because the thin soils of these flat coral islands are not suited for agriculture, for years the country struggled to develop a strong economic base. The solution was tourism, which capitalizes on the islands' most valuable resource—a semitropical climate. Because it is a tax haven, the country is also an international finance center.

History and Politics. Christopher Columbus's first stop on his way to America in 1492, the Bahamas were originally the home of the Lucayo Indians, whom the Spaniards took for slave trade. The British arrived in the 1600s, and the islands became a British colony in 1717. The country achieved independence in 1973. In 1992 voters ended Sir Lynden Pindling's twenty-five-year tenure as Prime Minister. ■

BAHRAIN

Official name State of Bahrain
PEOPLE
Population 563,000. **Density** 2,109/mi2 (815/km2). **Urban** 83%. **Capital** Manama, Bahrain I., 82,700. **Ethnic groups** Bahraini 63%, Asian 13%, other Arab 10%. **Languages** Arabic, English, Farsi, Urdu. **Religions** Shiite Muslim 70%, Sunni Muslim 30%. **Life expectancy** 74 female, 69 male. **Literacy** 77%.
POLITICS
Government Monarchy. **Parties** None. **Suffrage** None. **Memberships** AL, UN. **Subdivisions** 12 regions.
ECONOMY
GDP $6,800,000,000. **Per capita** $12,121.
Monetary unit Dinar. **Trade partners** Exports: Saudi Arabia, Japan, United Arab Emirates.

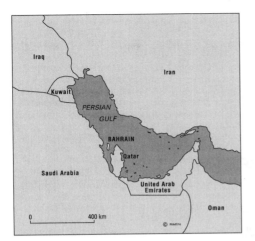

BALEARIC ISLANDS
See SPAIN.

BANGLADESH

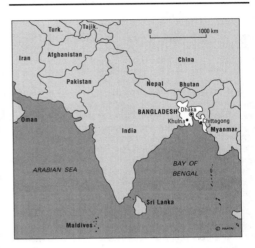

Imports: Saudi Arabia, U.K., U.S. **Exports** Petroleum products, aluminum. **Imports** Crude petroleum, machinery and transportation equipment, manufactures.
LAND
Description Southwestern Asian islands (in Persian Gulf). **Area** 267 mi^2 (691 km^2). **Highest point** Mt. Dukhan, 440 ft (134 m). **Lowest point** Sea level.

People. Most residents of Bahrain are native-born Muslims, with the Sunni sect predominating in urban areas and Shiites in the countryside. Many of the country's thirty-three islands are barren, and population is concentrated in the capital city—Manama, on Bahrain Island—and on the smaller island of Muharraq. The oil economy has resulted in an influx of foreign workers and considerable westernization, and Bahrain is a Persian Gulf leader in free health care and education.

Economy and the Land. The one-time pearl-and-fish economy was reshaped by exploitation of oil and natural gas, careful management, and diversification. A major refinery processes crude oil piped from Saudi Arabia as well as the country's own oil, and Bahrain's aluminum industry is the Gulf's largest non-oil activity. Because of its location, Bahrain is able to provide Gulf countries with services such as dry docking, and the country has become a Middle Eastern banking center. Agriculture exists on northern Bahrain Island, where natural springs provide an irrigation source. Their newest industry is tourism, providing a "playground" for Saudis and American military. Much of the state is desert. Summers are hot and dry and winters are mild.

History and Politics. From about 2000 to 1800 B.C., the area of Bahrain flourished as a center for trade. After early periods of Portuguese and Iranian rule, the Al Khalifa family came to power in the eighteenth century, and it has governed ever since. Bahrain became a British protectorate in the nineteenth century, and independence was gained in 1971. Recent attempts at democratization have been quashed by the Al Khalifa family. ∎

Official name People's Republic of Bangladesh
PEOPLE
Population 119,370,000. **Density** 2,147/mi^2 (829/km^2). **Urban** 16%. **Capital** Dhaka, 3,637,892. **Ethnic groups** Bengali 98%. **Languages** Bangla, English. **Religions** Muslim 83%, Hindu 16%. **Life expectancy** 53 female, 53 male. **Literacy** 35%.
POLITICS
Government Republic. **Parties** Awami League, Jamaat-e-Islami, Jatiyo, Nationalist, others. **Suffrage** Universal, over 18. **Memberships** CW, UN. **Subdivisions** 5 divisions.
ECONOMY
GDP $12,200,000,000. **Per capita** $101. **Monetary unit** Taka. **Trade partners** Exports: U.S., Italy, Japan, U.K. Imports: Japan, U.S., United Arab Emirates. **Exports** Clothing, jute, leather, shrimp. **Imports** Machinery, petroleum, food, textiles.
LAND
Description Southern Asia. **Area** 55,598 mi^2 (143,998 km^2). **Highest point** Reng Mtn., 3,141 ft (957 m). **Lowest point** Sea level.

People. Bangladesh's population is characterized by extremes. The people, mostly peasant farmers, are among Asia's poorest and most rural. With a relatively small area and a high birthrate, the country is also one of the world's most densely populated. Many Bangladeshis are victims of disease, floods, and ongoing medical and food shortages. Islam, the major religion, has influenced almost every aspect of life. Bangla is the official language.

Economy and the Land. Fertile flood plain soil is the chief resource of this mostly flat, river-crossed country, and farming is the main activity. Rice and jute are among the major crops. Farm output fluctuates greatly, however, subject to the frequent monsoons, floods, and droughts of a semitropical climate. Because of this and other factors, foreign aid, imports, and an emphasis on agriculture have not assuaged the continuing food shortages. In 1988 floods put 75 percent of the country under water and left twenty-five million people in dire straits. A cyclone in 1991 killed more than one hundred thousand people and left millions at risk from lack of fresh water and food.

History and Politics. Most of Bangladesh lies in eastern Bengal, an Asian region whose western sector encompasses India's Bengal province. Early religious influences in Bengal included Buddhist rulers in the eighth century A.D. and Hindus in the eleventh. In A.D.1200 Muslim rule introduced the religion to which the majority of eastern Bengalis eventually converted, while most western Bengalis retained their Hindu beliefs. British control in India, beginning in the seventeenth century, expanded until all Bengal was part of British India by the 1850s. When British India gained independence in 1947, Muslim population centers were united into the single nation of Pakistan in an attempt to end Hindu-Muslim hostilities. More than 1,000 miles (1,600 km) separated West Pakistan, formed from northwest India, from East Pakistan, comprised mostly of eastern Bengal. The bulk of Pakistan's population resided in the eastern province and felt the west wielded political and economic power at its expense. A civil war began in 1971, and the eastern province declared itself an independent nation called Bangladesh, or "Bengal nation." That same year, West Pakistan surrendered to eastern guerrillas joined with Indian troops. The state has seen political crises since independence, including two leader assassinations and several coups. In 1982 General Ershad took control in a bloodless coup, and assumed the office of president in 1983. Violent protests led to Ershad's resignation in December 1990 and his subsequent sentence for misappropriation of funds. Local elections in January 1994 were met with violence. ∎

Trinidad and Tobago, U.K. **Exports** Sugar and molasses, chemicals, electrical equipment, clothing, rum. **Imports** Food, consumer goods, raw materials, machinery, petroleum.
LAND
Description Caribbean island. **Area** 166 mi^2 (430 km^2). **Highest point** Mt. Hillaby, 1,115 ft (340 m). **Lowest point** Sea level.

People. A history of British rule is reflected in the Anglican religion and English language of this easternmost West Indian island. It is one of the world's most densely populated countries, and most citizens are black descendants of African slaves.

Economy and the Land. Barbados's pleasant tropical climate and its land have determined its economic mainstays: tourism and sugar. Sunshine and year-round warmth attract thousands of visitors and, in conjunction with the soil, provide an excellent environment for sugar cane cultivation. Manufacturing consists mainly of sugar processing. The coral island's terrain is mostly flat, rising to a central ridge.

History and Politics. Originally settled by South American Arawak Indians, followed by Carib Indians, Barbados was uninhabited when the first British settlers arrived in the 1600s. More colonists followed, developing sugar plantations and bringing slaves from Africa to work them. The country remained under British control until it became independent in 1966. ∎

BARBADOS

Official name Barbados
PEOPLE
Population 261,000. **Density** 1,572/mi^2 (607/km^2). **Urban** 45%. **Capital** Bridgetown, 5,928. **Ethnic groups** Black 80%, mixed 16%, white 4%. **Languages** English. **Religions** Anglican 40%, Pentecostal 8%, Methodist 7%, Roman Catholic 4%. **Life expectancy** 78 female, 73 male. **Literacy** 99%.
POLITICS
Government Parliamentary state. **Parties** Democratic Labor, Labor, National Democratic. **Suffrage** Universal, over 18. **Memberships** CW, OAS, UN. **Subdivisions** 11 parishes.
ECONOMY
GDP $2,200,000,000. **Per capita** $8,527.
Monetary unit Dollar. **Trade partners** Exports: U.S., U.K., Trinidad and Tobago. Imports: U.S.,

BELARUS

Official name Republic of Belarus
PEOPLE
Population 10,425,000. **Density** 130/mi^2 (50/km^2). **Urban** 65%. **Capital** Minsk, 1,633,600. **Ethnic groups** Belarussian 78%, Russian 13%, Polish 4%, Ukrainian 3%. **Languages** Belarussian, Russian. **Religions** Russian Orthodox. **Life expectancy** 76 female, 66 male. **Literacy** 99%.
POLITICS
Government Republic. **Parties** Popular Front, Social Democratic, United Democratic, Workers Union. **Suffrage** Universal, over 18. **Memberships** CIS, UN. **Subdivisions** 6 oblasts.
ECONOMY
GDP $61,000,000,000. **Per capita** $5,865.
Monetary unit Rubel. **Trade partners** Former Soviet republics. **Exports** Food, textiles, agricultural machinery. **Imports** Steel, industrial raw materials.

LAND
Description Eastern Europe, landlocked. **Area** 80,155 mi² (207,600 km²). **Highest point** Mt. Dzerzhinskaya, 1,132 ft (345 m). **Lowest point** Along Neman River, 279 ft (85 m).

People. Most people speak Belarussian, a Slavic language closely related to Russian and Ukrainian, and belong to the Orthodox church. There is also a substantial Roman Catholic minority. Belarussian people also predominate in a large area of surrounding Russian territory.

Economy and the Land. Most of the land is either forest or swamp, and the terrain is flat. The country is a net exporter of food, including meat, milk, eggs, flour, and potatoes. Peat is the major mineral resource, and is used to fuel several major electrical power plants.

History and Politics. The Belarussians are descendants of Slavic peoples who came to the area around the seventh century. The area was conquered first by Kiev, then by Lithuania, and later by Poland. Russia gained control of Belorussia in the late 1700s. Emancipation of the serfs did not come until 1861, while the area remained backward and poor. Following the Bolshevik Revolution, Belorussia enjoyed a short period of independence before joining the Soviet Union in 1922. Despite its status as part of the Soviet Union, Belorussia retained its seat in the United Nations. Poland controlled part of Belorussia from 1921 until 1939, and the country suffered vast devastation under German occupation during World War II. Belorussia became known as Belarus after it gained its independence following the demise of the Soviet Union in 1991. The new country is struggling to create a stable market economy in the face of rampant inflation and economic chaos. In 1994 an anti-corruption candidate was elected. The country maintains close ties with Russia. ∎

BELGIUM

Official name Kingdom of Belgium
PEOPLE
Population 10,075,000. **Density** 855/mi²

(330/km²). **Urban** 96%. **Capital** Brussels, 136,424. **Ethnic groups** Fleming 55%, Walloon 33%, mixed and others 12%. **Languages** Dutch (Flemish), French, German. **Religions** Roman Catholic 75%. **Life expectancy** 79 female, 73 male. **Literacy** 99%.
POLITICS
Government Constitutional monarchy. **Parties** Flemish: Liberal, Social Christian, Socialist. Walloon: Liberal, Social Christian, Socialist, others. **Suffrage** Universal, over 18. **Memberships** EU, NATO, OECD, UN. **Subdivisions** 9 provinces.
ECONOMY
GDP $177,500,000,000. **Per capita** $17,697. **Monetary unit** Franc. **Trade partners** Exports: France, Germany, Netherlands. Imports: Germany, Netherlands, France. **Exports** Iron and steel, transportation equipment, tractors, diamonds, petroleum. **Imports** Fuel, grains, chemicals, food.
LAND
Description Western Europe. **Area** 11,783 mi² (30,518 km²). **Highest point** Botrange, 2,277 ft (694 m). **Lowest point** Sea level.

People. Language separates Belgium into two main regions. Northern Belgium, known as Flanders, is dominated by Flemings, or Flemish-speaking descendants of Germanic Franks. French-speaking Walloons, descendants of the Celts, inhabit southern Belgium, or Wallonia. Both groups are found in centrally located Brussels. In addition, a small German-speaking population is concentrated in the east. Flemish and French divisions often result in discord, but diversity has also been a source of cultural richness. Belgium has often been at the hub of European cultural movements.

Economy and the Land. The economy, as well as the population, was affected by Belgium's location at the center of European activity. Flanders, formerly a poor, rural area, is now more prosperous than the southern Wallonia. Industry was early established as the economic base, and today the country is heavily industrialized. Although agriculture plays a minor economic role, Belgium is nearly self-sufficient in food production. The north and west are dominated by a flat fertile plain, the central region by rolling hills, and the south by the Ardennes Forest, often a tourist destination. The climate is cool and temperate.

History and Politics. Belgium's history began with the settlement of the Belgae tribe in the second century B.C. The Romans invaded the area around 50 B.C. and were overthrown by Germanic Franks in the A.D. 400s. Trade, manufacturing, and art prospered as various peoples invaded, passed through, and ruled the area. In 1794 Napoleon annexed Belgium to France. He was defeated at Waterloo in Belgium in 1815, and the country passed into Dutch hands. Dissatisfaction under Netherlands rule led to revolt and, in 1830, the formation of the independent country of Belgium. Linguistic divisions mark nearly all political activity, from parties split by language to government decisions based on linguistic rivalries. ■

BELIZE

Official name Belize
PEOPLE
Population 212,000. **Density** 24/mi² (9.2/km²).
Urban 51%. **Capital** Belmopan, 5,256. **Ethnic groups** Mestizo 44%, Creole 30%, Mayan 11%, Garifuna 7%. **Languages** English, Spanish, Mayan, Garifuna. **Religions** Roman Catholic 62%, Anglican 12%, Methodist 6%, Mennonite 4%. **Life expectancy** 70 female, 66 male. **Literacy** 91%.
POLITICS
Government Parliamentary state. **Parties** National Alliance, People's United, United Democratic. **Suffrage** Universal, over 18.
Memberships CW, OAS, UN. **Subdivisions** 6 districts.
ECONOMY
GDP $550,000,000. **Per capita** $2,957. **Monetary unit** Dollar. **Trade partners** U.S., U.K., Mexico.
Exports Sugar, clothing, seafood, molasses, citrus, wood. **Imports** Machinery and transportation equipment, food, manufactures, fuels.
LAND
Description Central America. **Area** 8,866 mi²

(22,963 km²). **Highest point** Victoria Pk., 3,675 ft (1,120 m). **Lowest point** Sea level.

People. With the lowest population of any Central American country, Belize has a mixed populace, including descendants of black Africans, mestizos of Spanish-Indian ancestry, and Indians. Population is concentrated in six urban areas along the coast. Most people are poor, but participation in the educational system has led to a high literacy rate.

Economy and the Land. An abundance of timberland resulted in an economy based on forestry until woodlands began to be depleted in the twentieth century. Today the economy focuses on agriculture, with sugar the major crop and export. Arable land is the primary resource, but only a small portion has been cultivated. Industrial activity is limited. The recipient of much foreign aid, Belize hopes to expand export of agricultural surpluses and to develop a tourist industry based on its climate and sandy beaches. The coastal region consists of swampy lowlands rising to the Maya Mountains inland. The hot, humid climate is offset by sea breezes.

History and Politics. Until about the eleventh century A.D., Belize was the site of a flourishing Mayan civilization. Spain claimed the region in the sixteenth century. A British shipwreck in 1638 resulted in the first European settlement and began a process of British colonization, accompanied by extensive logging, piracy, and occasional Spanish and Indian attacks. In 1862 the area officially became the crown colony of British Honduras. Its name was changed to Belize in 1973, and independence was achieved in 1981. A July 1993 election resulted in an upset victory for the opposition United Democratic Party. ■

BENIN

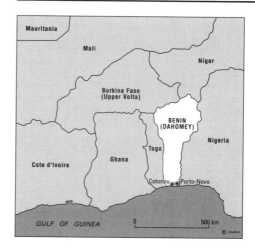

Official name Republic of Benin
PEOPLE
Population 5,433,000. **Density** 125/mi² (48/km²).
Urban 38%. **Capital** Porto-Novo (designated), 164,000; Cotonou (de facto), 533,212. **Ethnic**

groups Fon 39%, Yoruba 12%, Adja 10%, others.
Languages French, Fon, Yoruba, indigenous.
Religions Voodoo and other African religions,
70%, Muslim 15%, Christian. **Life expectancy** 48
female, 45 male. **Literacy** 23%.
POLITICS
Government Republic. **Parties** Democratic Union
for the Forces of Progress, Movement for
Democracy and Social Progress, others. **Suffrage**
Universal, over 18. **Memberships** OAU, UN.
Subdivisions 6 provinces.
ECONOMY
GDP $6,200,000,000. **Per capita** $1,220.
Monetary unit CFA franc. **Trade partners**
Exports: Netherlands, U.S., Spain. Imports:
France, U.K., Netherlands. **Exports** Oil, cotton,
palm products, cocoa. **Imports** Food, beverages,
tobacco, petroleum, manufactures.
LAND
Description Western Africa. **Area** 43,475 mi^2
(112,600 km^2). **Highest point** Unnamed, 2,235 ft
(681 m). **Lowest point** Sea level.

People. Numerous peoples comprise the mostly
black population of Benin. The main groups are the
Fon, the Adja, the Yoruba, and the Bariba. The
nation's linguistic diversity reflects its ethnic variety;
French is the official language, a result of former French
rule. Most Beninese are farmers, although urban
migration is increasing. Indigenous beliefs predominate, but there are also Christians, especially in the
south, and Muslims in the north.

Economy and the Land. Political instability has
been both the cause and effect of Benin's economic problems. The agricultural economy is largely
undeveloped, and palm trees and their by-products
provide the chief source of income and activity for both
farming and industry. Some economic relief may be
found in the exploitation of offshore oil. The predominately flat terrain features coastal lagoons and
dense forests, with mountains in the northwest. Heat
and humidity characterize the coast, with less humidity and varied temperatures in the north.

History and Politics. In the 1500s, Dahomey, a
Fon kingdom, became the power center of the Benin
area. European slave traders came to the coast in the
seventeenth and eighteenth centuries, establishing
posts and bartering with Dahomey royalty for slaves.
As the slave trade prospered, the area became
known as the Slave Coast. France defeated Dahomey's
army in the 1890s and subsequently made the area
a territory of French West Africa. In 1960 the country gained independence, which was followed by
political turmoil, various coups, and a military overthrow
that installed a socialist government in 1972. In 1975
the nation changed its name from Dahomey to Benin.
Economic difficulties in the late 1980s have led the
country away from socialism and towards private
enterprise. In March 1991 elections resulted in the first
popularly elected president and the present government is attempting to pay off foriegn debt. ∎

BERMUDA
See UNITED KINGDOM.

BHUTAN

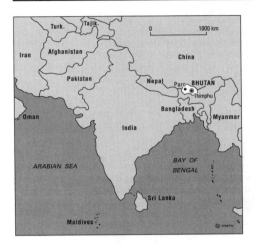

Official name Kingdom of Bhutan
PEOPLE
Population 1,758,000. **Density** 98/mi^2 (38/km^2).
Urban 5%. **Capital** Thimphu, 12,000. **Ethnic
groups** Bhotia 60%, Nepalese 25%, indigenous
15%. **Languages** Dzongkha, Tibetan and
Nepalese dialects. **Religions** Buddhist 75%, Hindu
25%. **Life expectancy** 49 female, 48 male.
POLITICS
Government Monarchy (Indian protection).
Parties None. **Suffrage** One vote per family.
Memberships UN. **Subdivisions** 18 districts.
ECONOMY
GDP $500,000,000. **Per capita** $298. **Monetary
unit** Ngultrum, Indian rupee. **Trade partners** India.
Exports Cardamom, gypsum, timber, handicrafts,
cement, fruit. **Imports** Fuel, grain, machinery,
transportation equipment, textiles.
LAND
Description Southern Asia, landlocked. **Area**
17,954 mi^2 (46,500 km^2). **Highest point** Kula
Kangri, 24,784 ft (7,554 m). **Lowest point** Along
Manãs River, 318 ft (97 m).

People. A mountainous terrain long isolated Bhutan
from the outside world and limited internal mingling
of its peoples. The population is ethnically divided
into the Bhotia, Nepalese, and various tribes. Of Tibetan
ancestry, the Bhotes are a majority and as such have
determined the major religion, Buddhism, and language, Dzongkha, a Tibetan dialect. The Nepalese
are mostly Hindu and speak Nepalese; tribal dialects
diversify language further. A largely rural population,
many villages grew up around dzongs, or monastery
fortresses built in strategic valley locations during
Bhutan's past. In 1989 a controversial program

began in which settlers who could not prove Bhutanese descent were evicted.

Economy and the Land. Partially due to physical isolation, Bhutan has one of the world's least developed economies and remains dependent on foreign aid. There is potential for success, however. Forests cover much of the land, limiting agricultural area but offering opportunity for the expansion of forestry. Farming is concentrated in the more densely populated, fertile valleys of the Himalayas, and the country is self-sufficient in food production. The climate varies with altitude; the icy Himalayas in the north give way to temperate central valleys and a subtropical south.

History and Politics. Bhutan's early history remains mostly unknown, but it is thought that by the early sixteenth century, descendants of Tibetan invaders were ruling their lands from strategically located dzongs. In the 1600s a Tibetan lama consolidated the area and became the political and religious leader. Proximity to and interaction with British India resulted in British control of Bhutan's foreign affairs in the nineteenth and early twentieth centuries. In 1907 the current hereditary monarchy was established. India gained independence from Britain in 1947 and soon assumed the role of adviser in Bhutan's foreign affairs. Bhutan became independent in 1949 but ties with India were strengthened in the late 1950s to counter Chinese influence. In recent years the King has instituted a policy of expelling people he considers refugees, causing widespread hardship. ∎

BOLIVIA

Official name Republic of Bolivia
PEOPLE
Population 6,790,000. **Density** 16/mi² (6.12/km²).
Urban 51%. **Capital** La Paz (seat of government), 713,378; Sucre (legal capital), 131,769. **Ethnic groups** Quechua 30%, Aymara 25%, mixed 25-30%, European 5-15%. **Languages** Aymara, Quechua, Spanish. **Religions** Roman Catholic 95%, Methodist and other Protestant. **Life**

expectancy 64 female, 59 male. **Literacy** 78%.
POLITICS
Government Republic. **Parties** Civic Solidarity Union, Condepa, Nationalist Revolutionary Movement, Patriotic Accord. **Suffrage** Universal adult (married, 18; single, 21). **Memberships** OAS, UN. **Subdivisions** 9 departments.
ECONOMY
GDP $15,800,000,000. **Per capita** $2,132.
Monetary unit Boliviano. **Trade partners** Exports: Argentina, U.S., U.K. Imports: U.S., Brazil, Argentina. **Exports** Metals, natural gas, coffee, soybeans, sugar, cotton, lumber. **Imports** Food, petroleum, consumer goods, capital goods.
LAND
Description Central South America, landlocked.
Area 424,165 mi² (1,098,581 km²). **Highest point** Nevado Sajama, 21,463 ft (6,542 m). **Lowest point** Along Paraguay River, 226 ft (69 m).

People. Indians compose the majority of Bolivia's population, while minorities include mestizos, of Spanish-Indian descent, and Europeans. Although most people live at a subsistence level, Bolivia has a rich cultural heritage, evidenced by early Aymaran and Quechuan artifacts; Spanish-influenced Indian and mestizo art; and twentieth-century achievements. Roman Catholicism is the major religion, and is frequently combined with Indian beliefs.

Economy and the Land. Although the underdeveloped Bolivia is among South America's poorest nations, it is rich in natural resources. While farming is the main activity, mining makes the largest contribution to the gross national product. Population, industry, and major cities are concentrated on the western altiplano, an Andean high plateau where many continue to practice agriculture according to ancestral methods. The eastern llano, or lowland plain, contains fuel deposits and is the site of commercial farming. The yungas (hills and valleys) between the altiplano and the llano form the most developed agricultural region. Successful development of Bolivia's rich resources is partially dependent upon political stability. The climate varies from tropical to semiarid and cool, depending on altitude.

History and Politics. The Aymara Indian culture flourished in the area that is now Bolivia between the seventh and tenth centuries. In the mid-1400s the area was absorbed into the expanding empire of the Incas, who controlled the region until ousted by the Spanish in 1535. Simón Bolívar, the Venezuelan organizer of the South American movement to free Spanish colonies, helped lead the way to independence, which was gained in 1825. As Bolivia developed economically, the Indian population remained ensconced in poverty and enjoyed few rights. After years of turmoil, a 1952 revolution installed a government that introduced suffrage, land and educational reforms. Several military coups followed, and civilian control was re-established in 1982. The government elected in 1993 has created stability and reduced foreign debt. ∎

BOSNIA AND HERZEGOVINA

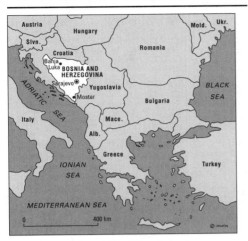

Official name Republic of Bosnia and Herzegovina
PEOPLE
Population 4,481,000. **Density** 227/mi² (88/km²).
Urban 36%. **Capital** Sarajevo, 341,200. **Ethnic groups** Muslim 44%, Serb 31%, Croat 17%.
Languages Serbo-Croatian. **Religions** Muslim 40%, Orthodox 31%, Roman Catholic 15%. **Life expectancy** 78 female, 72 male. **Literacy** 86%.
POLITICS
Government Republic. **Parties** Croatian Democratic Union, Democratic Action, Muslim-Bosnian Organization, Serbian Democratic, others.
Suffrage Universal, over 18; over 16 if employed.
Memberships UN. **Subdivisions** none.
ECONOMY
GDP $14,000,000,000. **Per capita** $3,098.
Monetary unit Yugoslavian dinar, Croatian dinar.
Trade partners Former Yugoslavian republics.
Exports Manufactures, machinery and transportation equipment, raw materials. **Imports** Fuels, machinery and transportation equipment, chemicals, raw materials, food.
LAND
Description Eastern Europe. **Area** 19,741 mi² (51,129 km²). **Highest point** Maglić, 7,828 ft (2,386 m). **Lowest point** Sea level.

People. Before the outbreak of war in 1992, Muslims accounted for about 40% of the population, and Serbians comprised about 30%. Subsequent war-related refugee movements and ethnic cleansing have had a profound effect on the population structure.

Economy and the Land. The main activity is agriculture, and there is limited industrial development. The country has ample mineral and hydroelectric resources. The region was one of the poorer of the former Yugoslavian republics. Bosnia, in the north, is a land of mountains and dense forests, while the Herzegovina region, in the south, is a rocky plateau. Bosnia and Herzegovina has many spas, which have historically been popular tourist destinations.

History and Politics. The Serbs and the Croats settled Bosnia in the seventh century, and the country later became part of the Roman Empire. Bosnia established itself as a self-governing country under Hungarian rule in the 1100s. Bosnia and Herzegovina were joined when they were conquered by the Ottoman Turks in the fifteenth century. Bosnia and Herzegovina was one of the few areas of Europe that converted to Islam during this period. In 1878 the region was relinquished to Austro-Hungarian rule, and was annexed by Austria-Hungary in 1908. Following World War I, both Bosnia and Herzegovina were incorporated into Serbia, and later into Yugoslavia. When Yugoslavia began to break up in the early 1990s, ethnic Muslims and Croatians overwhelmingly favored independence, but most of the region's ethnic Serbians resisted the notion and boycotted the referendum. Fighting over independence broke out following the country's secession from Yugoslavia in 1992. The bitter war and its many broken cease-fire agreements have left the survival of the nation in doubt. ∎

BOTSWANA

Official name Republic of Botswana
PEOPLE
Population 1,438,000. **Density** 6.4/mi² (2.5/km²).
Urban 25%. **Capital** Gaborone, 133,468. **Ethnic groups** Tswana 95%; Kalanga, Baswara, and Kgalagadi 4%; white 1%. **Languages** English, Tswana. **Religions** Khoisan 50%, Roman Catholic and other Christian 50%. **Life expectancy** 64 female, 58 male. **Literacy** 72%.
POLITICS
Government Republic. **Parties** Democratic, National Front. **Suffrage** Universal, over 21.
Memberships CW, OAU, UN. **Subdivisions** 10 districts.
ECONOMY
GDP $6,000,000,000. **Per capita** $4,351.
Monetary unit Pula. **Trade partners** Switzerland, U.K., Southern African countries. **Exports** Diamonds, copper, nickel, meat. **Imports** Food,

motor vehicles, textiles, petroleum.
LAND
Description Southern Africa, landlocked. **Area** 224,711 mi² (582,000 km²). **Highest point** Unnamed, 4,969 ft (1,515 m). **Lowest point** Confluence of Shashi and Limpopo rivers, 1,684 ft (513 m).

People. The population of this sparsely-populated country is composed mostly of Tswana, Bantu peoples of various groups. Following settlement patterns laid down centuries ago, Tswana predominate in the more fertile eastern region, and the minority Bushmen are concentrated in the Kalahari Desert. There is also a white minority population. English is an official language, reflecting years of British rule, but the majority speak Tswana. Half of the people follow traditional beliefs, while the rest are Christian.

Economy and the Land. Agriculture and livestock raising are the primary activities, although they are limited by the southwestern Kalahari Desert. The most productive farmland lies in the east and north, where rainfall is higher and grazing lands are plentiful. Since the early 1970s, when increased exploitation of natural resources began, the economy has developed rapidly. Diamond mining is the main focus of this growth, together with development of copper, nickel, and coal. The climate is mostly subtropical.

History and Politics. In Botswana's early history, Bushmen, the original inhabitants, retreated into the Kalahari region when the Tswana invaded and established their settlements in the more fertile east. Intertribal wars in the early nineteenth century were followed by conflicts with the Boers, settlers of Dutch or Huguenot descent. These conflicts led the Tswana to seek British assistance, and the area of present-day Botswana became part of the British protectorate of Bechuanaland. When the Union of South Africa was created in 1910, those living in Bechuanaland (later Botswana), Basutoland (later Lesotho), and Swaziland requested and were granted exclusion from the Union. British rule continued until 1966, when the protectorate of Bechuanaland became the Republic of Botswana. With outstanding leadership and a tribal history of democracy Botswana has developed Africa's oldest and most prosperous democracy. ∎

BRAZIL

Official name Federative Republic of Brazil
PEOPLE
Population 159,690,000. **Density** 49/mi² (19/km²). **Urban** 75%. **Capital** Brasília, 1,513,470. **Ethnic groups** White 55%, mixed 38%, black 6%. **Languages** Portuguese, Spanish, English, French. **Religions** Roman Catholic 90%. **Life expectancy** 69 female, 64 male. **Literacy** 81%.
POLITICS
Government Republic. **Parties** Labor, Liberal, Liberal Front, Social Democracy, Workers', others. **Suffrage** Universal, over 16. **Memberships** OAS, UN. **Subdivisions** 26 states, 1 federal district.

ECONOMY
GDP $785,000,000,000. **Per capita** $4,918.
Monetary unit Real. **Trade partners** Exports: U.S., Netherlands, Japan. Imports: U.S., Germany, Argentina, Iraq. **Exports** Iron ore, soybeans, orange juice, shoes, coffee. **Imports** Petroleum, machinery, chemicals, food, coal.
LAND
Description Eastern South America. **Area** 3,286,500 mi² (8,511,996 km²). **Highest point** Pico da Neblina, 9,888 ft (3,014 m). **Lowest point** Sea level.

People. The largest South American nation, Brazil is also the most populous. Indigenous Indians, Portuguese colonists, black African slaves, and European and Japanese immigrants shaped the mixed population. Today, native Indians compose less than 1% of the population, and the group is disappearing rapidly due to contact with modern cultures and other factors. Brazil is the only Portuguese-speaking nation in the Americas, and Roman Catholicism is the major religion.

Economy and the Land. Brazil's prosperous economy stems from a diversified base of agriculture, mining, and industry. Most commercial farms and ranches lie in the southern plateau region, and coffee, cocoa, soybeans, and beef are important products. Mineral resources include iron ore deposits, many found in the central and southern plateau regions. Additional mineral deposits have recently been discovered in the Amazon area. During and after World War II, the country focused on industrial expansion in the southeast, and in 1960 it moved the capital from Rio de Janeiro to Brasília to redistribute activity. Undeveloped states have been targeted for development, but such programs may require displacement of the Indian population. Forests cover about half the country, and the Amazon River basin is the site of the world's largest rain forest. The northeast consists of semiarid grasslands, and the central west and south are marked by hills, mountains, and rolling plains. Overall the climate is semitropical to tropical, with heavy rains.

History and Politics. Portugal obtained rights to the region in a 1494 treaty with Spain and claimed Brazil in 1500. As the native Indian population died out, blacks were brought from Africa to work the plantations. In the 1800s, during the Napoleonic Wars, the Portuguese royal family fled to Rio de Janeiro, and in 1815 the colony became a kingdom. In 1821 the Portuguese king departed for Portugal, leaving Brazil's rule to his son, who declared Brazil an independent country and himself emperor in 1822. Economic development in the mid-1800s brought an influx of Europeans. Following a military takeover in 1889, Brazil became a republic. In recent years key political issues have been the massive foreign debt and worldwide concern over the destruction of the rain forest. Corruption at high government levels has been extensive. October 1994 elections were won by the Social Democracy Party. ■

BRITISH INDIAN OCEAN
TERRITORY See UNITED KINGDOM.

BRUNEI

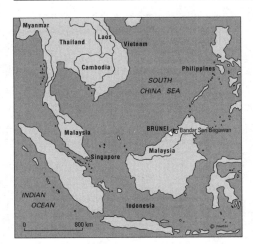

Official name Negara Brunei Darussalam
PEOPLE
Population 289,000. **Density** 130/mi² (50/km²).
Urban 58%. **Capital** Bandar Seri Begawan, 22,777. **Ethnic groups** Malay 64%, Chinese 20%, indigenous 8%, Tamil 3%. **Languages** Malay, English, Chinese. **Religions** Muslim 63%, Buddhist 14%, Roman Catholic and other Christian 8%. **Life expectancy** 76 female, 73 male. **Literacy** 77%.
POLITICS
Government Monarchy. **Parties** None. **Suffrage** None. **Memberships** ASEAN, CW, UN. **Subdivisions** 4 districts.
ECONOMY
GDP $2,500,000,000. **Per capita** $9,579. **Monetary unit** Dollar. **Trade partners** Exports: Japan, Thailand, Korea. Imports: Singapore,

Japan, U.S. **Exports** Petroleum, natural gas. **Imports** Machinery and transportation equipment, manufactures, food, chemicals.
LAND
Description Southeastern Asia (island of Borneo). **Area** 2,226 mi² (5,765 km²). **Highest point** Mt. Pagon, 6,070 ft (1,850 m). **Lowest point** Sea level.

People. The majority of Brunei's population is Malay, with minorities of Chinese and indigenous peoples. Most Malays are Muslim, and the Chinese are mainly Christian or Buddhist. Many Chinese, although wealthy, are unable to become citizens due to language-proficiency exams and strict residency requirements. The standard of living is high because of Brunei's oil-based economy, yet wealth is not equally distributed.

Economy and the Land. Oil and natural gas are the economic mainstays, giving Brunei a high per capita gross domestic product. Much food is imported, however, and the country has failed to diversify. Situated on northeastern Borneo, Brunei is generally flat and covered with dense rain forests. The climate is tropical.

History and Politics. Historical records of Brunei date back to the seventh century. The country was an important trading center, and by the sixteenth century the sultan of Brunei ruled Borneo and parts of nearby islands. In 1888 Brunei became a British protectorate, and in 1984, it gained independence from Great Britain. The nation is ruled by a sultan who has been on the throne since 1967. ■

BULGARIA

Official name Republic of Bulgaria
PEOPLE
Population 8,787,000. **Density** 205/mi² (79/km²).
Urban 68%. **Capital** Sofia, 1,136,875. **Ethnic groups** Bulgarian (Slavic) 85%, Turkish 9%, Gypsy 3%, Macedonian 3%. **Languages** Bulgarian, Turkish. **Religions** Bulgarian Orthodox

85%, Muslim 13%. **Life expectancy** 75 female, 69 male. **Literacy** 93%.
POLITICS
Government Republic. **Parties** Movement for Rights and Freedoms, Socialist, New Union for Democracy, Union of Democratic Forces.
Suffrage Universal, over 18. **Memberships** NATO, UN. **Subdivisions** 9 regions.
ECONOMY
GDP $33,900,000,000. **Per capita** $3,834.
Monetary unit Lev. **Trade partners** Exports: Former Soviet republics, Czechoslovakia, Poland. Imports: Former Soviet republics, Germany, Poland. **Exports** Machinery, agricultural products, manufactures. **Imports** Fuel and minerals, machinery and equipment, manufactures, food.
LAND
Description Eastern Europe. **Area** 42,855 mi^2 (110,994 km^2). **Highest point** Musala, 9,596 ft (2,925 m). **Lowest point** Sea level.

People. Bulgaria's ethnic composition was determined early in its history when Bulgar tribes conquered the area's Slavic inhabitants. Bulgarians, descendants of these peoples, are a majority today, while Turks, Gypsies, and Macedonians compose the main minority groups. Postwar development is reflected in an agriculture-to-industry shift in employment and a resultant rural-to-urban population movement.

Economy and the Land. A market economy is the declared goal of the post-Soviet government. However, the pace of reform is slow with 90% of the economy still under control of the state. Rich soils in river valleys, as well as a climate similar to that of the American Midwest, make the area well suited for raising livestock, growing grain and other crops. The overall terrain is mountainous.

History and Politics. The area of modern Bulgaria was absorbed by the Roman Empire by A.D. 15, and was subsequently invaded by the Slavs. In the seventh century Bulgars conquered the region and settled alongside Slavic inhabitants. Rule by the Ottoman Turks began in the late fourteenth century and lasted until 1878, when the Bulgarians defeated the Turks with the aid of Russia and Romania. The Principality of Bulgaria emerged in 1885, with boundaries approximating those of today, and in 1908 Bulgaria was declared an independent kingdom. Increased territory and a desire for access to the Aegean Sea were partially responsible for Bulgaria's involvement in the Balkan Wars of 1912 and 1913 and alliances with Germany during both World Wars. Following Bulgaria's declaration of war on the United States and Britain in World War II, the Soviet Union declared war on Bulgaria. Defeat came in 1944, when the monarchy was overthrown and a Communist government was established shortly thereafter. In 1989 pressure from the people for more participation in the government resulted in the resignation of General Zhivkov, Bulgaria's leader for thirty-five years. A severe economic downturn forced multiparty elections in 1990, with the Bulgarian Socialist (formerly Communist) Party retaining control. Worsening economic conditions in late 1990 led to the collapse of the governing party. Elections in late 1991 were won by the Union of Democratic

Forces, in forced coalition with the Muslim Turkish minority. The Bulgarian Socialist Party regained control in 1994 after years of disheartening economic hardship.■

BURKINA FASO

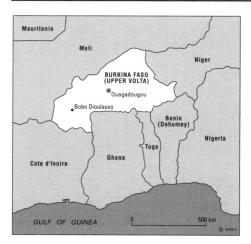

Official name Burkina Faso
PEOPLE
Population 10,275,000. **Density** 97/mi^2 (38/km^2).
Urban 15%. **Capital** Ouagadougou, 441,514.
Ethnic groups Mossi 30%, Fulani, Lobi, Malinke, Bobo, Senufo, Gurunsi, others. **Languages** French, indigenous. **Religions** Animist 65%, Muslim 25%, Roman Catholic and other Christian 10%. **Life expectancy** 50 female, 47 male.
Literacy 18%.
POLITICS
Government Republic. **Parties** National Convention of Progressive Patriots, Organization for Popular Democracy-Labor Movement, others.
Suffrage None. **Memberships** OAU, UN.
Subdivisions 30 provinces.
ECONOMY
GDP $7,000,000,000. **Per capita** $714. **Monetary unit** CFA franc. **Trade partners** Exports: France, Cote d'Ivoire, Switzerland. Imports: France, Cote d'Ivoire, U.S. **Exports** Oilseed, cotton, live animals, gold. **Imports** Grain and other food, petroleum, machinery.
LAND
Description Western Africa, landlocked. **Area** 105,869 mi^2 (274,200 km^2). **Highest point** Téna Kourou, 2,451 ft (747 m). **Lowest point** Along Pendjari River, 443 ft (135 m).

People. The agricultural Mossi, descendants of warrior migrants, are Burkina Faso's majority population. Other groups include the Fulani, Lobi, Malinke, Bobo, Senufo, and Gurunsi. Ethnic languages vary, although French is the official language.

Economy and the Land. Burkina Faso's agricultural economy suffers from frequent droughts and an underdeveloped transportation system. Most people engage in subsistence farming or livestock raising, and industrialization is minimal. Resources are limited but include gold and manganese. The country remains dependent on foreign aid, much of it from France. The land is marked by northern desert, central savanna, and southern forests, while the climate is generally tropical.

History and Politics. The Mossi arrived from central or eastern Africa during the eleventh century and established their kingdom in the area of Burkina Faso. The French came in the late nineteenth century. In 1919 France united various provinces and created the colony of Upper Volta. The colony was divided among other French colonies in 1932, reinstituted in 1937 as an administrative unit called the Upper Coast, and returned to territorial status as Upper Volta in 1947. It gained independence in 1960. Economic problems and accusations of government corruption led to leadership changes and military rule, including numerous coups. In 1984 the country changed its name from Upper Volta to Burkina Faso. It has since functioned under a civilian, multiparty government. ∎

BURMA
See MYANMAR

BURUNDI

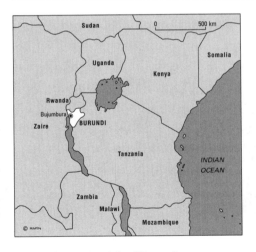

Official name Republic of Burundi
PEOPLE
Population 6,192,000. **Density** 576/mi² (222/km²). **Urban** 5%. **Capital** Bujumbura, 226,628. **Ethnic groups** Hutu 85%, Tutsi 14%, Twa (Pygmy) 1%. **Languages** French, Kirundi, Swahili. **Religions** Roman Catholic 62%, Animist 32%, Protestant 5%, Muslim 1%. **Life expectancy** 50 female, 46 male. **Literacy** 50%.

POLITICS
Government Republic. **Parties** Front for Democracy, People's, Reconciliation of the People, Unity and Progress. **Suffrage** Universal adult. **Memberships** OAU, UN. **Subdivisions** 15 provinces.
ECONOMY
GDP $4,400,000,000. **Per capita** $719. **Monetary unit** Franc. **Trade partners** Exports: Germany, Finland. Imports: Belgium, Germany, Iran, France. **Exports** Coffee, tea, hides and skins. **Imports** Machinery, petroleum, food, manufactures.
LAND
Description Eastern Africa, landlocked. **Area** 10,745 mi² (27,830 km²). **Highest point** Mt. Heha, 8,760 ft (2,670 m). **Lowest point** Lake Tanganyika, 2,534 ft (772 m).

People. One of Africa's most densely populated nations, Burundi has a populace composed mainly of three Bantu groups. The Hutu are a majority, while the Tutsi, descendants of invaders from Ethiopia, wield most of the power. The Twa are Pygmy hunters, probably descended from the area's inhabitants prior to the influx of the Hutu. Most Burundians are subsistence farmers and Roman Catholic, evidence of foreign influence and rule.

Economy and the Land. An undeveloped country, Burundi relies mainly on agriculture, although undependable rainfall, depleted soil, and erosion occasionally combine for famine. Coffee is a major export. Exploitation of nickel deposits, industrial development through foreign investment, and expansion of tourism offer potential for growth. Although the country is situated near the equator, its high altitude and hilly terrain result in a pleasant climate.

History and Politics. In the fourteenth century, invading pastoral Tutsi warriors conquered the Hutu and Pygmy Twa and established themselves as the region's power base. The areas of modern Burundi and Rwanda were absorbed into German East Africa in the 1890s. Following Belgian occupation during World War I, in 1919 the League of Nations placed present-day Burundi and Rwanda under Belgian rule as part of Ruanda-Urundi. After World War II Ruanda-Urundi was made a United Nations trust territory under Belgian administration. In 1962 Urundi became Burundi, an independent monarchy, and political turmoil soon followed. A Tutsi-dominated government replaced the monarchy in 1966. The country's first multiparty elections were held in June 1993. The new president, a member of the majority Hutu ethnic tribe, was assassinated in October. Ensuing warfare between the Hutu and the minority Tutsi continues unabated, although Burundi has managed to avoid some of the chaos and bloodshed of neighboring Rwanda. ∎

CAMBODIA

Official name Kingdom of Cambodia
PEOPLE
Population 9,713,000. **Density** 139/mi² (54/km²). **Urban** 12%. **Capital** Phnom Penh, 620,000.

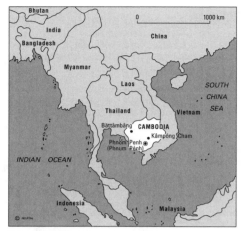

Ethnic groups Khmer 90%, Vietnamese 5%.
Languages Khmer, French. **Religions** Buddhist
95%. **Life expectancy** 52 female, 50 male.
Literacy 35%.
POLITICS
Government Constitutional monarchy. **Parties**
Buddhist Liberal Democratic, FUNCINPEC,
People's. **Suffrage** Universal, over 18.
Memberships UN. **Subdivisions** 20 provinces.
ECONOMY
GDP $6,000,000,000. **Per capita** $672. **Monetary
unit** Riel. **Trade partners** Vietnam, former Soviet
countries, Eastern European countries. **Exports**
Rubber, rice, pepper, wood. **Imports** Fuel, con-
sumer goods, machinery.
LAND
Description Southeastern Asia. **Area** 69,898 mi^2
(181,035 km^2). **Highest point** Mt. Aoral, 5,948 ft
(1,813 m). **Lowest point** Sea level.

People. The Khmer, one of the oldest peoples in
Southeast Asia, constitute the major ethnic group in
Cambodia. The population has declined significantly since the mid-1970s due to war, famine, human-
rights abuses, and emigration. Because of an urban-
evacuation campaign initiated by the Khmer Rouge,
Cambodia's previous regime, most Cambodians live
in rural areas, working as farmers or laborers. Although
religious activity was often punished by death during
the Khmer Rouge era and discouraged by the communists, the practice of Buddhism, the main religion, is on the rise.

Economy and the Land. Cambodia's flat central region
and wet climate make it well suited for rice production. Along with rubber, rice was the mainstay of the
economy before the seventies, but the Vietnam and
civil wars all but destroyed agriculture. This sector of
the economy has begun to recover recently, but a shortage of skilled labor, combined with the effects of
war, have held back development. The terrain is
marked by the central plain, forests, and mountains
in the south, west, and along the Thai border. The climate is tropical, with high rainfall and humidity.

History and Politics. Cambodia traces its roots to
the Hindu kingdoms of Funan and Chenla, which
reigned in the early centuries A.D. The Angkor Empire
dominated until the fifteenth century, incorporating
much of present-day Laos, Thailand, and Vietnam and

constructing the stone temples of Angkor Wat, considered one of Southeast Asia's greatest architectural
achievements. By 1431 the Siamese had overrun the
region, and subsequent years saw the rise of the
Siamese, Vietnamese, and Lao. By the mid-1700s
Cambodia's boundaries approximated those of
today. During the 1800s, as French control in
Indochina expanded, the area became a French
protectorate. Cambodia gained independence in
1953 under King Sihanouk, who, after changing his
title to "prince," became prime minister in 1955 and
head of state in 1960. In 1970, after Sihanouk was
ousted, Lon Nol was installed as prime minister,
and the monarchy of Cambodia changed to the
Khmer Republic. During this time the Vietnam War
spilled over the Khmer Republic's borders, as United
States forces made bombing raids against what
they claimed were North Vietnamese bases. Resulting
anti-American sentiment gave rise to discontent
with Lon Nol's pro-United States regime. The Khmer
Communists, or Khmer Rouge, seized power in
1975 and, led by Pol Pot, exiled most Cambodians
to the countryside. An estimated three million died under
the Khmer Rouge; many were executed because they
were educated or had links to the former government.
Vietnamese troops supported by some Cambodian
Communists invaded Cambodia in late 1978, and by
early 1979 they had overthrown the Khmer Rouge.
While 1993 elections and a new constitution resulted in Prince Sihanouk again becoming King of
Cambodia, the Khmer Rouge have regained much
of their former power. ∎

CAMEROON

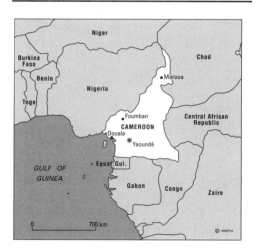

Official name Republic of Cameroon
PEOPLE
Population 13,330,000. **Density** 73/mi^2 (28/km^2).
Urban 40%. **Capital** Yaoundé, 560,785. **Ethnic
groups** Cameroon Highlander 31%, Equatorial
Bantu 19%, Kirdi 11%, Fulani 10%. **Languages**
English, French, indigenous. **Religions** Bangwa
and other African religions 51%, Christian 33%,
Muslim 16%. **Life expectancy** 58 female, 55 male.
Literacy 54%.

POLITICS
Government Republic. **Parties** National Union for Democracy and Progress, People's Democratic Movement, Union of the Peoples. **Suffrage** Universal, over 20. **Memberships** OAU, UN. **Subdivisions** 10 provinces.
ECONOMY
GDP $19,100,000,000. **Per capita** $1,483. **Monetary unit** CFA franc. **Trade partners** Exports: France, Belgium, U.S. Imports: France, Netherlands, Japan, Germany. **Exports** Petroleum, coffee, cocoa, lumber, manufactures. **Imports** Machinery and electrical equipment, transportation equipment, chemicals.
LAND
Description Central Africa. **Area** 183,568 mi^2 (475,440 km^2). **Highest point** Cameroon Mtn., 13,451 ft (4,100 m). **Lowest point** Sea level.

People. Immigration and foreign rule shaped Cameroon's diverse population, composed of some two hundred groups speaking twenty-four major African languages. Both English and French are official languages, resulting from the merging of former French-ruled eastern and British-ruled western territories. Population is concentrated in the French-speaking eastern region. The majority of people practice indigenous beliefs that often influence Islamic and Christian practices as well.

Economy and the Land. Recent economic plans have focused on agriculture, industry, and the development of oil deposits. Agriculture is still the country's economic base, but oil is a major export. A varied terrain features southern coastal plains and rain forests, central plateaus, mountainous western forests, and northern savanna and marshes. Although this has hindered transportation development and thus slowed economic growth, improvements are being made. Climate varies from a hot, humid coastal region to fluctuating temperatures and less humidity northward.

History and Politics. The Sao people reached the Cameroon area in the tenth century. The Portuguese arrived in the 1500s, and the following three centuries saw an influx of European and African peoples and an active slave trade along the coast. In 1884 Germany set up a protectorate that included modern Cameroon by 1914. During World War I British and French troops occupied the area, and in 1919, following the war, the League of Nations divided Cameroon into eastern French and western British mandates. The Cameroons became trust territories in 1946, and French Cameroon became an independent republic in 1960. In 1961 the northern region of British Cameroon elected to join Nigeria, and the southern area chose to unite with the eastern Republic of Cameroon. This resulted in a two-state Federal Republic of Cameroon. A 1972 referendum combined the states into the United Republic of Cameroon and, in 1984, the official name became the Republic of Cameroon. An election in October 1992 returned an authoritarian government to power despite widespread claims of electoral fraud by foreign observers. Rioting and mass arrests ensued. ∎

CANADA

Official name Canada
PEOPLE
Population 28,285,000. **Density** 7.3/mi^2 (2.8/km^2). **Urban** 77%. **Capital** Ottawa, 313,987. **Ethnic groups** British origin 40%, French origin 27%, other European 23%, native Canadian 2%. **Languages** English, French. **Religions** Roman Catholic 47%, United Church 16%, Anglican 10%, other Christian. **Life expectancy** 81 female, 74 male. **Literacy** 99%.
POLITICS
Government Parliamentary state. **Parties** Bloc Quebecois, Liberal, New Democratic, Progressive Conservative, Reform. **Suffrage** Universal, over 18. **Memberships** CW, NATO, OAS, OECD, UN. **Subdivisions** 10 provinces, 2 territories.
ECONOMY
GDP $617,700,000,000. **Per capita** $20,233. **Monetary unit** Dollar. **Trade partners** U.S., Japan, U.K. **Exports** Newsprint, wood pulp, timber, petroleum, machinery, natural gas, aluminum. **Imports** Petroleum, chemicals, transportation equipment, manufactures, computers.
LAND
Description Northern North America. **Area** 3,849,674 mi^2 (9,970,610 km^2). **Highest point** Mt. Logan, 19,551 ft (5,959 m). **Lowest point** Sea level.

People. Canada was greatly influenced by French and British rule, and its culture reflects this dual nature. Descendants of British and French settlers compose the two main population groups, and languages include both English and French. French-speaking inhabitants are concentrated in the Province of Quebec. Minorities include descendants of various European groups, indigenous Indians, and Inuit. Because of the rugged terrain and harsh climate of northern Canada, population is concentrated near the United States border.

Economy and the Land. Rich natural resources—including extensive mineral deposits, fertile land, forests, and lakes—helped shape Canada's diversified economy, which ranks among the world's most prosperous. Economic problems are those common to most modern industrial nations. Agriculture, mining, and industry are highly developed. Canada is a major wheat producer; mineral output includes asbestos, zinc, silver, and nickel; and crude petroleum is an important export. The service sector is also active. Second only to Russia in land area, Canada has a terrain that varies from eastern rolling hills and plains to mountains in the west. The Canadian Shield consists of ancient rock and extends from Labrador to the Arctic Islands. It is covered by thick forests in the south and tundra in the north. Overall, summers are moderate and winters long and cold.

History and Politics. Canada's first inhabitants were Asian Indians and Inuit, an Arctic people. Around the year 1000, Vikings were the first Europeans to reach North America, and in 1497 John Cabot claimed the Newfoundland coastal area for Britain. Jacques Cartier established French claim when he landed at the Gaspé Peninsula in the 1500s. Subsequent French and British rivalry culminated in several wars during the late seventeenth and eighteenth centuries. The wars ended with the 1763 Treaty of Paris, by which France lost Canada and other North American territory to Britain. To aid in resolving the continued conflict between French and English residents, the British North America Act of 1867 united the colonies into the Dominion of Canada. Canada fought on the side of the British during World War I. In 1926, along with other dominions, Canada declared itself an independent member of the British Commonwealth and, in 1931, Britain recognized the declaration through the Statute of Westminster. Canada once again allied itself with Britain during World War II. In 1988 Canada saw vigorous debate over a free trade pact with the United States, which narrowly won approval. The Quebec separatist movement is striving for independent status for French-speaking Quebec. ∎

CANARY ISLANDS See SPAIN.

CAPE VERDE

Official name Republic of Cape Verde
PEOPLE
Population 429,000. **Density** 276/mi² (106/km²).
Urban 29%. **Capital** Praia, São Tiago I., 61,644.
Ethnic groups Creole (mulatto) 71%, African 28%, European 1%. **Languages** Portuguese, Crioulo. **Religions** Roman Catholic, Nazarene and other Protestant. **Life expectancy** 69 female, 67 male. **Literacy** 66%.
POLITICS
Government Republic. **Parties** African Party for Independence, Movement for Democracy.
Suffrage Universal, over 18. **Memberships** OAU,

UN. **Subdivisions** 14 districts.
ECONOMY
GDP $415,000,000.
Per capita $1,089.
Monetary unit Escudo.
Trade partners Exports: Algeria, Portugal. Imports: Portugal, Netherlands, Japan. **Exports** Bananas, fish, salt.
Imports Petroleum, food, manufactures, industrial products.
LAND
Description Western African islands. **Area** 1,557 mi² (4,033 km²). **Highest point** Pico, 9,281 ft (2,829 m). **Lowest point** Sea level.

People. The Portuguese-African heritage of Cape Verde's population is a result of Portuguese rule and the forced transmigration of Africans for slavery. Although Portuguese is an official language, the majority speaks Crioulo, a creole dialect. Most people are Roman Catholic, but indigenous practices exist, sometimes in combination with Catholicism. The mainly poor population is largely undernourished and plagued by unemployment. The country consists of five islets and ten main islands, and all but one are inhabited.

Economy and the Land. The volcanic, mountainous islands have few natural resources and low rainfall; thus the country's economy remains underdeveloped. Fishing and agriculture are important for both subsistence and commercial purposes. Much of the land is too dry for farming, and drought is a frequent problem. Cape Verde's location on air and sea routes and its tropical climate offer potential for expansion into services and tourism. However, Cape Verde will most likely continue to rely on foreign aid for some time.

History and Politics. The islands that make up Cape Verde were uninhabited when the Portuguese arrived around 1460. Settlement began in 1462, and by the sixteenth century Cape Verde had become a shipping center for the African slave trade. Until 1879 Portugal ruled Cape Verde and present-day Guinea-Bissau as a single colony. A movement for the independence of Cape Verde and Guinea-Bissau began in the 1950s, and a 1974 coup in Portugal ultimately resulted in autonomy for both countries, with Cape Verde proclaiming independence in 1975. Plans to unify Cape Verde and Guinea-Bissau were abandoned following a 1980 coup in Guinea-Bissau. ∎

CAYMAN ISLANDS
See UNITED KINGDOM.

CENTRAL AFRICAN REPUBLIC

Official name Central African Republic
PEOPLE
Population 3,177,000. **Density** 13/mi² (5.1/km²).
Urban 47%. **Capital** Bangui, 596,800. **Ethnic
groups** Baya 34%, Banda 27%, Mandjia 21%,
Sara 10%. **Languages** French, Sango, Arabic,
indigenous. **Religions** Protestant 25%, Roman
Catholic 25%, Kimbanguist and other African reli-
gions 24%, Muslim 15%. **Life expectancy** 49
female, 45 male. **Literacy** 27%.
POLITICS
Government Republic. **Parties** Democratic Rally,
People's Liberation, others. **Suffrage** Universal,
over 21. **Memberships** OAU, UN. **Subdivisions**
16 prefectures, 1 autonomous commune.
ECONOMY
GDP $2,500,000,000. **Per capita** $815. **Monetary
unit** CFA franc. **Trade partners** Exports: Belgium,
France, Switzerland. Imports: France, Cameroon,
Japan. **Exports** Diamonds, cotton, coffee, lumber,
tobacco. **Imports** Food, textiles, petroleum,
machinery, electrical equipment.
LAND
Description Central Africa, landlocked. **Area**
240,535 mi² (622,984 km²). **Highest point** Mont
Ngaoui, 4,626 ft (1,410 m). **Lowest point** Along
Ubangi River, 1,100 ft (335 m).

People. Lying near Africa's geographical center, the
Central African Republic was the stopping point for
many pre-colonial nomadic groups. The resultant
multiethnic populace was further diversified by migrations during the slave-trade era. Of the country's
many languages, Sango is most widely used. Overall,
the population is rural and suffers from poverty and
a low literacy rate.

Economy and the Land. Fertile land, extensive
forests, and mineral deposits provide adequate bases
for agriculture, forestry, and mining. Economic development remains minimal, however, impeded by poor
transportation routes, a landlocked location, lack of

skilled labor, and political instability. Subsistence
farming continues as the major activity, and agriculture is the chief contributor to the economy. The
country consists of a plateau region with southern rain
forests and a northeastern semidesert. The climate
is temperate, and ample rainfall sometimes results in
impassable roads.

History and Politics. Little is known of the area's early
history except that it was the site of many migrations.
European slave trade in the nineteenth century led to
the 1894 creation of a French territory called the
Ubangi-Chari. This in turn combined with the areas
of the present-day Congo, Chad, and Gabon in 1910
to form French Equatorial Africa. The Central African
Republic gained independence in 1960. A 1966 military coup installed military chief Jean-Bedel Bokassa,
who in 1976 assumed the title of emperor, changed
the republic to a monarchy, and renamed the nation
the Central African Empire. A 1979 coup ended the
monarchy and reinstated the name Central African
Republic. The country enacted a new constitution in
1986. The country held its first free elections in
August 1993. Voters overwhelmingly rejected the
incumbent dictator in favor of reform candidates. ■

CHAD

Official name Republic of Chad
PEOPLE
Population 6,396,000. **Density** 13/mi² (5.0/km²).
Urban 32%. **Capital** N'Djamena, 500,000. **Ethnic
groups** Sara and other African, Arab. **Languages**
Arabic, French, indigenous. **Religions** Muslim
44%, Christian 33%, Animist 23%. **Life expectan-
cy** 49 female, 46 male. **Literacy** 30%.
POLITICS
Government Republic. **Parties** National
Recovery, Patriotic Salvation Movement. **Suffrage**
Universal adult. **Memberships** OAU, UN.
Subdivisions 14 prefectures.
ECONOMY
GDP $2,700,000,000. **Per capita** $510. **Monetary**

unit CFA franc. **Trade partners** Exports: France, Nigeria, Cameroon. Imports: U.S., France, Nigeria. **Exports** Cotton, cattle, textiles, fish. **Imports** Machinery and transportation equipment, industrial goods, petroleum, food.
LAND
Description Central Africa, landlocked. **Area** 495,755 mi² (1,284,000 km²). **Highest point** Mt. Koussi, 11,204 ft (3,415 m). **Lowest point** Bodélé Depression, 525 ft (160 m).

People. Centuries ago, Islamic Arabs mixed with indigenous black Africans and established Chad's diverse population. This variety has led to a rich but often troubled culture. Descendants of Arab invaders mainly inhabit the north, where Islam predominates and nomadic farming is the major activity. In the south—traditionally the economic and political center—the black Sara predominate, operating small farms and practicing indigenous or Christian beliefs. Chad's many languages also reflect its ethnic variety.

Economy and the Land. Natural features and instability arising from ethnic and regional conflict have combined to prevent Chad from prospering. Agriculture and fishing are economic mainstays and are often conducted at subsistence levels. The Sahara extends into Chad's northern region, and the southern grasslands with their heavy rains compose the primary agricultural area. The relative prosperity of the region, in conjunction with its predominantly Sara population, has fueled much of the political conflict. Future growth is greatly dependent on political equilibrium. Climate varies from the hot, dry northern desert to the semiarid central region and rainier south.

History and Politics. African and Arab societies began prospering in the Lake Chad region around the eighth century A.D. Subsequent centuries saw the landlocked area become an ethnic crossroads for Muslim nomads and African groups. European traders arrived in the late 1800s, and by 1900 France had gained control. When created in 1910, French Equatorial Africa's boundaries included modern Chad, Gabon, the Congo, and the Central African Republic. Following Chad's independence in 1960, the southern Sara gained dominance over the government. A northern rebel group has emerged and government-rebel conflict has continued. Libyan troops entered Chad in 1980, and conflict continued until a cease-fire was implemented in 1987. Isolated incursions continue. The pro-Western government fell to rebel forces in December 1990. A 1993 national conference established an interim constitution and a transitional government. ∎

CHANNEL ISLANDS
See UNITED KINGDOM.

CHILE

Official name Republic of Chile
PEOPLE
Population 14,050,000. **Density** 48/mi² (19/km²).

Urban 85%. **Capital** Santiago, 232,667. **Ethnic groups** White and mestizo 95%, Amerindian 3%. **Languages** Spanish. **Religions** Roman Catholic 89%, Pentecostal and other Protestant 11%. **Life expectancy** 76 female, 69 male. **Literacy** 93%.
POLITICS
Government Republic. **Parties** Christian Democratic, Democracy, National Renewal, others. **Suffrage** Universal, over 18. **Memberships** OAS, UN. **Subdivisions** 13 regions.
ECONOMY
GDP $96,000,000,000. **Per capita** $7,041. **Monetary unit** Peso. **Trade partners** Exports: U.S., Japan, Germany. Imports: U.S., Japan, Brazil, Germany. **Exports** Copper and other metals, lumber, fish, fruit. **Imports** Petroleum, wheat, manufactures, raw materials.
LAND
Description Southern South America. **Area** 292,135 mi² (756,626 km²). **Highest point** Nevado Ojos del Salado, 22,615 ft (6,893 m). **Lowest point** Sea level.

People. Chile's land barriers—the eastern Andes, western coastal range, and northern desert—have resulted in a mostly urban population concentrated in a central valley. Mestizos, of Spanish-Indian heritage, and descendants of Spanish immigrants predominate. In addition to an Indian minority, the population includes those who trace their roots to Irish and English colonists or nineteenth-century German immigrants. The country enjoys a relatively high literacy rate, but poverty remains a problem.

Economy and the Land. Chile's land provides the natural resources necessary for a successful economy. Economic growth has been high in the post-Pinochet era but there is concern over the increasing gap between the rich and the poor. The northern desert region is the site of mineral deposits, and mining is a major component of trade, making Chile vulnerable to outside market forces. An agricultural zone lies in the central valley, while the South offers forests, grazing land, and some petroleum deposits. The climate varies from region to region but is generally mild.

History and Politics. Upon their arrival in the 1500s, the Spanish defeated the northern Inca Indians, although many years were spent in conflict with Araucanian Indians of the central and southern regions. From the sixteenth through nineteenth centuries, Chile received little attention from ruling Spain, and colonists established a successful agriculture. In 1818 Bernardo O'Higgins led the way to victory over the Spanish and became ruler of independent Chile.

By the 1920s, dissent arising from unequal power and land distribution united the middle and working classes, but social welfare, education, and economic programs were unable to eliminate inequalities rooted in the past. A 1960 earthquake and tidal wave added to the country's problems. Leftist Salvador Allende Gossens was elected to power in 1970, governing until his death in 1973 in a military coup, which installed Augusto Pinochet. Civil disturbances and grave human-rights abuses marked his right-wing government. This dictatorship ended in 1989 although Pinochet continued as the army's commander-in-chief. ∎

CHINA

Official name People's Republic of China
PEOPLE
Population 1,196,980,000. **Density** 324/mi² (125/km²). **Urban** 26%. **Capital** Beijing (Peking), 6,710,000. **Ethnic groups** Han Chinese 93%, Zhuang, Uygur, Hui, Yi, Tibetan, Miao, Manchu, others. **Languages** Chinese dialects. **Religions** Taoist, Buddhist, and Muslim 3%. **Life expectancy** 73 female, 69 male. **Literacy** 73%.
POLITICS
Government Socialist republic. **Parties** Communist. **Suffrage** Universal, over 18.
Memberships UN. **Subdivisions** 22 provinces, 5 autonomous regions, 3 municipalities.
ECONOMY
GDP $2,610,000,000,000. **Per capita** $2,214.
Monetary unit Yuan. **Trade partners** Hong Kong, Japan, U.S. **Exports** Textiles, clothing, telecommunications and recording equipment, petroleum. **Imports** Machinery, chemicals, manufactures, steel, textile yarn, fertilizer.
LAND
Description Eastern Asia. **Area** 3,689,631 mi² (9,556,100 km²). **Highest point** Mt. Everest, 29,028 ft (8,848 m). **Lowest point** Turfan

Depression, -505 ft (-154 m).
The above information excludes Taiwan.

People. China is the world's most populous nation. Its population is concentrated in the east, and Han Chinese are the majority group. Zhuang, Hui, Uygur, Yi, Miao, Manchu, and Tibetan peoples compose minorities. Many Chinese languages are spoken, but the national language is Modern Standard Chinese, or Mandarin, based on a northern dialect. Following a Communist revolution in 1949, religious activity was discouraged. It is now on the increase, and religions include Taoism and Buddhism, as well as Islam and Christianity. China's population has soared to over 1.1 billion, and family-planning programs have been implemented to aid population control. With a recorded civilization going back about 3,500 years, China has contributed much to world culture.

Economy and the Land. Economic progress dates from 1949, when the new People's Republic of China faced a starving, war-torn, and unemployed population. As of 1993, the Chinese economy was the third largest in the world. Industry is expanding, but agriculture continues as the major activity. Natural resources include coal, oil, natural gas, and minerals, many of which remain to be explored. A current economic plan focuses on growth in agriculture, industry, science and technology, and national defense. China's terrain is varied: two-thirds consists of mountainous or semiarid land, with fertile plains and deltas in the east. The climate is marked by hot, humid summers, while the dry winters are often cold.

History and Politics. China's civilization ranks among the world's oldest. The first dynasty, the Shang, began sometime during the second millennium B.C. Kublai Khan's thirteenth-century invasion brought China the first of its various foreign rulers. In the nineteenth century, despite government efforts to the contrary, foreign influence and intervention grew. The government was weakened by the Opium War with Britain in the 1840s; the Taiping Rebellion, a civil war; and a war with Japan from 1894 to 1895. Opposition to foreign influences erupted in the antiforeign and anti-Christian Boxer Rebellion of 1900. After China became a republic in 1912, the death of the president in 1916 triggered the warlord period, in which conflicts were widespread and power was concentrated among military leaders. Attempts to unite the nation began in the 1920s with Sun Yat-sen's Nationalist party, initially allied with the Communist party. Under the leadership of Chiang Kai-shek, the Nationalist party overcame the warlords, captured Beijing, and executed many Communists. Remaining Communists reorganized under Mao Zedong, and the Communist-Nationalist conflict continued, along with Japanese invasion and occupation. By 1949 the Communists controlled most of the country, and the People's Republic of China was proclaimed. Chiang Kai-shek fled to Taiwan, proclaiming T'aipei as China's provisional capital. After Mao's death in 1976, foreign trade and contact expanded. In 1979 the United States recognized Beijing, rather than T'aipei, as China's capital. When a retrenchment of the government from liberalization erupted violently in student demonstrations in 1989, many people were killed or arrested. A repressive political climate remains and rural unrest as well as high unemployment have made China more vulnerable. See also TAIWAN. ∎

CHRISTMAS ISLAND
See AUSTRALIA.

COCOS ISLANDS See AUSTRALIA.

COLOMBIA

Official name Republic of Colombia
PEOPLE
Population 34,870,000. **Density** 79/mi² (31/km²).
Urban 70%. **Capital** Santa Fe de Bogotá,
3,982,941. **Ethnic groups** Mestizo 58%, white
20%, mulatto 14%, black 4%. **Languages**
Spanish. **Religions** Roman Catholic 95%. **Life
expectancy** 72 female, 66 male. **Literacy** 87%.
POLITICS
Government Republic. **Parties** Conservative,
Liberal, others. **Suffrage** Universal, over 18.
Memberships OAS, UN. **Subdivisions** 32 depart-
ments, 1 capital district.
ECONOMY
GDP $192,000,000,000. **Per capita** $5,543.
Monetary unit Peso. **Trade partners** Exports:
U.S., Germany, Netherlands. Imports: U.S., Japan,
Germany. **Exports** Petroleum, coffee, coal,
bananas, flowers. **Imports** Machinery and trans-
portation equipment, food, chemicals, paper prod-
ucts.
LAND
Description Northern South America. **Area**
440,831 mi² (1,141,748 km²). **Highest point** Pico
Cristóbal Colón, 19,029 ft (5,800 m). **Lowest point**
Sea level.

People. Colombia's mixed population traces its
roots to indigenous Indians, Spanish colonists, and
black African slaves. Most numerous today are mestizos, those of Spanish-Indian descent. Roman
Catholicism, the Spanish language, and Colombia's

overall culture evidence the long-lasting effect of Spanish
rule. Over the past decades the population has shifted from mainly rural to urban as the economy has
expanded into industry.

Economy and the Land. Industry now keeps pace
with traditional agriculture in economic contributions, and mining is also important. Natural resources
include oil, coal, natural gas, most of the world's emer-
alds, plus fertile soils. The traditional coffee crop also
remains important for Colombia, a leading coffee producer. The terrain features a flat coastal region,
central highlands, and wide eastern llanos, or plains.
The climate is tropical on the coast and in the west,
with cooler temperatures in the highlands.

History and Politics. In the 1500s Spaniards conquered the native Indian groups and established the
area as a Spanish colony. In the early 1700s Bogotá
became the capital of the viceroyalty of New Granada,
which included modern Colombia, Venezuela,
Ecuador, and Panama. Rebellion in Venezuela in 1796
sparked revolts elsewhere in New Granada, including Colombia, and in 1813 independence was
declared. In 1819 the Republic of Greater Colombia
was formed and included all the former members of
the Spanish viceroyalty. Independence leader Simón
Bolívar became president. By 1830 Venezuela and
Ecuador had seceded from the republic, followed by
Panama in 1903. The Conservative and Liberal
parties, dominating forces in Colombia's political history, arose from differences between supporters
of Bolívar and Santander. Conservative-Liberal
conflict led to a violent civil war from 1899 to 1902,
as well as to *La Violencia*, The Violence, a civil
disorder that continued from the 1940s to the 1960s
and resulted in about three hundred thousand
deaths. From the late 1950s through the 1970s, the
government alternated between conservative and liberal rule. Political unrest reduced the effectiveness
of both parties. By the 1980s growing drug traffic presented Colombia with new problems. The government is now faced with widespread corruption and
increasing violence. ∎

COMOROS

Official name Federal Islamic Republic of the
Comoros
PEOPLE
Population 540,000. **Density** 626/mi² (242/km²).
Urban 28%. **Capital** Moroni, Njazidja I., 23,432.
Ethnic groups African-Arab descent (Antalote,
Cafre, Makoa, Oimatsaha, Sakalava). **Languages**
Arabic, French, Comoran. **Religions** Sunni Muslim
86%, Roman Catholic 14%. **Life expectancy** 57
female, 56 male. **Literacy** 48%.
POLITICS
Government Islamic republic. **Parties** Rally for
Democracy and Renewal, Union for Democracy
and Decentralization, Union for Progress, others.
Suffrage Universal, over 18. **Memberships** OAU,
UN. **Subdivisions** 3 islands.
ECONOMY
GDP $360,000,000. **Per capita** $716. **Monetary
unit** Franc. **Trade partners** Exports: France, U.S.,

Mauritius. Imports: France and other European countries. **Exports** Vanilla, cloves, perfume oils, copra. **Imports** Rice and other food, cement, petroleum, manufactures.

LAND

Description Southeastern African islands. **Area** 863 mi² (2,235 km²). **Highest point** Kartala, 7,746 ft (2,361 m). **Lowest point** Sea level.
The above information excludes Mayotte.

People. The ethnic groups of Comoros' Njazidja, Nzwani, and Mwali islands are mainly of Arab-African descent, practice Islam, and speak Comoran, a Swahili dialect. Arab culture, however, predominates throughout the island group. Poverty, disease, a shortage of medical care, and low literacy continue to plague the nation.

Economy and the Land. Comoros' economic mainstay is agriculture, and most Comorans practice subsistence farming and fishing. Plantations employ workers to produce the main cash crops, which include spices and essential (perfume) oils. Of volcanic origin, the islands have soils of varying quality, and some are unsuited for farming. Terrain varies from the mountains of Njazidja to the hills and valleys of Mwali. The climate is cool and dry, with a winter rainy season.

History and Politics. The Comoro Islands saw invasions by coastal African, Persian Gulf, Indonesian, and Malagasy peoples. Portuguese explorers landed in the 1500s, around the same time Arab Shirazis, most likely from Persia, introduced Islam. The French took Mayotte in 1843 and had established colonial rule over the four main islands by 1912. Comoros declared unilateral independence in 1975. Mayotte, however, voted to remain under French administration. In 1992 a new constitution was adopted, but the country's first election since the country's independence was marred by violence. ∎

CONGO

Official name Republic of the Congo
PEOPLE
Population 2,474,000. **Density** 19/mi² (7.2/km²).

Urban 41%. **Capital** Brazzaville, 693,712. **Ethnic groups** Kongo 48%, Sangho 20%, Bateke 17%, Mbochi 12%. **Languages** French, Lingala, Kikongo, indigenous. **Religions** Christian 50%, Animist 48%, Muslim 2%. **Life expectancy** 54 female, 49 male. **Literacy** 57%.

POLITICS

Government Republic. **Parties** Labor, Movement for Democracy and Integral Development, Pan-African Union for Social Democracy, others. **Suffrage** Universal, over 18. **Memberships** OAU, UN. **Subdivisions** 9 regions, 1 federal district.

ECONOMY

GDP $7,000,000,000. **Per capita** $2,901. **Monetary unit** CFA franc. **Trade partners** Exports: U.S., Spain, France. Imports: France, Spain, U.S. **Exports** Petroleum, lumber, coffee, cocoa, sugar, diamonds. **Imports** Food, manufactures, machinery.

LAND

Description Central Africa. **Area** 132,047 mi² (342,000 km²). **Highest point** Mt. Nabeba, 3,219 ft (981 m). **Lowest point** Sea level.

People. The Congo's main groups, the Kongo, Sangho, Bateke, and Mbochi create an ethnically and linguistically diverse populace. The official language, French, reflects former colonial rule. Population is concentrated in the south, away from the dense forests, heavy rainfall, and hot climate of the north. Educational programs have improved, although rural inhabitants remain relatively isolated.

Economy and the Land. Brazzaville was the commercial center of the former colony called French Equatorial Africa. The Congo now benefits from the early groundwork laid for service and transport industries. Subsistence farming occupies most Congolese, however, and takes most of the cultivated land. Low productivity and a growing populace create a need for foreign aid, much of it from France. Offshore petroleum is the most valuable mineral resource and a major economic contributor. The land is marked by coastal plains, a south-central valley, a central plateau, and the Congo River basin in the north. The climate is tropical.

History and Politics. Several tribal kingdoms existed in the area during its early history. The Portuguese arrived on the coast in the 1400s, and slave trade flourished until it was banned in the 1800s. A Teke king then signed a treaty placing the area, known as Middle Congo, under French protection. In 1910 Middle Congo, the present-day Central African Republic, Gabon, and Chad were joined to form French Equatorial Africa. The Republic of the Congo became independent in 1960. Subsequent years saw unrest, including coups, a presidential assassination, and accusations of corruption and human rights violations. Democratic reforms and the legalization of opposition parties have unleashed intense ethnic and regional rivalries that threaten the nation's stability. ∎

COOK ISLANDS
See NEW ZEALAND.

CORSICA See FRANCE.

COSTA RICA

Official name Republic of Costa Rica
PEOPLE
Population 3,379,000. **Density** 171/mi² (66/km²).
Urban 47%. **Capital** San José, 278,600. **Ethnic groups** White and mestizo 96%, black 2%, Amerindian 1%. **Languages** Spanish. **Religions** Roman Catholic 95%. **Life expectancy** 79 female, 74 male. **Literacy** 93%.
POLITICS
Government Republic. **Parties** National Liberation, Social Christian Unity, others. **Suffrage** Universal, over 18. **Memberships** OAS, UN. **Subdivisions** 7 provinces.

ECONOMY
GDP $19,300,000,000. **Per capita** $5,984.
Monetary unit Colon. **Trade partners** Exports: U.S., Germany, Italy. Imports: U.S., Venezuela, Japan. **Exports** Coffee, bananas, textiles, sugar. **Imports** Petroleum, machinery, manufactures, chemicals, fertilizer, food.
LAND
Description Central America. **Area** 19,730 mi² (51,100 km²). **Highest point** Cerro Chirripó, 12,530 ft (3,819 m). **Lowest point** Sea level.

People. Compared with most other Central American countries, Costa Rica has a relatively large population of European descent, mostly Spanish with minorities of German, Dutch, and Swiss ancestry. Together with mestizos, people of Spanish-Indian heritage, they compose the bulk of the population. Descendants of black Jamaican immigrants inhabit mainly the Caribbean coastal region. Indigenous Indians in scattered enclaves continue traditional lifestyles; some, however, have been assimilated into the country's majority culture.

Economy and the Land. Costa Rica's economy, one of the most prosperous in Central America, has not been without problems, some resulting from falling coffee prices and rising oil costs. Agriculture remains important, producing traditional coffee and banana crops, while the country attempts to expand industry. Population and agriculture are concentrated in the central highlands. Much of the country is forested, and the mountainous central area is bordered by coastal plains on the east and west. The climate is semitropical to tropical.

History and Politics. In 1502 Christopher Columbus arrived and claimed the area for Spain. Spaniards named the region Rich Coast, and settlers soon flocked to the new land to seek their fortune. Rather than riches, they found an Indian population unwilling to surrender its land. But many Spaniards remained, establishing farms in the central area. In 1821 the Central American provinces of Costa Rica, Guatemala, El Salvador, Honduras, and Nicaragua declared themselves independent from Spain, and by 1823 they had formed the Federation of Central America. Despite efforts to sustain it, the federation was in a state of virtual collapse by 1838, and Costa Rica became an independent republic. Since the first free elections in 1889, Costa Rica has experienced a presidential overthrow in 1919 and a civil war in 1948, which arose over a disputed election. In the 1980s the country worked to promote peaceful solutions to armed conflicts in the region. It is Central America's oldest and most stable democracy. ∎

COTE D'IVOIRE

Official name Republic of Cote d'Ivoire
PEOPLE
Population 14,540,000. **Density** 117/mi² (45/km²). **Urban** 40%. **Capital** Abidjan (de facto), 1,929,079; Yamoussoukro (future), 106,786.
Ethnic groups Baule 23%, Bete 18%, Senoufou 15%, Malinke 11%, other African. **Languages**

in 1637, but European settlement was hindered by the rugged coastline and intertribal conflicts. Cote d'Ivoire became a French colony in 1893. Movements toward autonomy began after World War II, and in 1960 Cote d'Ivoire declared itself an independent republic. The nation has enjoyed political stability since independence and has maintained close economic ties with France. The nation enjoyed many years of political stability under the rule of President Houphouet-Boigny. However, protests against the government and against one-party rule led to Cote d'Ivoire's first multiparty election in 1990. The ruling party won an overwhelming victory, leading to charges of fraud by the opposition. Houphouet-Boigny's death in 1993 was followed by a smooth transition of power. ■

French, Dioula and other indigenous. **Religions** Animist 63%, Muslim 25%, Christian 12%. **Life expectancy** 53 female, 50 male. **Literacy** 54%.
POLITICS
Government Republic. **Parties** Democratic, Popular Front. **Suffrage** Universal, over 21.
Memberships OAU, UN. **Subdivisions** 49 departments.
ECONOMY
GDP $21,000,000,000. **Per capita** $1,526.
Monetary unit CFA franc. **Trade partners** Exports: Netherlands, France, U.S. Imports: France, Nigeria. **Exports** Cocoa, coffee, wood, cotton, bananas, pineapples, palm oil. **Imports** Manufactures, raw materials and fuel.
LAND
Description Western Africa. **Area** 124,518 mi² (322,500 km²). **Highest point** Mont Nimba, 5,748 ft (1,752 m). **Lowest point** Sea level.

People. Cote d'Ivoire is composed almost entirely of black Africans from more than sixty ethnic groups. French is the nation's official language, a result of former French rule, but many indigenous languages are spoken as well. Traditional religions predominate, though a significant number of Ivorians are Muslim or Christian. Most Ivorians live in huts in small villages, but increased numbers have moved to the cities to find work. Overcrowding is a major problem in the cities.

Economy and the Land. Once solely dependent upon the export of cocoa and coffee, Cote d'Ivoire now produces and exports a variety of agricultural goods. Forest land, when cleared, provides rich soil for agriculture—still the country's main activity. Petroleum, textile, and apparel industries also contribute to the strong economy. Cote d'Ivoire pursues a policy of economic liberalism in which foreign investment is encouraged. As a result, foreigners hold high-level positions in most Cote d'Ivoire industries. The hot, humid coastal region gives way to inland tropical forest. Beyond the forest lies savanna, and to the northwest are highlands.

History and Politics. Cote d'Ivoire once consisted of many African kingdoms. French sailors gave the region its present name when they began trading for ivory and other goods in 1483. Missionaries arrived

CROATIA

Official name Republic of Croatia
PEOPLE
Population 4,801,000. **Density** 220/mi² (85/km²).
Urban 51%. **Capital** Zagreb, 697,925. **Ethnic groups** Croat 78%, Serb 12%, Muslim 1%.
Languages Serbo-Croatian. **Religions** Roman Catholic 77%, Orthodox 11%, Muslim 1%. **Life expectancy** 77 female, 70 male. **Literacy** 97%.
POLITICS
Government Republic. **Parties** Democratic Change, Democratic Union, Peasant, Social Democratic, Social Liberal, others. **Suffrage** Universal, over 18; over 16 if employed.
Memberships UN. **Subdivisions** 21 counties.
ECONOMY
GDP $21,800,000,000. **Per capita** $4,542.
Monetary unit Kuna. **Trade partners** Former Yugoslavian republics. **Exports** Machinery and transportation equipment, manufactures, food, raw materials. **Imports** Machinery and transportation equipment, fuel and lubricants, food, chemicals.
LAND
Description Eastern Europe. **Area** 21,829 mi² (56,538 km²). **Highest point** Troglav, 6,276 ft

(1,913 m). **Lowest point** Sea level.

People. Despite a common heritage with the Serbian people of Yugoslavia, the Croats have their own distinct culture and traditions. The basis of the continuing friction between the Croats and Serbs is religious in origin: the Croats are Roman Catholic, while the Serbs are mainly Orthodox. The religious difference resulted in a more Western European cultural orientation for the Croats and an eastern affiliation for the Serbs. Most of Croatia's Serbian minority lives in northwestern Croatia.

Economy and the Land. Croatia is a land of extremely varied terrain, and includes the historic regions of Croatia, Dalmatia, Slavonia, and part of Istria. Croatia's fertile plains produce ample supplies of grains. Grapes, olives, and citrus fruits are grown along the mountainous coast. Croatia has a well-developed industrial sector, and leading industries include petrochemicals, food processing, and shipbuilding. The Adriatic coast attracts tourists from all over the world.

History and Politics. Slavic people settled in Croatia in the seventh century and established their own independent state. The original tribal organization of the people was eventually replaced by a feudal one. In 1102 the country chose to merge with Hungary. Turkey invaded Croatia in 1463, but in 1699, Croatia was reclaimed by the Austro-Hungarian Hapsburg Empire. Tiring of foreign rule, the Croats began to agitate for independence in the mid-1800s, but Croatia nevertheless joined the Serbs and Slovenes in the new state of Yugoslavia in 1918. In 1941 Germany invaded Yugoslavia, and Croatia was set up as an independent state. Allied with the Nazis, this government was responsible for the deaths of thousands of Serbs and Jews. The end of World War II marked the end of Croatian independence and, in 1946, Croatia became a state of the new Yugoslavia, united under the dictator Tito. Enmity between the Croats and Serbs continued to simmer in the postwar period, and terrorism was common. Tito's death in 1980 plunged the country into a political and economic crisis, and Croats began to demand greater autonomy. Croatia claimed home rule in February 1991, and fighting between the Croats and the Yugoslavian army began shortly thereafter. Along with neighboring Slovenia, Croatia declared its independence on June 25, 1991. The war between Croatia and Serbian Yugoslavia continued to escalate throughout 1991. More than ten thousand people were killed by the time a cease-fire was reached in early 1992, when a United Nations peacekeeping force was sent in. Ethnic Serbs in western Croatia have declared the independence of their homeland, Krajina, and tensions remain high. ∎

CUBA

Official name Republic of Cuba
PEOPLE
Population 11,560,000. **Density** 270/mi²
(104/km²). **Urban** 74%. **Capital** Havana,
2,119,059. **Ethnic groups** Mulatto 51%, white
37%, black 11%, Chinese 1%. **Languages**

Spanish. **Religions** Roman Catholic, Pentecostal, Baptist. **Life expectancy** 78 female, 74 male. **Literacy** 94%.
POLITICS
Government Socialist republic. **Parties** Communist. **Suffrage** Universal, over 16.
Memberships UN. **Subdivisions** 13 provinces, 1 city, 1 municipality.
ECONOMY
GDP $13,700,000,000. **Per capita** $1,257.
Monetary unit Peso. **Trade partners** Former Soviet republics, Germany. **Exports** Sugar, nickel, medical supplies, shellfish, fruit, tobacco, coffee.
Imports Petroleum, machinery, raw materials, food.
LAND
Description Caribbean island. **Area** 42,804 mi² (110,861 km²). **Highest point** Pico Turquino, 6,470 ft (1,972 m). **Lowest point** Sea level.

People. Most Cubans are descendants of Spanish colonists, African slaves, or a blend of the two. The government provides free education and health care. Although religious practices are discouraged, most people belong to the Roman Catholic church. Personal income, health, education, and housing have improved since the 1959 revolution, but most food products and consumer goods remain in short supply.

Economy and the Land. Cuba's economy is largely dependent on sugar, although other forms of agriculture are also important. The most fertile soils lie in the central region between mountain ranges, while mineral deposits, including oil and nickel, are found in the northeast. In addition to agriculture and mining, industry is an economic contributor. Most economic activity is nationalized, and has, until recently, been dependent on aid from the former Soviet Union. Mountains, plains, and a scenic coastline make Cuba one of the most beautiful islands in the West Indies. The climate is tropical.

History and Politics. Christopher Columbus claimed Cuba for Spain in 1492, and Spanish settlement began in 1511. When the native Indian population died out, African slaves were brought to work plantations. The United States joined with Cuba against Spain in the Spanish-American War in 1898. Cuba gained full independence in 1902. Unrest continued, however, and the United States again intervened from 1906 to 1909 and in 1917. A 1933 coup ousted a nine-year dictatorship, and a subsequent government over-throw in 1934 ushered in an era dominated by Sergeant Fulgencio Batista. After ruling through other presidents and serving an elected term himself, Batista seized power in a 1952 coup that established an unpopular and oppressive regime. Led by lawyer Fidel Castro, a revolutionary group opposed to Batista gained quick support, and Batista fled the country on January 1, 1959, leaving the government to Castro. Early United States support of Castro soured when nationalization of American busi-nesses began. American aid soon ceased, and Cuba looked to the Soviet Union for assistance. The United States ended diplomatic relations with Cuba in 1961. In 1962 the United States and the Soviet Union became embroiled in a dispute over Soviet missile bases in Cuba that ended with removal of the missiles. Fidel Castro remains in power despite a weakened economy following the withdrawal of Soviet support. Political and economic sanctions as well as massive illegal emigration continue to sour relations with the U.S.   ∎

CURAÇAO See NETHERLANDS.

CYPRUS

Official name Republic of Cyprus
PEOPLE
Population 551,000. **Density** 242/mi^2 (93/km^2). **Urban** 53%. **Capital** Nicosia (Levkosía), 48,221. **Ethnic groups** Greek. **Languages** Greek, English. **Religions** Greek Orthodox. **Life expectancy** 79 female, 75 male. **Literacy** 94%.
POLITICS
Government Republic. **Parties** Democratic, Democratic Rally, Progressive Party of the Working People. **Suffrage** Universal, over 18. **Memberships** CW, UN. **Subdivisions** 6 districts.
ECONOMY
GDP $6,700,000,000. **Per capita** $9,397. **Monetary unit** Pound. **Trade partners** Exports: U.K., Greece, Lebanon. Imports: U.K., Japan, Italy. **Exports** Fruit, potatoes, grapes, wine, cement, clothing and shoes. **Imports** Manufactures, petro-leum, food, machinery.

LAND
Description Southern part of the island of Cyprus. **Area** 2,276 mi^2 (5,896 km^2). **Highest point** Olim-bos, 6,401 ft (1,951 m). **Lowest point** Sea level.

People. Most Cypriots occupying the southern two thirds of the island are of Greek ancestry, and their religion, language, and general culture reflect this heritage. Family and religion are a dominant influence in the community. Decades of British rule had little impact.

Economy and the Land. Conflict between the Greek and Turkish Cypriots has severely disrupted the economy of the island. With foreign assistance, Greek Cypriots have made considerable progress, expanding traditional southern agriculture to light manufacturing and tourism. Known for its scenic beauty and tourist appeal, southern Cyprus is marked by a fertile southern plain bordered by the rugged Troodos Mountains to the southwest. Sandy beach-es dot the coastline. The Mediterranean climate brings hot, dry summers and damp, cool winters.

History and Politics. History of Cyprus and North Cyprus follows NORTH CYPRUS.

CYPRUS, NORTH

Official name Turkish Republic of Northern Cyprus
PEOPLE
Population 182,000. **Density** 141/mi^2 (54/km^2). **Capital** Nicosia (Lefkoşa), 37,400. **Ethnic groups** Turkish 99%, Greek, Maronite, and others 1%. **Languages** Turkish. **Religions** Sunni Muslim.
POLITICS
Government Republic. **Parties** Democratic Struggle, National Unity. **Memberships** None. **Subdivisions** 3 districts.
ECONOMY
GDP $550,000,000. **Per capita** $2,865. **Monetary unit** Turkish lira. **Trade partners** Turkey, U.K., Germany. **Exports** Food and livestock, manufac-tures, crude materials. **Imports** Manufactures, machinery and transportation equipment, mineral fuels.
LAND
Description Northern part of the island of Cyprus. **Area** 1,295 mi^2 (3,355 km^2). **Highest point** Unnamed, 3,360 ft (1,024 m). **Lowest point** Sea level.

People. The northern part of the island is occupied by Cypriots of Turkish ancestry who speak Turkish and are Sunni Muslims. The 1974 Turkish invasion result-ed in a formal segregation of this settlement pattern. The Turkish Cypriot ancestors arrived on the island during the three centuries of Ottoman rule.

Economy and the Land. Since the partition of the island, North Cyprus has become somewhat iso-lated. Lacking in capital, foreign aid, and official recognition, it remains agriculturally based and dependent upon Turkey for tourism, trade, and assis-tance. The mostly barren Kyrenia Range dominates North Cyprus.

History and Politics. In the Late Bronze Age—from 1600 to 1050 B.C.—a Greek culture flourished in Cyprus. Rule by various peoples followed, including Assyrians, Egyptians, Persians, Romans, Byzantines, French, and Venetians. The Ottoman Turks invaded in 1571. In the nineteenth century, Turkey ceded the island to the British as security for a loan. Although many Turks remained on Cyprus, the British declared it a crown colony in 1925. A growing desire for *enosis*, or union, with Greece led to rioting and guerrilla activity by Greek Cypriots. The Turkish government, opposed to absorption by Greece, desired separation into Greek and Turkish sectors. Cyprus became independent in 1960, with treaties forbidding either enosis or partition, but Greek-Turkish conflicts continued. A 1974 coup by pro-enosis forces led to an invasion by Turkey. The resulting partition runs east-west across the island dividing Nicosia, which serves as a capital for both countries. North Cyprus, which is not recognized internationally, maintains a separate government with a prime minister and a president. The United Nations, in an attempt to force a resolution of the continuing conflict, is threatening withdrawal of its peacekeeping forces. ∎

CZECH REPUBLIC

Official name Czech Republic
PEOPLE
Population 10,430,000. **Density** 343/mi² (132/km²). **Capital** Prague, 1,212,010. **Ethnic groups** Czech 94%, Slovak 3%. **Languages** Czech, Slovak. **Religions** Roman Catholic 39%, Protestant 5%, Orthodox 3%. **Life expectancy** 77 female, 69 male.
POLITICS
Government Republic. **Parties** Civic Democratic, Left Bloc, Liberal National Socialist, Liberal Social Union, Social Democracy, others. **Suffrage** Universal, over 18. **Memberships** NATO, UN. **Subdivisions** 8 regions.
ECONOMY
GDP $75,000,000,000. **Per capita** $7,257.

Monetary unit Koruna. **Trade partners** Exports: Slovakia, Germany, Poland. Imports: Slovakia, former Soviet republics, Germany. **Exports** Manufactures, machinery and transportation equip., chemicals, fuels, minerals. **Imports** Machinery and transportation equip., fuel, manufactures, raw materials.
LAND
Description Eastern Europe, landlocked. **Area** 30,450 mi² (78,864 km²). **Highest point** Sněžka, 5,256 ft (1,602 m). **Lowest point** Along Elbe River, 377 ft (115 m).

People. Although the Czechs are Slavic in origin, their culture has been profoundly influenced by the Germans as a result of centuries of Austrian rule. By eastern European standards, the people are well educated and highly skilled. The language is Czech, and the predominate religion is Roman Catholic. There is a small Slovak minority.

Economy and the Land. An industrial nation, the Czech Republic has moved aggressively since 1991 to establish a free market economy. Unlike other eastern European nations, the Czech Republic has managed to keep unemployment and government spending in check during the transition from communism to capitalism. Coal deposits have traditionally formed the base for the development of glass, chemical, and machine industries. Most of the land is low hills and plateaus bounded on three sides by mountain ranges. The climate is temperate.

History and Politics. Slavic tribes were established in the region by the fifth century, and the area fell under the rule of the Roman Empire. An important Moravian state rose in the ninth century, followed by the advent of a strong Bohemian kingdom that reached its zenith in the thirteenth century. Austria gained control of the area in the 1500s, and sovereignty later passed to Austria-Hungary. With the collapse of Austria-Hungary at the end of World War I, an independent Czechoslovakia, consisting of Bohemia, Moravia, Silesia, and Slovakia, was formed. Nazi Germany invaded Czechoslovakia in 1939, and the Soviet Union liberated the nation from German occupation during 1944 and 1945. By 1948 Communists controlled the government, and political purges continued from 1949 to 1952. A 1968 invasion by the Soviet Union, Bulgaria, Hungary, Poland, and East Germany resulted when the Czechoslovakian Communist party leader introduced liberal reforms. Demonstrations forced the Communist party to relinquish its hold on power in 1989. Growing economic differences between the rural east and the industrialized west led to the breakup of Czechoslovakia into the Czech Republic and Slovakia in 1993. ∎

DENMARK

Official name Kingdom of Denmark
PEOPLE
Population 5,207,000. **Density** 313/mi² (121/km²). **Urban** 85%. **Capital** Copenhagen, 464,566. **Ethnic groups** Danish (Scandinavian), German. **Languages** Danish. **Religions** Lutheran

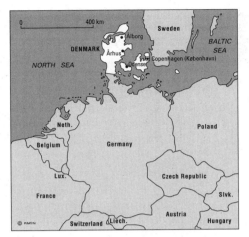

91%. **Life expectancy** 79 female, 73 male.
Literacy 99%.
POLITICS
Government Constitutional monarchy. **Parties**
Conservative, Liberal, Social Democratic, Socialist
People's, others. **Suffrage** Universal, over 18.
Memberships EU, NATO, OECD, UN.
Subdivisions 14 counties, 2 cities.
ECONOMY
GDP $95,600,000,000. **Per capita** $18,495.
Monetary unit Krone. **Trade partners** Germany,
Sweden, U.K. **Exports** Meat, dairy products,
ships, fish, chemicals, machinery. **Imports**
Petroleum, machinery, chemicals, food, textiles,
paper.
LAND
Description Northern Europe. **Area** 16,639 mi^2
(43,094 km^2). **Highest point** Yding Skovhøj, 568 ft
(173 m). **Lowest point** Lammefjord, -23 ft (-7 m).
*The above information excludes Greenland and
the Faeroe Is.*

People. Denmark is made up of the Jutland Peninsula
and more than four hundred islands, about one
hundred of which are inhabited. Greenland, which
is situated northeast of Canada, and the Faeroe
Islands, which are located between Scotland and
Iceland in the North Atlantic, are also part of
Denmark. Lutheran, Danish-speaking Scandinavians
constitute the homogenous population of the peninsula and surrounding islands, although a German
minority is concentrated near the German border. The
government provides extensive social services and
programs. The literacy rate is high, and Denmark has
made significant contributions to science, literature, and the arts.

Economy and the Land. Despite limited natural
resources, Denmark has a diversified economy.
Agriculture contributes to trade, and pork and bacon
are important products. Postwar expansion focused
on industry, and the country now imports the raw materials it lacks and exports finished products. The
North Sea is the site of oil and natural gas deposits.
On the Faeroe Islands, traditional fishing continues
as the economic mainstay. Most of Denmark's terrain is rolling, with hills covering much of the penin-

sula and the nearby islands. Coastal regions are
marked by fjords and sandy beaches, especially in
the West. The climate is temperate, with North Sea
winds moderating temperatures. The rugged Faeroe
Islands are damp, cloudy, and windy.

History and Politics. By the first century, access
to the sea had brought contact with other civilizations. This led to the Viking era, which lasted from
the ninth to eleventh centuries and resulted in temporary Danish rule of England. In the fourteenth century, Sweden, Norway, Finland, Iceland, the Faeroe
Islands, and Greenland were united under Danish
rule. Sweden and Finland withdrew from the union
in the 1500s, and Denmark lost Norway to Sweden
in 1814. A constitutional monarchy was instituted in
1849. Late nineteenth-century social reform, reflected in a new constitution in 1915, laid the groundwork
for Denmark's current welfare state. The country
remained neutral in World War I. Iceland gained independence following the war but maintained its
union with Denmark until 1944. Despite declared neutrality in World War II, Denmark was invaded and
occupied by Germany from 1940 to 1945.
Compromise and gradual change characterize
Danish politics.   ∎

DJIBOUTI

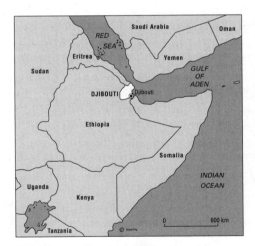

Official name Republic of Djibouti
PEOPLE
Population 557,000. **Density** 62/mi^2 (24/km^2).
Urban 81%. **Capital** Djibouti, 329,337. **Ethnic
groups** Somali 60%, Afar 35%. **Languages**
French, Arabic, Somali, Afar. **Religions** Muslim
94%, Christian 6%. **Life expectancy** 51 female,
47 male. **Literacy** 48%.
POLITICS
Government Republic. **Parties** Democratic
Renewal, National Democratic, People's Progress
Assembly, others. **Suffrage** Universal adult.
Memberships AL, OAU, UN. **Subdivisions** 5
districts.

ECONOMY

GDP $500,000,000. **Per capita** $1,263. **Monetary unit** Franc. **Trade partners** Exports: France, Yemen, Somalia. Imports: France, Ethiopia, Italy. **Exports** Hides and skins, coffee. **Imports** Food, beverages, transportation equipment, chemicals, petroleum.

LAND

Description Eastern Africa. **Area** 8,958 mi^2 (23,200 km^2). **Highest point** Moussa 'Ali, 6,631 ft (2,021 m). **Lowest point** Lake Assal, -515 ft (-157 m).

People. Characterized by strong cultural unity, Islam, and ethnic ties to Somalia, Somali Issas compose Djibouti's majority. Afars, who make up another main group, are also mostly Muslim and are linked ethnically with Afars in Ethiopia. Rivalry between the two groups has marked the nation's history. Because of unproductive land, much of the population is concentrated in the capital city of Djibouti.

Economy and the Land. Traditional nomadic herding continues as a way of life for many Djiboutians, despite heat, aridity, and limited grazing area. Several assets promote Djibouti as a port and trade center: a strategic position on the Gulf of Aden, an improved harbor, and a railway linking the city of Djibouti with Addis Ababa in Ethiopia. Marked by mountains that divide a coastal plain from a plateau region, the terrain is mostly desert. The climate is extremely hot and dry.

History and Politics. In the ninth century Arab missionaries introduced Islam to the population, and by the 1800s a pattern of conflict between the Issas and Afars had developed. The French purchased the port of Obcock from Afar sultans in 1862, and their territorial control expanded until the region became French Somaliland. The goal of the pro-independence Issas was defeated in elections in 1958 and 1967 when the majority voted for continued French control. The country became the French Territory of Afars and Issas in 1967, and as the Issa population grew, so did demands for independence. A 1977 referendum created the independent Republic of Djibouti. The country has been involved in ethnic conflict since 1991. ∎

Exports: U.K., Jamaica, U.S. Imports: U.S., U.K., Trinidad and Tobago. **Exports** Bananas, coconuts, grapefruit, soap, galvanized sheets. **Imports** Food, oils and fats, chemicals, fuels and lubricants, manufactures.

LAND

Description Caribbean island. **Area** 305 mi^2 (790 km^2). **Highest point** Morne Diablotins, 4,747 ft (1,447 m). **Lowest point** Sea level.

People. Dominica's population consists of descendants of black Africans, brought to the island as slaves, and Carib Indians descended from early inhabitants. The Carib population is concentrated in the northeastern part of the island, and maintains its own customs and lifestyle. English is widely spoken in urban areas, but villagers, who compose a majority, speak mainly a French-African blend, resulting from French rule and the importation of Africans.

Economy and the Land. Of volcanic origin, the island has soils suitable for farming, but a mountainous and densely-forested terrain limits land accessible to cultivation. Agriculture is the economic mainstay, although hurricanes have hindered production. Forestry and fishing offer potential for expansion, and a tropical climate and scenic landscape create a basis for tourism.

History and Politics. In the fourteenth century Carib Indians conquered the Arawak, who originally inhabited the island. Although Christopher Columbus arrived at Dominica in 1493, Carib hostilities discouraged Spanish settlement. French and British rivalry for control of the island followed, and British possession was recognized in 1783. Dominica gained independence in 1978. ∎

DOMINICA

Official name Commonwealth of Dominica
PEOPLE
Population 89,000. **Density** 292/mi^2 (113/km^2). **Urban** 27%. **Capital** Roseau, 9,348. **Ethnic groups** Black 91%, mixed 6%, West Indian 2%. **Languages** English, French. **Religions** Roman Catholic 77%, Methodist 5%, Pentecostal 3%. **Life expectancy** 80 female, 74 male. **Literacy** 83%.
POLITICS
Government Republic. **Parties** Freedom, Labor. **Suffrage** Universal, over 18. **Memberships** CW, OAS, UN. **Subdivisions** 10 parishes.
ECONOMY
GDP $185,000,000. **Per capita** $2,126. **Monetary unit** East Caribbean dollar. **Trade partners**

DOMINICAN REPUBLIC

Official name Dominican Republic
PEOPLE
Population 7,896,000. **Density** 422/mi^2 (163/km^2). **Urban** 60%. **Capital** Santo Domingo, 2,411,900. **Ethnic groups** Mulatto 73%, white 16%, black 11%. **Languages** Spanish. **Religions** Roman Catholic 95%. **Life expectancy** 70 female, 65 male. **Literacy** 83%.
POLITICS
Government Republic. **Parties** Liberation, Revolutionary, Social Christian Reformist, others. **Suffrage** Universal, over 18 or married. **Memberships** OAS, UN. **Subdivisions** 29 provinces, 1 district.

ECONOMY

GDP $23,000,000,000. **Per capita** $3,030.
Monetary unit Peso. **Trade partners** Exports:
U.S., Netherlands. Imports: U.S., western
European countries. **Exports** Sugar, coffee,
cocoa, gold, ferronickel. **Imports** Food, petroleum,
cotton and fabrics, chemicals and pharmaceuticals.

LAND

Description Caribbean island (eastern
Hispaniola). **Area** 18,704 mi² (48,442 km²).
Highest point Pico Duarte, 10,417 ft (3,175 m).
Lowest point Lago Enriquillo, -131 ft (-40 m).

People. Occupying eastern Hispaniola Island, the
Dominican Republic borders Haiti and has a population of mixed ancestry. Haitians, other blacks,
Spaniards, and European Jews compose minority
groups. Population growth has resulted in unemployment and made it difficult for the government to
meet food and service needs.

Economy and the Land. Agriculture remains important, with sugar a main component of trade, and sugar
refining a major manufacturing activity. Farmland is
limited, however, by a northwest-to-southeast mountain range and an arid region west of the range. Mineral
exploitation and iron exports contribute to trade,
and a number of American firms have subsidiaries
here. Tourism is growing, aided by the warm, tropical climate.

History and Politics. In 1492 Christopher Columbus
arrived at Hispaniola Island. Spanish colonists followed, and the Indian population was virtually wiped
out, although some intermingling with Spanish probably occurred. In 1697 the western region of the island,
which would become Haiti, was ceded to France. The
entire island came under Haitian control as the
Republic of Haiti in 1822, and an 1844 revolution established the independent Dominican Republic. Since
independence the country has experienced periods
of instability, evidenced by military coups, United States
military intervention, and human rights abuses. In May
1994 an aged and ill President Balaguer was re-elect-
ed for a seventh term. Political unrest following
claims of vote fraud forced Balaguer to agree to a
reduced mandate of 18 months. ■

ECUADOR

Official name Republic of Ecuador

PEOPLE

Population 11,015,000. **Density** 105/mi²
(40/km²). **Urban** 56%. **Capital** Quito, 1,100,847.
Ethnic groups Mestizo 55%, Amerindian 25%,
white 10%, black 10%. **Languages** Spanish,
Quechua, indigenous. **Religions** Roman Catholic
95%. **Life expectancy** 69 female, 65 male.
Literacy 86%.

POLITICS

Government Republic. **Parties** Democratic Left,
Republican Unity, Roldosist, Socialist, Social
Christian, others. **Suffrage** Universal, over 18.
Memberships OAS, UN. **Subdivisions** 21
provinces.

ECONOMY

GDP $41,800,000,000. **Per capita** $3,781.
Monetary unit Sucre. **Trade partners** Exports:
U.S., Peru, Chile. Imports: U.S., Japan, Germany.
Exports Petroleum, coffee, bananas, cocoa,
shrimp, fish. **Imports** Transportation equipment,
vehicles, machinery, chemicals.

LAND

Description Western South America. **Area**
105,037 mi² (272,045 km²). **Highest point**
Chimborazo, 20,702 ft (6,310 m). **Lowest point**
Sea level.

People. Ecuador's ethnicity was established by an
indigenous Indian population and Spanish colonists.
Minority whites, of Spanish or other European
descent, live mainly in urban areas or operate large
farms called haciendas. Of mixed Spanish-Indian blood,
mestizos compose over half the population, although
economic and political power is concentrated among
whites. Minority Indians speak Quechua or other Indian
languages and maintain traditional customs in
Andean villages or nomadic jungle tribes. Blacks are
concentrated on the northern coastal plain. Recent
trends show a movement from the interior highlands to the fertile coastal plain and a rural-to-urban
shift. A history of economic inequality has produced

a literary and artistic tradition that has focused on social reform.

Economy and the Land. Despite an oil boom in the 1970s, Ecuador remains underdeveloped. Minor oil production began in 1911, but since a 1967 petroleum discovery in the *oriente*, a jungle region east of the Andes, Ecuador has become an oil exporter. Agriculture remains important for much of the population, although primitive and inefficient practices continue among the poor. Rich soils of the *costa*, extending from the Pacific to the Andes, support most of the export crops. Forestry and fishing have growth potential, and the waters around the Galapagos Islands are rich in tuna. Manufacturing is mainly devoted to meeting domestic needs. The oriente and costa lie on either side of the sierra, a region of highland plateaus between the two Andean chains. Varied altitudes result in a climate ranging from tropical in the lowlands to temperate in the plateaus and cold in the high mountains. A variety of wildlife inhabits the Galapagos Islands, five large and nine small islands about 600 miles (966 km) off Ecuador's coast in the Pacific Ocean.

History and Politics. In the fifteenth century Incas conquered and subsequently united the area's various tribes. In the 1500s the Spanish gained control, using Indians and African slaves to work the plantations. Weakened by the Napoleonic Wars, Spain lost control of Ecuador in 1822, and Simón Bolívar united the independent state with the Republic of Greater Colombia. Ecuador left the union as a separate republic in 1830, and subsequent years saw instability and rule by presidents, dictators, and juntas. From 1925 to 1948 no leader was able to complete a full term in office. A new constitution was established in 1978. Elections in 1992 were won by the right-wing United Republican Party committed to a privatization policy. The fall in world crude oil prices in 1993 caused an economic crisis and riots over the increase in gasoline prices, as well as general political unrest. Border skirmishes renewed a dispute with Peru over a part of the rain forest thought to be mineral-rich. ∎

EGYPT

Official name Arab Republic of Egypt
PEOPLE
Population 56,100,000. **Density** 150/mi² (58/km²). **Urban** 44%. **Capital** Cairo, 6,068,695. **Ethnic groups** Egyptian (Eastern Hamitic) 90%. **Languages** Arabic. **Religions** Muslim 94%, Coptic Christian and others 6%. **Life expectancy** 63 female, 60 male. **Literacy** 48%.
POLITICS
Government Socialist republic. **Parties** National Democratic, National Progressive Unionist Grouping, others. **Suffrage** Universal, over 18. **Memberships** AL, OAU, UN. **Subdivisions** 26 governorates.
ECONOMY
GDP $139,000,000,000. **Per capita** $2,436. **Monetary unit** Pound. **Trade partners** Exports: Italy, former Soviet republics, France. Imports:

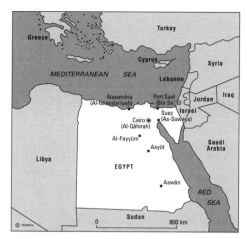

U.S., Germany, France. **Exports** Petroleum, cotton, textiles, metals, chemicals. **Imports** Machinery, food, fertilizer, wood products, manufactures.
LAND
Description Northeastern Africa. **Area** 386,662 mi² (1,001,449 km²). **Highest point** Mt. Katrina, 8,668 ft (2,642 m). **Lowest point** Qattara Depression, -436 ft (-133 m).

People. Egypt's population is relatively homogeneous, and Egyptians compose the largest group. Descended from ancient Nile Valley inhabitants, Egyptians have intermixed somewhat with Mediterranean and Asiatic peoples in the north and with black Africans in the south. Minorities include Bedouins, Arabic-speaking desert nomads; Nubians, black descendants of migrants from the Sudan; and Copts, a Christian group. Islam, the major religion, is also a cultural force; many Christians and Muslims follow Islamic lifestyles. A desert terrain confines about 99 percent of the population to less than 4 percent of the land, in the fertile Nile River valley and along the Suez Canal.

Economy and the Land. Egypt's economy has suffered from wars, shifting alliances, and limited natural resources. Government-sponsored expansion and reform in the 1950s concentrated on manufacturing, and most industry was nationalized during the 1960s. Agriculture, centered in the Nile Valley, remains an economic mainstay, and cotton, a principal crop, is both exported and processed. Petroleum is found, mainly in the Gulf of Suez. Tourism is one of the nation's most important economic activities. Much of Egypt is desert, with hills and mountains in the east and along the Nile River, while the climate is warm and dry.

History and Politics. Egypt's recorded history began when King Menes united the region in about 3100 B.C., beginning a series of Egyptian dynasties. Art and architecture flourished during the Age of the Pyramids, from 2700 to 2200 B.C. In time native dynasties gave way to foreign conquerors, including Alexander the Great in the fourth century B.C. The Coptic Christian church emerged between the fourth and sixth centuries A.D., but in the 600s Arabs conquered the area and established Islam as the main religion. Ruling parties changed frequently, and in 1517 the Ottoman Turks added Egypt to their empire. Upon completion of the strategically important Suez Canal in 1869, foreign interest in Egypt increased. In 1875 Egypt sold its share of the canal to Britain, and a rebellion against foreign intervention ended with British occupation in 1882. Turkey sided with Germany in World War I, and the United Kingdom made Egypt a British protectorate in 1914. The country became an independent monarchy in 1922, but the British presence remained. In 1945 Egypt and six other nations formed the Arab League. The founding of Israel in 1948 initiated an era of Arab-Israeli hostilities, including periodic warfare in which Egypt often had a major role. Dissatisfaction over dealings with Israel and continued British occupation of the Suez Canal led to the overthrow of the king, and Egypt became a republic in 1953. Following a power struggle, Gamal Abdel Nasser was elected president in 1956, and the British agreed to remove their troops. Upon the death of Nasser in 1970, Vice President Anwar Sadat came to power. Negotiations between Egyptian president Sadat and Israeli prime minister Menachem Begin began in 1977, and in 1979 the leaders signed a peace treaty ending conflicts between Egypt and Israel. As a result, Egypt was suspended from the Arab League until 1989. In 1981 President Sadat was assassinated and was succeeded by Hosni Mubarek, who is faced with a growing fundamentalist Muslim campaign of violence targeting tourists and government officers. ■

EL SALVADOR

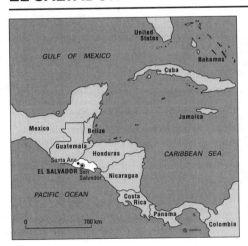

Official name Republic of El Salvador
PEOPLE
Population 5,280,000. **Density** 650/mi²
(251/km²). **Urban** 44%. **Capital** San Salvador,
462,652. **Ethnic groups** Mestizo 94%, Amerindian
5%, white 1%. **Languages** Spanish, Nahua.
Religions Roman Catholic 75%. **Life expectancy**
69 female, 64 male. **Literacy** 73%.
POLITICS
Government Republic. **Parties** Authentic

Christian Movement, Christian Democratic, National Republican Alliance, others. **Suffrage** Universal, over 18. **Memberships** OAS, UN. **Subdivisions** 14 departments.
ECONOMY
GDP $14,200,000,000. **Per capita** $2,520.
Monetary unit Colon. **Trade partners** Exports: U.S., Guatemala, Germany. Imports: U.S., Guatemala, Mexico. **Exports** Coffee, sugar, cotton, shrimp. **Imports** Petroleum, manufactures, food, machinery, construction materials, fertilizer.
LAND
Description Central America. **Area** 8,124 mi² (21,041 km²). **Highest point** Cerro El Pital, 8,957 ft (2,730 m). **Lowest point** Sea level.

People. Most Salvadorans are Spanish-speaking mestizos, people of Spanish-Indian descent. An Indian minority is mainly descended from the Pipil, a Nahuatl group related to the Aztecs. The Nahuatl dialect is still spoken among some Indians. El Salvador, the smallest Central American country in area, has the highest population density in mainland Latin America, with inhabitants concentrated in a central valley-and-plateau region.

Economy and the Land. El Salvador's economy has been plagued by political instability, low literacy, high population density, and high unemployment. Agriculture remains the economic mainstay, and most arable land has been cultivated. Coffee, cotton, and sugar are produced on large commercial plantations, while subsistence farmers rely on corn, bean, and sorghum crops. East-to-west mountain ranges divide El Salvador into a southern coastal region, central valleys and plateaus, and northern mountains. The climate is subtropical.

History and Politics. Maya and Pipil predominated in the area of El Salvador prior to Spanish arrival. In the 1500s Pipil defeated invading Spaniards but were conquered in a subsequent invasion. In 1821 the Spanish-controlled Central American colonies declared independence, and in 1823 they united as the Federation of Central America. By 1838 the problem-ridden federation was in a state of collapse, and as the union dissolved, El Salvador became independent. Instability and revolution soon followed. The expansion of the coffee economy in the late 1800s exacerbated problems by further concentrating wealth and power among large-estate holders. A dictatorship from 1931 to 1944 was followed by instability under various military rulers. In 1969 a brief war with Honduras arose from resentment toward land-ownership laws, border disputes, and nationalistic feelings following a series of soccer games between the two countries. During the 1980s, the United States provided extensive military and economic aid in an attempt to moderate the government. A twelve-year civil war erupted which did not end until 1992. Elections in 1994 were won by the National Republican Alliance (ARENA), the ruling rightist party. Their economic reform plan is strongly opposed by labor unions. ■

EQUATORIAL GUINEA

Official name Republic of Equatorial Guinea

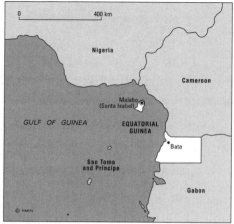

PEOPLE
Population 394,000. **Density** 36/mi² (14/km²).
Urban 29%. **Capital** Malabo, Bioko I., 31,630.
Ethnic groups Fang 80%, Bubi 15%. **Languages**
Spanish, indigenous, English. **Religions** Roman
Catholic 83%, other Christian, tribal religionist. **Life
expectancy** 50 female, 46 male. **Literacy** 50%.
POLITICS
Government Republic. **Parties** Democratic.
Suffrage Universal adult. **Memberships** OAS,
UN. **Subdivisions** 7 provinces.
ECONOMY
GDP $280,000,000. **Per capita** $711. **Monetary
unit** CFA franc. **Trade partners** Exports: Spain,
Italy, Netherlands. Imports: France, Spain, Italy.
Exports Coffee, wood, cocoa. **Imports** Petroleum,
food, beverages, clothing, machinery.
LAND
Description Central Africa. **Area** 10,831 mi²
(28,051 km²). **Highest point** Pico de Santa Isabel,
9,869 ft (3,008 m). **Lowest point** Sea level.

People. Several ethnic groups inhabit Equatorial
Guinea's five islands, as well as the mainland
region of Río Muni. Although the majority Fang, a
Bantu people, are concentrated in Río Muni, they
also inhabit Bioko, the largest island. Found mainly on Bioko Island are the minority Bubi, also a Bantu
people. Coastal groups known as *playeros*, or
"those who live on the beach," live on both the
mainland and the small islands. The Fernandino, of
mixed African heritage, are concentrated on Bioko.
Equatorial Guinea is the only black African state with
Spanish as its official language.

Economy and the Land. Equatorial Guinea's
economy is based on agriculture and forestry;
cocoa, coffee, and wood are the main products. Cocoa
production is centered on fertile Bioko Island, and
coffee in Río Muni. The mainland's rain forests
also provide for forestry. Mineral exploration has
revealed petroleum and natural gas in the waters
north of Bioko, and petroleum, iron ore, and radioac-
tive materials exist in Río Muni. Bioko is of volcanic origin, and Río Muni consists of a coastal plain and
interior hills. The climate is tropical, with high temperatures and humidity.

History and Politics. Pygmies most likely inhabited the Río Muni area prior to the thirteenth century, when mainland Bubi came to Bioko. From
the seventeenth to the nineteenth centuries, Bantu
migrations brought first the coastal tribes and then
the Fang. Portugal claimed Bioko and part of the mainland in the 1400s, then ceded them to Spain in 1778.
From 1827 to 1843, British antislavery activities were
based on Bioko, which became the home of many
former slaves, the ancestors of the Fernandino
population. In 1959 the area became the Spanish
Territory of the Gulf of Guinea, and the name was
changed to Equatorial Guinea in 1963. Independence
was achieved in 1968. November 1993 elections were
boycotted by opposition parties and a dictatorship
remains in place. ∎

ERITREA

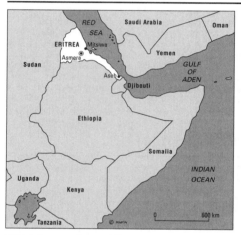

Official name State of Eritrea
PEOPLE
Population 3,458,000. **Density** 96/mi² (37/km²).
Urban 15%. **Capital** Asmera, 358,100. **Ethnic
groups** Tigray 50%, Tigre and Kunama 30%, Afar
4%, Saho 3%. **Languages** Tigre, Kunama,
Cushitic dialects, Nora Bana, Arabic. **Religions**
Muslim, Coptic Christian, Roman Catholic,
Protestant.
POLITICS
Government Republic. **Parties** Liberation Front,
Liberation Front-United Organization, People's
Liberation Front. **Suffrage. Memberships** OAU,
UN. **Subdivisions** 3 administrative regions.
ECONOMY
GDP $1,700,000,000. **Per capita** $496.
LAND
Description Eastern Africa. **Area** 36,170 mi²
(93,679 km²). **Highest point** Soira, 9,806 ft (2,989
m). **Lowest point** Unnamed, -515 ft (-157 m).

People. Eritrea is a land of diverse languages and religions. The main ethnic groups are the Tigre and
Afar, although there are also Kunama, Saho, Agau,
and others. Tige and Kunama is one of the predominate languages along with Arabic and others. About

half of the population are Coptic Christian, and the other half practice Islam.

Economy and the Land. Eritrea's climate is dry and the region suffers from chronic drought. Some cotton and oilseed crops are grown, but fish provide the major source of food. Crop failure resulted in severe food shortages in 1994. Thirty years of war with Ethiopia left the country's infrastructure in disrepair, but the rebuilding process has been swift. Despite many advances, the country is still dependent on foreign aid. Eritrea hopes to develop its Red Sea coastline as a tourist attraction.

History and Politics. Eritrea was originally settled by people who migrated across the Red Sea from Yemen. In 950 A.D. the region now known as Eritrea was part of the Ethiopian empire. In 1557 the city of Massawa and surrounding areas were captured by the Ottoman Turks, who established loose control of the region until it was overtaken by the Egyptians in 1846. Sovereignty shifted between Turkey and Egypt until 1890, when the Italians invaded the region and established the colony of Eritrea in 1890. Fifty years of Italian rule left Eritrea with sound industrial, educational, governmental, and transportation systems that were rare elsewhere in Africa. It also left the Eritreans with a strong sense of national identity, despite their cultural diversity. After the British captured the region from the Italians in World War II, the United Nations handed it over to Ethiopia in 1952, despite claims by some that Eritrea should be granted its independence. The Ethiopians were instructed to administer Eritrea as a self-governing territory within Ethiopia, but they violated the arrangement by annexing Eritrea in 1962. This action ignited a civil war which lasted for more than thirty years. After defeating the Marxist regime in 1991, the Eritreans agreed to wait almost two years before legalizing their status as an independent nation. In May 1993 Eritrea became independent and a transitional government was elected to function until a constitution is drafted. Disastrous crop failures following independence failed to rock the stability or dampen the spirit of this new country. ■

ESTONIA

Official name Republic of Estonia
PEOPLE
Population 1,515,000. **Density** 87/mi² (34/km²).
Urban 72%. **Capital** Tallinn, 481,500. **Ethnic groups** Estonian 62%, Russian 30%, Ukrainian 3%. **Languages** Estonian, Latvian, Lithuanian, Russian. **Religions** Lutheran. **Life expectancy** 76 female, 67 male. **Literacy** 99%.
POLITICS
Government Republic. **Parties** Fatherland, Moderates, National Independence, Popular Front, Safe Home. **Suffrage** Universal, over 18.
Memberships NATO, UN. **Subdivisions** 15 counties, 6 municipalities.
ECONOMY
GDP $8,800,000,000. **Per capita** $5,456.
Monetary unit Kroon. **Trade partners** Former Soviet republics. **Exports** Machinery, food, chemicals, electricity. **Imports** Machinery, oil, chemicals.

LAND
Description Eastern Europe. **Area** 17,413 mi² (45,100 km²). **Highest point** Suur Munamägi, 1,043 ft (318 m). **Lowest point** Sea level.

People. The Estonians have retained their own unique language and culture for centuries, despite almost continuous foreign intervention. Before the Soviet invasion in 1940, the Estonians, who are related to the Finns, accounted for almost all of the population. Since then, massive immigration has increased the Russians' share of the population to almost one-third. Estonia has a relatively high urban population, and most people are engaged in industry.

Economy and the Land. Most of Estonia's industry is centered on shale oil, its only major industrial raw material. Shale oil has permitted Estonia to develop a sound manufacturing base. Agriculture is based on livestock and dairy products, and most crops are grown to supply animal feed. Estonia's natural landscape is plains and poorly drained marshes, although much of the land has been drained for agriculture. More than a third of the land is forested.

History and Politics. Prior to incorporation into the Soviet Union, Estonia enjoyed only twenty years of independence during its long history. Danes conquered the territory in 1219 and sold it to the Teutonic Knights in 1346. The Swedes invaded in 1561 and domination alternated between Sweden and Poland until Peter the Great of Russia conquered it in 1721. The country was granted independence in 1918, but freedom lasted only until the Soviet invasion of 1940, after which Estonia was forced to become a Soviet Socialist Republic. Estonians enjoyed the highest overall standard of living in the Soviet Union. Estonia's "home rule" legislation led the Baltic states' drive for independence following the introduction of glasnost in the Soviet Union. International recognition as an independent nation was achieved in 1991, several months before the breakup of the Soviet Union. The first free elections in any former Soviet Union country were held in late 1992. Tensions exist between Estonians and ethnic Russians over discrimination and language laws. A 1995 election voted out the youthful Fatherland Party in favor of older, more cautious politicians but this was not expected to slow down their rapid economic growth. ■

ETHIOPIA

Official name Ethiopia

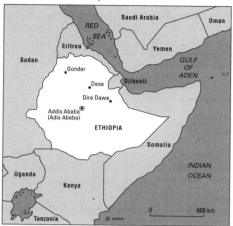

PEOPLE
Population 55,070,000. **Density** 123/mi²
(48/km²). **Urban** 12%. **Capital** Addis Ababa,
1,912,500. **Ethnic groups** Oromo (Galla) 40%,
Amhara and Tigrean 32%, Sidamo 9%, Shankella
6%, Somali 6%. **Languages** Amharic, Tigrinya,
Orominga, Guaraginga, Somali, Arabic. **Religions**
Muslim 40-50%, Ethiopian Orthodox 35-40%,
Animist 12%. **Life expectancy** 49 female, 45
male. **Literacy** 62%.
POLITICS
Government Provisional military government.
Parties Ethiopian People's Revolutionary Party,
Oromo Liberation Front, others. **Suffrage**
Universal, over 18. **Memberships** OAU, UN.
Subdivisions 14 administrative regions.
ECONOMY
GDP $22,700,000,000. **Per capita** $412.
Monetary unit Birr. **Trade partners** Exports:
Germany, Japan, U.S. Imports: Italy, former Soviet
republics, U.S. **Exports** Coffee, animal hides.
Imports Food, fuel, manufactures.
LAND
Description Eastern Africa, landlocked. **Area**
446,953 mi² (1,157,603 km²). **Highest point** Ras
Dashen Mtn., 15,158 ft (4,620 m). **Lowest point**
Asālē, -410 ft (-125 m).

People. Ethiopia is ethnically, linguistically, and reli-
giously diverse, but the Oromo, Amhara, and Tigre predominate. The Oromo include agricultural Muslims,
Christians, and nomadic herders with traditional religions. Mainly Christian and agricultural, the Amhara
have dominated the country politically. The official language is Amharic; Arabic and indigenous languages
are also spoken. Ethiopia's boundaries encompass
over forty ethnic groups.

Economy and the Land. In addition to problems caused
by political instability, drought has plagued Ethiopia's
agricultural economy. Existing problems of soil erosion and deforestation resulted in disaster in 1982 when
planting-season rains failed to fall in much of the country. The consequences of drought are especially
severe in the north and west. A grain shortfall in
1993 was predicted to produce widespread famine.
Subsistence farming remains a major activity, and much
arable land is uncultivated. Mines produce gold, copper, and platinum, and there is potential for expansion.
A central plateau is split diagonally by the Great Rift
Valley, with lowlands on the west and plains in the southeast. The climate is temperate on the plateau and hot
in the lowlands.

History and Politics. Ethiopia's history is one of
the oldest in the world. Its ethnic patterns were established by indigenous Cushites and Semite settlers, who
probably arrived from Arabia about 3,000 years ago.
Christianity was introduced in the early fourth century.
During the 1800s modern Ethiopia began to develop
under Emperor Menelik II. Ras Tafari Makonnen
became emperor in 1930, taking the name Haile
Selassie. Italians invaded in the 1930s and occupied
the country until 1941, when Selassie returned to the
throne. Discontent with the feudal society increased
until Selassie was ousted by the military in 1974. Reform
programs and the change in leadership did little to ease
political tensions, which sometimes erupted in governmental and civilian violence. Government troops
continued their battle with separatists in Eritrea, a former Italian colony and autonomous province incorporated into Ethiopia in 1962. Since the 1980s, widespread famine and drought aggravated political
problems. Civil war hampered worldwide relief efforts.
Over 250,000 people died in the war which ended in
1991 when the country's Marxist regime fell to Eritrean
and Tigrean rebels. Eritrea gained full independence
in 1993, leaving Ethiopia a landlocked country. A new
constitution adopted in December 1994 establishes
a federal system of government. The country's first
multiparty election was held in May 1995. ∎

FAEROE ISLANDS See DENMARK.

FALKLAND ISLANDS

Official name Colony of the Falkland Islands
PEOPLE
Population 2,100. **Density** 0.2/mi² (0.2/km²).
Urban 59%. **Capital** Stanley, East Falkland I.,
1,557. **Ethnic groups** British descent. **Languages**
English. **Religions** Anglican, Roman Catholic,
United Free Church.
POLITICS
Government Dependent territory (U.K.). **Parties**.
Suffrage Universal, over 18. **Memberships** None.
Subdivisions None.
ECONOMY
Monetary unit Pound. **Trade partners** Exports:
U.K., Netherlands, Japan. Imports: U.K.,
Netherlands Antilles, Japan. **Exports** Wool, animal
hides. **Imports** Food, clothing, fuel, machinery.
LAND
Description South Atlantic islands (east of
Argentina). **Area** 4,700 mi² (12,173 km²). **Highest**

point Mt. Usborne, 2,312 ft (705 m). **Lowest point** Sea level.

People. Most Falkland Island inhabitants are of British descent, an ancestry reflected in their official language, English, and majority Anglican religion.

Economy and the Land. Sheep raising is the main activity, supplemented by fishing. In 1982 Britain funded the Falkland Islands Development Corporation, which began operation in 1984. Situated about 300 miles (482 km) east of southern Argentina, East and West Falkland compose the main and largest islands. Numerous small islands are also part of the Falklands. The climate is cool, damp, and windy.

History and Politics. Although the British sighted the islands in 1592, the French established the first settlement in 1764, on East Falkland. The British settled on West Falkland the next year. Spain, which ruled the Argentina territories to the west, purchased the French area and drove out the British in 1770. When Argentina gained independence from Spain in 1816, it claimed Spain's right to the islands. Britain reasserted its rule over the islands in the 1830s. The Falklands became a British colony in 1892, with dependencies annexed in 1908. Continued Argentine claim resulted in a 1982 Argentine invasion and occupation. The British won the subsequent battle and continue to govern the Falklands. The dependencies of South Georgia and the South Sandwich Islands became a separate British colony in 1985. ■

FIJI

Official name Republic of Fiji

PEOPLE
Population 775,000. **Density** 110/mi^2 (42/km^2). **Urban** 39%. **Capital** Suva, Viti Levu I., 69,665. **Ethnic groups** Fijian 49%, Indian 46%. **Languages** English, Fijian, Hindustani. **Religions** Methodist and other Christian 52%, Hindu 38%, Muslim 8%. **Life expectancy** 74 female, 70 male. **Literacy** 86%.
POLITICS
Government Republic. **Parties** Alliance, Labor, National Federation. **Suffrage** None. **Memberships** UN. **Subdivisions** 4 divisions.
ECONOMY
GDP $3,000,000,000. **Per capita** $3,979. **Monetary unit** Dollar. **Trade partners** Exports: U.K., Malaysia, New Zealand. Imports: Australia, New Zealand, Japan, Singapore. **Exports** Sugar, gold, clothing, copra, fish, lumber. **Imports**

Machinery and transportation equipment, food, petroleum products.
LAND
Description South Pacific islands. **Area** 7,056 mi^2 (18,274 km^2). **Highest point** Tomanivi (Victoria), 4,341 ft (1,323 m). **Lowest point** Sea level.

People. Almost half of Fiji's population is descended from laborers brought from British India between 1879 and 1916. Most Indians are Hindu, but a Muslim minority also exists. Native Fijians are of Melanesian and Polynesian heritage, and most are Christian. English is the official language, a result of British rule; but Indians speak Hindustani, and the main Fijian dialect is Bauan. Tensions between the two groups occasionally arise because plantation owners, who are mainly Indian, must often lease their land from Fijians, the major landowners. About a hundred of the several hundred islands are inhabited.

Economy and the Land. The traditional sugar cane crop continues as the basis of Fiji's economy, and agricultural diversification is a current goal. Tourism is another economic contributor, and expansion of forestry is planned. Terrain varies from island to island and is characterized by mountains, valleys, rain forests, and fertile plains. The tropical islands are cooled by ocean breezes.

History and Politics. Little is known of Fiji's history prior to the arrival of Europeans. Melanesians probably migrated from Indonesia, followed by Polynesian settlers in the second century. After a Dutch navigator sighted Fiji in 1643, Captain James Cook of Britain visited the island in the eighteenth century. The nineteenth century saw the arrival of European missionaries, traders, whalers, and several native wars. In 1874 tribal chiefs ceded Fiji to the British, who established sugar plantations and brought indentured Indian laborers. The country became independent in 1970. Fiji was ejected from the British Commonwealth in 1987 after declaring itself a republic and limiting participation by Indians in the government. A new constitution in 1990 institutionalized the domination of ethnic Fijians. ■

FINLAND

Official name Republic of Finland
PEOPLE
Population 5,098,000. **Density** 39/mi^2 (15/km^2). **Urban** 60%. **Capital** Helsinki, 501,514. **Ethnic groups** Finnish (mixed Scandinavian and Baltic), Swedish, Lappic, Gypsy, Tatar. **Languages** Finnish, Swedish, Lapp, Russian. **Religions** Jehovah's Witness, Free Church, Adventist, Confessional Lutheran. **Life expectancy** 80 female, 72 male. **Literacy** 100%.
POLITICS
Government Republic. **Parties** Center, Leftist Alliance, National Coalition, Social Democratic, others. **Suffrage** Universal, over 18. **Memberships** EU, NATO, OECD, UN. **Subdivisions** 12 provinces.
ECONOMY

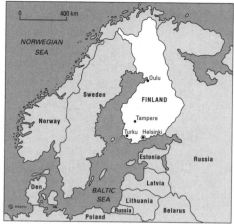

GDP $81,100,000,000. **Per capita** $15,983.
Monetary unit Markkaa. **Trade partners** Exports:
Former Soviet republics, Sweden, Germany.
Imports: Germany, Sweden, former Soviet
republics. **Exports** Lumber, paper and pulp, ships,
machinery, clothing and footwear. **Imports** Food,
petroleum, chemicals, transportation equipment,
iron and steel.

LAND

Description Northern Europe. **Area** 130,559 mi²
(338,145 km²). **Highest point** Haltiatunturi, 4,357
ft (1,328 m). **Lowest point** Sea level.

People. The mainly Finnish population includes
minorities of Swedes—a result of past Swedish
rule—and indigenous Lapps. As part of northern
Finland lies within the Arctic Circle, population is concentrated in the south. Finland's rich cultural tradition has contributed much to the arts. Its highly
developed social welfare programs provide free
education through the university level, as well as national health insurance.

Economy and the Land. Much of Finland's economy is based on its rich forests, which support
trade and manufacturing activities. The steel industry is also important. Agriculture focuses on dairy farming and livestock raising; hence many fruits and
vegetables must be imported. Coastal islands and
lowlands, a central lake region, and northern hills mark
Finland's scenic terrain. Summers in the south and
central regions are warm, and winters long and
cold. Northern Finland—located in the "Land of the
Midnight Sun"—has periods of uninterrupted daylight
in the summer and darkness in the winter.

History and Politics. The indigenous nomadic
Lapps migrated north in the first century when the
Finns arrived, probably from west-central Russia. A
Russian-Swedish struggle for control of the area ended
with Swedish rule in the 1100s. Finland was united
with Denmark from the fourteenth through the sixteenth centuries. Russia and Sweden fought several
wars for control of the country. In 1809 Finland
became an autonomous grand duchy within the
Russian Empire. After the Russian czar was overthrown in the 1917 Bolshevik Revolution, the new
Russian government recognized Finland's declaration

of independence. During World War II, Finland
fought against the Soviets and, by the peace treaty
signed in 1947, lost a portion of its land to the
Soviet Union. During the postwar years, Finland and
the Soviet Union developed strong economic ties that
resulted in prosperity for Finland. The dissolution of
the Soviet Union and a worldwide recession have
threatened its economic stability.   ■

FRANCE

Official name French Republic

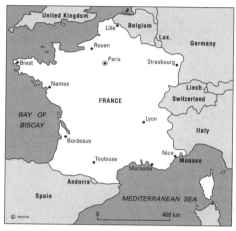

PEOPLE

Population 58,010,000. **Density** 275/mi²
(106/km²). **Urban** 73%. **Capital** Paris, 2,152,423.
Ethnic groups French (mixed Celtic, Latin, and
Teutonic). **Languages** French. **Religions** Roman
Catholic 90%, Protestant 2%, Jewish 1%, Muslim
1%. **Life expectancy** 81 female, 73 male.
Literacy 99%.

POLITICS

Government Republic. **Parties** Left Radical
Movement, Rally for the Republic, Socialist, Union
for Democracy, others. **Suffrage** Universal, over
18. **Memberships** EU, NATO, OECD, UN.
Subdivisions 96 departments.

ECONOMY

GDP $1,050,000,000,000. **Per capita** $18,239.
Monetary unit Franc. **Trade partners** Germany,
Italy, Belgium. **Exports** Machinery and transporta-
tion equipment, chemicals, food. **Imports**
Petroleum, machinery, agricultural products,
chemicals, iron and steel.

LAND

Description Western Europe. **Area** 211,208 mi²
(547,026 km²). **Highest point** Mt. Blanc, (Monte
Bianco), 15,771 ft (4,807 m). **Lowest point** Lac de
Cazaux et de Sanguinet, -10 ft (-3 m).
*The above information excludes French overseas
departments.*

People. Many centuries ago, Celtic and Teutonic tribes

and Latins established France's current ethnic patterns. The French language developed from the Latin of invading Romans but includes Celtic and Germanic influences as well. Language and customs vary somewhat from region to region, but most people who speak dialects also speak French. France has long contributed to learning and the arts, and Paris is a world cultural center. In addition to mainland divisions, the country has overseas departments and territories.

Economy and the Land. The French economy is highly developed. The nation is a leader in agriculture and industry; its problems of inflation and unemployment are common to other modern countries. Soils in the north and northeast are especially productive, and grapes are grown in the south. Minerals include iron ore and bauxite. Industry is diversified, centered in the Paris manufacturing area, and tourism is important. About two-thirds of the country is flat to rolling, and about one-third is mountainous, including the Pyrenees in the South and the Alps in the east. In the west and north, winters are cool and summers mild. Climate varies with altitude. The southern coast has a Mediterranean climate with hot summers and mild winters.

History and Politics. In ancient times Celtic tribes inhabited the area that encompasses present-day France. The Romans, who called the region Gaul, began to invade about 200 B.C., and by the 50s B.C. the entire region had come under Roman rule. Northern Germanic tribes—including the Franks, Visigoths, and Burgundians—spread throughout the region as Roman control weakened. The Franks defeated the Romans in A.D. 486. In the 800s Charlemagne greatly expanded Frankish-controlled territory, which was subsequently divided into three kingdoms. The western kingdom and part of the central kingdom included modern France. In 987 the Capetian dynasty began when Hugh Capet came to the throne, an event which is often considered the start of the French nation. During subsequent centuries, the power of the kings increased and France became a leading world power. Ambitious projects, such as the palace built by Louis XIV at Versailles, and several military campaigns, resulted in financial difficulties. The failing economy and divisions between rich and poor led to the French Revolution in 1789 and the First French Republic in 1792. Napoleon Bonaparte, who had gained prominence during the revolution, overthrew the government in 1799 and established the First Empire, which ended in 1815 with his defeat at Waterloo in Belgium. The subsequent monarchy resulted in discontent, and an 1848 revolution established the Second French Republic with an elected president, who in turn proclaimed himself emperor and set up the Second Empire in 1852. Following a war with Prussia in 1870, the emperor was ousted, and the Third Republic began. This republic repulsed Germany's invasion in World War I but ended in 1940 when invading Germans defeated the French. By 1942 the Nazis had control of the entire country. The Allies liberated France in 1944, and General Charles de Gaulle headed a provisional government until 1946, when the Fourth Republic was established. Colonial revolts in Africa and French Indochina took their toll on the economy during the fifties. Controversy over a continuing Algerian war for independence brought de Gaulle to power once more and resulted in the Fifth Republic in 1958. Dissension and national strikes erupted during the 1960s, a result of dissatisfaction with the government, and de Gaulle resigned in 1969. In 1987 François Mitterand was reelected, giving the Socialists a plurality until 1993. Since then the country has moved steadily to the right. Conservative President Jacques Chirac took office in 1995, replacing the ailing Mitterand. ∎

Places and Possessions of FRANCE

Entity	Status	Area	Population	Capital/Population
Corsica (Mediterranean island)	Part of France	3,367 mi^2 (8,720 km^2)	256,000	None
French Guiana (Northeastern South America)	Overseas department	35,135 mi^2 (91,000 km^2)	138,000	Cayenne, 38,091
French Polynesia (South Pacific islands)	Overseas territory	1,359 mi^2 (3,521 km^2)	217,000	Papeete, 23,555
Guadeloupe (Caribbean islands)	Overseas department	687 mi^2 (1,780 km^2)	432,000	Basse-Terre, 13,656
Kerguelen Islands (Indian Ocean)	Territory	2,700 mi^2 (6,993 km^2)	100	None
Martinique (Caribbean island)	Overseas department	425 mi^2 (1,100 km^2)	384,000	Fort-de-France, 99,844
Mayotte (Southeastern African islands)	Territorial collectivity	144 mi^2 (374 km^2)	95,000	Mamoutzou, 5,865
New Caledonia (South Pacific islands)	Overseas territory	7,358 mi^2 (19,058 km^2)	183,000	Nouméa, 65,110
Reunion (Indian Ocean island)	Overseas department	969 mi^2 (2,510 km^2)	660,000	Saint-Denis, 84,400
St. Pierre and Miquelon (North Atlantic islands; south of Newfoundland)	Territorial collectivity	93 mi^2 (242 km^2)	6,700	Saint-Pierre, 5,371
Wallis and Futuna (South Pacific islands)	Overseas territory	98 mi^2 (255 km^2)	14,000	Mata-Utu, 815

FRENCH GUIANA

Official name Department of Guiana
PEOPLE
Population 138,000. **Density** 3.9/mi² (1.5/km²).
Urban 75%. **Capital** Cayenne, 38,091. **Ethnic groups** Black or mulatto 66%; white 12%; East Indian, Chinese, and Amerindian 12%.
Languages French. **Religions** Roman Catholic.
Life expectancy 78 female, 72 male. **Literacy** 82%.
POLITICS
Government Overseas department (France).
Parties Democratic Action, Rally for the Republic, Socialist, Union for French Democracy. **Suffrage** Universal, over 18. **Memberships** None.
Subdivisions 2 arrondissements.
ECONOMY
GDP $421,000,000. **Per capita** $5,012. **Monetary unit** French franc. **Trade partners** Exports: France, Guadeloupe, Spain. Imports: France, Trinidad and Tobago, Germany. **Exports** Shrimp, timber, rum, rosewood essence. **Imports** Food, manufactures, petroleum.
LAND
Description Northeastern South America. **Area** 35,135 mi² (91,000 km²). **Highest point** Unnamed, 2,723 ft (830 m). **Lowest point** Sea level.

People. French Guiana has a majority population of black descendants of African slaves and people of mixed African-European ancestry. Population is concentrated in the more accessible coastal area, but the interior wilderness is home to minority Indians and the descendants of slaves who fled to pursue traditional African lifestyles. French is the predominant language, but a French-English creole is also spoken. Two Indo-Chinese refugee settlements were established in 1977 and 1979.

Economy and the Land. Shrimp production and a growing timber industry are French Guiana's economic mainstays. The land remains largely undeveloped, however, and reliance on French aid continues.

Agriculture is limited by wilderness, but mineral deposits offer potential for mining. The fertile coastal plains of the north give way to hills and mountains along the Brazilian border. Rain forests cover much of the landscape, which features a tropical climate.

History and Politics. Indigenous Indians and a hot climate defeated France's attempt at settlement in the early 1600s. The first permanent French settlement was established in 1634, and the area became a French colony in 1667. For almost one hundred years, beginning in the 1850s, penal colonies such as Devils Island brought an influx of European prisoners. The region became a French overseas department in 1946. A minority nationalist group strives for greater autonomy. ∎

FRENCH POLYNESIA

Official name Territory of French Polynesia
PEOPLE
Population 217,000. **Density** 160/mi² (62/km²).
Urban 65%. **Capital** Papeete, Tahiti I., 23,555.
Ethnic groups Polynesian 78%, Chinese 12%, French descent 6%. **Languages** French, Tahitian.
Religions Evangelical and other Protestant 54%, Roman Catholic 30%. **Life expectancy** 73 female, 68 male. **Literacy** 98%.
POLITICS
Government Overseas territory (France). **Parties** Amuitahiraa Mo Porinesia, Ia Mana, Pupu Here Ai'a, Tahoeraa Huiraatira. **Suffrage** Universal, over 18. **Memberships** None. **Subdivisions** 5 circumscriptions.
ECONOMY
GDP $1,500,000,000. **Per capita** $7,212.
Monetary unit CFP franc. **Trade partners** Exports: France, Japan, U.S. Imports: France, U.S., Greece. **Exports** Coconut products, mother-of-pearl, vanilla, shark meat. **Imports** Fuel, food, machinery.
LAND
Description South Pacific islands. **Area** 1,359 mi² (3,521 km²). **Highest point** Mont Orohena, 7,352 ft (2,241 m). **Lowest point** Sea level.

People. Most inhabitants are Polynesian, with minorities including Chinese and French. More than one hundred islands compose the five archipelagoes, and population and commercial activity is concentrated in Papeete on Tahiti. Although per capita income is relatively high, wealth is not equally distributed. Emigration from the poorer islands to Tahiti is common. Polynesia's reputation as a tropical paradise has attracted European and American writers and artists, including French painter Paul Gauguin.

Economy and the Land. The islands' economy is based on natural resources; coconut, mother-of-pearl, and tourism contribute. This South Pacific territory, located south of the equator and midway between South America and Australia, is spread over roughly 1.5 million square miles (3.9 million square km) and is made up of the Marquesas Islands, the Society Islands, the Tuamotu Archipelago, the Gambier Islands, and the Austral Islands. The

Marquesas, known for their beauty, form the north-ernmost group. The Society Islands, southwest of the Marquesas, include Tahiti and Bora-Bora, both pop-ular tourist spots. The Tuamoto Archipelago lies south of the Marquesas and east of the Society Islands, the Gambier Islands are situated at the southern tip of the Tuamotu group, and the Austral Islands lie to the southwest. The region includes both volcanic and coral islands, and the climate is tropi-cal, with a rainy season extending from November to April.

History and Politics. The original settlers prob-ably came from Micronesia and Melanesia in the east. Europeans began arriving around the sixteenth century. By the late 1700s they had reached the five major island groups, and visitors to the area included mutineers from the British vessel Bounty By the 1880s the islands had come under French rule, although they did not become an overseas ter-ritory until 1946. The country has since moved toward internal autonomy with discussion of eventual independence. ∎

GABON

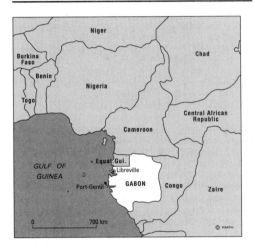

Official name Gabonese Republic
PEOPLE
Population 1,035,000. **Density** 10/mi² (3.9/km²).
Urban 46%. **Capital** Libreville, 235,700. **Ethnic groups** Fang, Eshira, Bapounou, Bateke.
Languages French, Fang, indigenous. **Religions** Roman Catholic and other Christian 55-75%, Muslim. **Life expectancy** 55 female, 52 male.
Literacy 61%.
POLITICS
Government Republic. **Parties** Democratic, National Recovery Movement-Lumberjacks, Party for Progress. **Suffrage** Universal, over 21.
Memberships OAU, OPEC, UN. **Subdivisions** 9 provinces.
ECONOMY
GDP $5,400,000,000. **Per capita** $4,843.

Monetary unit CFA franc. **Trade partners** Exports: France, U.S., Spain. Imports: France, U.S., Japan. **Exports** Petroleum, manganese, wood, uranium. **Imports** Food, chemicals, petrole-um, construction materials, manufactures.
LAND
Description Central Africa. **Area** 103,347 mi² (267,667 km²). **Highest point** Unnamed, 3,360 ft (1,024 m). **Lowest point** Sea level.

People. Of Gabon's more than forty ethnic groups, the Fang are a majority and inhabit the area north of the Ogooué River. Other major groups include the Eshira, Bapounou, and Bateke. The French, who col-onized the area, compose a larger group today than during colonial times. Each of the groups has its own distinct language and culture, but French remains the official language.

Economy and the Land. Gabon is located astride the equator, and its many resources include petro-leum, manganese, uranium, and dense rain forests. The most important activities are oil production, forestry, and mining. The economy depends great-ly on foreign investment and imported labor, how-ever, and many native Gabonese continue as sub-sistence farmers. While the labor shortage hinders economic development, the country has a high per capita income. The terrain is marked by a coastal plain, inland forested hills, and savanna in the east and south. The climate is hot and humid.

History and Politics. First inhabited by Pygmies, Gabon was the site of migrations by numerous Bantu peoples during its early history. The thick rain forests isolated the migrant groups from one anoth-er and thus preserved their individual cultures. The Portuguese arrived in the fifteenth century, followed by the Dutch, British, and French in the 1700s. The slave and ivory trades flourished, and the Fang, drawn by the prosperity, migrated to the coast in the 1800s. A group of freed slaves found-ed Libreville, which later became the capital. By 1885 France had gained control of the area, and in 1910 it was united with present-day Chad, the Congo, and the Central African Republic as French Equatorial Africa. Gabon became independent in 1960, and in 1964 French assistance thwarted a military takeover. After anti-government protests in 1990, opposi-tion parties were legalized. ∎

GALAPAGOS ISLANDS
See ECUADOR.

GAMBIA

Official name Republic of the Gambia
PEOPLE
Population 1,082,000. **Density** 262/mi² (101/km²). **Urban** 23%. **Capital** Banjul, 44,188.
Ethnic groups Malinke 42%, Fulani 18%, Wolof 16%, Jola 10%, Serahuli 9%. **Languages** English, Malinke, Wolof, Fula, indigenous.

Religions Muslim 90%, Christian 9%, tribal religionist 1%. **Life expectancy** 47 female, 43 male. **Literacy** 27%.
POLITICS
Government Provisional military government.
Parties National Convention, People's, People's Progressive. **Suffrage** Universal, over 21.
Memberships CW, OAU, UN. **Subdivisions** 5 divisions, 1 city.
ECONOMY
GDP $740,000,000. **Per capita** $808. **Monetary unit** Dalasi. **Trade partners** Exports: Japan, European countries, African countries. Imports: European countries, Asian countries. **Exports** Peanuts, fish, cotton, palm kernels. **Imports** Food, manufactures, raw materials, fuel.
LAND
Description Western Africa. **Area** 4,127 mi^2 (10,689 km^2). **Highest point** Unnamed, 174 ft (53 m). **Lowest point** Sea level.

People. Gambia's population includes the Mandingo, or Malinke; Fulani; Wolof; Jola; and Serahuli. Most people are Muslim, and language differs from group to group, although the official language is English. Gambians are mainly rural farmers, and literacy is low, with educational opportunities focused in the Banjul area. The population's size varies with the arrival and departure of seasonal Senegalese farm laborers.

Economy and the Land. Gambia's economy relies on peanut production, and crop diversification is a current goal. Subsistence crops include rice, and the government hopes increased rice production will decrease dependence on imports and foreign aid. Fishing and tourism have expanded in the past years. In addition, the Gambia River, which provides a route to the African interior, offers potential for an increased role in trade. Dense mangrove swamps border the river, giving way to flat ground that floods in the rainy season. Behind this lie sand hills and plateaus. Low-lying Gambia, with its subtropical climate, is virtually an enclave within Senegal.

History and Politics. From the thirteenth to the fifteenth centuries the flourishing Mali Empire included the Gambia area. The Portuguese arrived in the fifteenth century, established slave trading posts, and sold trade rights to Britain in 1588. During the seventeenth and eighteenth centuries France and Britain competed for control of the river trade. By the late 1800s the Banjul area had become a British colony and the interior a British protectorate. Gambia achieved independence as a monarchy in 1965 and became a republic in 1970. Many years of electoral democracy were interrupted by a bloodless coup in July 1994. The new regime promised reforms, including a new constitution, followed by free elections. ∎

GEORGIA

Official name Republic of Georgia
PEOPLE
Population 5,704,000. **Density** 212/mi^2 (82/km^2). **Urban** 56%. **Capital** Tbilisi, 1,279,000. **Ethnic groups** Georgian 70%, Armenian 8%, Russian 6%, Azeri 6%, Ossetian 3%, Abkhaz 2%.
Languages Georgian, Russian, Armenian, Azeri. **Religions** Georgian Orthodox 65%, Muslim 11%, Russian Orthodox 10%. **Life expectancy** 76 female, 69 male. **Literacy** 99%.
POLITICS
Government Republic. **Parties** Round Table-Free Georgia, others. **Suffrage** Universal, over 18.
Memberships CIS, NATO, UN. **Subdivisions** 2 republics.
ECONOMY
GDP $7,800,000,000. **Per capita** $1,148. **Monetary unit** Coupon. **Trade partners** Former Soviet republics. **Exports** Fruit, tea, machinery, metals, textiles. **Imports** Machinery, fuel, transportation equipment, textiles.
LAND
Description Southwestern Asia. **Area** 26,911 mi^2 (69,700 km^2). **Highest point** Mt. Shkhara, 16,627 ft (5,068 m). **Lowest point** Sea level.

People. Georgians are the descendants of the original inhabitants of the Caucasus region, and are proud of their ancient culture and language. Georgians have been Christians since the fourth century, and are world renowned for their many important contributions to the arts. Georgia is also home to Armenian, Russian, Abkhazian, and Ossetian minorities.

Economy and the Land. Despite its small size, Georgia has a variety of climates and terrains. Most of Georgia is mountainous or forested, but there are also fertile plains and valleys that are highly suitable for agriculture. Vineyards and orchards are scattered throughout the country. The area on the shores of the Black Sea is subtropical and is used for growing tea and citrus fruit. Georgia also has a well-developed industrial base as a result of its enormous hydroelectric power resources. The country has abundant mineral deposits, including coal and manganese. Georgia also has an active tourism industry that has been recently weakened by political instability.

History and Politics. Civilization has flourished in the Georgian region since 3000 B.C. The country's great wealth attracted a variety of invaders, including the Roman, Byzantine, and Persian empires. Arabs invaded the region in the seventh century. The early thirteenth century marked a high point in Georgia's cultural influence throughout the region, but this era was brought to a sudden end by the invasion of the Mongols. The country was later divided between the Turks and the Persians before it was annexed by Russia in 1801. Georgia, the birthplace of Joseph Stalin, played an important role in the Russian revolution of 1917. After the revolution, Georgia declared its independence, but Soviet troops invaded the country and forced its surrender in 1921. Resistance continued until great purges in the late 1930s eliminated Georgia's enemies of communism. After Soviet troops attacked Georgian demonstrators with poison gas in 1990, Georgia declared its independence in April 1991. It achieved full independence after the Soviet Union fell the following December, but freedom did not bring peace. Fighting immediately resumed as pro-democracy elements battled to force the resignation of the country's first-elected president, the controversial Zviad Gamsakhurdia. In 1992 the former Soviet foreign minister Eduard Shevardnadze was elected head of state. Georgia has been troubled by secessionist wars ignited by ethnic minorities in the Georgian territory of Abkhazia. Russia aided the government after Georgia agreed to join the Commonwealth of Independent States in 1994. ∎

GERMANY

Official name Federal Republic of Germany
PEOPLE
Population 81,710,000. **Density** 593/mi² (227/km²). **Urban** 85%. **Capital** Berlin (designated), 3,433,695; Bonn (de facto), 292,234. **Ethnic groups** German (Teutonic) 95%, Turkish 2%.
Languages German. **Religions** Evangelical and other Protestant 45%, Roman Catholic 37%. **Life expectancy** 79 female, 73 male. **Literacy** 99%.
POLITICS
Government Republic. **Parties** Christian Democratic Union, Christian Social Union, Free Democratic, Social Democratic, others. **Suffrage** Universal, over 18. **Memberships** EU, NATO,

OECD, UN. **Subdivisions** 16 states.
ECONOMY
GDP $1,331,000,000,000. **Per capita** $16,516.
Monetary unit Mark. **Trade partners** Exports: France, Italy, Netherlands, U.K. Imports: France, Netherlands, Italy, Belgium. **Exports** Machinery, chemicals, transportation equipment, iron and steel. **Imports** Manufactures, agricultural products, raw materials, fuel.
LAND
Description Northern Europe. **Area** 137,822 mi² (356,955 km²). **Highest point** Zugspitze, 9,718 ft (2,962 m). **Lowest point** Freepsum Lake, -7 ft (-2 m).

People. Germany has a homogeneous, German-speaking population with a very small Turkish minority. Roman Catholics, Evangelicals, and other Protestants are the largest religious groups. Germans are well-educated and boast a rich cultural heritage of achievements in music, literature, philosophy, and science. Germany has the largest population of any European nation, excluding Russia.

Economy and the Land. Despite the devastating effects of World War II and Germany's forty-five year division into two countries, the country has one of the world's strongest economies. Industry is the basis of its prosperity, with mining, manufacturing, construction, and utilities as important contributors. The Ruhr district, which is the nation's most important industrial region, is located near the Rhine River in west-central Germany and includes cities such as Essen and Dortmund. Agriculture remains important in the southern and central regions. Germany's terrain varies from northern plains to central uplands and hills that rise to the southern Bavarian Alps. A mild climate is tempered by the sea in the north; in the south the winters are colder because of the Alps.

History and Politics. In ancient times Germanic tribes overcame Celtic inhabitants in the area of Germany and established a northern stronghold against Roman expansion of Gaul. As the Roman Empire weakened, the Germanic peoples invaded, deposing the Roman governor of Gaul in the fifth century A.D. The Franks composed the strongest tribe, and in the ninth century Frankish-controlled territory was expanded and united under Charlemagne. Unity did not last, however, and Germany remained a disjointed territory of warring feudal states, duchies, and independent cities. The Reformation, a movement led by German monk Martin Luther, began in 1517 and evolved into the Protestant branch of Christianity. The rise of Prussian power and growing nationalism eventually united the German states into the German Empire in 1871, and Prussian chancellor Otto von Bismarck installed Prussian King Wilhelm I as emperor. In a few short years, Germany rose to become Europe's foremost industrial and military power. In 1914 Germany allied with Austria; their subsequent invasions of France and Russia led to World War I. Hardships imposed by the victors against Germany led to instability and economic collapse. Promising prosperity, Adolf Hitler and his National Socialists, or Nazi, party rose to power in 1933. Hitler's ruthless nationalist policies included a genocidal program to eliminate Jews and many other peoples, and his ambitions to conquer all of Europe led to World War II. The Allied Forces defeated Germany in 1945 only after enormous casualties had been inflicted on both sides. The United States, Britain, the Soviet Union, and France subsequently divided Germany into four zones of occupation. The eastern, Soviet-occupied zone became a Communist country called the German Democratic Republic, or East Germany. The three remaining zones of Germany were combined to form the capitalist Federal Republic of Germany, or West Germany. Berlin, not included in occupation zones, was divided between the east and west. The Berlin Wall became a symbol of the cold war between the United States and the Soviet Union. In the late 1980s the Soviet Union began to loosen its grip on its satellite nations, and in 1989 East Germans began a mass exodus to West Germany. In October 1990 East Germany was officially absorbed into West Germany. Elation over reunification has been followed by unforeseen economic problems and rising political violence. ∎

GHANA

Official name Republic of Ghana

PEOPLE
Population 17,210,000. **Density** 187/mi² (72/km²). **Urban** 34%. **Capital** Accra, 949,113. **Ethnic groups** Akan 44%, Moshi-Dagomba 16%, Ewe 13%, Ga 8%. **Languages** English, Akan and other indigenous. **Religions** Tribal religionist 38%, Muslim 30%, Christian 24%. **Life expectancy** 58 female, 54 male. **Literacy** 60%.
POLITICS
Government Republic. **Parties** None. **Suffrage** Universal, over 18. **Memberships** CW, OAU, UN. **Subdivisions** 10 regions.
ECONOMY
GDP $25,000,000,000. **Per capita** $1,520. **Monetary unit** Cedi. **Trade partners** Exports: Switzerland, U.S. Imports: Nigeria, U.S., Germany. **Exports** Cocoa, gold, timber, tuna, bauxite, aluminum. **Imports** Petroleum, manufactures, food, machinery.
LAND
Description Western Africa. **Area** 92,098 mi² (238,533 km²). **Highest point** Afadjoto, 2,905 ft (885 m). **Lowest point** Sea level.

People. Nearly all Ghanaians are black Africans. The Akan, the majority group, are further divided into the Fanti, who live mainly along the coast, and the Ashanti, who inhabit the forests north of the coast. The Ewe and Ga live in the south and southeast. Other groups include the Guan, living on the Volta River plains, and the Moshi-Dagomba in the North. Ghana's more than fifty languages and dialects reflect this ethnic diversity, and English, the official language, is spoken by a minority. Islam and traditional African religions predominate, but a Christian minority also exists. Most people live in rural areas, and the literacy rate is low.

Economy and the Land. Agriculture is the economic base, but Ghana's natural resources are diverse. Production of cocoa, the most important export, is concentrated in the Ashanti region, a belt of tropical rain forest extending north from the coastal plain. Resources include forests and mineral deposits, and exploitation of bauxite, gold, diamonds, and manganese ore is currently underway. Ghana has enjoyed steady economic growth since the 1980s. Its coastal lowlands give way to scrub and plains, the Ashanti rain forest, and northern savanna. A dam on the Volta River has created the world's largest reservoir. The climate is tropical.

History and Politics. The ancestors of today's Ghanaians probably migrated from the northern areas of Mauritania and Mali in the thirteenth century. The Portuguese reached the shore around 1470 and called the area the Gold Coast. Many countries competed for the region, but in 1874 the Gold Coast was made a British colony. By 1901 Britain had extended its control to the inland Ashanti area, which became a colony, and the northern territories, which became a protectorate. The three regions were merged with British Togoland, a onetime German colony under British administration since 1922. In 1957 the four regions united as independent Ghana. Instability resulted, arising from a history of disunity and economic problems. The parliamentary state became a republic in 1960, and civilian rule has alternated with military governments. The leader of the 1981 military coup was elected as a civilian president in 1992 and has overseen a successful economic recovery program. ∎

GIBRALTAR

Official name Gibraltar
PEOPLE
Population 32,000. **Density** 13,913/mi² (5,333/km²). **Urban** 100%. **Capital** Gibraltar, 32,000. **Ethnic groups** Gibraltarian (mixed Italian, English, Maltese, Portuguese, and Spanish) 75%, British 14%. **Languages** English, Spanish, Italian, Portuguese, Russian. **Religions** Roman Catholic 74%, Anglican 8%, Muslim 8%, Jewish 2%, Hindu 1%. **Life expectancy** 79 female, 73 male.
POLITICS
Government Dependent territory (U.K.). **Parties** National, Social Democratic, Socialist Labor. **Suffrage** Universal, over 18. **Memberships** None. **Subdivisions** None.
ECONOMY
GNP $182,000,000. **Per capita** $5,871. **Monetary unit** Pound. **Trade partners** Exports: U.K., Morocco, Portugal. Imports: U.K., Spain, Japan. **Exports** Petroleum, manufactures. **Imports** Fuel, manufactures, food.
LAND
Description Southwestern Europe (peninsula on Spain's southern coast). **Area** 2.3 mi² (6.0 km²). **Highest point** Unnamed, 1,398 ft (426 m). **Lowest point** Sea level.

People. Occupying a narrow peninsula on Spain's southern coast, the British colony of Gibraltar has a mixed population of Italian, English, Maltese, Portuguese, and Spanish descent. A number of British residents—many of whom are military personnel—also reside here. Most are bilingual in English and Spanish.

Economy and the Land. With land unsuited for agriculture and a lack of mineral resources, Gibraltar depends mainly on the British military and tourism. Shipping-related activities and a growing service industry also provide jobs and income. Connected to Spain by an isthmus, Gibraltar consists mainly of the limestone-and-shale ridge known as the Rock of Gibraltar. The climate is mild.

History and Politics. Drawn by Gibraltar's strategic location at the Atlantic entrance to the Mediterranean Sea, Phoenicians, Carthaginians, Romans, Vandals, Visigoths, and Moors all played a role in the land's history. After nearly three hundred years under Spanish control, Gibraltar was captured by Britain in 1704, during the War of the Spanish Succession. It was officially ceded to the British in the 1713 Peace of Utrecht. In a 1967 referendum, residents voted to remain under British control. British-Spanish competition for the colony continues. ∎

GREECE

Official name Hellenic Republic
PEOPLE
Population 10,475,000. **Density** 206/mi² (79/km²). **Urban** 63%. **Capital** Athens, 748,110. **Ethnic groups** Greek 98%. **Languages** Greek, English, French. **Religions** Greek Orthodox 98%, Muslim 1%. **Life expectancy** 80 female, 75 male. **Literacy** 93%.
POLITICS
Government Republic. **Parties** New Democracy, Left Alliance, Panhellenic Socialist Movement, others. **Suffrage** Universal, over 18. **Memberships** EU, NATO, OECD, UN. **Subdivisions** 13 regions.
ECONOMY
GDP $93,200,000,000. **Per capita** $9,251. **Monetary unit** Drachma. **Trade partners** Germany, Italy, France. **Exports** Manufactures, food and beverages, fuel and lubricants. **Imports** Manufactures, machinery, food, fuels and lubricants.
LAND
Description Southeastern Europe. **Area** 50,949 mi² (131,957 km²). **Highest point** Mt. Olympus, 9,570 ft (2,917 m). **Lowest point** Sea level.

People. Greece has played a central role in European, African, and Asian cultures for thousands of years, but today its population is almost homogeneous. Native Greek inhabitants are united by a language that dates back 3,000 years and a religion that influences many aspects of everyday life. Athens, the capital, was the cultural center of an ancient civilization that produced masterpieces of art and literature and broke ground in philosophy, political thought, and science.

Economy and the Land. The economy of Greece takes its shape from terrain and location. Dominated by the sea and long a maritime trading power, Greece has one of the largest merchant fleets in the world and depends greatly on commerce. The mountainous terrain and poor soil limit agriculture, although Greece is a leading producer of lemons and olives. The service sector, including tourism, provides most of Greece's national income. Inhabitants enjoy a temperate climate, with mild, wet winters, and hot, dry summers.

History and Politics. Greece's history begins with the early Bronze Age cultures of the Minoans and the Mycenaeans. The city-state, or *polis*, began to develop around the tenth century B.C., and Athens, a democracy, and Sparta, an oligarchy, gradually emerged as Greece's leaders. The Persian Wars, in which the city-states united to repel a vastly superior army, ushered in the Golden Age of Athens, a cultural explosion in the fifth century B.C. The Parthenon, perhaps Greece's most famous building, was built at this time. Athens was defeated by Sparta in the Peloponnesian War, and by 338 B.C. Philip II of Macedon had conquered all of Greece. His son, Alexander the Great, defeated the Persians and spread Greek civilization and language all over the known world. Greece became a Roman province in 146 B.C. and part of the Byzantine Empire in A.D. 395, but its traditions had a marked influence on these empires. Absorbed into the Ottoman Empire in the 1450s, Greece had gained independence by 1830 and became a constitutional monarchy about fifteen years later. For much of the twentieth century the nation was divided between republicans and monarchists. During World War II Germany occupied Greece, and postwar instability led to a civil war, which Communist rebels eventually lost. A repressive military junta ruled Greece from 1967 until 1974, followed by a civilian government. The Greeks voted for a republic, over a monarchy, and in 1993 Socialists regained power. ∎

GREENLAND

Official name Greenland
PEOPLE
Population 57,000. **Density** 0.07/mi² (0.03/km²).
Urban 78%. **Capital** Godthåb, 12,217. **Ethnic groups** Greenlander (Inuit and native-born whites) 86%, Danish 14%. **Languages** Danish, Greenlandic, Inuit dialects. **Religions** Lutheran.

Life expectancy 71 female, 62 male.
POLITICS
Government Self-governing territory (Danish protection). **Parties** Forward (Siumut), Inuit Movement, Polar (Issittrup), Unity (Atassut). **Suffrage** Universal, over 18. **Memberships** None. **Subdivisions** 3 municipalities.
ECONOMY
GNP $500,000,000. **Per capita** $9,091. **Monetary unit** Danish krone. **Trade partners** Exports: Denmark, U.K., Germany. Imports: Denmark, Norway, U.S. **Exports** Fish, minerals. **Imports** Manufactures, machinery and transportation equipment, food, petroleum.
LAND
Description North Atlantic island. **Area** 840,004 mi² (2,175,600 km²). **Highest point** Gunnbjorn Mtn., 12,139 ft (3,700 m). **Lowest point** Sea level.

People. Most Greenlanders are native-born descendants of mixed Inuit-Danish ancestry. Lutheranism, the predominant religion, reflects Danish ties. Descended from an indigenous Arctic people, pure Inuit are a minority and usually follow traditional lifestyles. Most of the island lies within the Arctic Circle, and population is concentrated along the southern coast.

Economy and the Land. Fishing is the state's economic backbone. Despite a difficult arctic environment, mining of zinc and lead continues; but iron, coal, uranium, and molybdenum deposits remain undeveloped. The largest island in the world, Greenland is composed of an inland plateau, coastal mountains and fjords, and offshore islands. More than 80 percent of the island lies under permanent ice cap. Greenland is situated in the "Land of the Midnight Sun," and certain areas have twenty-four consecutive hours of daylight in summer and darkness in winter. The climate is cold, with warmer temperatures and more precipitation in the southwest.

History and Politics. Following early migration of Arctic Inuit, Norwegian Vikings sighted Greenland in the ninth century, and in the tenth century Erik the Red brought the first settlers from Iceland. Greenland united with Norway in the 1200s, and the two regions, along with several others, came under Danish rule in the 1300s. Denmark retained control of Greenland when Norway left the union in 1814. American troops defended the island during World War II. In 1953 the island became a province of Denmark and in 1979 it gained home rule. ∎

GRENADA

Official name Grenada
PEOPLE
Population 92,000. **Density** 692/mi² (267/km²).
Urban 15%. **Capital** St. George's, 4,439. **Ethnic groups** Black 82%, mixed 13%, East Indian 3%. **Languages** English, French. **Religions** Roman Catholic 59%, Anglican 17%, Seventh Day Adventist 6%. **Life expectancy** 73 female, 68 male. **Literacy** 98%.

POLITICS
Government
Parliamentary state.
Parties National,
National Democratic
Congress, New
National, United Labor.
Suffrage Universal,
over 18.
Memberships CW,
OAS, UN.
Subdivisions 7
parishes.
ECONOMY
GDP $250,000,000.
Per capita $2,551.
Monetary unit East
Caribbean dollar.
Trade partners
Exports: U.K.,
Netherlands, Germany. Imports: U.S., U.K.,
Trinidad and Tobago. **Exports** Nutmeg, cocoa
beans, bananas, mace, textiles. **Imports** Food,
manufactures, machinery, chemicals, fuel.
LAND
Description Caribbean island. **Area** 133 mi² (344
km²). **Highest point** Mt. St. Catherine, 2,757 ft
(840 m). **Lowest point** Sea level.

People. Grenada's culture bears the influences of former British and French rule. The most widely spoken
language is English, although a French patois is
also spoken, and the majority of the population is Roman
Catholic. Most Grenadians are black, descended
from African slaves brought to the island by the
British, but there are small East Indian and European
populations.

Economy and the Land. Rich volcanic soils and heavy
rainfall have made agriculture the chief economic activity. Also known as the Isle of Spice, Grenada is one
of the world's leading producers of nutmeg and
mace. Many tropical fruits are also raised, and the small
plots of peasant farmers dot the hilly terrain. Another
mainstay of the economy is tourism, with visitors
drawn by the beaches and tropical climate. Grenada
has little industry; high unemployment has plagued
the nation in recent years.

History and Politics. The Carib Indians resisted
European attempts to colonize Grenada for more than
100 years after Christopher Columbus discovered the
island in 1498. The French established the first settlement in 1650 and slaughtered the Caribs, but the
British finally gained control in 1783. In 1974 Grenada
achieved full independence under Prime Minister
Eric Gairy, despite widespread opposition to his policies. In 1979 foes of the regime staged a coup and
installed a Marxist government headed by Maurice
Bishop. Power struggles resulted, and a military
branch of the government seized power in 1983 and
executed Bishop, along with several of his ministers.
The United States led a subsequent invasion that
deposed the Marxists. A centrist government has ruled
since 1984 . ■

GUADELOUPE See FRANCE.

GUAM See UNITED STATES.

GUATEMALA

Official name Republic of Guatemala
PEOPLE
Population 10,420,000. **Density** 248/mi²
(96/km²). **Urban** 39%. **Capital** Guatemala,
1,057,210. **Ethnic groups** Ladino (mestizo) 56%,
Amerindian 44%. **Languages** Spanish,
Amerindian. **Religions** Roman Catholic,
Protestant, tribal religionist. **Life expectancy** 67
female, 62 male. **Literacy** 55%.
POLITICS
Government Republic. **Parties** Christian
Democratic, Democratic Party of National
Cooperation, National Centrist Union,
Revolutionary, others. **Suffrage** Universal, over
18. **Memberships** OAS, UN. **Subdivisions** 22
departments.
ECONOMY
GDP $31,300,000,000. **Per capita** $3,225.
Monetary unit Quetzal. **Trade partners** Exports:
U.S., El Salvador, Germany. Imports: U.S.,
Venezuela, Germany, Japan. **Exports** Coffee,
sugar, bananas, beef. **Imports** Fuel, machinery,
grain, fertilizer, transportation equipment.
LAND
Description Central America. **Area** 42,042 mi²
(108,889 km²). **Highest point** Volcán Tajumulco,
13,845 ft (4,220 m). **Lowest point** Sea level.

People. Guatemala's population is made up of majority ladinos and minority Indians. Ladinos include
both mestizos, those of Spanish-Indian origin, and west-
ernized Indians of Mayan descent. Classified on the

basis of culture rather than race, ladinos follow a Spanish-American lifestyle and speak Spanish. Non-ladino Indians are of Mayan descent and speak several Mayan dialects. Many are poor, uneducated, and suffer from persecution. Roman Catholicism often combines with traditional Mayan religious practice. Population is concentrated in the central highlands.

Economy and the Land. Most Guatemalans practice agriculture in some form. Indians generally operate small, unproductive subsistence farms. Export crops are mainly produced on large plantations on the fertile southern plain that borders the Pacific. Although light industry is growing, it is unable to absorb rural immigrants seeking employment in the cities. Much of the landscape is mountainous, with the Pacific plain and Caribbean lowlands bordering central highlands. Northern rain forests and grasslands are sparsely populated and largely undeveloped. The climate is tropical in low areas and temperate in the highlands.

History and Politics. Indians in the region were absorbed into the Mayan civilization that flourished in Central America by the fourth century. In 1523 the Spanish defeated the indigenous Indians and went on to establish one of the most influential colonies in Central America. Guatemala joined Costa Rica, El Salvador, Nicaragua, and Honduras in 1821 to declare independence from Spain, and the former Spanish colonies formed the Federation of Central America in 1823. Almost from the start, the federation was marked by dissension, and by 1838 it had, in effect, been dissolved. Following a series of dictatorships, social and economic reform began in 1944 and continued under two successive presidents. The government was ousted in a United States-backed 1954 coup, and military rule was established. In 1985 the country returned to a civilian government. The years since have been filled with corruption and some of the worst human rights abuses in Central America. Peace talks between the government and many dissident groups, including that of Nobel Peace Prize winner Rigoberta Menchú, are ongoing. ∎

GUERNSEY See UNITED KINGDOM.

GUINEA

Official name Republic of Guinea
PEOPLE
Population 6,469,000. **Density** 68/mi² (26/km²). **Urban** 26%. **Capital** Conakry, 800,000. **Ethnic groups** Fulani 35%, Malinke 30%, Susu 20%, others. **Languages** French, indigenous. **Religions** Muslim 85%, Christian 8%, Animist 7%. **Life expectancy** 45 female, 44 male. **Literacy** 24%.
POLITICS
Government Provisional military government.
Parties Party of Unity and Progress, Rally of the People, Union for the New Republic, others.
Suffrage Universal adult. **Memberships** OAU, UN. **Subdivisions** 33 regions.

ECONOMY
GDP $3,100,000,000. **Per capita** $406. **Monetary unit** Franc. **Trade partners** Exports: U.S., European countries, former Soviet republics. Imports: U.S., France, Brazil. **Exports** Alumina, bauxite, diamonds, coffee, pineapples, bananas, palm kernels. **Imports** Petroleum, metals, machinery and transportation equipment, food.
LAND
Description Western Africa. **Area** 94,926 mi² (245,857 km²). **Highest point** Mont Nimba, 5,748 ft (1,752 m). **Lowest point** Sea level.

People. Guinea's population is composed of several ethnic groups, with three—the Fulani, Malinke, and Susu—forming the majority. Most Guineans are rural farmers, living in hamlets, and the only true urban center is Conakry. Mortality as well as emigration rates are high. Eight languages besides French, the language of the colonial power, are taught in the schools.

Economy and the Land. Rich soil and a varied terrain suited for diverse crop production have made agriculture an important economic activity. Guinea also has vast mineral reserves, including one of the world's largest bauxite deposits. Centralized economic planning and state enterprise have characterized the republic, but Guinea now encourages private and foreign investments. The terrain is mostly flat along the coast and mountainous in the interior. The climate is tropical on the coast, hot and dry in the north and northeast, and cooler with less humidity in the highlands.

History and Politics. As part of the Ghana, Mali, and Songhai empires that flourished in West Africa between the fourth and fifteenth centuries, Guinea was a trading center for gold and slaves. The Portuguese arrived on the coast in the 1400s, and European competition for Guinean trade soon began. In the 1890s France declared the area a colony and named it French Guinea. A movement for autonomy began after World War II with a series of reforms by the French and the growth of a labor movement headed by Sékou Touré, later the nation's first president. The first of the French colonies in West Africa to attain independence, in 1958 Guinea was also the only colony to reject membership in the French Community. The country's first multiparty elections were held in December 1993 amid violence and confusion. The results were not accepted by opposition leaders and the winner, President Lansana Conte, has since resumed a military title. ∎

GUINEA-BISSAU

Official name Republic of Guinea-Bissau
PEOPLE
Population 1,111,000. **Density** 80/mi^2 (31/km^2).
Urban 20%. **Capital** Bissau, 125,000. **Ethnic groups** Balanta 30%, Fulani 20%, Manjaca 14%, Malinke 13%, Papel 7%. **Languages** Portuguese, Crioulo, indigenous. **Religions** Tribal religionist 65%, Muslim 30%, Christian 5%. **Life expectancy** 45 female, 42 male. **Literacy** 36%.
POLITICS
Government Republic. **Parties** African Party for Independence, Democratic Front, Democratic Social Front. **Suffrage** Universal, over 15.
Memberships OAU, UN. **Subdivisions** 9 regions.
ECONOMY
GDP $860,000,000. **Per capita** $211. **Monetary unit** Peso. **Trade partners** Exports: Portugal, Senegal, France. Imports: Portugal, Netherlands, Senegal. **Exports** Cashews, fish, peanuts, palm kernels. **Imports** Manufactures, food, petroleum.
LAND
Description Western Africa. **Area** 13,948 mi^2 (36,125 km^2). **Highest point** Unnamed, 860 ft (262 m). **Lowest point** Sea level.

People. Guinea-Bissau's largest ethnic group, the Balanta, mainly inhabit the coastal area. Most practice traditional beliefs, although some are Christian. Predominately Muslim peoples, the Fulani and Malinke are concentrated in the northwest. The Manjaca inhabit the northern and central coastal regions. Although the official language is Portuguese, many speak Crioulo, a creole dialect also spoken in Cape Verde.

Economy and the Land. Guinea-Bissau's economy is underdeveloped and dependent upon agriculture. Peanuts, cotton, corn, and sorghum are grown in the north, and palm-oil production is concentrated along the coast. Timber is produced primarily in the south. Fishing, especially shrimp production, has increased since 1976. Bauxite deposits have been located, and exploration for additional resources continues. Mineral exploitation is hindered by a lack of transportation routes, however. A swamp-covered coastal plain rises to an eastern savanna. The climate is tropical. The country includes the Bijagos Archipelago, which lies just off the coast.

History and Politics. The area of Guinea-Bissau was inhabited by diverse peoples prior to the arrival of the Portuguese in 1446. Ruled as a single colony with Cape Verde, the region soon developed into a base for the Portuguese slave trade. In 1879 it was separated from Cape Verde as Portuguese Guinea, and its status changed to overseas province in 1951. A movement for the independence of Guinea-Bissau and Cape Verde developed in the 1950s, and a coup in Portugal in 1974 resulted in independence the same year. Attempts to unite Guinea-Bissau and Cape Verde were unsuccessful, and a 1980 coup installed an anti-unification government. The country's first multiparty presidential elections were held in July 1994. The incumbent party retained power. ∎

GUYANA

Official name Co-operative Republic of Guyana
PEOPLE
Population 726,000. **Density** 8.7/mi^2 (3.4/km^2).
Urban 33%. **Capital** Georgetown, 78,500. **Ethnic groups** East Indian 51%, black 30%, mixed 11%, Amerindian 5%. **Languages** English, indigenous. **Religions** Anglican and other Christian 57%, Hindu 33%, Muslim 9%. **Life expectancy** 68 female, 62 male. **Literacy** 95%.
POLITICS
Government Republic. **Parties** People's National

Congress, People's Progressive, others. **Suffrage**
Universal, over 18. **Memberships** CW, OAS, UN.
Subdivisions 10 regions.
ECONOMY
GDP $1,400,000,000. **Per capita** $1,900.
Monetary unit Dollar. **Trade partners** Exports:
U.K., U.S., Trinidad and Tobago. Imports: Trinidad
and Tobago, U.S., U.K. **Exports** Bauxite, sugar,
gold, rice, shrimp, molasses, timber, rum. **Imports**
Manufactures, machinery, food, petroleum.
LAND
Description Northeastern South America. **Area**
83,000 mi^2 (214,969 km^2). **Highest point** Mt.
Roraima, 9,432 ft (2,875 m). **Lowest point** Sea
level.

People. Guyana's population includes descendants
of black African slaves and East Indian, Chinese, and
Portuguese laborers who were brought to work
sugar plantations. Amerindians, the indigenous
peoples of Guyana, are a minority. Ninety percent
of the people live along the fertile coastal plain,
where farming and manufacturing are concentrated.

Economy and the Land. Agriculture and mining compose the backbone of the Guyanese economy.
Sugar and rice continue to be important crops, and
mines produce bauxite, manganese, diamonds,
and gold. Guyana's inland forests give way to
savanna and a coastal plain. The climate is tropical.

History and Politics. First gaining European notice
in 1498 with the voyages of Christopher Columbus,
Guyana was the stage for competing colonial interests—British, French, and Dutch—until it officially
became British Guiana in 1831. Slavery was abolished several years later, causing the British to
import indentured laborers, the ancestors of today's
majority group. A constitution, adopted in 1953,
was suspended when Britain feared a Communist
victory at the polls. In the early 1960s racial tensions
erupted into riots between East Indians and blacks.
In 1966 the country gained independence, and
adopted the name Guyana. Guyana became a
republic in 1970 and has pursued socialist policies. The two main political parties continue to
reflect its ethnic divisions: the People's National
Congress (PNC) is supported by blacks, and the
People's Progressive Party (PPP) by East Indians.
A 1992 election was won by the PPP ∎

HAITI

Official name Republic of Haiti
PEOPLE
Population 7,069,000. **Density** 660/mi^2
(255/km^2). **Urban** 29%. **Capital** Port-au-Prince,
797,000. **Ethnic groups** Black 95%, mulatto and
white 5%. **Languages** Creole, French. **Religions**
Roman Catholic 80%, Baptist 10%, Pentecostal
4%. **Life expectancy** 58 female, 55 male.
Literacy 53%.
POLITICS
Government Provisional military government.
Parties Christian Democratic, Movement to Install
Democracy, National Alliance Front, Social

Christian. **Suffrage** Universal, over 18.
Memberships OAS, UN. **Subdivisions** 9 depart-
ments.
ECONOMY
GDP $5,220,000,000. **Per capita** $948. **Monetary
unit** Gourde. **Trade partners** Exports: U.S., Italy.
Imports: U.S., Canada, Japan. **Exports**
Manufactures, coffee and other food. **Imports**
Machinery and manufactures, food, petroleum,
chemicals, fats and oils.
LAND
Description Caribbean island (western
Hispaniola). **Area** 10,714 mi^2 (27,750 km^2).
Highest point Mt. La Selle, 8,773 ft (2,674 m).
Lowest point Sea level.

People. The world's oldest black republic, Haiti
has a population composed mainly of descendants
of African slaves. Most people are poor and rural.
Although French is an official language, Haitian Creole,
a combination of French and West African languages, is more widely spoken. Roman Catholicism
is the major religion. Voodooism, which blends
Christian and African beliefs, is also practiced.

Economy and the Land. Haiti's economy remains
underdeveloped. Most people rely on subsistence
farming, though productivity is hampered by high population density in productive regions. Coffee is a main
commercial crop and export. Recent growth of
light industry is partially attributable to tax exemp-
tions and low labor costs. Occupying the western
third of Hispaniola Island, Haiti has an overall
mountainous terrain and a tropical climate.

History and Politics. Christopher Columbus
reached Hispaniola in 1492, and the indigenous
Arawak Indians almost completely died out during
subsequent Spanish settlement. Most Spanish settlers had gone to seek their fortunes in other
colonies by the 1600s, and western Hispaniola
came under French control in 1697. Slave importation increased rapidly, and in less than a hundred
years black Africans far outnumbered the French.
In a 1791 revolution led by Toussaint L'Ouverture,
Jean Jacques Dessalines, and Henri Christophe, the
slaves rose against the French. By 1804 the country achieved independence from France, and the area
was renamed Haiti. In the 1820s Haitians con-

quered the eastern region of the island, now the Dominican Republic, and it remained part of Haiti until 1844. Instability increased under various dictatorships from 1843 to 1915, and United States marines occupied the country from 1915 to 1934. After a time of alternating military and civilian rule, François Duvalier came to office in 1957, declaring himself president-for-life in 1964. His rule was marked by repression, corruption, and human-rights abuses. His son, Jean-Claude, succeeded him as president-for-life in 1971. The Duvalier dictatorship ended in 1986 when Jean-Claude fled the country. Continued unrest resulted in six different governments between 1987 and 1990. There were hopes that an internationally monitored election in 1990 would bring peace and democracy. However, a coup in September 1991 forced the winner, Jean-Bertrand Aristide, into exile. International pressure and sanctions resulted in his return in 1994. ■

HONDURAS

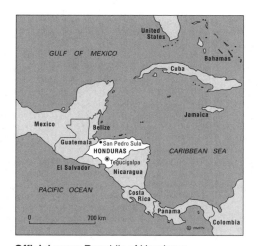

Official name Republic of Honduras
PEOPLE
Population 5,822,000. **Density** 135/mi² (52/km²).
Urban 44%. **Capital** Tegucigalpa, 576,661. **Ethnic groups** Mestizo 90%, Amerindian 7%, black 2%, white 1%. **Languages** Spanish, indigenous.
Religions Roman Catholic 97%. **Life expectancy** 68 female, 64 male. **Literacy** 73%.
POLITICS
Government Republic. **Parties** Liberal, National, others. **Suffrage** Universal, over 18.
Memberships OAS, UN. **Subdivisions** 18 departments.
ECONOMY
GDP $10,000,000,000. **Per capita** $1,936.
Monetary unit Lempira. **Trade partners** Exports: U.S., Germany, Japan. Imports: U.S., Japan, Mexico. **Exports** Bananas, coffee, shrimp, lobster, minerals, lumber. **Imports** Machinery and transportation equipment, chemicals, manufactures, fuel.

LAND
Description Central America. **Area** 43,277 mi² (112,088 km²). **Highest point** Cerro Las Minas, 9,347 ft (2,849 m). **Lowest point** Sea level.

People. Most Hondurans are mestizos—people of Spanish-Indian descent. Other groups include Indians and descendants of black Africans and Europeans. Most Indians have been assimilated into the majority culture, but a minority continues to practice a traditional Indian lifestyle. The Spanish language predominates, and English is spoken by a small population of British descent on the northern coast and Bay Islands. Poverty is an ongoing problem for the mainly rural population, and economic and educational improvements mostly affect urban inhabitants.

Economy and the Land. Honduras has an underdeveloped economy based on banana cultivation. Other activities include livestock raising, coffee production, forestry, and some mining. Honduras's terrain is mostly mountainous, with lowlands along some coastal regions. The climate varies from tropical in the lowlands to temperate in the mountains.

History and Politics. Early in its history Honduras was part of the Mayan Empire. By 1502, when Christopher Columbus arrived to claim the region for Spain, the decline of the Maya had rendered the Indians weak and unable to stave off Spanish settlement. The Spanish colonial period introduced gold and silver mines, cattle ranches, and African slaves. In 1821 Honduras, El Salvador, Nicaragua, Costa Rica, and Guatemala declared independence from Spain and, in 1823, formed the Federation of Central America. The unstable union had virtually collapsed by 1838, and the member states became independent as the federation dissolved. Instability, Guatemalan political influence, and the development of a banana economy based on United States-owned plantations marked the 1800s and early 1900s. Frequent revolutions have characterized the twentieth century, and a dictator governed from 1933 to 1948. Since the 1950s civilian governments have alternated with military coups and rule. Controversies focus on issues of poverty and land distribution. Amnesty International continues to report extensive human rights abuses. Presidential elections in 1993 brought reformers to power who promise to confront the military and to stop abuses. ■

HONG KONG

Official name Hong Kong
PEOPLE
Population 5,927,000. **Density** 14,316/mi² (5,529/km²). **Urban** 94%. **Capital** Hong Kong (Victoria), Hong Kong I., 1,250,993. **Ethnic groups** Chinese 98%. **Languages** Chinese (Cantonese), English, Putonghua. **Religions** Buddhist and Taoist 90%, Christian 10%. **Life expectancy** 80 female, 75 male. **Literacy** 77%.
POLITICS
Government Chinese territory under British administration. **Parties** Democratic Foundation, Liberal Democratic Federation, United Democrats, others. **Suffrage** Universal, over 21.

Memberships None. **Subdivisions** 4 areas.
ECONOMY
GDP $119,000,000,000. **Per capita** $21,326.
Monetary unit Dollar. **Trade partners** Exports:
China, U.S., Germany. Imports: China, Japan,
U.S. **Exports** Clothing, textiles, yarn and fabric,
footwear, electrical appliances. **Imports** Food,
transportation equipment, raw materials, manufac-
tures, petroleum.
LAND
Description Eastern Asia (islands and mainland
area on China's southeastern coast). **Area** 414 mi^2
(1,072 km^2). **Highest point** Tai Mo Mtn., 3,140 ft
(957 m). **Lowest point** Sea level.

People. Hong Kong has a majority Chinese population. Cantonese, a Chinese dialect, is spoken by
most of the people, and English and Chinese are the
official languages. Major religions are Taoism,
Christianity, and Buddhism. Hong Kong is one of the
world's most densely populated areas.

Economy and the Land. Low taxes, duty-free status, an accessible location, and an excellent natural
harbor have helped make Hong Kong an Asian
center of trade, finance, manufacturing, and transportation. Situated on the coast of China, Hong
Kong borders Guangdong province. The colony
consists of the islands of Hong Kong and Lantau, the
Kowloon Peninsula, and the New Territories, which
include a mainland area and many islands. In addition to mountains, the New Territories contain some
level areas suitable for agriculture, while the islands
are hilly. The climate is tropical, with hot, rainy
summers and cool, humid winters.

History and Politics. Inhabited since ancient
times, Hong Kong came under Chinese rule around
the third century B.C. In 1839 British opium smuggling led to the Opium War between Britain and China,
and a victorious Britain received the island of Hong
Kong in an 1842 treaty. In 1860 the British gained
control of the Kowloon Peninsula, and in 1898 the
New Territories came under British rule through a
ninety-nine-year lease with China. Hong Kong will
be returned to China in 1997 under a negotiated
agreement whereby the present economic system
will be retained for fifty years. Liberal democratic candidates defeated China-backed candidates in Hong
Kong's first direct legislative elections in 1991.
British-Chinese discussions regarding democratic
and economic freedoms under Chinese rule ended
in 1993 with no resolution. China will disband the
Hong Kong legislature when it takes over. Despite
Chinese vows to limit intervention in economic
affairs, scores of people are emigrating. ∎

HUNGARY

Official name Republic of Hungary
PEOPLE
Population 10,270,000. **Density** 286/mi^2
(110/km^2). **Urban** 64%. **Capital** Budapest,
2,016,774. **Ethnic groups** Hungarian (Magyar)
90%, Gypsy 4%, German 3%, Serb 2%.
Languages Hungarian. **Religions** Roman

Catholic 68%, Calvinist 20%, Lutheran 5%. **Life
expectancy** 74 female, 66 male. **Literacy** 99%.
POLITICS
Government Republic. **Parties** Democratic
Forum, Free Democrats, Independent
Smallholders, Workers', others. **Suffrage**
Universal, over 18. **Memberships** NATO, UN.
Subdivisions 19 counties, 1 autonomous city.
ECONOMY
GDP $57,000,000,000. **Per capita** $5,531.
Monetary unit Forint. **Trade partners** Former
Soviet republics, Germany, Austria. **Exports**
Machinery, food, manufactures, fuel. **Imports**
Machinery, fuel, manufactures, agricultural
products.
LAND
Description Eastern Europe, landlocked. **Area**
35,919 mi^2 (93,030 km^2). **Highest point** Kékes,
3,327 ft (1,014 m). **Lowest point** Along Tisza
River, 256 ft (78 m).

People. Hungary's major ethnic group and language evolved from Magyar tribes who settled the
region in the ninth century. Gypsies, Germans, and
other peoples compose minorities. Most people
are Roman Catholic and the literacy rate is high.
Growth of industry since the 1940s has caused a rural-
to-urban population shift.

Economy and the Land. Following World War II,
Hungary pursued a program of industrialization,
which is now in the process of being privatized.
Agriculture, socialized under Communist rule, will also
be returned to private ownership. Farming remains
important, with productivity aided by fertile soils
and a mild climate. Economic planning was decentralized in 1968, thus Hungary's economy differed
from that of other Soviet-bloc nations, permitting some
private enterprise. A flat plain dominates the landscape, and the lack of varied terrain results in a temperate climate throughout the country.

History and Politics. In the late 800s Magyar tribes
from the east overcame Slavic and Germanic residents and settled the area. Invading Mongols
caused much destruction in the thirteenth century.
In the early 1500s, after repeated attacks, the
Ottoman Turks dominated central Hungary. By the

late seventeenth century, the entire region had come under the rule of Austria's Hapsburgs. Hungary succeeded in obtaining equal status with Austria in 1867, and the dual monarchy of Austria-Hungary emerged. Discontent and nationalistic demands increased until 1914, when a Bosnian Serb killed the heir to the Austro-Hungarian throne. Austria-Hungary declared war on Serbia, and World War I began, resulting in both territory and population losses for Hungary. At the end of the war, in 1918, Hungary became a republic, only to revert to monarchical rule in 1919. Hungary entered World War II on the side of Germany, and Adolf Hitler set up a pro-Nazi government in Hungary in 1944. The Soviet Union invaded that same year, and a Hungarian-Allied peace treaty was signed in 1947. Coalition rule evolved into a Communist government in 1949. In 1956 discontent erupted into rebellion, a new premier declared Hungary neutral, and Soviet forces entered Budapest to quell the uprising. A new constitution, which went into effect in 1990, helped move the nation away from Communist domination. Discontent with the following years of free-market policy resulted in a heavy victory for the Worker's Party, formerly the Socialist Party, in 1994. ∎

ICELAND

Official name Republic of Iceland
PEOPLE
Population 265,000. **Density** 6.7/mi² (2.6/km²).
Urban 91%. **Capital** Reykjavík, 100,850. **Ethnic groups** Icelander (mixed Norwegian and Celtic).
Languages Icelandic. **Religions** Lutheran 96%, other Christian 3%. **Life expectancy** 81 female, 76 male. **Literacy** 100%.
POLITICS
Government Republic. **Parties** Independence, Progressive, Social Democratic, others. **Suffrage** Universal, over 18. **Memberships** NATO, OECD, UN. **Subdivisions** 8 regions.
ECONOMY
GDP $4,200,000,000. **Per capita** $16,154.

Monetary unit Krona. **Trade partners** Exports: U.K., Germany, U.S. Imports: U.S., Germany, Netherlands. **Exports** Fish, animal products, aluminum, diatomite. **Imports** Machinery and transportation equipment, petroleum, food, textiles.
LAND
Description North Atlantic island. **Area** 39,769 mi² (103,000 km²). **Highest point** Hvannadalshnúkur, 6,952 ft (2,119 m). **Lowest point** Sea level.

People. Most Icelanders are of Norwegian or Celtic ancestry, live in coastal cities, and belong to the Lutheran church. Icelandic, the predominant language, has changed little from the Old Norse of the original settlers and still resembles the language of twelfth-century Nordic sagas.

Economy and the Land. Fish, found in the island's rich coastal waters, are the main natural resource and export. Iceland has a long tradition based on fishing, but the industry has recently suffered from decreasing markets and catches. Glaciers, lakes, hot springs, volcanoes, and a lava desert limit agricultural land but provide a scenic terrain. Although the island lies just south of the Arctic Circle, the climate is moderated by the Gulf Stream. Summers are damp and cool, and winters relatively mild but windy. Proximity to the Arctic Circle puts Iceland in the "Land of the Midnight Sun," resulting in periods of twenty-four-hour daylight in June.

History and Politics. Norwegians began settlement of Iceland around the ninth century. The world's oldest parliament, the Althing, was established in Iceland in A.D. 930. Civil wars and instability during the thirteenth century led to the end of independence in 1262, when Iceland came under Norwegian rule. In the fourteenth century Norway was joined to Denmark's realm, and rule of Iceland passed to the Danes. The Althing was abolished in 1800 but reestablished in 1843. In the 1918 Act of Union, Iceland became a sovereign state but retained its union with Denmark under a common king. Germany occupied Denmark in 1940 during World War II. British troops, replaced by Americans in 1941, protected Iceland from invasion. Following a 1944 plebiscite, Iceland left its union with Denmark and became an independent republic. ∎

INDIA

Official name Republic of India
PEOPLE
Population 909,150,000. **Density** 735/mi² (284/km²). **Urban** 26%. **Capital** New Delhi, 301,297. **Ethnic groups** Indo-Aryan 72%, Dravidian 25%, Mongoloid and other 3%.
Languages English, Hindi, Telugu, Bengali, indigenous. **Religions** Hindu 80%, Muslim 11%, Christian 2%, Sikh 2%. **Life expectancy** 61 female, 60 male. **Literacy** 48%.
POLITICS
Government Republic. **Parties** Congress (I), Communist (Marxist), Janata, Janata Dal, others.
Suffrage Universal, over 18. **Memberships** CW, UN. **Subdivisions** 25 states, 7 union territories.

ECONOMY

GDP $1,170,000,000,000. **Per capita** $1,339.
Monetary unit Rupee. **Trade partners** Exports:
U.S., former Soviet republics, Japan. Imports:
U.S., Japan, Germany. **Exports** Gems and jewelry, engineering goods, clothing, textiles, chemicals,
tea. **Imports** Petroleum, machinery, gems, jewelry,
chemicals, iron and steel.

LAND

Description Southern Asia. **Area** 1,237,062 mi²
(3,203,975 km²). **Highest point** Kānchenjunga,
28,208 ft (8,598 m). **Lowest point** Sea level.
*The above information includes part of Jammu
and Kashmir.*

People. India's population is composed of two main
ethnic groups: the Indo-Aryans and the Dravidians.
Found mostly in the north are the Indo-Aryans, a central Asian people who arrived in India around 1500 B.C.,
pushing the Dravidians to the south, where they
remain concentrated today. A Mongoloid minority
inhabits the mountains of the far north, and aboriginal groups live in the central forests and mountains.
There are fifteen official indigenous languages, as well
as English, which is spoken by the majority of educated people. India is second only to China in population, and although Hindus are the religious majority, the country also has one of the world's largest Muslim
populations. Christians, Sikhs, Jains, and Buddhists
comprise additional religious minorities.

Economy and the Land. Economic conditions have
improved since India became independent in 1947.
Agriculture, upon which most Indians depend, is
now more efficient, a result of modernization programs.
Industry has expanded as well, and the country
ranks high in its number of scientists and skilled
laborers. Poverty, unemployment, and underemployment continue to plague the nation, however, partly due to rapid population growth and improved life
expectancy. Many natural resources, including coal,
iron ore, bauxite, and manganese, remain undeveloped. India comprises three land regions: the
Himalayas along the northern border; the Gangetic
plain, a fertile northern region; and the peninsula, made
up mostly of the Deccan, a plateau region. The climate
ranges from temperate to tropical monsoon.

History and Politics. India's civilization dates back
to 2500 B.C., when the Dravidians flourished in the region.
Aryan tribes invaded about one thousand years later,
bringing the indigenous beliefs that evolved into
Hinduism, and various empires followed. In the sixth
or fifth century B.C., Siddhārtha Gautama, who came
to be called Buddha, founded Buddhism, a major influence on Indian life until about A.D. 800. Invasions beginning around A.D. 450 brought the Huns and, during the
seventh and eighth centuries, Arab conquerors introduced Islam. The Mogul Empire, under a series of
Muslim rulers, began in the 1500s, and the British East
India Company established trading posts in the
1600s. By 1757 the East India Company had become
India's major power, and by the 1850s the company
controlled nearly all present-day India, Pakistan, and
Bangladesh. An Indian rebellion in 1857 caused
Britain to take over the East India Company's rule.
Demands for independence increased after a controversial massacre of Indians by British troops in 1919.
By 1920 Mohandas Gandhi had emerged as the
leader of an independence campaign based on nonviolent disobedience and noncooperation. The nation
gained independence in 1947 and established
Pakistan as a separate Muslim state because of
Muslim-Hindu hostilities. Ongoing disputes include a
border conflict with China that erupted into fighting in
1959 and 1962 and a disagreement with Pakistan over
the mainly Muslim region of Kashmir. ∎

INDONESIA

Official name Republic of Indonesia
PEOPLE
Population 193,680,000. **Density** 257/mi²
(99/km²). **Urban** 29%. **Capital** Jakarta, Java I.,
8,227,746. **Ethnic groups** Javanese 45%,
Sundanese 14%, Madurese 8%, coastal Malay
8%. **Languages** Bahasa Indonesia (Malay),
English, Dutch, indigenous. **Religions** Muslim
87%, Protestant 6%, Catholic 3%, Hindu 2%. **Life
expectancy** 65 female, 61 male. **Literacy** 77%.

POLITICS
Government Republic. **Parties** Democracy, Golkar, United Development. **Suffrage** Universal, over 17 or married. **Memberships** ASEAN, OPEC, UN. **Subdivisions** 27 provinces.
ECONOMY
GDP $571,000,000,000. **Per capita** $3,067.
Monetary unit Rupiah. **Trade partners** Exports: Japan, U.S., Singapore. Imports: Japan, U.S., Germany. **Exports** Petroleum and natural gas, timber, textiles, rubber, coffee. **Imports** Machinery, chemicals, manufactures.
LAND
Description Southeastern Asian islands. **Area** 752,410 mi^2 (1,948,732 km^2). **Highest point** Jaya Pk., 16,503 ft (5,030 m). **Lowest point** Sea level.

People. Indonesia is the fourth most populous nation in the world. The majority of the people are of Malay stock, which includes several subgroups, such as Javanese, Sundanese, Madurese, and coastal Malay. More than two hundred indigenous languages are spoken, but the official, unifying language is Bahasa Indonesia, a Malay dialect. Most people live in small farm villages and follow ancient customs stressing cooperation. Muslim traders brought Islam to Indonesia, and most of the population is Muslim. Many Indonesians combine spirit worship with Islam or Christianity. Indonesia's rich cultural heritage includes many ancient temples.

Economy and the Land. Indonesia is a leading producer of petroleum in the Far East. The area also has large deposits of minerals and natural gas. Agriculture is still a major economic activity, and rice remains an important crop, though overpopulation threatens the economy and food supply. The nation's more than 13,600 islands form a natural barrier between the Indian and Pacific oceans, making the straits between the islands important for world trade and military strategy. Java, the most industrial and heavily populated island, is characterized by volcanic mountains and narrow fertile plains along the northern coast. Indonesia includes most of Borneo, the third largest island in the world. Other major Indonesian islands are Sulawesi, Sumatra, and Irian Jaya (the western half of New Guinea), which also feature inland mountains and limited coastal plains. The climate is tropical, with seasonal monsoons.

History and Politics. Indonesian civilization is more than 2,500 years old and has produced two major empires with influence throughout Southeast Asia. The Portuguese arrived in the sixteenth century but were outnumbered by the Dutch, who eventually gained control of most of the islands and established a plantation colony. An independence movement began early in the twentieth century and slowly gained momentum. Japan encouraged Indonesian nationalism during World War II. Shortly after the Japanese surrendered in 1945, Indonesia proclaimed itself an independent republic. Economic and political instability led to an attempted Communist coup in 1965. The government has outlawed the Communist party and strengthened relations with the West, at the same time establishing trade talks with China. In annexed East Timor, reports of labor rights violations and human rights abuses continue. ∎

IRAN

Official name Islamic Republic of Iran
PEOPLE
Population 63,810,000. **Density** 101/mi^2 (39/km^2). **Urban** 57%. **Capital** Tehrān, 6,042,584. **Ethnic groups** Persian 51%, Azeri 24%, Kurdish 7%. **Languages** Farsi, Turkish dialects, Kurdish. **Religions** Shiite Muslim 95%, Sunni Muslim 4%. **Life expectancy** 68 female, 67 male. **Literacy** 54%.
POLITICS
Government Islamic republic. **Parties** Militant Clerics Association, Fedaiyin Islam Organization. **Suffrage** Universal, over 15. **Memberships** OPEC, UN. **Subdivisions** 24 provinces.
ECONOMY
GNP $303,000,000,000. **Per capita** $5,008.
Monetary unit Rial. **Trade partners** Exports: Japan, Italy, France. Imports: Germany, Japan, Italy. **Exports** Petroleum, carpets, fruit, nuts, hides. **Imports** Machinery, military supplies, metal works, food, pharmaceuticals.
LAND
Description Southwestern Asia. **Area** 632,457 mi^2 (1,638,057 km^2). **Highest point** Mt. Demavend, 18,386 ft (5,604 m). **Lowest point** Caspian Sea, -92 ft (-28 m).

People. Most Iranians are of Aryan ancestry, descended from an Asiatic people who migrated to the area in ancient times. The Aryan groups include majority Persians and minority Gilani, Mazanderani, Kurds, Lur, Bakhtiari, and Baluchi. Turks and Azeries are the major non-Aryan minorities. Until 1935, when the shah officially changed its name, Iran was known as Persia. Farsi, or Persian, remains the main language. Nearly all Iranians are Muslim, mainly of the Shiite sect, and the country is an Islamic republic, with law based on Islamic teachings. Minority religious groups, especially Baha'is, have been victims of persecution. Due to aridity and a harsh mountain-and-desert terrain, the population is concentrated in the west and north.

Economy and the Land. Iran's previously rapid economic development has slowed as a result of a 1979 revolution and a war with Iraq. Small-scale farming, manufacturing, and trading appear to be current economic trends. Oil remains the most important export, although output has decreased due to changes in economic policy and other factors. Persian carpets also continue as elements of trade. Iran's terrain consists mainly of a central plateau marked by desert and surrounded by mountains; thus agriculture is limited, and the country remains dependent on imported food. The central region is one of the most arid areas on Earth, and summers throughout most of the country are long, hot, and dry, with higher humidity along the Persian Gulf and Caspian coast. Winters are cold in the mountains of the northwest, but mild on the plain. The Caspian coastal region is generally subtropical.

History and Politics. Iran's history is one of the world's oldest, with a civilization dating back several thousand years. Around 1500 B.C., Aryan immigrants began arriving from central Asia, calling the region Iran, or land of the Aryans, and splitting into two groups: the Medes and the Persians. In the sixth century B.C., Cyrus the Great founded the Persian, or Achaemenian, Empire, which came to encompass Babylonia, Palestine, Syria, and Asia Minor. Alexander the Great conquered the region in the fourth century B.C. Various dynasties followed, and Muslim Arabs invaded in the A.D. 600s and established Islam as the major religion. The following centuries saw Iran's boundaries expand and recede under various rulers, and increasing political awareness resulted in a 1906 constitution and parliament. In 1908 oil was discovered in the region, and modernization programs began during the reign of Reza Shah Pahlavi, who came to power in 1925. Despite Iran's declared neutrality in World War II, the Allies invaded, obtaining rights to use the country as a supply route to the Soviet Union. The presence of foreign influences caused nationalism to increase sharply after the war. Mohammad Reza Pahlavi—who succeeded his father, Reza Shah Pahlavi, as shah—instituted social and economic reforms during the sixties, although many Muslims felt the reforms violated religious law, and resented the increasing Western orientation of the country and the absolute power of the shah. Led by Muslim leader Ayatollah Ruholla Khomeini, revolutionaries seized the government in 1979, declaring Iran an Islamic republic based upon fundamental Islamic principles. Khomeini remained the religious leader of Iran until his death in 1989. In 1988 a long and destructive war with Iraq ended. Hashemi Rafsanjani was elected president two years later. Recent signs of military build-up and the growing strength of the fundamentalist movement throughout the world continue to cause concern in the West. ∎

IRAQ

Official name Republic of Iraq
PEOPLE
Population 20,250,000. **Density** 120/mi²
(46/km²). **Urban** 72%. **Capital** Baghdād,
3,841,268. **Ethnic groups** Arab 75%-80%;

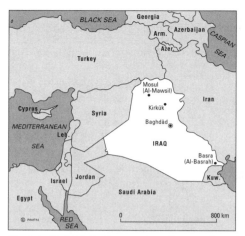

Kurdish 15-20%; Turkoman, Assyrian, or other 5%.
Languages Arabic, Kurdish, Assyrian, Armenian.
Religions Shiite Muslim 60-65%, Sunni Muslim 32-37%, Christian and others 3%. **Life expectancy** 68 female, 65 male. **Literacy** 60%.
POLITICS
Government Republic. **Parties** Ba'th. **Suffrage** Universal, over 18. **Memberships** AL, OPEC, UN.
Subdivisions 15 governorates, 3 autonomous regions.
ECONOMY
GNP $38,000,000,000. **Per capita** $2,020.
Monetary unit Dinar. **Trade partners** Exports: U.S., Brazil, Turkey, Japan. Imports: Germany, U.S., Turkey, France, U.K. **Exports** Petroleum, fertilizer, sulphur. **Imports** Manufactures, food.
LAND
Description Southwestern Asia. **Area** 169,235 mi² (438,317 km²). **Highest point** Unnamed, 11,835 ft (3,607 m). **Lowest point** Sea level.

People. Descendants of the founders of one of the world's oldest civilizations inhabit Iraq. Most Iraqis are Muslim Arabs and speak Arabic. The minority Kurds, also mainly Muslim, are concentrated in the northwest; speak their own language, Kurdish; and follow a non-Arab lifestyle. Kurdish demands for self-rule have led to occasional rebellion.

Economy and the Land. Oil is the mainstay of Iraq's economy, and nearly all economic development has focused on the petroleum industry, nationalized in the 1970s. Despite its oil wealth, the Iraqi economy, like the Iranian, was drained by the Iran-Iraq war. Most farmland lies near the Tigris and Euphrates rivers. The terrain is marked by northeastern mountains, southern and western deserts, and the plains of upper and lower Iraq, which lie between the Tigris and Euphrates rivers. The climate is generally hot and dry.

History and Politics. Civilizations such as the Sumerian, Babylonian, and Parthian flourished in the area of the Tigris and Euphrates in ancient times. Once known as Mesopotamia, the region was the setting for many biblical events. After coming under Persian rule in the sixth century B.C., Mesopotamia fell to Alexander the Great in the fourth century B.C.

Invading Arabs brought the Muslim religion in the seventh century A.D. and for a time Baghdād was the capital and cultural center of the Arab empire. Thirteenth-century Mongol invaders were followed by Ottoman Turks in the sixteenth century. Ottoman rule continued and, following a British invasion during World War I, Mesopotamia became a British mandate at the end of the war. In 1921 the monarchy of Iraq was established, and independence was gained in 1932. Iraq and other nations formed the Arab League in 1945 and participated in a war against Israel in 1948. Opposition to monarchical rule increased during the 1950s, and after a 1958 military coup, the country was declared a republic. Instability, evidenced by coups, continued into the 1970s. The political climate was further complicated by occasional uprisings by Kurds demanding autonomy. War with Iran, which caused heavy losses on both sides, continued intermittently through the early 1980s, ending in a 1988 cease-fire agreement. In August 1990 Iraq invaded Kuwait and forced the government into exile. A coalition of countries under the military direction of the United States forced Iraq to withdraw in early 1991. After the war the United Nations established "no-fly" zones in northern and southern Iraq to protect Kurdish and Shiite rebels. The UN continues an embargo on trade until Iraq downsizes its military capabilities. ∎

IRELAND

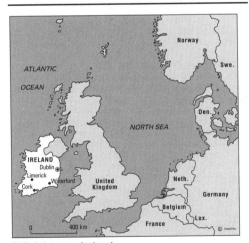

Official name Ireland
PEOPLE
Population 3,546,000. **Density** 131/mi² (50/km²).
Urban 57%. **Capital** Dublin, 502,749. **Ethnic groups** Irish (Celtic), English. **Languages** English, Irish Gaelic. **Religions** Roman Catholic 93%, Church of Ireland 3%. **Life expectancy** 78 female, 73 male. **Literacy** 98%.
POLITICS
Government Republic. **Parties** Fianna Fail, Fine Gael, Labor, others. **Suffrage** Universal, over 18. **Memberships** EU, OECD, UN. **Subdivisions** 26 counties.

ECONOMY
GDP $46,300,000,000. **Per capita** $13,135.
Monetary unit Pound (punt). **Trade partners** Exports: U.K., Germany, France. Imports: U.K., U.S., Germany. **Exports** Chemicals, data processing equipment, machinery, live animals. **Imports** Food, animal feed, chemicals, petroleum, machinery, textiles, clothing.
LAND
Description Northwestern European island (five-sixths of island of Ireland). **Area** 27,137 mi² (70,285 km²). **Highest point** Carrauntoohil, 3,406 ft (1,038 m). **Lowest point** Sea level.

People. Most of Ireland's population is descended from the Celts, a people who flourished in Europe and Great Britain in ancient times. Irish Gaelic, a form of ancient Celtic, and English are official languages. Most people are Roman Catholic. Protestants mainly belong to the Church of Ireland, a member of the Anglican Communion. With a long literary tradition, the country has contributed greatly to world literature.

Economy and the Land. Ireland's economy was agricultural until the 1950s, when a program of rapid industrialization began. This expansion resulted in significant foreign investment, especially by the United States. Most of the Irish labor force is unionized. Agriculture continues to play an important role, however, and food is produced for domestic and foreign consumption. The country of Ireland occupies most of the island but excludes Northern Ireland, which is part of the United Kingdom. The fertile central region features green, rolling hills, suitable for farming and pastureland, and is surrounded by coastal highlands. The climate is temperate maritime, with mild summers and winters and plentiful rainfall.

History and Politics. Around the fourth century B.C., Ireland's indigenous population was conquered by Gaels, a Celtic tribe, from continental Europe and Great Britain. Christianity was introduced by St. Patrick in A.D. 432, and periodic Viking raids began near the end of the eighth century. In the twelfth century the pope made the Norman king of England, Henry II, overlord of the island; the English intervened in a dispute between Irish kings; and centuries of British influence began. As British control grew, so did Irish Catholic hostility, arising from seizure of land by English settlers, the Protestant Reformation, and the elimination of political and religious freedoms. The Protestant majority of present-day Northern Ireland was established in the 1600s, when land taken from the Irish was distributed to English and Scottish Protestants. In 1801 the British Act of Union established the United Kingdom of Great Britain, and Northern Ireland. Religious freedom was regained in 1829, but the struggle for independence continued. Most of the Irish depended upon potatoes as a staple food, and hundreds of thousands died or emigrated in the 1840s when the crop failed because of a plant disease. Following an armed rebellion, the Irish Free State, a dominion of Great Britain, was created in 1921, with the predominantly Protestant countries in the north remaining under British rule. The nation became a republic in 1949. The volitile issue of reunification with Northern Ireland continues to dominate Irish politics. ∎

ISLE OF MAN See UNITED KINGDOM.

ISRAEL

Official name State of Israel

PEOPLE
Population 5,059,000. **Density** 631/mi² (244/km²). **Urban** 92%. **Capital** Jerusalem, 524,500. **Ethnic groups** Jewish 83%, Arab and other 17%. **Languages** Hebrew, Arabic. **Religions** Jewish 82%, Muslim 14%, Christian 2%, Druze 2%. **Life expectancy** 78 female, 75 male. **Literacy** 92%.
POLITICS
Government Republic. **Parties** Labor, Likud, others. **Suffrage** Universal, over 18. **Memberships** UN. **Subdivisions** 6 districts.
ECONOMY
GDP $65,700,000,000. **Per capita** $14,304. **Monetary unit** Shekel. **Trade partners** Exports: U.S., Japan, U.K. Imports: U.S., Belgium, Germany. **Exports** Diamonds, fruit, textiles and clothing, food, fertilizer. **Imports** Military equipment, diamonds, oil, chemicals, machinery, iron and steel.
LAND
Description Southwestern Asia. **Area** 8,019 mi² (20,770 km²). **Highest point** Mt. Meron, 3,963 ft (1,208 m). **Lowest point** Dead Sea, -1,322 ft (-403 m).
The above information excludes Israeli-occupied areas.

People. Most Israelis are Jewish immigrants or descendants of Jews who settled in the region in the late 1800s. The two main ethnic groups are the Ashkenazim of central and eastern European origin and the Sephardim of the Mediterranean and Middle East. The non-Jewish population is predominantly Arab and Muslim, and many Palestinians inhabit the Israeli-occupied West Bank, the status of which is still in dispute. Hebrew and Arabic are the official languages, and both are used on documents and currency. Conflict between conservative and liberal Jewish groups has spilled over into the nation's political life.

Economy and the Land. Despite drastic levels of inflation and a constant trade deficit, Israel has experienced continuous economic growth. Skilled labor supports the market economy based on services, manufacturing, and commerce. Taxes are a major source of revenue, as are grants and loans from other countries and income from tourism. The country is poor in natural resources, but through improved irrigation and soil conservation, Israel now produces much of its own food. Because of its limited natural resources, Israel must import most of the raw materials it needs for industry. The region's varied terrain includes coastal plains, central mountains, the Jordan Rift Valley, and the desert region of the Negev. Except in the Negev, the climate is temperate.

History and Politics. Israel comprises much of the historic region of Palestine, known in ancient times as Canaan and the site of most biblical history. Hebrews arrived in this region around 1900 B.C. The area experienced subsequent immigration and invasion by diverse peoples, including Assyrians, Babylonians, and Persians. In 63 B.C. it became part of the Roman Empire, was renamed Judaea and finally, Palestine. In the A.D. 600s, invading Arabs brought Islam to the area and, by the early 1500s when Ottoman Turks conquered the region, Muslims comprised a majority. During the late 1800s, as a result of oppression in eastern Europe, many Jews immigrated to Palestine, hoping to establish a Jewish state. This movement, called Zionism, and the increasing Jewish population led to Arab-Jewish tensions. Turkey sided with Germany in World War I, and after the war the Ottoman Empire collapsed. Palestine became a mandated territory of Britain in 1920. Jewish immigration and Arab-Jewish hostility increased during the years of Nazi Germany. Additional unrest arose from conflicting interpretations of British promises and the terms of the mandate. In 1947 Britain turned to the United Nations for help, and in 1948 the nation of Israel was established. Neighboring Arab countries invaded immediately, and war ensued, during which Israel gained some land. A truce was signed in 1949, but Arab-Israeli wars broke out periodically throughout the fifties, sixties, and seventies. Israel signed a peace treaty with Egypt in 1979, annexed the Golan Heights in 1981, and returned the Sinai to Egypt the following year. The years since have seen continual conflict over the occupation of the Gaza Strip and West Bank. In 1993 an historic accord between Israel and the Palestinians was reached, which gives the Palestinians limited autonomy over the Gaza Strip and the town of Jericho. Continuing peace talks have paved the way for expanded Jewish/Arab relations. ∎

ITALY

Official name Italian Republic
PEOPLE
Population 57,330,000. **Density** 493/mi² (190/km²). **Urban** 69%. **Capital** Rome, 2,693,383. **Ethnic groups** Italian (Latin). **Languages** Italian, German, French, Slovene. **Religions** Roman Catholic. **Life expectancy** 80 female, 74 male. **Literacy** 97%.
POLITICS
Government Republic. **Parties** Democratic Party of the Left, Popular, Socialist, others. **Suffrage** Universal, over 18. **Memberships** EU, NATO, OECD, UN. **Subdivisions** 20 regions.

Following the demise of the Roman Empire, rulers and influences included Byzantines; Lombards, an invading Germanic tribe; and the Frankish King Charlemagne, whom the pope crowned emperor of the Romans in 800. During the eleventh century, Italy became a region of city-states, and its cultural life led to the Renaissance, which started in the 1300s. As the city-states weakened, Italy fell victim to invasion and rule by France, Spain, and Austria, with these countries controlling various regions at different times. In 1861 Victor Emmanuel II, the king of Sardinia, proclaimed Italy a kingdom, and by 1871 the nation included the entire peninsula, with Rome as the capital and Victor Emmanuel as king. In 1922 Benito Mussolini, the leader of Italy's Fascist movement, came to power and ruled as dictator until his death at the hands of Italian partisans in 1945. The country allied with Germany in World War II, and a popular resistance movement evolved. Recent politics have been marked by a volatility that has produced frequent changes in government. ∎

IVORY COAST see COTE D'IVOIRE

ECONOMY
GDP $967,600,000,000. **Per capita** $17,100. **Monetary unit** Lira. **Trade partners** Exports: Germany, France, U.S. Imports: Germany, France, Netherlands. **Exports** Textiles, clothing, metals, transportation equipment, chemicals. **Imports** Petroleum, machinery, chemicals, metals, food, agricultural products.
LAND
Description Southern Europe. **Area** 116,324 mi^2 (301,277 km^2). **Highest point** Mont Blanc (Monte Bianco), 15,771 ft (4,807 m). **Lowest point** Sea level.

People. Italy is populated mainly by Italian Roman Catholics. Most speak Italian, although dialects often differ from region to region. Despite an ethnic homogeneity, the people exhibit diversity in terms of politics and culture. The country has about twelve political parties, and northern inhabitants are relatively prosperous, employed primarily in industry, whereas southerners are generally farmers and often poor. The birthplace of the Renaissance, Italy has made substantial contributions to world culture.

Economy and the Land. The Italian economy is based on private enterprise, although the government is involved in some industrial and commercial activities. Industry and commercial agriculture are centered in the north, which produces steel, textiles, and chemicals. A hilly terrain makes parts of the south unsuited for crop raising, and livestock grazing is a main activity. Tourism is also important; visitors are drawn by the northern Alps, the sunny south, and the Italian cultural tradition. The island of Sicily, lying off the southwest coast, produces fruits, olives, and grapes. Sardinia, a western island, engages in some sheep and wheat raising. Except for the northern Po Valley, narrow areas along the coast, and a small section of the southern peninsula, Italy's terrain is mainly rugged and mountainous. The climate varies from cold in the Alps to mild and Mediterranean in other regions.

History and Politics. Early influences in Italy included Greeks, Etruscans, and Celts. From the fifth century B.C. to the fifth century A.D., the dominant people were Romans descended from Sabines and neighboring Latins, who inhabited the Latium coast.

JAMAICA

Official name Jamaica
PEOPLE
Population 2,568,000. **Density** 605/mi^2 (234/km^2). **Urban** 52%. **Capital** Kingston, 587,798. **Ethnic groups** Black 75%, mixed 13%, East Indian 1%. **Languages** English, Creole. **Religions** Church of God 18%, Baptist 10%, Anglican 7%, Seventh-Day Adventist 7%. **Life expectancy** 76 female, 71 male. **Literacy** 98%.
POLITICS
Government Parliamentary state. **Parties** Labor, People's National. **Suffrage** Universal, over 18. **Memberships** CW, OAS, UN. **Subdivisions** 14 parishes.

ECONOMY
GDP $8,000,000,000. **Per capita** $3,199.
Monetary unit Dollar. **Trade partners** Exports:
U.S., U.K., Canada. Imports: U.S., U.K.,
Venezuela. **Exports** Bauxite, alumina, sugar,
bananas. **Imports** Petroleum, machinery, food,
manufactures.

LAND
Description Caribbean island. **Area** 4,244 mi^2
(10,991 km^2). **Highest point** Blue Mountain Pk.,
7,402 ft (2,256 m). **Lowest point** Sea level.

People. Most Jamaicans are of African or Afro-
European descent, and the majority are Christian.
English is the official language, but many Jamaicans
also speak Creole. Population is concentrated on
the coastal plains, where the main commercial
crops are also grown.

Economy and the Land. Agriculture is the traditional
mainstay, and more than a third of the population
is engaged in farming. Sugar cane and bananas are
principal crops. Mining is also important, and
Jamaica is a leading producer of bauxite. The tropical climate, tempered by ocean breezes, makes the
island a popular tourist destination. A mountainous
inland region is surrounded by coastal plains and
beaches.

History and Politics. Christopher Columbus claimed
the island for Spain in 1494. As the enslaved native
population died out, blacks were brought from
Africa to work plantations. Britain invaded and
gained control of Jamaica in the seventeenth century, and for a time the island was one of the most
important sugar and slave centers of the New
World. In 1838 the British abolished slavery, the plantation economy broke down, and most slaves
became independent farmers. Local political control began in the 1930s, and the nation became fully
independent in 1962. Since independence the
nation has faced problems of unemployment, inflation, and poverty, with periodic social unrest. ∎

JAPAN

Official name Japan
PEOPLE
Population 125,360,000. **Density** 859/mi^2
(332/km^2). **Urban** 77%. **Capital** Tōkyō, Honshū I.,
8,163,573. **Ethnic groups** Japanese 99%,
Korean. **Languages** Japanese. **Religions**
Buddhist and Shinto. **Life expectancy** 82 female,
76 male. **Literacy** 99%.
POLITICS
Government Constitutional monarchy. **Parties**
Liberal Democratic, Shinseito, Social Democratic,
others. **Suffrage** Universal, over 20.
Memberships OECD, UN. **Subdivisions** 47 pre-
fectures.
ECONOMY
GDP $2,549,000,000,000. **Per capita** $20,439.
Monetary unit Yen. **Trade partners** Exports:
U.S., Germany, Korea. Imports: U.S., Indonesia,
Korea. **Exports** Machinery, motor vehicles, consumer electronics. **Imports** Manufactures, fuel,
food and raw materials.
LAND
Description Eastern Asian islands. **Area** 145,870
mi^2 (377,801 km^2). **Highest point** Mt. Fuji, 12,388
ft (3,776 m). **Lowest point** Hachiro-gata reclama-
tion area, Honshū I., -13 ft (-4 m).

People. The Japanese constitute Japan's major
ethnic group; there is a small Korean minority.
Shintoism and Buddhism are the principal religions.
Almost all the population lives on the coastal plains.
Japan's culture blends East and West, with karate,
tea ceremonies, and kimonos balanced by baseball,
fast food, and business suits. Although its arts have
been greatly influenced by China, Japan has developed distinctive music, literature, and painting.

Economy and the Land. One of the world's leading
industrial powers, Japan is remarkable for its economic
growth rate since World War II, considering it has few
natural resources. It has also become famous for its
innovative technology. Manufacturing is the basis of
the economy, and Japan is a leading producer of ships,
machinery, cars, and electronic equipment. Its chemical, iron, and steel industries are extremely profitable.
Agriculture's part in the economy is small, since little of the rugged island terrain is arable. Fishing
still plays a significant role in Japan's economy as Japan
maintains one of the world's largest fishing fleets.
Overseas trade has expanded rapidly since the
1960s, as Japan requires raw materials for its many
industries. Trade barriers and the competitiveness
of Japanese products overseas have led to trade deficits
among Western nations. Japan's mountainous terrain includes both active and dormant volcanoes; earthquakes occasionally occur. The climate ranges from
subtropical to temperate.

History and Politics. Legend states that Japan's first
emperor was descended from the sun goddess
and came to power around 600 B.C. The arrival of
Buddhism, Confucianism, and new technologies
from China in the fifth and sixth centuries A.D. rev-
olutionized society. Feuding nobles controlled Japan
between 1192 and 1867 and ruled as *shoguns*, or
generals, in the name of the emperor. The warrior
class, or *samurai*, developed early in this period. The
arrival of Europeans in the sixteenth century caused

fear of an invasion among the shoguns, and in the 1630s they dissolved all foreign contacts. Japan's isolation lasted until 1854, when Commodore Matthew Perry of the United States opened the nation to the West with a show of force. The subsequent Meiji Restoration modernized Japan by adopting Western technologies and legal systems, and by stressing industrialization and education. Japan embarked on military expansion in the late nineteenth century, annexing Korea in 1910 and adding to its holdings after participating in World War I as a British ally. It occupied Manchuria in 1931 and invaded China in 1937. As part of the Axis powers in World War II, Japan attacked United States military bases in Pearl Harbor, Hawaii, in 1941. After the United States dropped atomic bombs on Hiroshima and Nagasaki in 1945, Japan surrendered. Allied forces occupied the nation until 1952, by which time the Japanese had approved a constitution that shifted power from the emperor to the people and abolished the military. With the help of U.S. aid Japan experienced a rapid economic recovery. Foreign trade issues and an economic slump dominated the early 1990s. ■

JERSEY See UNITED KINGDOM.

JORDAN

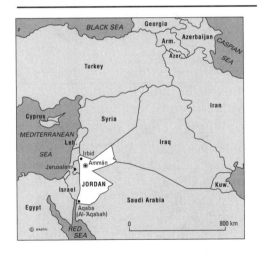

Official name Hashemite Kingdom of Jordan
PEOPLE
Population 4,028,000. **Density** 115/mi² (44/km²).
Urban 68%. **Capital** 'Ammān, 936,300. **Ethnic groups** Arab 98%, Circassian 1%, Armenian 1%.
Languages Arabic. **Religions** Sunni Muslim 92%, Christian 8%. **Life expectancy** 70 female, 66 male. **Literacy** 80%.
POLITICS
Government Constitutional monarchy. **Parties** Muslim Brotherhood. **Suffrage** Universal, over 20.

Memberships AL, UN. **Subdivisions** 8 governorates.
ECONOMY
GDP $11,500,000,000. **Per capita** $3,166.
Monetary unit Dinar. **Trade partners** Exports: India, Iraq, Saudi Arabia. Imports: U.S., Iraq, France. **Exports** Phosphates, fertilizer, potash, agricultural products, manufactures. **Imports** Petroleum, machinery, transportation equipment, food, live animals.
LAND
Description Southwestern Asia. **Area** 35,135 mi² (91,000 km²). **Highest point** Mt. Ramm, 5,755 ft (1,754 m). **Lowest point** Dead Sea, -1,322 ft (-403 m).

People. Most Jordanians are Arabs, but there are Circassian, Armenian, and Kurdish minorities, as well as a small nomadic population, the Bedouins, in desert areas. About one-third of all Jordanians are Palestinian refugees, displaced by Arab-Israeli wars. Jordan is the only Arab nation that has granted citizenship to the Palestinians. Arabic is the official language, and most people are Sunni Muslim, legacies of the Muslim conquest in A.D. 600s.

Economy and the Land. A nation with few natural resources, limited rainfall, and little arable land, Jordan has suffered further economic damage from an influx of refugees and the chronic political instability of the Middle East. In a 1967 war with Israel, Jordan lost control of Jerusalem and the West Bank, which made up about half the country's farmland. Agriculture remains the most important activity, and tourism has helped boost a weak economy that relies heavily on foreign aid and investment from the United States and Arab nations. There is some light industry and mining. The Jordan River forms the country's westernmost boundary, and the terrain is marked by deserts, mountains, and rolling plains. The climate ranges from Mediterranean in the West to desert in the East.

History and Politics. Jordan is the site of one of the world's oldest settlements, dating back to about 8000 B.C. The area came under the rule of the Hebrews, Assyrians, Egyptians, Persians, Greeks, and Romans, and around A.D. 636, Arab Muslims. Rule by the Ottoman Turks began in the sixteenth century, and in World War I Arab armies helped the British defeat Turkey. At the end of the war present-day Israel and Jordan became the British mandate of Palestine, which in 1922 was divided into the mandates of Transjordan, lying east of the Jordan River, and Palestine, lying to the West. Transjordan gained full independence in 1946. In 1948 the Palestine mandate created Israel, and Arab-Israeli fighting ensued. After capturing the West Bank, Transjordan was renamed Jordan in 1949. During the Arab-Israeli Six-Day War in 1967, this region and the Jordanian section of Jerusalem fell to Israel. After each war, Jordan's Palestinian-refugee population grew. A 1970 civil war pitted the Jordanian monarchy against Palestinian guerrillas who sought to overthrow the government. The guerrillas were expelled following the war, but subsequent Arab-Israeli hostilities led to Jordan's recognition of the Palestine Liberation Organization. Although Jordan relinquished all claims to the Israeli-held West Bank area in 1988, the country continues to be involved in discussions on the fate of the

Palestinians who live there. Jordan is a constitutional monarchy and has been headed by King Hussein since 1953. In the 1990s, King Hussein's moderate policies were increasingly criticized not only by Palestinian radicals, but also by a growing number of Muslim fundamentalists. However, 1993 parliamentary elections were won by moderates endorsing peace efforts that resulted in an historic peace treaty with Israel in 1994. ■

KAZAKHSTAN

Official name Republic of Kazakhstan

PEOPLE
Population 17,025,000. **Density** 16/mi^2 (6.3/km^2). **Urban** 57%. **Capital** Alma-Ata (Almaty), 1,156,200. **Ethnic groups** Kazakh 42%, Russian 37%, Ukrainian 5%, German 5%. **Languages** Kazakh, Russian. **Religions** Muslim 47%, Russian Orthodox 15%, Lutheran. **Life expectancy** 73 female, 63 male. **Literacy** 98%.
POLITICS
Government Republic. **Parties** December Movement, Freedom (Azat), Peoples Congress, Socialist. **Suffrage** Universal, over 18.
Memberships CIS, NATO, UN. **Subdivisions** 19 oblasts.
ECONOMY
GNP $60,300,000,000. **Per capita** $3,508. **Monetary unit** Tenge. **Trade partners** Exports: Russia, Ukraine, Uzbekistan. Imports: Russia and other former Soviet republics. **Exports** Oil, metals, chemicals, grain, wool, meat. **Imports** Machinery and parts, industrial materials.
LAND
Description Central Asia, landlocked. **Area** 1,049,156 mi^2 (2,717,300 km^2). **Highest point** Khan-Tengri Peak, 22,949 ft (6,995 m). **Lowest point** Karagiye Basin, -433 ft (-132 m).

People. Kazakhstan is the traditional homeland of the Kazakh people, Turkic-speaking descendants of the Mongols. Prior to Soviet control, most Kazakhs were Muslim and nomadic. Immigration into Kazakhstan from other republics has left the Kazakhs with only 42% of the population. Russians are the next largest group, with more than one-third of the population.

Economy and the Land. The world's ninth-largest country in area, Kazakhstan is generally a vast tableland. The climate is harsh and dry, with hot summers and cold winters. Agriculture is concentrated in the north and the irrigated areas of the southeast. Industry, based mainly on the country's vast mineral resources, makes the largest contributions to the economy. Kazakhstan produces large amounts of coal and boasts tremendous undeveloped oil resources.

History and Politics. Two important trade routes brought early travelers through Kazakhstan on their way to China. The people known as the Kazakhs have inhabited the region since the sixteenth century. Russian expansion into the region began in the mid-1700s, and one of the area's most powerful states joined the Russian empire in the mid-1800s. After the Russian revolution, the region was organized into the Kirghiz Autonomous Republic, but then enlarged in 1925 to form the Kazakh Autonomous Republic. Kazakhstan became a Soviet Republic in 1936. As the heartland of the Soviet Union, Kazakhstan was home to the country's space program and hosted much of the nation's nuclear arsenal. Since the break-up of the Soviet Union in late 1991, Kazakhstan has emerged as the leader of the newly independent central Asian states, and has taken a lead in modernizing its economy. In 1993 Kazakhstan voted to dismantle its nuclear weapons. A large Russian minority threatens the stability of the government. ■

KENYA

Official name Republic of Kenya
PEOPLE

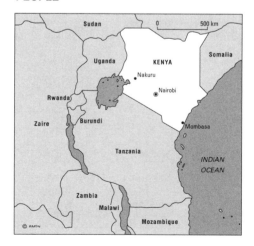

Population 28,380,000. **Density** 126/mi^2 (49/km^2). **Urban** 24%. **Capital** Nairobi, 1,505,000. **Ethnic groups** Kikuyu 21%, Luhya 14%, Luo

13%, Kamba 11%, Kalenjin 11%, Kisii 6%, Meru 5%. **Languages** English, Swahili, indigenous. **Religions** Roman Catholic 28%, Protestant 26%, Animist 18%, Muslim 6%. **Life expectancy** 61 female, 57 male. **Literacy** 69%.

POLITICS
Government Republic. **Parties** African National Union, Democratic, Forum for the Restoration of Democracy, others. **Suffrage** Universal, over 18. **Memberships** CW, OAU, UN. **Subdivisions** 7 provinces, 1 capital district.

ECONOMY
GDP $33,200,000,000. **Per capita** $1,246. **Monetary unit** Shilling. **Trade partners** Exports: U.K., Germany, Uganda. Imports: U.K., Japan, United Arab Emirates. **Exports** Tea, coffee, petroleum. **Imports** Machinery and transportation equipment, petroleum, iron and steel.

LAND
Description Eastern Africa. **Area** 224,961 mi^2 (582,646 km^2). **Highest point** Kirinyaga (Mt. Kenya), 17,058 ft (5,199 m). **Lowest point** Sea level.

People. Nearly all Kenyans are black Africans belonging to one of more than forty different groups, each with its own language and culture. Some groups are nomadic, like the Masai. Arab and European minorities—found mostly along the coast—reflect Kenya's history of foreign rule. Most Kenyans live in the southwestern highlands, raising crops or livestock. Over half of the citizens practice a form of Christianity, while the rest pursue indigenous beliefs or Islam. Swahili, a blend of Bantu and Arabic, is an official language; it serves as a communication link among Kenya's many ethnic groups. English is also an official language. The national slogan of *harambee*, or "pull together," illustrates the need for cooperation among Kenya's diverse groups. The government promotes such national unity.

Economy and the Land. Scenic terrain, tropical beaches, and abundant wildlife have given Kenya a thriving tourist industry, and land has been set aside for national parks and game preserves. Agriculture is the primary activity, even though the northern three-fifths of the country is semidesert. The most productive soils are found in the southwestern highlands where tea and coffee are the main export crops. Much of the land is also used for raising livestock, another leading economic contributor. Oil from other nations is refined in Kenya, and food processing and cement production are also significant activities. Kenya's climate varies from arid in the north to temperate in the highlands and tropical along the coast.

History and Politics. Remains of early humans dating back more than two million years have been found in Kenya. Settlers from other parts of Africa arrived about 1000 B.C. A thousand years later Arab traders reached the coast, and controlled the area by the eighth century A.D. The Portuguese ruled the coast between 1498 and the late 1600s. Kenya came under British control in 1895 and was known as the East African Protectorate. Opposition to British rule began to mount in the 1940s as Kenyans demanded a voice in government. The Mau Mau rebellion of the fifties, an armed revolt, was an outgrowth of this discontent.

Kenya gained independence from Britain in 1963 and became a republic in 1964. Its first president was Jomo Kenyatta, a Kikuyu who had been an active leader in the previous revolt. Recent administrations have pursued a policy of Africanization, under which land and other holdings have been transferred from European to African hands. The first multiparty elections in 26 years were held in December 1992. The incumbent, Daniel arap Moi, won reelection as president despite widespread allegations of voting fraud. Tribal fighting has become a serious problem in recent years. ∎

KERGUELEN ISLANDS
See FRANCE.

KIRIBATI

Official name Republic of Kiribati
PEOPLE
Population 79,000. **Density** 252/mi^2 (97/km^2). **Urban** 36%. **Capital** Bairiki, Tarawa Atoll, 2,226. **Ethnic groups** Kiribatian (Micronesian) 98%. **Languages** English, Gilbertese. **Religions** Roman Catholic 53%, Congregationalist 39%, Bahai 2%. **Life expectancy** 56 female, 53 male.

POLITICS
Government Republic. **Parties** Christian Democratic, Gilbertese National. **Suffrage** Universal, over 18. **Memberships** CW. **Subdivisions** 6 districts.

ECONOMY
GDP $36,800,000. **Per capita** $526. **Monetary unit** Australian dollar. **Trade partners** Exports: Netherlands, Denmark, Fiji. Imports: Australia, Japan, Fiji. **Exports** Fish, copra. **Imports** Food, fuel, transportation equipment.

LAND
Description Central Pacific islands. **Area** 313 mi^2 (811 km^2). **Highest point** Unnamed, 246 ft (75 m). **Lowest point** Sea level.

People. The people of Kiribati, a nation of thirty-three islands in the central Pacific, are mostly Micronesian. Almost all the population lives on the Gilbert Islands in small villages and practices Roman Catholicism or Protestantism. English, the official language, and Gilbertese are spoken.

Economy and the Land. A small, unskilled work force combined with small land area and few natural resources have given Kiribati a subsistence economy. Tourism is of increasing importance. Copra and fish are the main exports. Kiribati depends on economic aid from Australia, New Zealand, and Great Britain. The islands of Kiribati are almost all coral reefs, composed of hard sand and little soil; many surround a lagoon. The climate is tropical.

History and Politics. Samoa invaded Kiribati in the 1400s. The islands were declared a British protectorate in 1892 and, from 1916 until 1975, the islands were administered as part of the Gilbert and Ellice Islands.

Fighting between the United States and Japan took place during World War II on Tarawa Island. The Ellice Islands became independent in 1978 as the nation of Tuvalu and the Gilbert Islands gained independence as part of the Republic of Kiribati one year later. ◼

KOREA, NORTH

Official name Democratic People's Republic of Korea

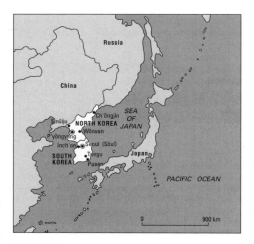

PEOPLE
Population 23,265,000. **Density** 500/mi² (193/km²). **Urban** 60%. **Capital** Pyŏngyang, 2,355,000. **Ethnic groups** Korean 100%. **Languages** Korean. **Religions** Buddhist, Chondoist, Confucian. **Life expectancy** 74 female, 68 male. **Literacy** 99%.
POLITICS
Government Socialist republic. **Parties** Chondoist Chongu, Social Democratic, Workers'. **Suffrage** Universal, over 17. **Memberships** UN. **Subdivisions** 9 provinces, 3 special cities.
ECONOMY
GDP $22,000,000,000. **Per capita** $989. **Monetary unit** Won. **Trade partners** Former Soviet republics, Japan, China, Hong Kong. **Exports** Minerals, metal products, food, manufactures. **Imports** Petroleum, machinery, coal, grain.
LAND
Description Eastern Asia. **Area** 46,540 mi² (120,538 km²). **Highest point** Paektu Mtn., 9,003 ft (2,744 m). **Lowest point** Sea level.

People. Despite a history of invasions, North Korea has a homogeneous population with virtually no minorities. Several dialects of Korean are spoken, and North Koreans use the Hankul, or Korean, alphabet exclusively. Korean religions have included Confucianism and Buddhism with Chondoist sects, though the government discourages religious activity. Urban population has grown rapidly since 1953 due to an emphasis on manufacturing. The nation remains more sparsely populated than

South Korea.

Economy and the Land. The division of the Korean peninsula after World War II left North Korea with most of the industry and natural resources but little agricultural land and few skilled workers. The country has succeeded in becoming one of the most industrialized nations in Asia and in overcoming its agricultural problems. Most industry is government owned, and mines produce a variety of minerals. Farming is collectivized, and output has been aided by irrigation and other modern practices. The Soviet Union and China aided North Korea's development, but the theory of self-reliance was the government's guiding principle. A central mountainous region is bounded by coastal plains, and the climate is temperate.

History and Politics. History of North and South Korea follows SOUTH KOREA. ◼

KOREA, SOUTH

Official name Republic of Korea
PEOPLE
Population 44,655,000. **Density** 1,168/mi² (451/km²). **Urban** 72%. **Capital** Seoul, 10,627,790. **Ethnic groups** Korean. **Languages** Korean. **Religions** Christian 49%, Buddhist 47%, Confucian 3%. **Life expectancy** 74 female, 68 male. **Literacy** 96%.
POLITICS
Government Republic. **Parties** Democratic Justice, New Democratic Republican, Peace and Democracy, Reunification Democratic, others. **Suffrage** Universal, over 20. **Memberships** UN. **Subdivisions** 9 provinces, 6 special cities.
ECONOMY
GNP $424,000,000,000. **Per capita** $9,711. **Monetary unit** Won. **Trade partners** Exports: U.S., Japan, Hong Kong. Imports: Japan, U.S., Germany. **Exports** Textiles, clothing, electronic and electrical equipment, footwear. **Imports** Machinery, electronic equipment, oil, steel, transportation equipment.
LAND
Description Eastern Asia. **Area** 38,230 mi² (99,016 km²). **Highest point** Halla Mtn., 6,398 ft (1,950 m). **Lowest point** Sea level.

People. The homogeneous quality of South Korea's population is similar to that of North Korea. Population density, however, is much greater in South Korea, where two million Koreans migrated following World War II. The major language, Korean, is written predominantly in the Hankul, or Korean, alphabet, with some Chinese characters. Christianity is practiced by most South Koreans, although Buddhism and Confucianism have influenced much of life.

Economy and the Land. South Korea was traditionally the peninsula's agricultural zone, and following the 1945 partition of the country, the south was left with little industry and few resources but abundant manpower. The economy has advanced rapidly since 1953, and today agriculture and industry are of almost equal importance. Rice, barley, and beans are principal crops; electronics and textiles are significant manufactured products. Central mountains give way to plains in the south and west, and the climate is temperate.

History and Politics. Korea's strategic location between Russia, China, and Japan has made it prey to foreign powers. China conquered the northern part of the peninsula in 108 B.C., influencing culture, religion, and government. Mongols controlled Korea for most of the thirteenth and fourteenth centuries. The rule of the Yi dynasty lasted from 1392 to 1910, when Japan annexed Korea. In 1945, following Japan's defeat in World War II, Soviet troops occupied northern Korea while the United States military occupied the south. The Soviet Union, the United States, and Great Britain tried to aid unification of the country but failed. The Soviets opposed a subsequent plan for United Nations-supervised elections. Separate governments were formed in 1948: the northern Democratic People's Republic of Korea and the southern Republic of Korea. Both governments claimed the peninsula, and relations became strained. After several border clashes, North Korea invaded South Korea in 1950. Chinese Communists fought on the side of North Korea, and United States/United Nations forces aided the south. An armistice ended the war in 1953, but a permanent peace treaty has never been signed.

North Korea. The Democratic People's Republic of Korea was established in 1948, several months after the formation of South Korea. The country incurred about three million casualties during the war with South Korea. Following the war, the government moved quickly to modernize industry and the military; North Korea maintains one of the world's largest armies. North Korea's reported development of its nuclear facilities has raised serious concerns worldwide.

South Korea. The Republic of Korea was established on August 15, 1948. The country has since experienced a presidential overthrow, military rule, and a presidential assassination. In 1980 it adopted its fifth constitution since 1948, which initiated the Fifth Republic. The first non-military president in more than thirty years was elected in December 1992. ■

KUWAIT

Official name State of Kuwait
PEOPLE
Population 1,866,000. **Density** 271/mi² (105/km²). **Urban** 96%. **Capital** Kuwait, 44,335. **Ethnic groups** Kuwaiti 45%, other Arab 35%, South Asian 9%, Iranian 4%. **Languages** Arabic, English. **Religions** Sunni Muslim 45%, Shiite Muslim 30%, Christian 6%. **Life expectancy** 78 female, 73 male. **Literacy** 73%.
POLITICS
Government Constitutional monarchy. **Parties** None. **Suffrage** Limited adult male. **Memberships** AL, OPEC, UN. **Subdivisions** 5 governorates.
ECONOMY
GDP $25,700,000,000. **Per capita** $10,762. **Monetary unit** Dinar. **Trade partners** Exports: Iraq, Saudi Arabia, China. Imports: U.S., Japan, Germany. **Exports** Petroleum. **Imports** Food, con-

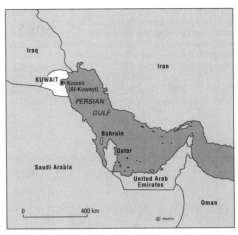

struction materials, motor vehicles, clothing.
LAND
Description Southwestern Asia. **Area** 6,880 mi² (17,818 km²). **Highest point** Unnamed, 922 ft (281 m). **Lowest point** Sea level.

People. Kuwait's recent prosperity has drawn emigrants from the Persian Gulf and beyond, giving it a diverse population with Palestinian, Iranian, and Pakistani minorities. The population has risen dramatically since the thirties, when the oil industry began. Arabic is the official language; English is also taught and widely spoken. Almost all residents of Kuwait observe Islam, the state religion. Most belong to the Sunni branch, but there is a sizable Shiite community.

Economy and the Land. The economy centers on the largely government-controlled petroleum industry. Kuwait is one of the world's largest oil producers, and its oil reserves are among the world's most extensive. Iraq's 1990 invasion of Kuwait brought the economy to a standstill when many Kuwaitis and virtually all of the large foreign work force fled the country. During 1991, burning oil fields, oil slicks, and massive aerial bombardments threatened the environment. Despite the destruction, the Kuwaiti government continues to profit from its many foreign investments as it rebuilds its oil production facilities.

History and Politics. Arab nomads settled Kuwait Bay around A.D. 1700. The Al Sabah dynasty has ruled the nation since the mid-1700s. Alarmed by Turk and Arabic expansion, in 1899 Kuwait signed an agreement with Britain to guarantee Kuwait's defense. Drilling for oil began in 1936, and by 1945 Kuwait had become a major exporter. Independence came in 1961. Iraq immediately made a claim to the state but was discouraged from attacking by the arrival of British troops. Official border agreements have never been made between Kuwait and Iraq. Kuwait briefly cut off oil shipments to Western nations in retaliation for their support of Israel in the 1967 and 1973 Arab-Israeli wars. Kuwait's remarkable oil wealth, which transformed it from a poor nation into an affluent one, has enabled it to offer its citizens a wide range of benefits and to aid other Arab states. Poised at the tip of the Persian Gulf, Kuwait must always be sensitive to the interests of its many neighbors. Kuwait allied itself with Iraq in the 1980-1988 Iran/Iraq war. This did not, however, prevent Iraq from invading Kuwait in August 1990. International outrage resulted in allied military action against Iraq in January 1991. Less than two months later Iraq was forced to withdraw. The constitution, which was suspended in 1976, was revived after the war. In 1992 elections a number of opposition candidates won seats in the National Assembly and the process of democratization had begun. ■

KYRGYZSTAN

Official name Kyrgyz Republic

PEOPLE
Population 4,541,000. **Density** 59/mi^2 (23/km^2). **Urban** 38%. **Capital** Bishkek (Frunze), 631,300. **Ethnic groups** Kirghiz 52%, Russian 22%, Uzbek 13%. **Languages** Kirghiz, Russian. **Religions** Muslim 70%, Russian Orthodox. **Life expectancy** 72 female, 63 male. **Literacy** 97%.
POLITICS
Government Republic. **Parties** Akayev, Asaba, Democratic Movement. **Suffrage** Universal, over 18. **Memberships** CIS, NATO, UN. **Subdivisions** 6 oblasts.
ECONOMY
GDP $11,300,000,000. **Per capita** $2,450. **Monetary unit** Som. **Trade partners** Russia, Ukraine, Uzbekistan, Kazakhstan. **Exports** Wool, chemicals, cotton, metals, footwear, machinery, tobacco. **Imports** Lumber industrial products, ferrous metals, fuel, machinery, textiles, shoes.
LAND
Description Central Asia, landlocked. **Area** 76,641 mi^2 (198,500 km^2). **Highest point** Pobeda Pk., 24,406 ft (7,439 m). **Lowest point** Along Chu River, 1,804 ft (550 m).

People. A little more than one-half of the people are Kirghiz, Turkic-speaking descendants of the region's original nomadic herdsmen. The Kirghiz are related to the Mongols. Russians are the next largest ethnic group, followed by the Uzbeks. Ethnic tension exists between the Kirghiz and the Uzbeks, and fighting between the two groups claimed hundreds of lives in 1990. Most people live in the countryside and are engaged in agriculture, although the Russians tend to live in the cities.

Economy and the Land. High, snow-capped mountains dominate the landscape of Kyrgyzstan. Most of the economic activity takes place in the Fergana and Chu Valleys. Temperature and precipitation vary widely with elevation but, in general, the climate is harsh. The land is rich in minerals, including gold, coal, petroleum, natural gas, uranium, lead, zinc, and mercury. Although the Kirghiz were forced to give up their nomadic lifestyle, livestock raising remains important, including goats, sheep, and horses.

History and Politics. The Kirghiz people have lived in the mountains and valleys of Kyrgyzstan since at least the second millennium B.C. Kirghiz warlords controlled the region when it was used as a trade route to China. One of the Kirghiz warlords first turned to Russia for protection in the mid-1800s. By 1870, central Kyrgyzstan had been conquered by Russia, and control was consolidated after the 1917 revolution. It became an autonomous oblast in 1924 and the Kirghiz Soviet Socialist Republic within the Soviet Union in 1936. The Republic of Kyrgyzstan declared itself independent in December 1990 and elected its first President in October 1991. Their independence was internationally recognized in December 1991, after the collapse of the Soviet Union. Kyrgyzstan stands today as an example of a developing democracy. ■

LAOS

Official name Lao People's Democratic Republic

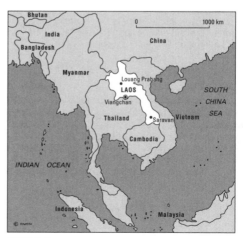

PEOPLE
Population 4,768,000. **Density** 52/mi^2 (20/km^2). **Urban** 19%. **Capital** Viangchan (Vientiane), 377,409. **Ethnic groups** Lao 50%; Thai 20%; Phoutheung 15%; Miao, Hmong, Yao, and others

15%. **Languages** Lao, French, English. **Religions** Buddhist 85%, Animist and other 15%. **Life expectancy** 53 female, 50 male. **Literacy** 84%.
POLITICS
Government Socialist republic. **Parties** People's Revolutionary. **Suffrage** Universal, over 18. **Memberships** UN. **Subdivisions** 16 provinces, 1 municipality.
ECONOMY
GDP $4,100,000,000. **Per capita** $910. **Monetary unit** Kip. **Trade partners** Exports: Thailand, Malaysia, Vietnam. Imports: Thailand, former Soviet republics, Japan, France. **Exports** Electricity, wood, coffee, tin. **Imports** Food, petroleum, consumer goods, manufactures.
LAND
Description Southeastern Asia, landlocked. **Area** 91,429 mi² (236,800 km²). **Highest point** Mt. Bia, 9,249 ft (2,819 m). **Lowest point** Along Mekong River, 230 ft (70 m).

People. Laos is populated by many ethnic groups, each with its own customs, religion, and language. Its history of culturally diverse communities is mirrored in the political divisions of recent years. The Lao are numerically and politically dominant, and Lao is the official language. Small Vietnamese and Chinese minorities exist. Most Laotians are rice farmers.

Economy and the Land. Years of warfare, a landlocked position, and a poor transportation system have hindered the development of Laos's economy. Although agriculture is the basis of the economy, very little of the fertile land is cultivated. Substantial mineral deposits and large timber reserves also have not been exploited to their potential. Manufacturing is limited, partly because of an unskilled work force. Situated in a mountainous, densely-forested region, Laos has a tropical climate and experiences seasonal monsoons.

History and Politics. By A.D. 900 the forerunners of the Lao had arrived from southern China. The first united Lao kingdom was founded in 1353 and included much of modern Thailand. It dissolved into three rival states by the early 1700s, setting the stage for interference by Burma, Vietnam, and Sigam, present-day Thailand. In 1899 France made Laos part of French Indochina. Laos gained some autonomy in 1949, but this period saw the growth of Communist and anti-Communist factions whose rivalry would prevent any unified government until 1975. Although Geneva peace agreements declared Laos neutral in 1954 and 1962, the nation became increasingly embroiled in the Vietnam War as both sides in that conflict entered Laos. A protracted civil war began in 1960 between the Pathet Lao, a Communist faction aided by the North Vietnamese, and government forces backed by the Thai and South Vietnamese. A cease-fire was signed in 1973 and a new coalition government was formed a year later. Following Communist victories in Vietnam and Cambodia, the Pathet Lao gained control in 1975 and established the Lao People's Democratic Republic. Laos began permitting private enterprise in 1986, but has allowed only limited contact with the outside world. Relief agencies were called upon for help after a drought in 1993 decimated the rice harvest. ■

LATVIA

Official name Republic of Latvia
PEOPLE
Population 2,532,000. **Density** 103/mi² (40/km²). **Urban** 71%. **Capital** Rīga, 910,200. **Ethnic groups** Latvian 52%, Russian 34%, Belorussian 5%, Ukrainian 3%, Polish 2%. **Languages** Lettish, Lithuanian, Russian, other. **Religions** Lutheran, Roman Catholic, Russian Orthodox. **Life expectancy** 76 female, 67 male. **Literacy** 99%.
POLITICS
Government Republic. **Parties** Harmony and Rebirth for the National Economy, Latvian Way, National Independence Movement, Peasants' Union. **Suffrage** Universal, over 18. **Memberships** NATO, UN. **Subdivisions** 26 counties, 7 municipalities.
ECONOMY
GNP $13,200,000,000. **Per capita** $4,823. **Monetary unit** Lat. **Trade partners** Russia, Ukraine, other former Soviet republics. **Exports** Food, railroad cars, chemicals. **Imports** Machinery, petroleum products, chemicals.
LAND
Description Eastern Europe. **Area** 24,595 mi² (63,700 km²). **Highest point** Gaizina Hill, 1,020 ft (311 m). **Lowest point** Sea level.

People. The Latvians are closely related to the neighboring Lithuanians, and the Latvian language is one of the oldest in Europe. Many Latvians were killed or deported during World War II and the subsequent Soviet invasion. Today, more than one-third of the people are Russian. Most Latvians are Lutheran or Roman Catholic.

Economy and the Land. Manufacturing is the foundation of the Latvian economy, despite its lack of energy resources. Industrial production is highly diversified. Latvia's farms are efficient, and food is plentiful and varied. Most of the land is low plains, and much is forested. The capital city of Rīga is one of the Baltic region's busiest ports.

History and Politics. Latvian history was profoundly affected by the Teutonic Knights, who ruled the country for more than two hundred years starting in the mid-1300s. They established themselves as landowners and forced the Latvians into serfdom. Latvia was subsequently captured by Poland, Sweden, and Russia. After one hundred years of Russian rule, serfdom in Latvia was eliminated in the early 1700s. An independent Latvian state was established in 1918. Political instability followed and the country descended into fascism. In 1940, the Soviet Union invaded Latvia, ending twenty-two years of Latvian independence. The Latvians resisted Soviet domination and regained their independence in 1991. They have begun a transition to a free market economy. ■

LEBANON

Official name Republic of Lebanon

PEOPLE
Population 3,660,000. **Density** 912/mi² (352/km²). **Urban** 84%. **Capital** Beirut, 509,000. **Ethnic groups** Arab 95%, Armenian 4%. **Languages** Arabic, French, Armenian, English. **Religions** Muslim 70%, Christian 30%. **Life expectancy** 71 female, 67 male. **Literacy** 80%.
POLITICS
Government Republic. **Parties** Progressive Socialist, Liberal Nationalist, Phalangist, others. **Suffrage** Females, over 21 (with elementary education); males, over 21. **Memberships** AL, UN.
Subdivisions 6 governorates.
ECONOMY
GDP $6,100,000,000. **Per capita** $1,759. **Monetary unit** Pound. **Trade partners** Exports: Saudi Arabia, Switzerland, Jordan. Imports: Italy, France, U.S., Turkey. **Exports** Agricultural products, chemicals, textiles, jewelry. **Imports** Food, textiles and clothing, machinery and transportation equipment, metals.
LAND
Description Southwestern Asia. **Area** 4,015 mi² (10,400 km²). **Highest point** Mt. Sawda, 10,115 ft (3,083 m). **Lowest point** Sea level.

People. Traditionally home to many diverse groups, Lebanon has recently been shaken by the conflicting demands of its population. Almost all Lebanese are of Arab stock, and Arabic and French are the official languages. Palestinian refugees have settled here since the creation of Israel in 1948, many of them living in refugee camps. Lebanon's religious makeup is notable for its variety, encompassing seventeen recognized sects. Islam is now the majority religion, although Christianity continues to be a strong presence. Muslims are divided among the majority Shiite, minority Sunni, and Druze sects, while most Christians are Maronites.

Economy and the Land. Situated strategically between the West and the Middle East, Lebanon has long been a center of commerce. Its economy is fueled by the service sector, particularly banking. Prolonged fighting, beginning with the 1975 civil war, has greatly damaged all economic activity. Much of the work force is engaged in agriculture, and various crops are grown. The coastal area consists of a plain, behind which lie mountain ranges separated by a fertile valley. The climate is Mediterranean.

History and Politics. The Phoenicians settled parts of Lebanon about 3000 B.C. and were followed by Egyptian, Assyrian, Persian, Greek, and Roman rulers. Christianity came to the area during the Byzantine Empire, around A.D. 325, and Islam followed in the seventh century. In 1516 Lebanon was incorporated into the Ottoman Empire. Between the end of World War I, when the Ottoman Empire collapsed, and 1943, when Lebanon became independent, the nation was a French mandate. After independence, Muslims and Christians shared government power. Opposition to Lebanon's close ties to the West led to a 1958 insurrection, which United States marines put down at the government's request. The Palestine Liberation Organization (PLO), a group working to establish a Palestinian state, began operating from bases in Lebanon. This led to clashes with Israel in the late 1970s and early 1980s. The presence of the PLO divided Muslims, who generally supported it, from Christians, who opposed it. The increasing Muslim population also demanded a greater voice in the government. Civil war between Muslims and Christians broke out in 1975, and fighting slowed the next year with the requested aid of Syrian deterrent forces. Internal instability continued, however, along with Israeli-Palestinian hostilities. In June 1982 Israel invaded Lebanon, driving the PLO from Beirut and the south. Hundreds of Palestinian refugees were killed by the Christian Lebanese forces in September. A multinational peacekeeping force left after falling victim to terrorist attacks. Israel began a gradual withdrawal from Lebanon in 1985, but maintains a buffer zone in southern Lebanon. Syrian troops also occupy parts of the country. An uneasy peace has returned to Beirut, but sporadic fighting continues in southern Lebanon. ■

LESOTHO

Official name Kingdom of Lesotho
PEOPLE
Population 1,967,000. **Density** 168/mi² (65/km²). **Urban** 19%. **Capital** Maseru, 109,382. **Ethnic groups** Sotho 99%. **Languages** English, Sesotho, Zulu, Xhosa. **Religions** Roman Catholic and other Christian 80%, tribal religionist 20%. **Life expectancy** 63 female, 58 male. **Literacy** 59%.
POLITICS
Government Constitutional monarchy under mili-

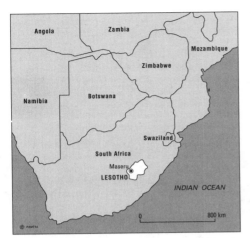

South Africa and became the independent kingdom of Lesotho in 1966. The military has effectively ruled since 1986, considerably reducing the powers of the hereditary monarchy. Surprise March 1993 election results have given an elected government at least some power. King Moshoeshoe II was restored to the throne in 1995. ∎

LIBERIA

tary rule. **Parties** Basotho National, Basutoland Congress, Democratic Alliance, others. **Suffrage** Universal, over 21 or married. **Memberships** CW, OAU, UN. **Subdivisions** 10 districts.
ECONOMY
GDP $2,800,000,000. **Per capita** $1,495.
Monetary unit Loti. **Trade partners** South Africa, Western European countries. **Exports** Wool, mohair, wheat, cattle, peas, beans, corn, hides and skins. **Imports** Corn, building materials, clothing, vehicles, machinery, pharmaceuticals.
LAND
Description Southern Africa, landlocked. **Area** 11,720 mi² (30,355 km²). **Highest point** Mt. Ntlenyana, 11,425 ft (3,482 m). **Lowest point** Along Orange River, 5,000 ft (1,524 m).

People. The Sotho, a black African group, comprise almost all of Lesotho's population. Most Sotho live in the lowlands and raise livestock and crops. The official languages are Sesotho, a Bantu tongue, and English, and the traditional religion is based on ancestor worship, though most Sotho are Roman Catholic. A system of tribal chieftaincy is followed locally.

Economy and the Land. Surrounded by South Africa and having few resources, Lesotho is almost entirely dependent on South Africa for economic survival. Much of the male population must seek employment there, usually spending several months a year in South African mines or industries. Agriculture remains at the subsistence level, and soil erosion threatens production. Livestock raising represents a significant part of Lesotho's economy. Wool and mohair are among the chief exports. Diamond mining, one of the few industries, employs a small portion of the population. Most of the terrain is mountainous; the fairly high elevations give Lesotho a temperate climate.

History and Politics. Refugees from tribal wars in southern Africa arrived in what is now Lesotho between the sixteenth and nineteenth centuries A.D. Chief Moshoeshoe united the Sotho tribes in 1818 and led them in war against the Boers, settlers of Dutch or Huguenot descent. At Moshoeshoe's request, Basutoland came under British protection in 1868. It resisted attempts at absorption by the Union of

Official name Republic of Liberia
PEOPLE
Population 2,771,000. **Density** 72/mi² (28/km²). **Urban** 45%. **Capital** Monrovia, 465,000. **Ethnic groups** Indigenous African 95%, descendants of freed American slaves 5%. **Languages** English, indigenous. **Religions** Animist 70%, Muslim 20%, Christian 10%. **Life expectancy** 57 female, 54 male. **Literacy** 40%.
POLITICS
Government Republic. **Parties** Action, National Democratic, others. **Suffrage** Universal, over 18. **Memberships** OAU, UN. **Subdivisions** 11 counties, 2 territories.
ECONOMY
GDP $2,300,000,000. **Per capita** $802. **Monetary unit** Dollar. **Trade partners** Exports: Germany, U.S., Italy. Imports: U.S., Germany, Netherlands. **Exports** Iron ore, rubber, timber, coffee. **Imports** Rice, fuel, chemicals, machinery, transportation equipment.
LAND
Description Western Africa. **Area** 38,250 mi² (99,067 km²). **Highest point** Mt. Wuteve, 4,528 ft (1,380 m). **Lowest point** Sea level.

People. Most Liberians belong to about twenty indigenous black groups. Few are descended from the freed American slaves who founded modern Liberia, but this group—known as Americo-Liberians—has traditionally been politically dominant. The official language is English, and more than twenty other tongues are also spoken. Most people are farmers and practice traditional religious beliefs, although Islam and

Christianity also have adherents. Liberia is the only black African state to escape colonialism.

Economy and the Land. Before the recent war, Liberia owed its healthy economy largely to an open-door policy, which had made its extensive resources attractive to foreign nations. Two of the most important activities, iron-ore mining and rubber production, were developed by western firms. Large timber reserves have not yet been fully exploited. Liberia also profits from the vast merchant fleet registered under its flag. The land is characterized by a coastal plain, plateaus, and low mountains, while the hot, humid climate is marked by distinct wet and dry seasons.

History and Politics. Early settlers are thought to have migrated from the north and east between the twelfth and seventeenth centuries A.D. Trade between Europeans and coastal groups developed after the Portuguese visited the area in the late 1400s. The American Colonization Society, a private United States organization devoted to resettling freed slaves, purchased land in Liberia, and in 1822 the first settlers landed at the site of Monrovia. The settlers declared their independence in 1847, setting up a government based on the United States model and creating Africa's first independent republic. For the next century, the Liberian government endured attempts at colonization by France and Britain, as well as internal tribal opposition. The string of Americo-Liberian rulers was broken in 1980, when a small group of soldiers of African descent toppled the government and imposed martial law. Civilian rule and some degree of harmony were restored in a 1985 election. Dissatisfaction with the growing corruption and waste of this government led to civil war in early 1990, resulting in the president's assassination. Peacekeeping forces of West African nations have been attempting to unify the various factions that have since divided the country. There are reports of 100,000 deaths from warfare and widespread starvation. ∎

LIBYA

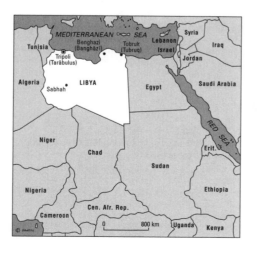

Official name Socialist People's Libyan Arab Jamahiriya
PEOPLE
Population 5,148,000. **Density** 7.6/mi² (2.9/km²). **Urban** 82%. **Capital** Tripoli, 591,062. **Ethnic groups** Arab-Berber 97%. **Languages** Arabic. **Religions** Sunni Muslim 97%. **Life expectancy** 65 female, 62 male. **Literacy** 64%.
POLITICS
Government Socialist republic. **Parties** None. **Suffrage** Universal, over 18. **Memberships** AL, OAU, OPEC, UN. **Subdivisions** 13 municipalities.
ECONOMY
GDP $32,000,000,000. **Per capita** $7,030. **Monetary unit** Dinar. **Trade partners** Exports: Italy, France, Greece. Imports: Italy, Japan, Germany. **Exports** Petroleum, peanuts, hides. **Imports** Machinery, transportation equipment, food, manufactures.
LAND
Description Northern Africa. **Area** 679,362 mi² (1,759,540 km²). **Highest point** Bīkkū Bīttī, 7,438 ft (2,267 m). **Lowest point** Sabkhat Ghuzzayil, -154 ft (-47 m).

People. Libya, originally settled by Berbers, is largely a mix of Arab and Berber today. Almost all Libyans live along the coast, with some nomadic groups in desert areas. Large migrations from rural areas to the cities have accompanied Libya's oil-based prosperity. Islam is the majority religion, and nearly all Libyans speak Arabic. Traditional social orders still exist, despite centuries of foreign rule.

Economy and the Land. The discovery of oil in 1959 propelled Libya from the ranks of the world's poorest nations to one of its leading oil producers. It has used these revenues to develop industry and agriculture to diversify its economy. Most of Libya is covered by the Sahara Desert, and the limited agriculture has been further hurt by Libyan farmers migrating to the cities. The climate is desert except for the coast, which has moderate temperatures.

History and Politics. For much of its history, Libya was dominated by Mediterranean empires: Phoenician, Carthaginian, Greek, and Roman. In the seventh century A.D. the area was taken by Muslim Arabs, whose language and religion transformed Libyan culture. Although the Ottoman Turks conquered the region in the sixteenth century, local rulers remained virtually autonomous. Italy invaded Libya in 1911, and the country became an Italian colony in 1912. Following World War II, British and French forces occupied the area until a United Nations resolution made Libya an independent nation in 1951. A monarchy ruled until 1969, when a military coup established a republic headed by Colonel Mu'ammar al-Qadhafi. Under his leadership, Libya has backed Arab unity and the Palestinian cause, opposed foreign influences, and created a welfare system. Libya's support of terrorist activities resulted in a controversial United States air strike against the country in 1986. Libya's refusal to turn over accused terrorists has led to United Nations sanctions. ∎

LIECHTENSTEIN

Official name Principality of Liechtenstein
PEOPLE
Population 30,000. **Density** 484/mi² (188/km²).
Urban 20%. **Capital** Vaduz, 4,887. **Ethnic groups**
Liechtensteiner (Alemannic) 95%. **Languages**
German. **Religions** Roman Catholic 87%,
Protestant 8%. **Life expectancy** 81 female, 74
male. **Literacy** 100%.
POLITICS
Government Constitutional monarchy. **Parties**
Fatherland Union, Progressive Citizens'. **Suffrage**
Universal, over 18. **Memberships** UN.
Subdivisions 11 communes.
ECONOMY
GDP $630,000,000. **Per capita** $22,500.
Monetary unit Swiss franc. **Trade partners**
Switzerland and other European countries.
Exports Machinery, dental products, stamps,
hardware, pottery. **Imports** Machinery, metal
goods, textiles, food, motor vehicles.
LAND
Description Central Europe, landlocked. **Area** 62
mi² (160 km²). **Highest point** Vorder-Grauspitz,
8,527 ft (2,599 m). **Lowest point** Ruggleller Riet,
1,411 ft (430 m).

People. In spite of its location at the crossroads of
Europe, Liechtenstein has retained a largely homogeneous ethnicity. Almost all Liechtensteiners are
descended from Germanic tribes, and German is the
official language. Roman Catholicism is the most widely practiced religion but a Protestant minority also exists.
Most of the country is mountainous, and population
is concentrated on the fertile plains adjacent to the
Rhine River, which forms the country's western
boundary. Most Liechtensteiners work in factories or
in trades.

Economy and the Land. The last few decades
have seen the economy shift from agricultural to highly industrialized. Despite this growth in industry,
Liechtenstein has not experienced a serious pollu-

tion problem, and the government continues its
work to prevent the problem from occurring. An
economic alliance with Switzerland dating from
1923 has been profoundly beneficial to Liechtenstein:
the two nations form a customs union and use the
same currency. Other important sources of revenue are tourism, the sale of postage stamps, and
taxation of foreign businesses headquartered here.
Most of Liechtenstein, one of the world's smallest
nations, is covered by the Alps; nonetheless, its climate is mild.

History and Politics. Early inhabitants of what is now
Liechtenstein included the Celts, Romans, and
Alemanni, who arrived about A.D. 500. The area
became part of the empire of the Frankish king
Charlemagne in the late 700s, and following
Charlemagne's death, it was divided into the lordships of Vaduz and Schellenberg. By 1719, when
the state became part of the Holy Roman Empire,
the Austrian House of Liechtenstein had purchased
both lordships, uniting them as the Imperial Principality
of Liechtenstein. The nation's independence dates
from the abolition of the empire by France's Napoleon
Bonaparte in 1806. Liechtenstein was neutral in both
world wars and has remained unaffected by European
conflicts. The government is a hereditary constitutional monarchy; the prince is the head of the
House of Liechtenstein, thus chief of state, and the
prime minister is the head of government. Women
gained the right to vote in 1984. ■

LITHUANIA

Official name Republic of Lithuania
PEOPLE
Population 3,757,000. **Density** 149/mi² (58/km²).
Urban 69%. **Capital** Vilnius, 596,900. **Ethnic
groups** Lithuanian 80%, Russian 9%, Polish 8%,
Byelorussian 2%. **Languages** Lithuanian, Polish,
Russian. **Religions** Roman Catholic, Lutheran.
Life expectancy 77 female, 68 male. **Literacy**
99%.

POLITICS
Government Republic. **Parties** Christian Democratic, Democratic Labor, Sajudis, Social Democratic. **Suffrage** Universal, over 18. **Memberships** NATO, UN. **Subdivisions** 44 regions, 11 municipalities.

ECONOMY
GDP $12,400,000,000. **Per capita** $3,260. **Monetary unit** Litas. **Trade partners** Russia, Ukraine, other former Soviet republics. **Exports** Electronics, petroleum products, food, chemicals. **Imports** Petroleum, machinery, chemicals, grain.

LAND
Description Eastern Europe. **Area** 25,212 mi² (65,300 km²). **Highest point** Juozapines Hill, 965 ft (294 m). **Lowest point** Sea level.

People. Lithuanians are a Baltic people related to the Latvians. Although about 80 percent of the people are ethnic Lithuanians, Russian immigrants held many key positions in Lithuania under Soviet rule. Lithuanians also chafed under Soviet rules restricting religion because most are devoutly Roman Catholic. Lithuanians are known for their fine singing and splendid choral festivals.

Economy and the Land. Prior to Soviet rule, Lithuania was predominately rural with an agricultural economy based on meat and dairy products. Today the Lithuanian economy is dependent on industrial production, although it lacks significant mineral fuel deposits. The nation has suffered from a severe oil shortage since independence when the Russians ceased to supply subsidized oil. The land is generally flat. There are fine white-sand beaches along the coastline of the Baltic Sea.

History and Politics. Unlike the neighboring Soviet republics of Latvia and Estonia, Lithuania has had a long tradition of independence. By the mid-1300s, Lithuania extended from the Baltic to the Black seas, and was a major regional power. Close political association with Poland led to a merger in 1569 and eventual annexation by Russia in the late nineteenth century. In 1918, Lithuania again claimed its independence, until it was overtaken by the Soviets in 1940. Stalin killed or deported about one-third of the Lithuanian population. Friction between Lithuania and the Soviet Union increased after the introduction of *glasnost* fueled Lithuanian aspirations for independence. A Soviet invasion in early 1991 was followed by international recognition of Lithuania as an independent state later in the year. Disillusionment with their lagging economy led to a surprise victory by the ex-communist Democratic Labor Party in October 1992. ■

LUXEMBOURG

Official name Grand Duchy of Luxembourg
PEOPLE
Population 396,000. **Density** 397/mi² (153/km²). **Urban** 84%. **Capital** Luxembourg, 75,377. **Ethnic groups** Luxembourger (mixed Celtic, French, and German). **Languages** French, Luxembourgish, German. **Religions** Roman Catholic 97%, Jewish

and Protestant 3%. **Life expectancy** 79 female, 72 male. **Literacy** 100%.

POLITICS
Government Constitutional monarchy. **Parties** Christian Socialist, Liberal, Socialist Workers, others. **Suffrage** Universal, over 18. **Memberships** EU, NATO, OECD, UN. **Subdivisions** 3 districts.

ECONOMY
GDP $8,700,000,000. **Per capita** $22,194. **Monetary unit** Franc. **Trade partners** Exports: Western European countries, U.S. Imports: Belgium, Germany, France. **Exports** Iron and steel products, chemicals, rubber products, glass. **Imports** Minerals, metals, food, consumer goods.

LAND
Description Western Europe, landlocked. **Area** 998 mi² (2,586 km²). **Highest point** Buurgplaatz, 1,834 ft (559 m). **Lowest point** Confluence of Moselle and Sûre rivers, 427 ft (130 m).

People. Luxembourg's population bears the imprint of foreign influences, yet retains an individual character. Most Luxembourgers are a blend of Celtic, French, and German stock. French is an official language, as is Luxembourgish, an indigenous German dialect. Roman Catholicism is observed by virtually all the population. There are significant communities of guest workers from several European nations.

Economy and the Land. Luxembourg's steel industry forms the basis of its economy, and the country has compensated for a worldwide drop in the steel market by developing financial services, notably banking. Manufacturing of plastics and chemicals is also important, as is tourism. Luxembourg's trade benefits from the country's membership in the European Community and the Benelux union. Luxembourg has two distinct regions: the mountainous, wooded north and the open, rolling south, known as Bon Pays. The climate is temperate.

History and Politics. The present city of Luxembourg developed from a castle built in A.D. 963 by Count Siegfried of Ardennes. Several heavily fortified towns grew up around the castle, and the area became known as the "Gibraltar of the North" because of those fortifications. The duchy remained semiautonomous until the Burgundians conquered the area in 1443. Various European powers ruled Luxembourg for most of the next four centuries, and in 1815 the duchy was elevated to a grand duchy. It became autonomous in 1839 and was recognized in 1867 as an independent state. Despite Luxembourg's declaration of neutrality, Germany occupied the country in both world wars. ∎

MACAO

Official name Macao
PEOPLE
Population 396,000. **Density** 57,571/mi² (22,000/km²). **Urban** 99%. **Capital** Macao, Macao I., 452,300. **Ethnic groups** Chinese 95%, Portuguese 3%. **Languages** Portuguese, Chinese (Cantonese). **Religions** Buddhist 45%, Roman Catholic 7%. **Life expectancy** 82 female, 77 male. **Literacy** 90%.
POLITICS
Government Chinese territory under Portuguese administration. **Parties** Association to Defend the Interests of Macau, Democratic Center, others. **Suffrage** Universal, over 18. **Memberships** None. **Subdivisions** 2 districts.
ECONOMY
GDP $3,500,000,000. **Per capita** $7,813. **Monetary unit** Pataca. **Trade partners** Exports: U.S., Hong Kong, Germany. Imports: Hong Kong, China, Japan. **Exports** Textiles, clothing, toys. **Imports** Raw materials, food, machinery.
LAND
Description Eastern Asia (islands and peninsula on China's southeastern coast). **Area** 7.0 mi² (18 km²). **Highest point** Coloane Alto, 571 ft (174 m). **Lowest point** Sea level.

People. Situated on the southeastern China coast, 17 miles (27.4 km) west of Hong Kong, Macao is populated almost entirely by Chinese. A former overseas province of Portugal, the island also includes people of Portuguese and mixed Chinese-Portuguese descent. Several Chinese dialects are widely spoken, and Portuguese is the official language. Buddhism is Macao's principal religion; a small percentage of its population are Roman Catholics.

Economy and the Land. Tourism, gambling, and light industry help make up Macao's economy; however, its leading industries are textiles and light manufacturing, which employ the majority of the labor force. Macao has been likened to Hong Kong because of its textile exports, yet it remains a heavy importer, relying on China for drinking water and much of its food supply. The province consists of the city of Macao, located on a peninsula, and the nearby islands of Taipa and Coloane. The climate is maritime tropical, with cool winters and warm summers.

History and Politics. Macao became a Portuguese trading post in 1557. It flourished as the midpoint for trade between China and Japan but declined when Hong Kong became a trading power in the mid-1800s. Macao remained a neutral port during World War II and was economically prosperous. Although the government is nominally directed by Portugal, any policies relating to Macao are subject to China's approval. Macao is the oldest European settlement in the Far East. It will be returned to China in 1999 under a negotiated agreement whereby the present capitalist system will be maintained for fifty years. ∎

MACEDONIA

Official name Republic of Macedonia
PEOPLE
Population 2,102,000. **Density** 212/mi² (82/km²). **Urban** 54%. **Capital** Skopje, 444,900. **Ethnic groups** Macedonian 67%, Albanian 21%, Turkish 4%, Serb 2%. **Languages** Macedonian, Albanian. **Religions** Eastern Orthodox 59%, Muslim 26%, Roman Catholic 4%. **Life expectancy** 75 female, 71 male. **Literacy** 89%.
POLITICS
Government Republic. **Parties** Internal Revolutionary Organization-Democratic National Unity, Social Democratic Alliance. **Suffrage** Universal, over 18. **Memberships** UN. **Subdivisions** 34 counties.
ECONOMY
GDP $2,200,000,000. **Per capita** $1,010. **Monetary unit** Denar. **Trade partners** Exports: Former Yugoslavian republics, Germany, Greece. Imports: Former Yugoslavian republics, Greece, Albania. **Exports** Manufactures, machinery and transportation equipment, raw materials, food. **Imports** Fuels and lubricants, manufactures, machinery and transport equipment.
LAND
Description Eastern Europe, landlocked. **Area** 9,928 mi² (25,713 km²). **Highest point** Korab, 9,035 ft (2,754 m). **Lowest point** Along Vardar River, 165 ft (50 m).

People. Most Macedonians are of mixed Serbian and Bulgarian descent, reflected in the country's Slavic dialect. Albanians are the most significant minority. Many Macedonians practice the Orthodox religion, although there is a significant Muslim minority in the western part of the country. Macedonians are proud of their folklore and traditional music.

Economy and the Land. Landlocked Macedonia is predominately mountainous, and most of the people are involved in agriculture and herding. Agricultural products include cereal grains, tobacco, and cotton. The country has deposits of iron ore, lead, zinc, nickel, and chromium, but there are no significant mineral fuels. Macedonia is the poorest and least developed of the former Yugoslavian republics.

History and Politics. The country of Macedonia is part of a larger historical region of the same name. Macedonia reached its zenith under the rule of Alexander the Great, who created a vast Macedonian empire in the fourth century B.C. that extended from Egypt to northern India. The empire fell apart after Alexander's death, and Rome then conquered the region. The Slavic people, who were the ancestors of today's Macedonians, migrated to the area in the sixth century A.D. The region suffered numerous invasions over the centuries. After 500 years of Turkish rule, it was finally split between Serbia, Greece, and Bulgaria in 1913, after serving as a battleground for two Balkan wars. In 1945, the Serbian portion of Macedonia became a full republic of Yugoslavia. It remained part of Yugoslavia until 1991, when it followed the lead of neighboring Yugoslavian republics and declared its independence. International peacekeeping forces in Macedonia are attempting to prevent a spillover of ethnic strife. Greece opposes use of the name "Macedonia." U.S. and European Union recognition of Macedonia in 1994 prompted Greece to cut off Macedonia's main trade route. ∎

MADAGASCAR

Official name Republic of Madagascar
PEOPLE
Population 13,645,000. **Density** 60/mi² (23/km²).
Urban 24%. **Capital** Antananarivo, 1,250,000.
Ethnic groups Merina 15%, Betsimisaraka 9%,

Betsileo 7%, Tsimihety 4%, Antaisaka 4%, other tribes. **Languages** Malagasy, French. **Religions** Animist 52%, Christian 41%, Muslim 7%. **Life expectancy** 57 female, 54 male. **Literacy** 80%.
POLITICS
Government Republic. **Parties** Advance Guard of the Revolution, Militants for the Establishment of a Proletarian Regime, others. **Suffrage** Universal, over 18. **Memberships** OAU, UN. **Subdivisions** 6 provinces.
ECONOMY
GDP $10,400,000,000. **Per capita** $813.
Monetary unit Franc. **Trade partners** Exports: France, U.S., Japan. Imports: France, U.S., former Soviet republics. **Exports** Coffee, vanilla, cloves, sugar, petroleum. **Imports** Manufactures, machinery, petroleum, food.
LAND
Description Southeastern African island. **Area** 226,658 mi² (587,041 km²). **Highest point** Maromokotro, 9,436 ft (2,876 m). **Lowest point** Sea level.

People. Most of the population is of mixed African and Indonesian descent. Those who live on the coast, the *cotiers*, are of predominantly African origin, while those on the inland plateau have Asian roots. There is a long-standing rivalry between the *cotiers* and the inland groups, most of whom belong to the Merina people. The official language is Malagasy. Sizable Christian communities exist, but most Malagasy practice indigenous Animist beliefs.

Economy and the Land. Madagascar is chiefly an agricultural nation, with the majority of the work force engaged in farming or herding. Overpopulation and outmoded cultivation have recently cut into yields of rice, an important crop, and other products. Varied mineral resources, including oil, point to possible expansion. The climate is tropical on the coastal plains and moderate in the inland highlands.

History and Politics. Madagascar's first settlers are thought to be Indonesians, who brought African wives and slaves around two thousand years ago. Arab traders established themselves on the coast in the seventh century. The Portuguese first sighted the island in the 1500s, and other Europeans followed. The Merina kingdom, based in the central plateau, gained control over most of the island in the 1790s. French influence grew throughout the nineteenth century, and in 1896 France made the island a colony after subduing the Merina. Resentment of French rule continued, culminating in an armed revolt in 1947. Full independence came in 1960. After twelve years of rule by the same president, a coup placed the military in power. A new constitution was adopted in 1975 that established the Democratic Republic of Madagascar. By 1991 there were major protests against the government, and a late 1992 election was won by the opposition. A new constitution was approved after much dissension; the highland people favoring a unitary form of government won over the coastal people who wanted a federal system with stronger regional control. ∎

MADEIRA ISLANDS
See PORTUGAL.

MALAWI

Official name Republic of Malawi
PEOPLE
Population 8,984,000. **Density** 196/mi² (76/km²).
Urban 12%. **Capital** Lilongwe, 233,318. **Ethnic groups** Chewa, Nyanja, Tumbuko, Yao, Lomwe, others. **Languages** Chichewa, English. **Religions** Protestant 55%, Roman Catholic 20%, Muslim 20%. **Life expectancy** 45 female, 44 male. **Literacy** 22%.
POLITICS
Government Republic. **Parties** Congress, others. **Suffrage** Universal, over 21. **Memberships** CW, OAU, UN. **Subdivisions** 3 regions.
ECONOMY
GDP $6.000,000,000. **Per capita** $619. **Monetary unit** Kwacha. **Trade partners** Exports: U.K., Germany, South Africa. Imports: South African countries, U.K., Japan. **Exports** Tobacco, tea, sugar, coffee, peanuts. **Imports** Food, petroleum, manufactures, transportation equipment.
LAND
Description Southern Africa, landlocked. **Area** 45,747 mi² (118,484 km²). **Highest point** Sapitwa, 9,849 ft (3,002 m). **Lowest point** Along Shire River, 120 ft (37 m).

People. Almost all Malawians are black Africans descended from Bantu peoples. The Chewa constitute the majority in the central area, while the Nyanja are dominant in the south and the Tumbuko in the north. Chichewa and English are official languages. The majority of the population is rural, and traditional village customs are prevalent. For the most part, the society is matriarchal. Many Malawians combine Christian or Muslim beliefs with traditional religious practices.

Economy and the Land. A landlocked nation with limited resources and a largely unskilled work force, Malawi relies almost entirely on agriculture. A recent series of poor harvests, combined with a tripling of the population between 1950 and 1989, has contributed to the decline in agricultural output and consequent food shortages. Among the main exports are tea and tobacco. Many Malawians work part of the year as miners in South Africa, Zambia, and Zimbabwe. Malawi, situated along the Great Rift Valley, has a varied terrain with highlands, plateaus, and lakes. The climate is subtropical, and rainfall varies greatly from north to south.

History and Politics. Archeological findings indicate that Malawi has been inhabited for at least 50,000 years. Bantu-speaking peoples, ancestors of the Malawians, immigrated from the north around A.D. 1400 and soon formed centralized kingdoms. In the 1830s, other Bantu groups, involved in the slave trade, invaded the region. The arrival of Scottish missionary David Livingstone in 1859 began a period of British influence; in 1891 the territory became the British protectorate of Nyasaland. Beginning in 1953, Nyasaland was part of the larger Federation of Rhodesia and Nyasaland. Malawi attained independence in 1964 and became a republic in 1966, with nationalist leader Dr. Hastings Banda as its first president. The Malawi Congress party appointed Banda as president-for-life in 1970, but a 1993 referendum strongly favored the creation of a multiparty system. In May 1994, President Banda, who was the oldest head of state in the world and Africa's longest-ruling dictator, was ousted from office and then charged with the murder of political foes. ∎

MALAYSIA

Official name Malaysia
PEOPLE
Population 19,505,000. **Density** 153/mi² (59/km²). **Urban** 43%. **Capital** Kuala Lumpur,

919,610. **Ethnic groups** Malay and other indigenous 59%, Chinese 32%, Indian 9%. **Languages** Malay, Chinese dialects, English, Tamil. **Religions** Muslim 53%, Buddhist 17%, Chinese religions 12%, Hindu 7%. **Life expectancy** 73 female, 69 male. **Literacy** 78%.

POLITICS

Government Constitutional monarchy. **Parties** Democratic Action, Islamic, National Front. **Suffrage** Universal, over 21. **Memberships** ASEAN, CW, UN. **Subdivisions** 13 states, 2 federal territories.

ECONOMY

GDP $141,000,000,000. **Per capita** $7,568. **Monetary unit** Ringgit. **Trade partners** Exports: Singapore, U.S., Japan. Imports: Japan, U.S., Singapore. **Exports** Manufactures, petroleum, timber, rubber, palm oil, textiles. **Imports** Food, petroleum, manufactures, machinery, chemicals.

LAND

Description Southeastern Asia (includes part of the island of Borneo). **Area** 127,320 mi² (329,758 km²). **Highest point** Mt. Kinabalu, 13,455 ft (4,101 m). **Lowest point** Sea level.

People. Malaysia's location at one of Southeast Asia's maritime crossroads has left it with a diverse population, including Malays, Chinese, Indians, and native non-Malay groups. The mostly rural Malays dominate politically, while the predominantly urban Chinese are very active in economic life. Considerable tension exists between the two groups. Although most Malays speak Malay and practice Islam, Malaysia's ethnic groups have resisted assimilation; Chinese, Indian, and Western languages and beliefs are also part of the culture. Most Malaysians live in Peninsular Malaysia.

Economy and the Land. The economy is one of the healthiest in the region, supported by multiple strengths in agriculture, mining, forestry, and fishing. The nation is one of the world's leading producers of rubber, palm oil, and tin, and one of the Far East's largest petroleum exporters. Manufacturing is also being developed. Malaysia consists of the southern portion of the Malay Peninsula and the states of Sarawak and Sabah on northern Borneo. The land features swampy areas, mountains, and rain forests. The climate is tropical and very humid.

History and Politics. The Malay Peninsula has been inhabited since the late Stone Age. Hindu and Buddhist influences were widespread from the ninth through the fourteenth centuries A.D., after which Islam was introduced. In 1511 the Portuguese seized Melaka, a trading center, but were soon replaced, first by the Dutch in 1641 and then by the British in 1795. By the early 1900s, Britain was in control of present-day Malaysia and Singapore, the areas which were occupied by Japan during World War II. Following the war, the Federation of Malaya was created, a semiautonomous state under British authority. A guerrilla war ensued, waged by Chinese Communists and others who opposed the British. The country gained full independence in 1963 with the unification of Malaysia. Singapore seceded in 1965. Government attempts in 1993 to curb the powers of hereditary rulers threatens peace in the country. ∎

MALDIVES

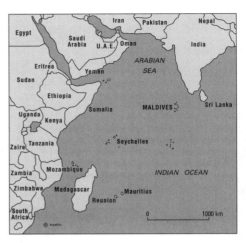

Official name Republic of Maldives

PEOPLE

Population 251,000. **Density** 2,183/mi² (842/km²). **Urban** 29%. **Capital** Male', Male I., 55,130. **Ethnic groups** Maldivian (mixed Sinhalese, Dravidian, Arab, and black). **Languages** Divehi. **Religions** Sunni Muslim. **Life expectancy** 62 female, 65 male. **Literacy** 92%.

POLITICS

Government Republic. **Parties** None. **Suffrage** Universal, over 21. **Memberships** CW, UN. **Subdivisions** 19 districts, 1 capital city.

ECONOMY

GDP $140,000,000. **Per capita** $651. **Monetary unit** Rufiyaa. **Trade partners** Exports: U.S., U.K., Sri Lanka. Imports: Singapore, Germany, Sri Lanka. **Exports** Fish, clothing. **Imports** Consumer goods, manufactures, petroleum products.

LAND

Description Indian Ocean islands. **Area** 115 mi² (298 km²). **Highest point** Unnamed, 10 ft (3 m). **Lowest point** Sea level.

People. Most Maldivians are descended from Sinhalese peoples from Sri Lanka; southern Indians, or Dravidians; and Arabs. Nearly all Maldivians are Sunni Muslims and speak Divehi. The population is concentrated on Male, the capital island.

Economy and the Land. The nation draws on its advantages as a union of eleven hundred islands to fuel its economy: tourism, shipping, and fishing are the mainstays. With limited arable land and infertile soil, agriculture is marginal. The Maldives, flat coral islands, form a chain of nineteen atolls. Seasonal monsoons mark the tropical climate.

History and Politics. The Maldives are believed to have been originally settled by southern Indian peoples. Arab sailors brought Islam to the islands in the twelfth century A.D. Although a Muslim sultanate remained in power with only two interruptions from 1153 until 1968, the Portuguese and Dutch controlled the islands intermittently between the

1500s and the 1700s. The Maldives were a British protectorate from 1887 to 1965, when they achieved independence. They declared the country a republic three years later. ■

MALI

Official name Republic of Mali
PEOPLE
Population 9,585,000. **Density** 20/mi^2 (7.2/km^2).
Urban 24%. **Capital** Bamako, 658,275. **Ethnic groups** Mande 50%, Fulani 17%, Voltaic 12%, Songhai 6%. **Languages** French, Bambara, indigenous. **Religions** Sunni Muslim 90%, Animist 9%, Christian 1%. **Life expectancy** 48 female, 44 male. **Literacy** 32%.
POLITICS
Government Republic. **Parties** Alliance for Democracy, National Committee for Democratic Initiative, Sudanese Union-African Democratic Rally. **Suffrage** Universal, over 21. **Memberships** OAU, UN. **Subdivisions** 8 regions, 1 capital district.
ECONOMY
GDP $5,800,000,000. **Per capita** $663. **Monetary unit** CFA franc. **Trade partners** Exports: Cote d'Ivoire, Senegal, former Soviet Union. Imports: France, Cote d'Ivoire, Senegal. **Exports** Livestock, peanuts, fish, cotton, animal hides. **Imports** Textiles, vehicles, petroleum, machinery, sugar, grain.
LAND
Description Western Africa, landlocked. **Area** 482,077 mi^2 (1,248,574 km^2). **Highest point** Hombori Mtn., 3,789 ft (1,155 m). **Lowest point** Along Senegal River, 72 ft (22 m).

People. The majority of Malians belong to one of several black groups, although there is a small non-black nomadic population. Most Malians are farmers who live in small villages. The official language is French, but most people communicate in Bambara, a market language. The population is concentrated in the basins of the Niger and Senegal rivers in the south. Heirs of three ancient empires, Malians have produced a distinct culture.

Economy and the Land. One of the world's poorest nations, Mali depends primarily on agriculture but is limited by a climate that produces drought and a terrain that is almost half desert. Mineral reserves have not been exploited because of poor transportation and power facilities. Food processing and textiles account for most industry. A landlocked country, Mali faces a growing national debt due to its dependence on foreign goods. The climate is hot and dry, with alternating dry and wet seasons.

History and Politics. Parts of present-day Mali once belonged to the Ghana, Mali, and Songhai empires. These wealthy empires, which ruled from about A.D. 300 to 1600, traded with the Mediterranean world and were centers of Islamic learning. Fierce native resistance delayed colonization by the French until 1904, when French Sudan, as the area was called, was made part of French West Africa. In 1959 it joined Senegal to form the Federation of Mali. Senegal soon withdrew from the union, and French Sudan declared itself the Republic of Mali in 1960. A military coup overthrew the republic, a socialist state, in 1968. This government, in turn, was overthrown and the country has since moved haltingly towards democracy. Nomadic Tuareg rebels have negotiated a peace agreement. ■

MALTA

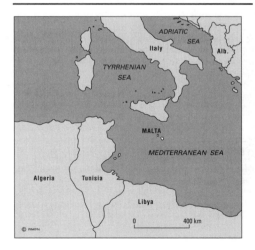

Official name Republic of Malta
PEOPLE
Population 368,000. **Density** 3,016/mi^2 (1,165/km^2). **Urban** 87%. **Capital** Valletta, 9,199. **Ethnic groups** Maltese (mixed Arab, Sicilian, Norman, Spanish, Italian, and English). **Languages** English, Maltese. **Religions** Roman Catholic 98%. **Life expectancy** 78 female, 74 male. **Literacy** 84%.

POLITICS
Government Republic. **Parties** Labor, Nationalist. **Suffrage** Universal, over 18. **Memberships** CW, UN. **Subdivisions** 6 regions.
ECONOMY
GDP $2,400,000,000. **Per capita** $6,723. **Monetary unit** Lira. **Trade partners** Exports: Italy, Germany, U.K. Imports: Italy, U.K., Germany. **Exports** Clothing, textiles, footwear, ships. **Imports** Food, petroleum, machinery, manufactures.
LAND
Description Mediterranean island. **Area** 122 mi^2 (316 km^2). **Highest point** Unnamed, 829 ft (253 m). **Lowest point** Sea level.

People. Malta's diverse population reflects centuries of rule by Arabs, Normans, and British. The official languages are English and Maltese, the latter a blend of Arabic and a Sicilian dialect of Italian. Roman Catholicism is practiced by the majority of residents. Malta is one of the world's most densely populated nations.

Economy and the Land. Situated strategically between Europe and Africa, Malta became an important military site for foreign powers with the opening of the Suez Canal in 1869. Its economy, shaped by the patterns of war and peace in the Mediterranean, has recently turned toward commercial shipbuilding, construction, manufacturing, and tourism. Its soil is poor, and most food is imported. Although there are many natural harbors and hundreds of miles of coastline, fishing is not a major source of income. Malta, with its hilly terrain, is subtropical in summer and temperate the rest of the year.

History and Politics. The Phoenicians and Carthaginians first colonized the island of Malta between 1000 and 600 B.C. After becoming part of the Roman and Byzantine empires, Malta was ruled successively by Arabs, Normans, and various feudal lords. In the 1500s the Holy Roman Emperor Charles V ceded Malta to the Knights of St. John of Jerusalem, an order of the Roman Catholic church. The Knights' reign, marked by cultural and architectural achievements, ended with surrender to France's Napoleon Bonaparte in 1798. The Maltese resisted French rule, however, and offered control to Britain, becoming part of the United Kingdom in 1814. Throughout both world wars, Malta was a vital naval base for the Allied forces. It achieved independence from Britain in 1964 and became a republic ten years later. In 1979 the last British and North Atlantic Treaty Organization (NATO) military forces departed, and Malta declared its neutrality. ∎

MARSHALL ISLANDS

Official name Republic of the Marshall Islands
PEOPLE
Population 55,000. **Density** 786/mi^2 (304/km^2). **Urban** 48%. **Capital** Majuro (island). **Ethnic groups** Micronesian. **Languages** English, indigenous, Japanese. **Religions** Protestant, Roman Catholic. **Life expectancy** 64 female, 61 male. **Literacy** 93%.

POLITICS
Government Republic (U.S. protection). **Parties** None. **Suffrage** Universal, over 18. **Memberships** UN. **Subdivisions** None.
ECONOMY
GDP $63,000,000. **Per capita** $1,575. **Monetary unit** U.S. dollar. **Trade partners** U.S., Japan. **Exports** Copra, agricultural products, handicrafts. **Imports** Food, beverages, building materials.
LAND
Description North Pacific islands. **Area** 70 mi^2 (181 km^2). **Highest point** Unnamed, 80 ft (24 m). **Lowest point** Sea level.

People. Most Marshall Islanders are Micronesian, although there is a Polynesian minority. Both English and Malay-Polynesian languages are spoken on the islands.

Economy and the Land. The main industry of the Marshall Islands is coconuts, and many islanders continue to practice subsistence farming and fishing. The islands remain dependent on economic aid from the United States. Part of the area of the Pacific Ocean known as Micronesia, the two major island groups are the eastern Ratak Chain and the western Ralik Chain. The coral islands are mostly flat and low-lying, and the climate is hot and rainy.

History and Politics. The history of the Marshall Islands prior to the arrival of Europeans is largely unknown, but it is likely that the earliest settlers came from Southeast Asia. The islands received their name from Captain John Marshall, a Briton who reached the Marshalls in 1788. In the 1880s, the Marshall Islands became a German protectorate, and in 1914, during World War I, Japan seized the islands. During World War II, the United States captured the islands from Japan, and in 1947, the Marshall Islands were incorporated into the Trust Territory of the Pacific Islands established by the United Nations, and placed under the protection of the United States. In the late 1940s and early 1950s, the United States conducted dozens of nuclear test explosions throughout the Marshall Islands. The United States continues to provide compensation to those victimized by radiation-related illnesses and destruction of property, but the displaced inhabitants of Bikini Atoll insist that the United States should restore their island's environment. In 1986, the Marshall Islands became self-governing, when a compact of free association with the United States was finalized. Official recognition of the new republic did not come until 1991, when the United Nations removed the Marshall Islands from the trusteeship. ∎

MARTINIQUE See FRANCE.

MAURITANIA

Official name Islamic Republic of Mauritania

land regions include a northern desert and southeastern grasslands. Mauritania has a hot, dry climate.

History and Politics. Berbers began settling in parts of the area around A.D. 300 and established a network of caravan trading routes. From this time until the late 1500s, sections of the south were dominated by the Ghana, the Mali, and finally the Songhai empires. Contact with Europeans grew between the 1600s and 1800s, and in 1920 France made Mauritania a colony. Mauritania attained independence in 1960, although Morocco claimed the area and did not recognize the state until 1970. During the late seventies, Mauritania became embroiled in a war with Morocco and the Polisario Front, a Western Saharan nationalist group, for control of Western Sahara. Mauritania withdrew its claim to the area in 1979. A new constitution providing for universal suffrage was approved in 1991 and multiparty elections have been held. There are repeated reports of discrimination against the black population. ∎

PEOPLE
Population 2,228,000. **Density** 5.6/mi^2 (2.2/km^2). **Urban** 47%. **Capital** Nouakchott, 285,000. **Ethnic groups** Mixed Moor and black 40%, Moor 30%, black 30%. **Languages** Arabic, Pular, Soninke, Wolof. **Religions** Sunni Muslim 100%. **Life expectancy** 50 female, 46 male. **Literacy** 34%.
POLITICS
Government Republic. **Parties** Assembly for Democratic Unity, Democratic and Social Republican, Union of Democratic Forces-New Era. **Suffrage** Universal, over 18. **Memberships** AL, OAU, UN. **Subdivisions** 12 regions, 1 capital district.
ECONOMY
GDP $2,200,000,000. **Per capita** $1086. **Monetary unit** Ouguiya. **Trade partners** Exports: Japan, France, Spain. Imports: France, Spain, Senegal. **Exports** Iron ore, fish. **Imports** Food, manufactures, petroleum, machinery.
LAND
Description Western Africa. **Area** 395,955 mi^2 (1,025,520 km^2). **Highest point** Mt. Jill, 3,002 ft (915 m). **Lowest point** Sebkha de Ndrhamcha, -10 ft (-3 m).

People. Most Mauritanians are Moors, descendants of Arabs and Berbers, or of mixed Arab, Berber, and black descent. The Moors, who speak Arabic, are mostly nomadic herdsmen. The remainder of the population is composed of black Africans, who speak several languages and farm in the Senegal River valley. Virtually all Mauritanians are Muslim. Proportionally, the nomadic population has declined recently because of long periods of drought, although overall population is increasing.

Economy and the Land. Mauritania's economy is based on agriculture, with many farmers producing only subsistence-level outputs. Crop production, confined chiefly to the Senegal River valley, has recently fallen because of drought and outmoded cultivation methods. Mining of high-grade iron-ore deposits is the main industrial activity, although fishing and fish processing are also important. Inadequate transportation and communication systems have crippled the economy. In addition to the river valley,

MAURITIUS

Official name Republic of Mauritius

PEOPLE
Population 1,120,000. **Density** 1,423/mi^2 (550/km^2). **Urban** 41%. **Capital** Port Louis, Mauritius I., 141,870. **Ethnic groups** Indo-Mauritian 68%, Creole 27%, Sino-Mauritian 3%, Franco-Mauritian 2%. **Languages** English, Creole, Bhojpuri, French, Hindi, Tamil, others. **Religions** Hindu 52%, Roman Catholic 28%, Muslim 17%. **Life expectancy** 74 female, 67 male. **Literacy** 83%.
POLITICS
Government Republic. **Parties** Labor, Militant Socialist Movement, Militant Movement, Social Democratic, others. **Suffrage** Universal, over 18. **Memberships** CW, OAU, UN. **Subdivisions** 9 districts.
ECONOMY

GDP $8,600,000,000. **Per capita** $7,847.
Monetary unit Rupee. **Trade partners** Exports:
U.K., France, U.S. Imports: France, China, U.S.,
South Africa. **Exports** Textiles, sugar, manufac-
tures. **Imports** Manufactures, machinery, food,
petroleum, chemicals.
LAND
Description Indian Ocean island. **Area** 788 mi^2
(2,040 km^2). **Highest point** Piton de la Petite
Rivière Noire, Piton, 2,717 ft (828 m). **Lowest
point** Sea level.
The above information includes dependencies.

People. Mauritius's diverse ethnicity is largely the
product of its past as a sugar-producing colony.
Creoles are descendants of African slaves and
European plantation owners, while the Indian com-
munity traces its roots to laborers who replaced
the Africans after slavery was abolished. There are
also people of Chinese and French descent. Franco-
Mauritians now compose most of the nation's elite.
English is the official tongue, although a French cre-
ole and many other languages are also spoken.
Religious activity is similarly varied and includes
Hinduism, Christianity and Islam.

Economy and the Land. Once heavily dependent
on the production of sugar, Mauritius was wise
enough to diversify its economy as the price of
sugar fell. Tourism has become important, as well
as international finance and light industry, earning
it the reputation as Africa's Hong Kong. The nation
includes the island of Mauritius, Rodrigues Island,
Agalega Islands, and Cargados Carajos Shoals.
The climate is tropical.

History and Politics. Although visited by Arab,
Malay, and Portuguese sailors between the tenth and
sixteenth centuries A.D., Mauritius was uninhabited
until 1598, when the Dutch claimed it. They aban-
doned the island in 1710, and five years later the
French made it their colony. During the 1700s, the
French used Mauritius, which they called Île de
France, as a naval base and established plantations
worked by imported slaves. The British ousted the
French in 1810 and outlawed slavery soon afterward.
In the nineteenth century indentured workers from
India replaced the slaves. Mauritius began its history as an independent state in 1968 with a system
of parliamentary democracy, and became a repub-
lic in 1992. ■

MAYOTTE See FRANCE.

MEXICO

Official name United Mexican States
PEOPLE
Population 93,860,000. **Density** 124/mi^2
(48/km^2). **Urban** 73%. **Capital** Mexico City,
8,235,744. **Ethnic groups** Mestizo 60%,
Amerindian 30%, white 9%. **Languages** Spanish,
indigenous. **Religions** Roman Catholic 89%,

Protestant 6%. **Life expectancy** 74 female, 67
male. **Literacy** 87%.
POLITICS
Government Republic. **Parties** Cardenist Front of
the Nationalist Reconstruction, Institutional
Revolutionary, National Action, others. **Suffrage**
Universal, over 18. **Memberships** OAS, UN.
Subdivisions 31 states, 1 federal district.
ECONOMY
GDP $740,000,000,000. **Per capita** $8,588.
Monetary unit Peso. **Trade partners** Exports:
U.S., Japan, Spain. Imports: U.S., Germany,
Japan. **Exports** Petroleum, petroleum products,
coffee, shrimp, engines, motor vehicles. **Imports**
Grain, manufactures, agricultural machinery, elec-
trical equipment.
LAND
Description Southern North America. **Area**
759,534 mi^2 (1,967,183 km^2). **Highest point** Pico
de Orizaba, 18,406 ft (5,610 m). **Lowest point**
Laguna Salada, -26 ft (-8 m).

People. Most Mexicans are mestizos, descended from
Indians and the Spaniards who conquered Mexico
in the 1500s. Spanish is spoken by most inhabitants,
and Roman Catholicism is the most popular religion.
Another major ethnic group is comprised of indigenous Indians, or Amerindians, some of whom speak
only Indian languages and hold traditional religious
beliefs. Mexico's rapid population growth has contributed to poverty among rural dwellers, spurring a
migration to the cities. Due to its mild climate and fertile soils, Mexico's central plateau is home to most
of the population.

Economy and the Land. Mexico is a leading producer
of petroleum and silver, a growing manufacturer of
iron, steel, and chemicals, and an exporter of coffee and cotton. Foreign visitors—drawn by archeological sites and warm, sunny weather—make
tourism an important activity. Despite economic
gains made since the mid-1900s in agriculture and
industry, Mexico recently has been troubled by
inflation, declining oil prices, rising unemployment,
and a trade deficit that has grown with the need for
imported materials. In recent years the peso has been
significantly devalued, and banks have been nation-

alized to help reduce a massive international debt. Austerity plans and foreign aid are expected to help revitalize the economy. Terrain and climate are greatly varied, ranging from tropical jungles along the coast to desert plains in the north. A temperate central plateau is bounded by rugged mountains in the south, east, and west.

History and Politics. Farm settlements grew in the Valley of Mexico between 6500 and 1500 B.C., and during the subsequent 3,000 years Mexico gave birth to the great civilizations of the Olmec, Maya, Toltec, and Aztec Indians. The Aztec Empire was overthrown by the Spanish in 1521, and Mexico became the viceroyalty of New Spain. Although there was much dissatisfaction with Spanish rule, rebellion did not begin until 1810. Formal independence came in 1821. Mexico lost considerable territory, including Texas, to the United States during the Mexican War, from 1846 to 1848. During subsequent years, power changed hands frequently as liberals demanding social and economic reforms battled conservatives. A brief span of French imperial rule, from 1864 to 1867, interrupted the struggle. Following a revolution that started in 1910, a new socialist constitution was adopted in 1917, and progress toward reform began, culminating in the separation of church and state and the redistribution of land. Mexico joined the U.S. and Canada in approving the North American Free Trade Agreement in 1992. Momentum for political change developed after the January 1994 peasant rebellion in the state of Chiapas. ∎

MICRONESIA, FEDERATED STATES OF

Official name Federated States of Micronesia
PEOPLE
Population 122,000. **Density** 450/mi^2 (174/km^2).
Urban 19%. **Capital** Kolonia, 6,169 (de facto); Paliker (future). **Ethnic groups** Micronesian, Polynesian. **Languages** English, indigenous.
Religions Protestant, Roman Catholic. **Life expectancy** 69 female, 65 male. **Literacy** 90%.
POLITICS
Government Republic (U.S. protection). **Parties** None. **Suffrage** Universal, over 18. **Memberships** UN. **Subdivisions** 4 states.
ECONOMY
GNP $150,000,000. **Per capita** $1,389. **Monetary unit** U.S. dollar. **Trade partners** U.S., Japan.
Exports Copra, pepper, fish, handicrafts, coconut oil.
LAND
Description North Pacific islands. **Area** 271 mi^2 (702 km^2). **Highest point** Ngihneni, 2,566 ft (782 m). **Lowest point** Sea level.

People. Most inhabitants of Chuuk, Yap, Kosrae, and Pohnpei—the four states of the Federated States of Micronesia—are Micronesian, a group of mixed Melanesian, Polynesian, and Malaysian origin. Eight native languages are spoken, and English is the unifying language.

Economy and the Land. Subsistence farming and fishing are the primary activities for most islanders. Coconuts are the main cash crop. The states are heavily dependent on economic assistance from the United States, which will continue until 2001. Each of the four states comprises a number of islands and, together with the territory of Palau, form the Caroline Islands, made up of volcanic and coral islands. The climate is tropical.

History and Politics. The ancestors of today's population probably arrived in the region more than twenty-five hundred years ago. Spanish and German competition for the islands came to an end in 1899, when Germany purchased the Caroline Islands and most of the Mariana Islands from Spain. Japan controlled the islands from World War I until 1947, when the islands became part of the Trust Territory of the Pacific Islands. The trust territory was established by the United Nations and placed under United States administration. In 1978, Chuuk, Yap, Kosrae, and Pohnpei, along with the Marshall Islands and Palau, voted on a constitution that would have united all of Micronesia into a single entity. The Marshall Islands and Palau rejected the proposal, but Chuuk, Yap, Kosrae, and Pohnpei elected to become the Federated States of Micronesia. The United States recognized the Micronesian constitution in 1979, and in 1982 a compact of free association was signed. The compact received final approval in 1986 and the country became self-governing. However, full independence was not achieved until 1991, when the United Nations officially removed the Federated States of Micronesia from trusteeship status. A new capital is planned at Palikir on the island of Pohnpei. ∎

MIDWAY ISLANDS
See UNITED STATES.

MOLDOVA

Official name Republic of Moldova

PEOPLE
Population 4,377,000. **Density** 336/mi^2 (130/km^2). **Urban** 47%. **Capital** Kishinev, 676,700. **Ethnic groups** Moldovan 65%, Ukrainian 14%, Russian 13%, Gagauz 4%, Jews 2%. **Languages** Romanian (Moldovan), Russian. **Religions** Eastern Orthodox 99%. **Life expectancy** 72 female, 64 male. **Literacy** 99%.

POLITICS
Government Republic. **Parties** Agrarian Democratic, Christian Democratic Popular Front, Democratic, Democratic Labor, Social Democratic. **Suffrage** Universal, over 18. **Memberships** NATO, UN. **Subdivisions** None.

ECONOMY
GNP $16,300,000,000. **Per capita** $3,643. **Monetary unit** Leu. **Trade partners** Former Soviet republics. **Exports** Food, wine, tobacco, textiles and footwear, machinery, chemicals. **Imports** Oil, gas, coal, machinery, food, automobiles, consumer durables.

LAND
Description Eastern Europe, landlocked. **Area** 13,012 mi^2 (33,700 km^2). **Highest point** Unnamed, 1,407 ft (429 m). **Lowest point** Along Dnestr River, 3 ft (1 m).

People. After the Soviet Union wrested Moldova from Romanian control, it claimed that the Moldovans were a distinct ethnic group with their own language. In fact, Moldovans claim Romanian ancestry, and their language is virtually the same as Romanian. Most people also speak Russian, and there are substantial Russian and Ukrainian minorities.

Economy and the Land. Most of Moldova is gently rolling plains, rising to wooded hills in the central part of the country. Much of the land is suitable for agriculture, and wheat, grapes, and other fruits are important crops. Although agriculture and food processing dominate the economy, Moldova also has some light manufacturing. The country has no significant energy resources.

History and Politics. Formerly known as Bessarabia, this region was ruled by Romanian-speaking Moldovan princes since the 1300s. Bessarabia fell under the control of the Ottoman Turks from the 1600s until 1812, when the Turks were defeated by Russia. In 1918 control went to Romania and the territory was subsequently shifted back and forth between the two countries. In 1944 the Soviet Union defeated Romania and the Moldavian Soviet Socialist Republic was established. Moldovans began agitating for greater autonomy within the Soviet Union as early as 1989. It gained its independence in December 1991, after the demise of the Soviet Union. A new 1994 constitution established Moldova as a neutral republic. A referendum provided for the withdrawal of foreign troops and special status for the Dniester region occupied by ethnic Russians. ∎

MONACO

Official name Principality of Monaco
PEOPLE

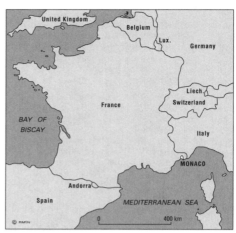

Population 31,000. **Density** 44,286/mi^2 (16,316/km^2). **Urban** 100%. **Capital** Monaco, 31,000. **Ethnic groups** French 47%, Monegasque 16%, Italian 16%, English 4%, Belgian 2%, Swiss 1%. **Languages** French, English, Italian, Monegasque. **Religions** Roman Catholic 95%. **Life expectancy** 81 female, 74 male.

POLITICS
Government Constitutional monarchy. **Parties** Action, Democractic Union Movement, National and Democratic Union, Socialist. **Suffrage** Universal, over 25. **Memberships** UN. **Subdivisions** 3 communes.

ECONOMY
GDP $475,000,000. **Per capita** $16,379. **Monetary unit** French franc.

LAND
Description Southern Europe (on the southeastern coast of France). **Area** 0.7 mi^2 (1.9 km^2). **Highest point** Unnamed, 459 ft (140 m). **Lowest point** Sea level.

People. Monaco is inhabited mostly by French citizens, while Monegasques—citizens of indigenous descent—and various Europeans form the rest of the population. Many foreigners have taken up residence, drawn by the country's tax benefits. French is the official language. Monegasque, a blend of French and Italian, is also spoken, as are French, Italian, and English. Most residents are Roman Catholic.

Economy and the Land. Monaco's scenic seaside location, mild Mediterranean climate, and renowned gambling casino in Monte Carlo make it a popular tourist haven. Consequently, tourism forms the backbone of the economy. Production of chemicals, food products, and perfumes, among other light industries, are additional sources of income. Monaco also profits from many foreign businesses, which are attracted by the favorable tax climate and headquartered in the principality. France and Monaco form a customs union for a mutually beneficial trade system; the French franc is Monaco's official currency. The world's second smallest independent state in area—after Vatican City—Monaco has four regions: the old city of Monaco-Ville,

site of the royal palace; Monte Carlo, the resort and

major tourist center; La Condamine, the port area; and Fontvieille, the rapidly growing industrial section.

History and Politics. Known to the Phoenicians, Greeks, and Romans, the region became a Genoese colony in the twelfth century A.D. Around the turn of the fourteenth century, the area was granted to the Grimaldi family of Genoa. France, Spain, and Sardinia had intermittent control of Monaco from 1400 until 1861, when its autonomy was recognized by the Franco-Monegasque Treaty. Another treaty, providing for French protection of Monaco, was signed in 1918. The absolute rule of Monaco's princes ended with the 1911 constitution. Monaco joined the United Nations in 1993. ■

MONGOLIA

Official name Mongolia

PEOPLE
Population 2,462,000. **Density** 4.1/mi² (1.6/km²). **Urban** 58%. **Capital** Ulan Bator, 575,000. **Ethnic groups** Mongol 90%, Kazakh 4%, Chinese 2%, Russian 2%. **Languages** Khalkha Mongol, Turkish dialects, Russian, Chinese. **Religions** Shamanic, Tibetan Buddhist, Muslim. **Life expectancy** 65 female, 62 male. **Literacy** 90%.
POLITICS
Government Republic. **Parties** Democratic, National Progress, National Renaissance, People's Revolutionary, Social Democratic. **Suffrage** Universal, over 18. **Memberships** UN. **Subdivisions** 18 provinces, 3 municipalities.
ECONOMY
GDP $2,800,000,000. **Per capita** $1,199. **Monetary unit** Tughrik. **Trade partners** Exports: Former Soviet republics, China, Japan. Imports: Former Soviet republics, Austria, China. **Exports** Copper, livestock, animal products, cashmere, wool, hides. **Imports** Machinery, fuel, food, consumer goods, chemicals, building materials.
LAND

Description Central Asia, landlocked. **Area** 604,829 mi² (1,566,500 km²). **Highest point** Kuiten Mtn., 14,350 ft (4,374 m). **Lowest point** Höh Lake, 1,814 ft (553 m).

People. Mongols, a central Asian people, make up the vast majority of Mongolia's population. Khalkha Mongol is the predominant language. Turkic-speaking Kazakhs, as well as Russians and Chinese, comprise minorities. Tibetan Buddhism was once the most common religion; however, during the years of communist rule the government discouraged religious practice. The traditional nomadic way of life is becoming less common, as recent government policies have led to urbanization and settled agriculture.

Economy and the Land. Mongolia's economy, long based on the raising of livestock, has been shaped by the ideal grazing land found in most of the country. Livestock outnumber people in Mongolia by a ratio of ten to one. Significant economic changes have taken place since the collapse of the Soviet economy because 90% of its trade was with Russia and Eastern Europe. Market reforms have produced economic hardship. Mongolia's terrain varies from mountains in the north and west to steppe in the east and desert in the south. Located in the heart of Asia, remote from any moderating body of water, Mongolia has a rigorous continental climate with little precipitation.

History and Politics. Mongolian tribes were united under the warlord Genghis Khan around A.D. 1200, and he and his successors built one of history's largest land empires. In 1691 the Manchu dynasty of China subdued Outer Mongolia, as the area was then known, but allowed the Mongol rulers autonomy. Until the Mongols ousted the Chinese in 1911, Outer Mongolia remained a Chinese province. In 1912 the state accepted Russian protection but was unable to prevent a subsequent Chinese advance, and in 1919 Outer Mongolia again became a Chinese province. In 1921 a combined Soviet and Mongolian force defeated Chinese and Belorussian, or White Russian, troops, and the Mongolian People's Republic was declared in 1924. A mutual-assistance pact was signed by Mongolia and Russia in 1966. In 1989 the Soviets agreed to withdraw most of their troops from Mongolia. Increasing pressure for democratization led to the country's first free, multiparty elections in August 1990. A new constitution, describing Mongolia as a republic with parliamentary government, was adopted in 1992. ■

MONTSERRAT
See UNITED KINGDOM.

MOROCCO

Official name Kingdom of Morocco
PEOPLE
Population 26,890,000. **Density** 156/mi² (60/km²). **Urban** 46%. **Capital** Rabat, 518,616. **Ethnic groups** Arab-Berber 99%. **Languages**

Arabic, Berber dialects, French. **Religions** Muslim 99%. **Life expectancy** 65 female, 62 male. **Literacy** 50%.

POLITICS
Government Constitutional monarchy. **Parties** Constitutional Union, Istiqlal, Popular Movement, Socialist Union of Popular Forces, others. **Suffrage** Universal, over 21. **Memberships** AL, UN. **Subdivisions** 36 provinces, 2 prefectures.

ECONOMY
GDP $70,300,000,000. **Per capita** $2,603. **Monetary unit** Dirham. **Trade partners** Exports: France, Spain, Italy. Imports: France, Spain, Iraq. **Exports** Food, manufactures, phosphates. **Imports** Machinery, manufactures, raw materials, fuel, food.

LAND
Description Northwestern Africa. **Area** 172,414 mi² (446,550 km²). **Highest point** Mt. Toubkal, 13,665 ft (4,165 m). **Lowest point** Sebkha Tah, -180 ft (-55 m).
The above information excludes Western Sahara.

People. Moroccans, virtually homogeneous in race and culture, are mostly a mix of Arab and Berber stocks and speak Arabic. A few Berber dialects are spoken in rural mountain areas, and French and Spanish, the colonial tongues, are common in business and government. The majority of people are Sunni Muslim. The population is concentrated west of the Atlas Mountains, which border the Sahara Desert. Rural people are migrating to cities, where the standard of living is higher.

Economy and the Land. Although agriculture employs much of the work force and is an important activity, the nation depends on mining for most of its income. Morocco is a leading exporter of phosphates, but has other mineral reserves as well. Fishing and tourism are growing sources of revenue. Recently, severe drought, rising dependency on imported oil, and a costly war in Western Sahara have slowed productivity, while investments by Arab countries have bolstered the economy. Morocco, with its varied terrain of desert, forests, and mountains, has an equally varied climate that is semitropical along the coast, and

desert beyond the Atlas Mountains.

History and Politics. In ancient times, Morocco was a province of Carthage and Rome. Vandals and Byzantine Greeks, the subsequent rulers, were followed in the A.D.700s by Arabs, who brought Islam. Morocco's strategic position awakened the interest of colonial powers in the 1800s, and by 1912 the area was divided into French and Spanish protectorates. A nationalist movement began in the 1920s, occasionally bringing violence, but not until 1956 did Morocco become independent from France. The last of Spain's holdings in Morocco were returned in 1969. War broke out in 1976, when Morocco claimed the northern part of Western Sahara and was challenged by the Saharan nationalist Polisario Front. Mauritania surrendered its claim in 1979 and Morocco quickly established claim to the entire territory. Negotiations over the final disposition of Western Sahara have been sporadic. King Hassan shares power with directly elected groups under a complex formula. ∎

MOZAMBIQUE

Official name Republic of Mozambique

PEOPLE
Population 17,860,000. **Density** 58/mi² (22/km²). **Urban** 27%. **Capital** Maputo, 1,069,727. **Ethnic groups** Makua, Lomwe, Thonga, others. **Languages** Portuguese, indigenous. **Religions** Tribal religionist 60%, Roman Catholic and other Christian 30%, Muslim. **Life expectancy** 48 female, 45 male. **Literacy** 33%.

POLITICS
Government Republic. **Parties** Front for the Liberation of Mozambique, others. **Suffrage** Universal, over 18. **Memberships** OAU, UN. **Subdivisions** 10 provinces, 1 independent city.

ECONOMY
GDP $9,800,000,000. **Per capita** $620. **Monetary unit** Metical. **Trade partners** Exports: U.S., Germany, Japan. Imports: Former Soviet

republics, South African countries, Portugal.
Exports Shrimp, cashews, sugar, copra, fruit.
Imports Food, clothing, farm equipment, petroleum.
LAND
Description Southern Africa. **Area** 308,642 mi² (799,380 km²). **Highest point** Monte Binga, 7,992 ft (2,436 m). **Lowest point** Sea level.

People. Black Africans belonging to about ten groups compose the vast majority of the population. Most black Mozambicans live in rural areas, while small European and Asian minorities live primarily in urban centers. Traditional African religions are followed by a majority, while others practice Islam and Christianity. Although Portuguese is the official language, most blacks speak Bantu tongues.

Economy and the Land. Mozambique's underdeveloped economy is largely the product of its colonial past, during which its human and natural resources were neglected. Recent political developments in southern Africa have created more economic woes, as lucrative trade agreements with racially divided neighbors have ceased. While the mainstays of the economy are agriculture and transport services, fishing and mining are also being developed. The Marxist government allowed some private enterprise, and foreign aid is important. The climate is tropical or subtropical along the coastal plain that covers nearly half of the country, with cooler conditions in the western high plateaus and mountains.

History and Politics. Bantu-speaking peoples settled in present-day Mozambique around the first century A.D. Subsequent immigrants included Arab traders in the 800s and the Portuguese in the late 1400s. European economic interest in the area was hindered by lucrative trading with other colonies, and Mozambique wasn't recognized as a Portuguese colony until 1885. Policies instituted by the Portuguese benefited European settlers and Portugal, but overlooked the welfare of Mozambique and its native inhabitants. In the early 1960s the country made clear its opposition to foreign rule, with the formation of the Front for the Liberation of Mozambique, a Marxist nationalist group that initiated an armed campaign against the Portuguese. In 1975 Mozambique became an independent state, but fighting between the socialist government and opposition forces continued. A new constitution passed in 1990 marked the end of single-party rule in Mozambique. The civil war, resulting in a million casualties and nearly two million refugees, finally ended in October 1992. A fragile peace and the return of over one million refugees was complicated by the worst drought of the century. The country's first multiparty elections were held in October 1994. ■

MYANMAR

Official name Union of Myanmar
PEOPLE
Population 44,675,000. **Density** 171/mi² (66/km²). **Urban** 25%. **Capital** Yangon (Rangoon), 2,513,023. **Ethnic groups** Bamar (Burmese) 69%, Shan 9%, Kayin 6%, Rakhine 5%. **Languages** Burmese, indigenous. **Religions** Buddhist 89%,

Muslim 4%, Christian 4%. **Life expectancy** 59 female, 56 male. **Literacy** 81%.
POLITICS
Government Provisional military government.
Parties National League for Democracy, National Unity Party, others. **Suffrage** Universal, over 18.
Memberships UN. **Subdivisions** 7 divisions, 7 states.
ECONOMY
GDP $41,000,000,000. **Per capita** $952.
Monetary unit Kyat. **Trade partners** Exports: Southeast Asian countries, India, Japan. Imports: Japan, Western European countries, China.
Exports Teak, rice, oilseed, metals, rubber, gems.
Imports Machinery and transportation equipment, chemicals, food.
LAND
Description Southeastern Asia. **Area** 261,228 mi² (676,577 km²). **Highest point** Hkakabo Razi, 19,296 ft (5,881 m). **Lowest point** Sea level.

People. The population of Myanmar is highly diverse, with many ethnic groups including Tibetan-related Bamar, who compose the majority; Kayin, who inhabit mainly the south and east; and Thai-related Shan, found on the eastern plateaus. Diversity results in many languages, although Burmese predominates. Buddhist monasteries and pagodas dot the landscape, and minority religions include Christianity, indigenous beliefs, and Islam. The primarily rural population is concentrated in the fertile valleys and on the delta of the Irrawaddy River.

Economy and the Land. Fertile soils, dense woodlands, and mineral deposits provide a resource base for agriculture, forestry, and mining. Myanmar has been beset with economic problems, however, caused mainly by the destruction of World War II, as well as post-independence instability. Today agriculture continues as the economic mainstay. The hot, wet climate is ideal for rice production. In addition, dense forests provide for a timber industry, and resource deposits include petroleum and various minerals. Myanmar's economic future most likely depends on exploitation of natural resources and political stability. The terrain is marked by mountains, rivers, and forests, and the climate is tropical.

History and Politics. Myanmar's Chinese and

Tibetan settlers were first united in the eleventh century. Independence ended with the invasion of Mongols led by Kublai Khan, followed by national unification in the fifteenth and eighteenth centuries. Annexation to British India in the nineteenth century ended Myanmar's monarchy. During World War II, Japanese occupation and subsequent Allied-Japanese conflicts caused much economic and physical damage. Myanmar officially became independent in 1948. After initial stability, the government was unable to withstand separatist and political revolts, and military rule has alternated with civilian governments. The latest attempts to reestablish democracy were thwarted when the results of elections in 1990 were contested by ninety-three opposition parties. The military government refused to relinquish control or hold new elections. The 1991 Nobel Peace Prize award to the country's main opposition leader, Aung San Suu Kyi, focused world attention on continued human rights abuses. Reforms were enacted in 1992 to appease public opinion, but reports of abuses continue. ∎

NAMIBIA

Official name Republic of Namibia

PEOPLE
Population 1,623,000. **Density** 5.1/mi² (2.0/km²). **Urban** 28%. **Capital** Windhoek, 114,500. **Ethnic groups** Ovambo 49%, Kavango 9%, Damara 8%, Herero 7%, white 7%, mixed 7%. **Languages** English, Afrikaans, German, indigenous. **Religions** Lutheran and other Protestant, Roman Catholic, Animist. **Life expectancy** 60 female, 58 male. **Literacy** 38%.
POLITICS
Government Republic. **Parties** Democratic Turnhalle Alliance, South West Africa People's Organization, United Democratic Front, others. **Suffrage** Universal, over 18. **Memberships** CW, OAU, UN. **Subdivisions** 13 regions.
ECONOMY
GDP 3,850,000,000. **Per capita** 2,402. **Monetary**

unit South African rand. **Trade partners** Exports: Switzerland, South Africa, Germany. Imports: South Africa, Germany, U.S. **Exports** Uranium, diamonds, zinc, copper, meat, fish. **Imports** Food, petroleum and fuel, machinery and equipment.
LAND
Description Southern Africa. **Area** 318,253 mi² (824,272 km²). **Highest point** Brandberg, 8,461 ft (2,579 m). **Lowest point** Sea level.

People. The largest ethnic group is black African, composed of many indigenous peoples. South Africans, Britons, and Germans constitute the white minority. Black Namibians speak various native dialects, while the majority of whites speak Afrikaans. Blacks still follow traditional customs and religions, but a considerable number have converted to Christianity.

Economy and the Land. Namibia's economy is based on the mining of diamonds, copper, lead, and other minerals. Agriculture makes a marginal contribution, but livestock raising is important. Manufacturing remains undeveloped because of an unskilled work force, and Namibia imports most of its finished goods from South Africa, its partner in a customs union. A variety of factors, including continuing drought and political instability, have held back economic growth. Namibia consists of a high plateau that encompasses the Namib Desert and part of the Kalahari Desert. The climate is subtropical.

History and Politics. Bushmen were probably the area's first inhabitants, followed by other African peoples. European exploration of the coast began in the A.D. 1500s, but the coastal desert prevented foreign penetration. In 1884 Germany annexed all of the territory except for the coastal enclave of Walvis Bay, which had been claimed by Britain in 1878. After South African troops ousted the Germans from the area during World War I, the League of Nations mandated Namibia, then known as South West Africa, to South Africa. Following World War II, the United Nations requested that the territory become a trusteeship. South Africa refused to cooperate. In 1966 the United Nations revoked South Africa's mandate, yet South Africa kept control of Namibia. Beginning in the 1960s, the South West Africa People's Organization, (SWAPO) a Namibian nationalist group with Communist support, made guerrilla raids on South African forces from bases in Zambia and later from Angola. In 1989, after years of continued pressure, an assembly was elected to draft a constitution. Independence was achieved in 1990. In 1994, Namibia's first post-independence election resulted in a major victory by SWAPO. ∎

NAURU

Official name Republic of Nauru
PEOPLE
Population 10,000. **Density** 1,235/mi² (476/km²). **Capital** Yaren District. **Ethnic groups** Nauruan 58%, other Pacific Islander 26%, Chinese 8%, European 8%. **Languages** Nauruan, English. **Religions** Congregationalist and other Protestant 67%, Roman Catholic 33%. **Life expectancy** 69

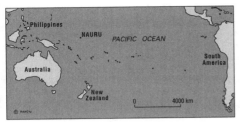

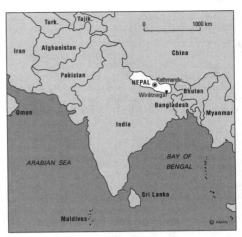

female, 64 male.
POLITICS
Government Republic. **Parties** None. **Suffrage**
Universal, over 20. **Memberships** CW.
Subdivisions 14 districts.
ECONOMY
GNP $90,000,000. **Per capita** $10,000. **Monetary**
unit Australian dollar. **Trade partners** Exports:
Australia, New Zealand. Imports: Australia, U.K.,
New Zealand, Japan. **Exports** Phosphates.
Imports Food, fuel, manufactures, building materi-
als, machinery.
LAND
Description South Pacific island. **Area** 8.1 mi^2 (21
km^2). **Highest point** Unnamed, 210 ft (64 m).
Lowest point Sea level.

People. Indigenous Nauruans are a mix of Polynesian,
Micronesian, and Melanesian stock, and many residents are from other Pacific islands. Nauruan is
the language of most inhabitants, but English is
widely spoken. Nearly all Nauruans are Christian.

Economy and the Land. The economy depends primarily on its sole resource, phosphates; the government
is establishing trust funds to support islanders when
the resource is depleted. Mining has destroyed 80 percent of the island and, with limited agriculture, nearly all food and water must be imported. Nauru is one
of the smallest countries in the world. Most of the coral
island is a plateau, and the climate is tropical.

History and Politics. Nauru was most likely settled
by castaways from nearby islands. Noted by a British
explorer in 1798, Nauru remained autonomous until
it came under German control in 1881. In 1914
Germany surrendered the island, and it was subsequently mandated to Australia, Britain, and New
Zealand. World War II brought occupation by Japan.
Nauru reverted to Australian rule in 1947 as a
trusteeship. It became independent in 1968 and
gained control of European interests in the phosphate
industry in 1970. The country is preparing for the near
future when phosphate is gone and the people must
develop a new economy and restore the land. ■

NEPAL

Official name Kingdom of Nepal
PEOPLE
Population 21,295,000. **Density** 375/mi^2
(145/km^2). **Urban** 11%. **Capital** Kathmandu,
421,258. **Ethnic groups** Newar, Indian, Tibetan,
Gurung, Magar, Tamang, Bhotia, Sherpa, others.
Languages Nepali, Maithali, Bhojpuri, other
indigenous. **Religions** Hindu 90%, Buddhist 5%,
Muslim 3%. **Life expectancy** 53 female, 54 male.
Literacy 26%.
POLITICS
Government Constitutional monarchy. **Parties**
Communist/United Marxist and Leninist, Congress,
United People's Front, others. **Suffrage** Universal,
over 18. **Memberships** UN. **Subdivisions** 14
zones.
ECONOMY
GDP $20,500,000,000. **Per capita** $1,009.
Monetary unit Rupee. **Trade partners** Exports:
U.S., Germany, India. Imports: India, Singapore,
Japan. **Exports** Clothing, carpets, leather goods,
grain. **Imports** Petroleum, fertilizer, machinery.
LAND
Description Southern Asia, landlocked. **Area**
56,827 mi^2 (147,181 km^2). **Highest point** Mt.
Everest, 29,028 ft (8,848 m). **Lowest point**
Unnamed, 197 ft (60 m).

People. Nepal's mixed population results from migrations over the centuries from India, Tibet, and central Asia. Most of Nepal's ruling families have been
of Indian descent, and Nepali, the official language,
is derived from Sanskrit, an ancient Indian language.
Although the majority of the population practices
Hinduism, Nepal is the birthplace of Buddha and has
been greatly influenced by Buddhism as well. The
importance of both religions is reflected in the more
than twenty-seven hundred shrines in the Kathmandu
Valley. Most Nepalese are rural farmers.

Economy and the Land. Because of geographic
remoteness and a political policy of isolation lasting
until the 1950s, Nepal's economy is one of the least
developed in the world. Agriculture, concentrated chiefly
in the south, is the most significant activity, even though
most of Nepal is covered by the Himalayas, the
world's highest mountains. This range—which
includes Mount Everest, the world's highest peak—
has made tourism increasingly lucrative. Nepal has
potential in hydroelectricity and forestry, but inadequate transportation routes, overpopulation, and
deforestation present obstacles to development.
Nepal has received financial aid from many nations,
partly because of its strategic location between India
and China. The climate varies from subtropical in the

flat, fertile south to temperate in the central hill country. Himalayan summers are cool and winters severe.

History and Politics. Several small Hindu-Buddhist kingdoms had emerged in the Kathmandu Valley by about A.D. 300. These states were unified in the late 1700s by the founder of the Shah dynasty. The Rana family wrested control from the Shahs in 1846 and pursued an isolationist course, which thwarted foreign influence but stunted economic growth. Opposition to the Ranas mounted during the 1930s and 1940s, and in 1951 the Shah monarchy was restored by a revolution. In 1962 the king established a government that gave the crown dominance and abolished political parties. A 1980 referendum narrowly upheld this system. In November 1990 a pro-democracy movement forced the king to approve a new constitution providing for a multiparty structure and the country's new status as a constitutional monarchy. In 1991 the Nepali Congress Party became the first democratically elected administration in Nepal, followed in 1994 by a reformist Communist Party which became the first democratically elected Communist government in Asia. ■

NETHERLANDS

Official name Kingdom of the Netherlands
PEOPLE

Population 15,425,000. **Density** 954/mi² (368/km²). **Urban** 89%. **Capital** Amsterdam (designated), 713,407; The Hague (seat of government), 445,287. **Ethnic groups** Dutch (mixed Scandinavian, French, and Celtic) 96%.
Languages Dutch. **Religions** Roman Catholic 36%, Dutch Reformed 19%, Calvinist 8%. **Life expectancy** 81 female, 74 male. **Literacy** 99%.
POLITICS
Government Constitutional monarchy. **Parties** Christian Democratic Appeal, Labor, Liberal, others. **Suffrage** Universal, over 18. **Memberships** EU, NATO, OECD, UN. **Subdivisions** 12 provinces.
ECONOMY
GDP $262,800,000,000. **Per capita** $17,301. **Monetary unit** Guilder. **Trade partners** Exports: Germany, Belgium, France. Imports: Germany, Belgium, U.K. **Exports** Agricultural products, food and tobacco, natural gas, chemicals. **Imports** Raw materials, consumer goods, transportation equipment, petroleum, food.
LAND
Description Western Europe. **Area** 16,164 mi² (41,864 km²). **Highest point** Vaalserberg, 1,053 ft (321 m). **Lowest point** Prins Alexander polder, -23 ft (-7 m).

People. The major ethnic group is the Dutch, for the most part a mixture of French, Scandinavian, and Celtic peoples. There are small minorities from the former Dutch possessions of Indonesia and Suriname. Dutch is the official language, but many Netherlanders also speak English or German. Although most Dutch are Christian, the nation has a history of religious tolerance that has drawn countless refugees of other faiths.

Economy and the Land. A variety of manufacturing strengths—notably the metal, chemical, and food-processing industries—fuels the prosperous economy. Tourism and the production of natural gas are also important. Due to a lack of natural resources, the Netherlands must import many goods. The country benefits from its strategic position and has enjoyed success in shipping and trade. Much of the Netherlands, including most farmland, has been reclaimed from the sea through artificial drainage. The land is almost uniformly flat, and proximity to the sea produces a mild, damp climate. The Kingdom of the Netherlands includes the Netherlands Antilles, two groups of Caribbean islands, and Aruba.

History and Politics. The Germanic tribes of the area were conquered in 58 B.C. by the Romans, who were driven out in the A.D. 400s by the Franks. As part of the Low Countries with Belgium and Luxembourg, the Netherlands was dominated successively by Charlemagne, the dukes of Burgundy, the Hapsburgs,

Places and Possessions of the NETHERLANDS

Entity	Status	Area	Population	Capital/Population
Aruba (Caribbean island)	Self-governing territory	75 mi² (193 km²)	67,000	Oranjestad, 20,045
Curaçao (Caribbean island)	Division of Netherlands Antilles	171 mi² (444 km²)	146,000	Willemstad, 31,883
Netherlands Antilles (Caribbean islands)	Self-governing territory	309 mi² (800 km²)	187,000	Willemstad, 31,883

and rulers of Spain. Spanish persecution of Dutch Protestants led to a revolt that in 1581 created the Republic of the United Netherlands. In the 1600s the Netherlands became a maritime as well as a colonial power and produced many masterpieces in painting. But a series of wars with England and France ending in 1714 spelled the end of Dutch influence, and the nation fell to France in 1795. With the defeat of Napoleon Bonaparte of France in 1815, the Netherlands was united with Belgium and became an independent kingdom. Belgium seceded in 1830. The Netherlands declared its neutrality in both world wars but was occupied by Germany from 1940 to 1945. The war cost the country many lives and much of its economic strength. Membership in several international economic unions aided recovery. In recent years the Netherlands has been actively involved in the European Union. ■

NETHERLANDS ANTILLES
See NETHERLANDS.

NEW CALEDONIA

Official name Territory of New Caledonia and Dependencies
PEOPLE
Population 183,000. **Density** 25/mi^2 (9.6/km^2).
Urban 60%. **Capital** Nouméa, New Caledonia I., 65,110. **Ethnic groups** Melanesian (Kanak) 45%, French 34%, Wallisian 9%, Indonesian 3%, Tahitian 3%. **Languages** French, indigenous. **Religions** Roman Catholic 60%, Protestant 30%. **Life expectancy** 77 female, 70 male. **Literacy** 91%.
POLITICS
Government Overseas territory (France). **Parties** Kanak Socialist National Liberation Front, National Front, Rally for the Republic, others. **Suffrage** Universal, over 18. **Memberships** None. **Subdivisions** 3 provinces.
ECONOMY
GNP $1,000,000,000. **Per capita** $5,882.
Monetary unit CFP franc. **Trade partners** Exports: France, Japan, U.S. Imports: France, Australia, Japan, U.S. **Exports** Nickel. **Imports** Food, fuel, minerals, machinery, electrical equipment.
LAND
Description South Pacific islands. **Area** 7,358 mi^2

(19,058 km^2). **Highest point** Mont Panié, 5,341 ft (1,628 m). **Lowest point** Sea level.

People. The Melanesian, or Kanak, comprise the largest ethnic group in New Caledonia, a group of Pacific islands northeast of Australia. People of French descent make up the second largest group, with Asians and Polynesians composing significant minorities. New Caledonia's status as an overseas French territory is reflected in its languages, which include French as well as regional dialects, and in a population that is largely Christian.

Economy and the Land. The principal economic activity, the mining and smelting of nickel, has fallen off in recent years. Small amounts of coffee and copra are exported, and tourism is important in the capital. Possessing few resources, New Caledonia imports almost all finished products from France. The main island, also called New Caledonia, is mountainous and accounts for almost 90 percent of the territory's land area. Smaller islands include the Isle of Pines, Loyalty and Bélep islands. The climate is tropical.

History and Politics. New Caledonia was settled by Melanesians about 2000 B.C. Europeans first reached the main island in 1774, when Captain James Cook of Britain gave it its present name. In 1853 France annexed New Caledonia and used the main island as a penal colony until the turn of the century. During World War II the islands served as a base for the United States military. Officially a French overseas territory since 1946, New Caledonia experienced violence in the 1980s, stemming from the desire of the Kanak population for independence. An independence referendum is planned for 1998, although the Kanaks may gain some form of autonomy earlier. ■

NEW ZEALAND

Official name New Zealand
PEOPLE
Population 3,558,000. **Density** 34/mi^2 (13/km^2).
Urban 84%. **Capital** Wellington, North I., 150,301.
Ethnic groups European origin 86%, Maori 10%, Samoan and other Pacific islander 4%.
Languages English, Maori. **Religions** Anglican 24%, Presbyterian 18%, Roman Catholic 15%, Methodist 5%. **Life expectancy** 79 female, 73 male. **Literacy** 99%.
POLITICS
Government Parliamentary state. **Parties**

Places and Possessions of NEW ZEALAND

Entity	Status	Area	Population	Capital/Population
Cook Islands (South Pacific)	Self-governing territory	91 mi^2 (236 km^2)	19,000	Avarua, 10,886
Niue (South Pacific island)	Self-governing territory	100 mi^2 (259 km^2)	1,900	Alofi, 706
Tokelau (South Pacific islands)	Island territory	4.6 mi^2 (12 km^2)	1,500	None

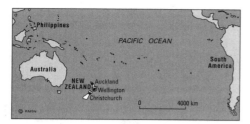

Alliance, Labor, National, others. **Suffrage** Universal, over 18. **Memberships** CW, OECD, UN. **Subdivisions** 14 regions.
ECONOMY
GDP $53,000,000,000. **Per capita** $15,241. **Monetary unit** Dollar. **Trade partners** Exports: Australia, Japan, U.S. Imports: Australia, U.S., Japan. **Exports** Wool, lamb, mutton, beef, fruit, fish, cheese, manufactures, chemicals. **Imports** Petroleum, manufactures, motor vehicles, machinery.
LAND
Description South Pacific islands. **Area** 104,454 mi^2 (270,534 km^2). **Highest point** Mt. Cook, 12,316 ft (3,754 m). **Lowest point** Sea level.

People. The majority of New Zealanders are descended from Europeans, mostly Britons, who arrived in the 1800s. The indigenous Maori, of Polynesian descent, form the largest minority. After a period of decline following the arrival of the Europeans, the Maori population has been increasing. The major languages are English, the official tongue, and Maori. Most New Zealanders live on North Island. Christian religions are observed by many residents, and the Maori have incorporated some Christian elements into their beliefs.

Economy and the Land. Success in agriculture and trade has allowed New Zealand to overcome its small work force, remoteness from major markets, and a relative lack of natural resources. A terrain with much ideal grazing land and a climate that is temperate year-round have encouraged cattle and sheep farming. Manufacturing, including the food-processing and paper industries, is an expanding sector, as is tourism. New Zealand consists of two large islands—North Island and South Island—and many smaller islands scattered throughout the South Pacific. The nation administers several island territories. The scenic terrain is greatly varied, ranging from fjords and mountains to a volcanic plateau.

History and Politics. The Maori, the original settlers, are thought to have arrived around A.D. 1000. In 1642 they fought off the Dutch, the first Europeans to reach the area. Captain James Cook of Britain charted the islands in the late 1700s. Soon after, European hunters and traders, drawn by the area's whales, seals, and forests, began to arrive. Maori chiefs signed the 1840 Treaty of Waitangi, establishing British sovereignty, and British companies began to send settlers to New Zealand. Subsequent battles between settlers and Maori ended with the Maori's defeat in 1872, but European diseases and weapons continued to reduce the Maori population. In 1907 New Zealand became a self-governing dominion of Britain; formal independence came forty years later. New Zealand sup-

ported Britain in both world wars, but foreign policy has recently focused on Southeast Asia and the South Pacific. The country has banned vessels carrying nuclear weapons through its waters. Compensation to Maori groups for land claims going back to 1840 has begun. ∎

NICARAGUA

Official name Republic of Nicaragua
PEOPLE

Population 4,438,000. **Density** 89/mi^2 (34/km^2). **Urban** 60%. **Capital** Managua, 682,000. **Ethnic groups** Mestizo 69%, white 17%, black 9%, Amerindian 5%. **Languages** Spanish, English, indigenous. **Religions** Roman Catholic 95%. **Life expectancy** 69 female, 65 male. **Literacy** 57%.
POLITICS
Government Republic. **Parties** National Opposition Union, Sandinista National Liberation Front. **Suffrage** Universal, over 16. **Memberships** OAS, UN. **Subdivisions** 16 departments.
ECONOMY
GDP $6,400,000,000. **Per capita** $1,628. **Monetary unit** Cordoba. **Trade partners** Exports: Belgium, Cuba, Germany. Imports: Former Soviet republics, Mexico. **Exports** Coffee, cotton, sugar, bananas, seafood, meat, chemicals. **Imports** Petroleum, food, chemicals, machinery, clothing.
LAND
Description Central America. **Area** 50,054 mi^2 (129,640 km^2). **Highest point** Mogotón, 6,913 ft (2,107 m). **Lowest point** Sea level.

People. Nicaraguan society closely reflects the nation's history as a Spanish colony: most of its inhabitants are Spanish speaking, Roman Catholic, and mestizo, a mix of Indian and European stocks. Indian and black communities are found mostly in the Caribbean region. The educational level has improved in the past decade.

Economy and the Land. Nicaragua is chiefly an agricultural nation, relying on the production of textiles, coffee, and sugar. A large foreign debt inherited from the previous regime, and continuing political instability, have severely hindered economic prosperity. The nation also suffers from a reliance on imported goods. In 1985 the currency was sharply devalued, and the United States, formerly a chief trading partner, announced a trade embargo. The terrain includes a low-lying Pacific region, central highlands, and a flat Caribbean area. The climate is tropical.

History and Politics. Spanish conquistadores, who came via Panama in 1522 to what is now Nicaragua, found a number of independent Indian states. Nicaragua was ruled by Spain as part of Guatemala until it became independent in 1821. In 1823 the former Spanish colonies of the region formed the Federation of Central America, a union which collapsed in 1838, resulting in the independent Republic of Nicaragua. For the next century, Nicaragua was the stage both for conflict between the Liberal and Conservative parties and for United States military and economic involvement. Members of the Somoza family, who had close ties to America, directed a repressive regime from 1936 to 1979, when the widely-supported Sandinistas overthrew the government. The Sandinistas, led by Daniel Ortega, were opposed by rival political parties and the Contras, rebels linked to the former Somoza administration and backed by the United States. Five Central American countries reached an agreement in 1987 on a plan to dismantle Contra forces. In 1990 elections, Ortega was defeated by Violeta Chamorro of the National Opposition Union. Despite the disbanding of the Contras in 1990, the situation remains unstable as Chamorro tries to placate the still powerful Sandinistas and revise the moribund economy. ∎

NIGER

Official name Republic of Niger

PEOPLE

Population 9,125,000. **Density** 19/mi² (7.2/km²). **Urban** 20%. **Capital** Niamey, 392,165. **Ethnic groups** Hausa 56%, Djerma 22%, Fulani 9%, Tuareg 8%, Beriberi 4%. **Languages** French, Hausa, Djerma, indigenous. **Religions** Muslim 80%, Animist and Christian 20%. **Life expectancy** 48 female, 45 male. **Literacy** 28%.

POLITICS
Government Provisional military government. **Parties** National Movement for the Development of Society, Social Democratic Convention, Unity and Democracy. **Suffrage** Universal, over 18. **Memberships** OAU, UN. **Subdivisions** 7 departments.

ECONOMY
GDP $5,400,000,000. **Per capita** $659. **Monetary unit** CFA franc. **Trade partners** Exports: France, Nigeria. Imports: France, U.S., Cote d'Ivoire, Nigeria. **Exports** Uranium, livestock products, cowpeas, onions. **Imports** Petroleum, raw materials, machinery, transportation equipment, electronics.

LAND
Description Western Africa, landlocked. **Area** 489,191 mi² (1,267,000 km²). **Highest point** Idoûkâl-en-Taghès, 6,634 ft (2,022 m). **Lowest point** Along Niger River, 650 ft (198 m).

People. Nearly all Nigeriens are black Africans belonging to culturally diverse groups. The Hausa and the Djerma, farmers who live mostly in the south, constitute the two largest groups. The remaining Nigeriens are nomadic herders who inhabit the northern desert regions. Although the official language is French, most inhabitants speak indigenous tongues. Islam is the most commonly observed religion, but some Nigeriens follow indigenous and Christian beliefs.

Economy and the Land. Niger's economy is chiefly agricultural, although arable land is scarce and drought common. The raising of livestock, grain, beans, and peanuts accounts for most farming activity. Uranium mining, a growing industry, has become less productive recently due to a slump in the world uranium market. Mountains and the Sahara Desert cover most of northern Niger, while the south is savanna. The climate is hot and dry.

History and Politics. Because of its central location in northern Africa, Niger was a crossroads for many peoples during its early history and was dominated by several African empires before European explorers arrived in the 1800s. The area was placed within the French sphere of influence in 1885, but not until 1922 did France make Niger a colony of French West Africa. Gradual moves toward autonomy were made during the forties and fifties, and Niger became fully independent in 1960. Unrest caused in part by a prolonged drought led to a coup in 1974 and the establishment of a military government. Frequent clashes with the Tuareg ethnic groups in the north have abated since a truce was signed in 1994. A December 1992 referendum gave overwhelming approval to a new multiparty constitution. ∎

NIGERIA

Official name Federal Republic of Nigeria
PEOPLE
Population 97,300,000. **Density** 273/mi^2
(105/km^2). **Urban** 35%. **Capital** Lagos (de facto),
1,213,000; Abuja (designated), 250,000. **Ethnic
groups** Hausa, Fulani, Yoruba, Ibo, others.
Languages English, Hausa, Fulani, Yorbua, Ibo,
indigenous. **Religions** Muslim 50%, Christian
40%, Animist 10%. **Life expectancy** 54 female, 51
male. **Literacy** 51%.
POLITICS
Government Provisional military government.
Parties National Republican Convention, Social
Democratic. **Suffrage** Universal, over 21.
Memberships CW, OAU, OPEC, UN.
Subdivisions 30 states, 1 capital territory.
ECONOMY
GDP $95,100,000,000. **Per capita** $1,037.
Monetary unit Naira. **Trade partners** Exports:
U.S., France, Netherlands. Imports: U.K.,
Germany, U.S., France. **Exports** Petroleum,
cocoa, rubber. **Imports** Manufactures, machinery,
chemicals, raw materials.
LAND
Description Western Africa. **Area** 356,669 mi^2
(923,768 km^2). **Highest point** Mt. Waddi, 7,936 ft
(2,419 m). **Lowest point** Sea level.

People. Nigeria, Africa's most populous nation, contains more than 200 distinct black African groups. The
largest groups are the Hausa and the Fulani, who dominate the north; the Yoruba, found primarily in the southwest; and the Ibo, who live in the southeast and have
historically been active in government and trade. Most
Hausa and Fulani are Muslim, and a sizable Christian
community is found mainly in the south. Religious violence between Christians and Muslims erupts periodically, as in 1982 when hundreds were killed.
Nigerians commonly combine traditional beliefs with
Islam or Christianity. Indigenous tongues are more
widely spoken than English, the official language.
Competition among Nigeria's many ethnic groups has
threatened national unity.

Economy and the Land. Nigeria's economy is
based on mining and agriculture. Petroleum is very
important to the Nigerian economy, but a number of
factors—including unskilled labor, poor power facilities, and the worldwide dip in oil prices—have
silenced the oil boom of the 1970s and slowed
development in other areas. In 1983 and 1985 the government expelled millions of illegal aliens in an effort
to revive the economy. The terrain is diverse, encompassing tropical forest, savanna, and semidesert. The
climate is predominantly tropical.

History and Politics. From around 500 B.C. to
about A.D. 200 the region was home to the sophisticated Nok civilization. Later cultures that dominated
parts of the area included the Hausa, Fulani, and
Yoruba. The Portuguese arrived in the 1400s, but
the British gained control over the following centuries,
uniting the region in 1914 as the Colony and
Protectorate of Nigeria. Nigerian calls for self-rule
culminated in independence in 1960. Internal tensions began to wrack the new nation, and in 1966
two military coups took place. After subsequent
massacres of Ibo, that group declared eastern
Nigeria the autonomous state of Biafra. A three-year
civil war followed, ending in 1970 with Biafra's surrender. Government development and the oil boom
speeded economic recovery. Subsequent years
have seen coups and elections which install short-
lived regimes, while political instability continues. In
a transparent attempt to retain control, June 1993
elections were annulled by the military, and democracy has been put on hold. ∎

NIUE See NEW ZEALAND.

NORFOLK ISLAND
See AUSTRALIA.

NORTHERN MARIANA
ISLANDS See UNITED STATES.

NORWAY

Official name Kingdom of Norway
PEOPLE
Population 4,339,000. **Density** 29/mi^2 (11/km^2).
Urban 75%. **Capital** Oslo, 470,204. **Ethnic
groups** Norwegian (Scandinavian), Lapp.
Languages Norwegian, Lapp, Finnish. **Religions**
Lutheran 89%, other Protestant and Roman
Catholic 4%. **Life expectancy** 81 female, 74 male.
Literacy 99%.
POLITICS
Government Constitutional monarchy. **Parties**
Center, Conservative, Labor, Progress, others.

royal line. It entered a union with Denmark in 1380, becoming a Danish province in 1536. Around the end of the Napoleonic Wars, in 1814, Norway became part of Sweden. A long struggle against Swedish rule ended in 1905 as Sweden recognized Norwegian independence, and a Danish prince was made king. Norway was neutral in World War I but endured German occupation during World War II. In 1967 the government initiated a wide-ranging social-welfare system. ∎

OMAN

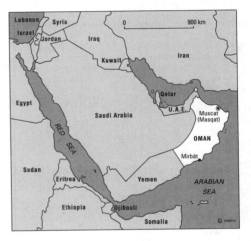

Official name Sultanate of Oman
PEOPLE
Population 2,089,000. **Density** 25/mi² (9.8/km²). **Urban** 11%. **Capital** Muscat, 30,000. **Ethnic groups** Arab, Baluchi, Zanzibari, Indian. **Languages** Arabic, English, Baluchi, Urdu, Indian dialects. **Religions** Ibadite Muslim 75%, Sunni Muslim, Shiite Muslim, Hindu. **Life expectancy** 72 female, 68 male.
POLITICS
Government Monarchy. **Parties** None. **Suffrage** None. **Memberships** AL, UN. **Subdivisions** 7 regions.
ECONOMY
GDP $16,400,000,000. **Per capita** $10,142. **Monetary unit** Rial. **Trade partners** Exports: United Arab Emirates, Saudi Arabia, U.K. Imports: United Arab Emirates, Japan, U.K. **Exports** Petroleum, fish, copper metal, fruits and vegetables. **Imports** Machinery, transportation equipment, manufactures, food, livestock.
LAND
Description Southwestern Asia. **Area** 82,030 mi² (212,457 km²). **Highest point** Mt. Sham, 9,957 ft (3,035 m). **Lowest point** Sea level.

People. Most of Oman's population is Arab, Arabic speaking, and belongs to the Ibadite sect of Islam. Other forms of Islam are also practiced. There is a significant foreign community that includes Indians,

Suffrage Universal, over 18. **Memberships** NATO, OECD, UN. **Subdivisions** 19 counties.
ECONOMY
GDP $89,500,000,000. **Per capita** $20,775. **Monetary unit** Krone. **Trade partners** Exports: U.K., Sweden, Germany. Imports: Sweden, Germany, U.K., U.S. **Exports** Petroleum, natural gas, fish, ships and boats, aluminum, pulp and paper. **Imports** Machinery, fuels and lubricants, transportation equipment, chemicals.
LAND
Description Northern Europe. **Area** 149,412 mi² (386,975 km²). **Highest point** Galdhøpiggen, 8,100 ft (2,469 m). **Lowest point** Sea level.
The above information includes Svalbard and Jan Mayen.

People. Because of its relatively remote location in far northern Europe, Norway has seen few population migrations and possesses a virtually homogeneous population, which is predominantly Germanic, Norwegian speaking, and Lutheran. Small communities of Lapps and Finns live in the far north, while most Norwegians live in the south and along the coast. The people enjoy many government-provided social services and programs.

Economy and the Land. Norway's economy, based on shipping, trade, and the mining of offshore oil and natural gas, takes its shape from the nation's proximity to several seas. Shipbuilding, fishing, and forestry are also important activities. Norway is a leading producer of hydroelectricity. Combined with some government control of the economy, these lucrative activities have given the nation a high standard of living and fairly low unemployment. Most of Norway is a high plateau covered with mountains. The Gulf Stream gives the nation a much milder climate than other places at the same latitude.

History and Politics. Parts of present-day Norway were inhabited by about 9000 B.C. Germanic tribes began immigrating to the area about 2000 B.C. Between A.D. 800 and 1100, Viking ships from Norway raided coastal towns throughout Western Europe and also colonized Greenland and Iceland. Unified around 900, Norway was subsequently shaken by civil war, plague, and the end of its

Baluchis from Pakistan, and East African blacks. Many of them are guest workers in the oil industry.

Economy and the Land. Once a mainstay of Oman's economy, oil revenues declined as prices fell throughout the 1980s. The mining of natural gas and copper is being developed, as are agriculture and fishing. A central position in the politically volatile Persian Gulf and revolutionary internal strife have led Oman to devote a considerable portion of its budget to defense. Land regions include a coastal plain and interior mountains and desert. Oman's land borders are undefined and in dispute. A desert climate prevails over most areas except the coast, which has humid conditions.

History and Politics. Islam came to Muscat and Oman, as the nation was known before 1970, in the seventh century A.D. The Portuguese gained control of parts of the coast in 1508 but were driven out in 1650 by the Arabs. At about this time the hereditary sultanate—which absorbed the political power formerly held by the Ibadite religious leaders, or imams—was founded. Close relations with Britain, cemented in a 1798 agreement and subsequent treaties, have continued to the present. Conflicts between the sultan and Omanis, who wanted to be ruled exclusively by their imam, erupted intermittently after 1900, and in 1959 the sultan defeated the rebels with British help and outlawed the office of imam. Marxist insurgency was put down in 1975. Sultan Qaboos bin Said, who overthrew his father's regime in 1970, has liberalized some policies and worked to modernize the nation. Oman is still somewhat isolated and discourages foreign contacts. ∎

ORKNEY ISLANDS
See UNITED KINGDOM.

PAKISTAN

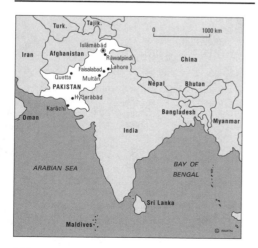

Official name Islamic Republic of Pakistan

PEOPLE
Population 126,630,000. **Density** 382/mi² (147/km²). **Urban** 32%. **Capital** Islāmābād, 204,364. **Ethnic groups** Punjabi, Sindhi, Pathan, Baluchi, others. **Languages** English, Urdu, Punjabi, Sindhi, Pashto. **Religions** Sunni Muslim 77%, Shiite Muslim 20%. **Life expectancy** 59 female, 59 male. **Literacy** 35%.
POLITICS
Government Islamic republic. **Parties** Muslim League (Nawaz), People's, others. **Suffrage** Universal, over 21. **Memberships** CW, UN. **Subdivisions** 4 provinces, 1 tribal area, 1 capital territory, 2 areas.
ECONOMY
GNP $239,000,000,000. **Per capita** $1,935. **Monetary unit** Rupee. **Trade partners** Exports: U.S., Japan, Germany. Imports: U.S., Japan, Kuwait. **Exports** Cotton, textiles, clothing, rice. **Imports** Petroleum, machinery, transportation equipment, vegetable oils, animal fats.
LAND
Description Southern Asia. **Area** 339,732 mi² (879,902 km²). **Highest point** K2, 28,250 ft (8,611 m). **Lowest point** Sea level.
The above information includes part of Jammu and Kashmir.

People. Pakistan's varied ethnicity is the product of centuries of incursions by different races. Today each people is concentrated in a different region and speaks its own language; English and Urdu, official languages, are not widely spoken. The Punjabis compose the largest ethnic group and traditionally have been influential in government and commerce. Virtually all of Pakistan, which was created as a Muslim homeland, follows Islam. Spurred by poor living conditions and a lack of jobs, many Pakistanis work abroad.

Economy and the Land. Despite recent progress in manufacturing, agriculture remains the economic mainstay. Improvement in farming techniques has increased productivity. Government planning and foreign assistance have aided all sectors, but Pakistan remains troubled by population growth, unskilled labor, a trade deficit, and an influx of refugees fleeing the war in Afghanistan. Pakistan's terrain includes mountains, fertile plains, and desert. The climate is continental, with extremes in temperature.

History and Politics. Around 2500 B.C., the Indus Valley civilization flourished in the area of modern Pakistan. Various empires and immigrants followed, including Aryans, Persians, and Greeks. Invading Arabs introduced Islam to the region in the A.D. 700s. In the 1500s the Mogul Empire of Afghanistan came to include nearly all of present-day Pakistan, India, and Bangladesh, and as that empire declined, various peoples ruled the area. Through wars and treaties, the British presence in Asia expanded, and by the early twentieth century British India included all of modern Pakistan. Because of hostilities between British India's Muslims and Hindus, the separate Muslim nation of Pakistan was created when British India gained independence in 1947. With its boundaries drawn around the Muslim population centers, Pakistan was formed from the northeastern and northwestern parts of India, and its eastern region was separated from the west by more than 1,000 miles (1,600 km). East Pakistanis felt that power was unfairly concentrated in the west, and in 1971 a civil war erupted. Aided by India, East Pakistan won the war and became the independent nation of Bangladesh. After the death of President Mohammed Zia in 1988, the people elected Benazir Bhutto, who revived the People's party of her father, a previous president. She was ousted in 1990 but reinstated as Prime Minister in 1993. Political violence has escalated as ethnic groups and Islamic fundamentalists struggle for power. ∎

PALAU See UNITED STATES.

PANAMA

Official name Republic of Panama
PEOPLE
Population 2,654,000. **Density** 91/mi² (35/km²).
Urban 53%. **Capital** Panamá, 411,549. **Ethnic groups** Mestizo 70%, West Indian 14%, white 10%, Amerindian 6%. **Languages** Spanish, English. **Religions** Roman Catholic 85%, Protestant 15%. **Life expectancy** 75 female, 71 male. **Literacy** 88%.
POLITICS
Government Republic. **Parties** Christian Democrat, Nationalist Republican Liberal Movement, Authentic Liberal, others. **Suffrage** Universal, over 18. **Memberships** OAS, UN.
Subdivisions 9 provinces, 1 intendency.
ECONOMY
GDP $11,600,000,000. **Per capita** $4,540.
Monetary unit Balboa. **Trade partners** Exports: U.S., Germany, Costa Rica. Imports: U.S., Ecuador, Japan. **Exports** Bananas, shrimp, sugar, clothing, coffee. **Imports** Machinery, petroleum, food, manufactures, chemicals.

LAND
Description Central America. **Area** 29,157 mi² (75,517 km²). **Highest point** Volcán Barú, 11,401 ft (3,475 m). **Lowest point** Sea level.

People. Most Panamanians are mestizos, a mixture of Spanish and Indian stocks. Indigenous Indians, blacks from the West Indies, and whites form the remaining population. A Spanish legacy is reflected by the official language, Spanish, and the predominance of Roman Catholicism. Most people live near the Panama Canal. A wealthy elite has traditionally directed the government and economy.

Economy and the Land. Because of its location, Panama has been a strategic center for trade and transportation. The 1914 opening of the Panama Canal, connecting the Atlantic and Pacific oceans, accentuated these strengths and has provided additional revenue and jobs; the canal area is now Panama's most economically developed region. Agriculture is an important activity; and oil refining, food processing, fishing, and financial services all contribute to the economy as well. Panama will have to adjust to the economic and technical losses that will accompany the end of United States operation of the canal in 1999. The country has a mountainous interior and a tropical climate.

History and Politics. Originally inhabited by Indians, Panama became a Spanish colony in the early 1500s and served as a vital transportation center. In 1821 it overcame Spanish rule and entered the Republic of Greater Colombia. After Colombia vetoed a United States plan to build a canal across the narrow isthmus, Panama, encouraged by the United States, seceded from the republic and became independent in 1903. Eleven years later, America completed the canal and established control over it and the Panama Canal Zone. Dissatisfaction with this arrangement resulted in several anti-American riots in the fifties and sixties. A 1968 coup placed the Panamanian National Guard in power, and the movement to end American control of the Canal Zone gained momentum. In 1979 the sovereignty of the Canal Zone was transferred to Panama; it will gain control of the canal in 1999. Beginning in 1994 military bases began reverting to Panamanian control. General Manuel Noriega maintained a repressive and corrupt control of the government until U.S. military forces invaded and overthrew him in 1989. Elections in May 1994 returned the reformed party of Noriega to power. ∎

PAPUA NEW GUINEA

Official name Independent State of Papua New Guinea
PEOPLE
Population 4,057,000. **Density** 23/mi² (8.8/km²).
Urban 16%. **Capital** Port Moresby, New Guinea I., 193,242. **Ethnic groups** Melanesian, Papuan, Negrito, Micronesian, Polynesian. **Languages** English, Motu, Pidgin, indigenous. **Religions** Roman Catholic 22%, Lutheran 16%, United Church 8%, Anglican 5%. **Life expectancy** 57

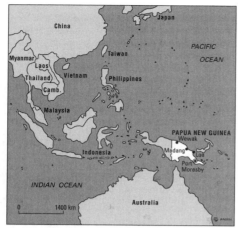

world War I. The League of Nations granted Australia a mandate to New Guinea in 1920. After being occupied by Japan in World War II, Papua and New Guinea were united as an Australian territory from 1945 to 1946. Papua New Guinea gained independence in 1975. A separatist movement in Bougainville continues to plague the central government. ■

female, 55 male. **Literacy** 52%.
POLITICS
Government Parliamentary state. **Parties** Pangu (United), People's Action, People's Democratic Movement, People's Progress, others. **Suffrage** Universal, over 18. **Memberships** CW, UN. **Subdivisions** 19 provinces, 1 capital district.
ECONOMY
GDP $8,200,000,000. **Per capita** $2,194. **Monetary unit** Kina. **Trade partners** Exports: Japan, Germany, Korea. Imports: Australia, Japan, U.S. **Exports** Copper, gold, coffee, lumber, palm oil, cocoa, lobster. **Imports** Machinery and transportation equipment, food, fuel, chemicals.
LAND
Description South Pacific islands. **Area** 178,704 mi^2 (462,840 km^2). **Highest point** Mt. Wilhelm, 14,793 ft (4,509 m). **Lowest point** Sea level.

People. Almost all inhabitants are Melanesians belonging to several thousand culturally diverse and geographically isolated communities. More than seven hundred languages are spoken, but most people also speak Motu or a dialect of English. European missionaries brought Christianity, but faiths based on spirit and ancestor worship predominate. The traditions of village life remain strong.

Economy and the Land. The economic supports are agriculture, which employs most of the work force, and copper and gold mining. Papua New Guinea has other mineral resources, as well as potential for forestry. The nation consists of the eastern half of New Guinea Island, plus New Britain, New Ireland, Bougainville, and six hundred smaller islands. Terrain includes mountains, volcanoes, broad valleys, and swamps; the climate is tropical.

History and Politics. Settlers from Southeast Asia are thought to have arrived as long as fifty thousand years ago. Isolated native villages were found by the Spanish and Portuguese in the early 1500s. In 1884 Germany annexed the northeastern part of the island of New Guinea and its offshore islands, and Britain took control of the southeastern section and its islands. Australia assumed administration of the British territory, known as Papua, in 1906 and seized the German regions, or German New Guinea, during

PARAGUAY

Official name Republic of Paraguay

PEOPLE
Population 4,400,000. **Density** 28/mi^2 (11/km^2). **Urban** 48%. **Capital** Asunción, 502,426. **Ethnic groups** Mestizo 95%, white and Amerindian 5%. **Languages** Spanish, Guarani. **Religions** Roman Catholic 90%, Mennonite and other Protestant. **Life expectancy** 70 female, 65 male. **Literacy** 90%.
POLITICS
Government Republic. **Parties** Authentic Radical Liberal, Colorado, others. **Suffrage** Universal, over 18. **Memberships** OAS, UN. **Subdivisions** 19 departments, 1 city.
ECONOMY
GDP $15,200,000,000. **Per capita** $3,038. **Monetary unit** Guarani. **Trade partners** Exports: Brazil, Netherlands. Imports: Brazil, Argentina, Algeria, U.S. **Exports** Cotton, soybeans, wood, vegetable oil, coffee, tung oil, meat. **Imports** Machinery, manufactures, petroleum, fuel, raw materials, food.
LAND
Description Central South America, landlocked. **Area** 157,048 mi^2 (406,752 km^2). **Highest point** Unnamed, 2,625 ft (800 m). **Lowest point** Confluence of Paraná and Paraguay rivers, 151 ft (46 m).

People. Paraguay's population displays a homogeneity unusual in South America; most people are a mix of Spanish and Guarani Indian ancestry, are Roman Catholic, and speak both Spanish and Guarani. The small number of unassimilated Guarani live mostly in western Paraguay, known as the Gran Chaco. There are some foreign communities, mostly German, Japanese, and Brazilian. Culture combines Spanish and Indian traditions.

Economy and the Land. Agriculture—based on cotton, soybeans, and cattle—forms the keystone of the economy. Forestry also contributes significantly to Paraguay's exports. the lack of direct access to the sea, unskilled labor, and a history of war and instability have resulted in an underdeveloped economy; manufacturing in particular has suffered. The world's largest hydroelectric project, the Itaipu Dam, was completed in 1988. Paraguay has two distinct regions, divided by the Paraguay River: the semiarid Gran Chaco plains in the west, and the temperate, fertile east, where most farming takes place.

History and Politics. The indigenous Guarani formed an agricultural society centered around what is now Asunción. Portuguese and Spanish explorers arrived in the early 1500s, and the region subsequently gained importance as the center of Spanish holdings in southern South America. During the 1700s, Jesuit missionaries worked to convert thousands of Indians to Roman Catholicism. After gaining independence in 1811, Paraguay was ruled by a succession of dictators. A disastrous war against Argentina, Brazil, and Uruguay from 1865 to 1870 cost the nation half its population. Another war against Bolivia from 1932 to 1935 increased Paraguay's territory but further weakened its stability. A military coup in 1989 ended the 35-year regime of General Stroessner, but the 1993 election of a civilian leader brought little change. The country is still controlled by the military. ∎

PERU

Official name Republic of Peru
PEOPLE
Population 23,095,000. **Density** 47/mi² (18/km²). **Urban** 70%. **Capital** Lima, 371,122. **Ethnic groups** Amerindian 45%, mestizo 37%, white 15%. **Languages** Quechua, Spanish, Aymara. **Religions** Roman Catholic. **Life expectancy** 67 female, 63 male. **Literacy** 85%.
POLITICS
Government Republic. **Parties** American Popular Revolutionary Alliance, New Majority-Change 90, Popular Action, United Left. **Suffrage** Universal, over 18. **Memberships** OAS, UN. **Subdivisions** 24 departments, 1 constitutional province.

ECONOMY
GDP $70,000,000,000. **Per capita** $3,044. **Monetary unit** Sol. **Trade partners** Exports: U.S., Japan, U.K. Imports: U.S., Panama, Germany, Argentina. **Exports** Copper, fishmeal, zinc, petroleum, lead, silver, coffee, cotton. **Imports** Food, machinery, transportation equipment, iron and steel, chemicals.
LAND
Description Western South America. **Area** 496,225 mi² (1,285,216 km²). **Highest point** Nevado Huascarán, 22,133 ft (6,746 m). **Lowest point** Sea level.

People. Peru's Indian population constitutes the nation's largest ethnic group and the largest Indian concentration in North or South America. Although whites make up the third-largest group after Indians and mestizos, they have historically controlled much of the wealth. The Indians are often geographically and culturally remote from the ruling classes and generally live in poverty. Most Peruvians practice Roman Catholicism.

Economy and the Land. Considerable natural resources have made Peru a leader in the production of minerals—notably copper, lead, and silver—and in fishing. The food-processing, textile, and oil-refining industries also contribute. Productivity has been slowed by a mountainous terrain that impedes transport and communication, earthquakes and other natural disasters, a largely unskilled work force, and years of stringent military rule. Climate varies from arid to mild in the coastal desert to temperate but cool in the Andean highlands, and hot and humid in the eastern jungles and plains.

History and Politics. Several Native American cultures arose in the region between 900 B.C. and A.D. 1200, the last of which was the Incan. Excavation began in 1987 of the richest pre-Hispanic ruler ever discovered, further documenting the sophistication of these cultures. Builders of an empire stretching from Colombia to Chile, the Inca were conquered by the Spanish in 1533. For almost the next three hundred years, Peru was a harshly ruled Spanish colony and center for colonial administration. Peru achieved independence from Spain in 1821, largely through the efforts of José de San Martín of Argentina and Simón Bolívar of Venezuela, although Spain did not formally recognize Peruvian independence until 1879. Military officers ruled the country through the rest of the century. In 1883, Chile and Bolivia defeated Peru in the War of the Pacific, and the country lost its valuable southern nitrite region. Fernando Belaúnde Terry, a moderate reformer, was elected in 1963. A military junta ousted him in 1968, nationalizing some industries and instituting land reform. Inflation and unemployment caused dissatisfaction and a 1975 coup. Elections in 1980 and 1985 restored democratic leadership. However, economic chaos has since destabilized the government and allowed the growth of the Shining Path, a terrorist guerrilla movement. Alberto Fujimori, elected in 1990, has controlled the Shining Path and improved the economy, although the distribution of wealth remains uneven. ∎

PHILIPPINES

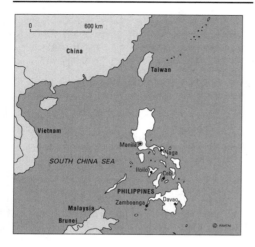

Official name Republic of the Philippines
PEOPLE
Population 67,910,000. **Density** 586/mi^2
(226/km^2). **Urban** 43%. **Capital** Manila, Luzon I.,
1,598,918. **Ethnic groups** Christian Malay 92%,
Muslim Malay 4%, Chinese 2%. **Languages**
English, Pilipino, Tagalog. **Religions** Roman
Catholic 83%, Protestant 9%, Muslim 5%,
Buddhist and others 3%. **Life expectancy** 67
female, 63 male. **Literacy** 90%.
POLITICS
Government Republic. **Parties** Democratic
Filipino Struggle, Nationalist People's Coalition,
People Power-Natl. Union of Christian Democrats.
Suffrage Universal, over 15. **Memberships**
ASEAN, UN. **Subdivisions** 73 provinces.
ECONOMY
GDP $171,000,000,000. **Per capita** $2,611.
Monetary unit Peso. **Trade partners** Exports:
U.S., Japan. Imports: U.S., Japan, Hong Kong.
Exports Electrical equipment, textiles, minerals,
agricultural products, coconut. **Imports** Raw mate-
rials, machinery, petroleum.
LAND
Description Southeastern Asian islands. **Area**
115,831 mi^2 (300,000 km^2). **Highest point** Mt.
Apo, 9,692 ft (2,954 m). **Lowest point** Sea level.

People. Nearly all Filipinos are descended from
Malay peoples. The majority are Roman Catholic, a
reflection of centuries of Spanish rule. A Muslim
minority has begun agitating for autonomy. Although
nearly ninety native languages and dialects are spoken, Pilipino and English are the official languages.
The wide gap between rich and poor, inherited from
a plantation economy, has concentrated wealth in the
hands of the landowners.

Economy and the Land. Philippines is a primarily
agricultural nation, relying on rice, sugar, coconuts,
and wood. Fishing is an important activity. Considerable
reserves of copper, nickel, and chromite make mining important. Manufacturing is developing through

government incentives. A dependence on imported
goods, along with inadequate but growing power and
transport systems, has hampered growth. The archipelago of more than seven thousand islands is
marked by mountains, volcanoes, forests, and
inland plains. The climate is tropical and includes a
typhoon season.

History and Politics. The islands are thought to have
been settled by Negritos about thirty thousand years
ago. Beginning about 3000 B.C., Malay immigrants
arrived. By 1565 the area was under Spanish control, and the Roman Catholic church had considerable influence throughout the Spanish period. In
the late 1800s a movement for independence developed but was put down first by the Spanish and then
by the United States, which gained the islands in 1898
after defeating Spain in the Spanish-American War.
Japan occupied the Philippines during World War II.
Independence came in 1946 and was followed by a
rebellion by Communists demanding land reform; the
rebels were defeated in 1954. Ferdinand Marcos was
elected president in 1965 and, in the face of opposition from many quarters, declared martial law in 1972.
Marcos lifted martial law in 1981 but was defeated
in a 1986 presidential elections by Corazon Aquino,
wife of assassinated opposition leader Benigno
Aquino. Marcos eventually fled the island, and
Aquino assumed power until 1992. The closing of Clark
Air Base and Subic Bay Naval Base in 1992 ended
an era of United States military presence in the
Philippines. There is increasing conflict between
Muslim-Christian factions, particularly in the Muslim-
majority southern islands. ∎

PITCAIRN See UNITED KINGDOM.

POLAND

Official name Republic of Poland

PEOPLE
Population 38,730,000. **Density** 320/mi^2 (123/km^2). **Urban** 62%. **Capital** Warsaw, 1,644,500. **Ethnic groups** Polish (mixed Slavic and Teutonic) 98%. **Languages** Polish. **Religions** Roman Catholic 95%. **Life expectancy** 76 female, 67 male. **Literacy** 99%.

POLITICS
Government Republic. **Parties** Democratic Left Alliance, Democratic Union, Labor, Peasant, others. **Suffrage** Universal, over 18. **Memberships** NATO, UN. **Subdivisions** 49 provinces.

ECONOMY
GDP $180,400,000,000. **Per capita** $4,706. **Monetary unit** Zloty. **Trade partners** Exports: Former Soviet republics, Germany, U.K. Imports: Former Soviet republics, Germany, Austria. **Exports** Machinery, metals, chemicals, fuel, food. **Imports** Machinery, fuel, chemicals, food, manufactures.

LAND
Description Eastern Europe. **Area** 121,196 mi^2 (313,895 km^2). **Highest point** Rysy, 8,199 ft (2,499 m). **Lowest point** Raczki Elbląskie, -7 ft (-2 m).

People. Poland's homogeneous population is partially a result of Nazi persecution during World War II, which virtually obliterated the Jewish community and led to the emigration of most minorities. Roman Catholicism, practiced by almost all Poles, remains a unifying force. The urban population has risen in the postwar period because of government emphasis on industrialization.

Economy and the Land. Government policies since the war transformed Poland from an agricultural nation into an industrial one. Machinery and textiles are important products. Since the collapse of communism in Eastern Europe an entreprenurial spirit has taken hold. Privatization is proceeding slowly in the hope of controlling inflation and unemployment. Poland has a mostly flat terrain—except for mountains in the south—and a temperate climate.

History and Politics. Slavic tribes inhabited the region of modern Poland several thousand years ago. The Piast dynasty began in the A.D. 900s and established Roman Catholicism as the official religion. In the sixteenth century, the Jagiellonian dynasty guided the empire to its height of expansion. A subsequent series of upheavals and wars weakened Poland, and from the 1770s to the 1790s it was partitioned three times, finally disappearing as an independent state. In 1918, following the Allies' World War I victory, Poland regained its independence and, through the 1919 Treaty of Versailles, much of its former territory. World War II began with Germany's invasion of Poland in 1939. With the end of the war, Poland came under Communist control and Soviet domination. Antigovernment strikes and riots, some spurred by rising food prices, erupted periodically. In the first free election since Communist control, the trade union Solidarity, led by Lech Walesa. won an overwhelming victory in 1989. The nation is still struggling with the transition from a communist to a capitalist economy, and communism remains a strong influence. ■

PORTUGAL

Official name Portuguese Republic
PEOPLE
Population 9,907,000. **Density** 279/mi^2 (108/km^2). **Urban** 34%. **Capital** Lisbon, 807,167. **Ethnic groups** Portuguese (Mediterranean), black. **Languages** Portuguese. **Religions** Roman Catholic 97%, Protestant 1%. **Life expectancy** 78 female, 71 male. **Literacy** 85%.
POLITICS
Government Republic. **Parties** Communist, Social Democratic, Socialist, others. **Suffrage** Universal, over 18. **Memberships** EU, NATO, OECD, UN. **Subdivisions** 18 districts, 2 autonomous regions.

Places and Possessions of PORTUGAL

Entity	Status	Area	Population	Capital/Population
Azores (North Atlantic islands)	Autonomous region	868 mi^2 (2,247 km^2)	241,000	Ponta Delgada, 21,187
Macao (Eastern Asia; islands and peninsula on China's southeastern coast)	Chinese territory under Portuguese administration	7.0 mi^2 (18 km^2)	396,000	Macau, 396,000
Madeira Islands (North Atlantic; northwest of Africa)	Autonomous region	307 mi^2 (794 km^2)	257,000	Funchal, 44,111

ECONOMY

GDP $91,500,000,000. **Per capita** $8,583.
Monetary unit Escudo. **Trade partners** Exports: Germany, France, Spain. Imports: Spain, Germany, France. **Exports** Textiles, cork and paper products, canned fish, wine, timber resin, machinery. **Imports** Machinery and transportation equipment, agricultural products, chemicals.

LAND

Description Southwestern Europe. **Area** 35,516 mi^2 (91,985 km^2). **Highest point** Ponta do Pico, 7,713 ft (2,351 m). **Lowest point** Sea level.

People. Although many foreign invaders have been drawn by Portugal's long coastline, today the population is relatively homogeneous. One group of invaders, the Romans, laid the basis for the chief language, Portuguese, which developed from Latin. The only significant minority is composed of black Africans from former colonies. Most Portuguese are rural and belong to the Roman Catholic church, which has had a strong influence on society.

Economy and the Land. The mainstays of agriculture and fishing were joined in the mid-1900s by manufacturing, chiefly of textiles, clothing, cork products, metals, and machinery. A variety of social and political ills contributing to Portugal's status as one of Europe's poorest nations include: past wars with African colonies, an influx of colonial refugees, and intraparty violence. Tourism is increasingly important, but agriculture has suffered from outdated techniques and a rural-to-urban population shift. The terrain is mostly plains and lowlands, with some mountains; the climate is mild and sunny.

History and Politics. Inhabited by an Iberian people about five thousand years ago, the area was later visited by Phoenicians, Celts, and Greeks before falling to the Romans around the first century B.C. The Romans were followed by Germanic Visigoths and in A.D. 711 by North African Muslims, who greatly influenced Portuguese art and architecture. Spain absorbed Portugal in 1094, and Portugal declared its independence in 1143. About one hundred years later, the last of the Muslims was expelled. Portugal's golden age—during which its navigators explored the globe and founded colonies in South America, Africa, and the Far East—lasted from 1385 to the late 1500s. Rival European powers soon began to seize Portuguese holdings. In 1580 Spain invaded Portugal, ruling until 1640, when the Spanish were driven out and independence reestablished. After the 1822 loss of Brazil, Portugal's most valuable colony, and decades of opposition, a weakened monarchy was overthrown in 1910. The hardships of World War I battered the newly established republic, and in 1926 its parliamentary democracy fell to a military coup. Antonio Salazar became prime minister in 1932, ruling as a virtual dictator until 1968. Salazar's favored treatment of the rich and his refusal to relinquish Portugal's colonies aggravated the economic situation. A 1974 coup toppled Salazar's successor and set up a military government, events that sparked violence among political parties. Almost all Portuguese colonies gained independence during the next two years, A democratic government was adopted in 1976; varying coalitions have since ruled the nation. ∎

PUERTO RICO

Official name Commonwealth of Puerto Rico

PEOPLE

Population 3,625,000. **Density** 1,031/mi^2 (398/km^2). **Urban** 74%. **Capital** San Juan, 426,832. **Ethnic groups** Puerto Rican (mixed Spanish and black). **Languages** Spanish, English. **Religions** Roman Catholic 85%, Protestant and other 15%. **Life expectancy** 78 female, 72 male. **Literacy** 89%.

POLITICS

Government Commonwealth (U.S. protection).
Parties New Progressive, Popular Democratic, others. **Suffrage** Universal, over 18.
Memberships None. **Subdivisions** 78 municipalities.

ECONOMY

GNP $26,800,000,000. **Per capita** $7,596.
Monetary unit U.S. dollar. **Trade partners** U.S.
Exports Pharmaceuticals, electronics, clothing, canned tuna, rum. **Imports** Chemicals, clothing, food, fish, petroleum.

LAND

Description Caribbean island. **Area** 3,515 mi^2 (9,104 km^2). **Highest point** Cerro de Punta, 4,389 ft (1,338 m). **Lowest point** Sea level.

People. Puerto Rico's chief language, Spanish, and religion, Roman Catholicism, reflect this American commonwealth's past under Spanish rule. Most of the population is descended from Spaniards and black African slaves. A rising population has caused housing shortages and unemployment. Many Puerto Ricans live in the United States, mostly in New York City.

Economy and the Land. Once dependent on such plantation crops as sugar and coffee, Puerto Rico is now a manufacturing nation, specializing in food processing and electrical equipment. Commonwealth incentives for foreign investors aided this transformation, also known as Operation Bootstrap, after World War II. Foreign visitors, attracted by the tropical climate, make tourism another important activity. A lack of natural resources and fluctuations in the United States economy have hurt economic development. The island's terrain is marked by mountains, lowlands, and valleys.

History and Politics. The original inhabitants, the Arawak Indians, were wiped out by Spanish colonists, who first settled the island in 1508. Despite successive attacks by the French, English, and Dutch, Puerto Rico remained under Spanish control until 1898, when the United States took possession after the Spanish-American War. A civil government under a United States governor was set up in 1900; seventeen years later Puerto Ricans were made United States citizens. In 1952 the island became a self-governing commonwealth. This status was upheld in a referendum in 1967, and again in 1993 after fierce internal debate. ■

QATAR

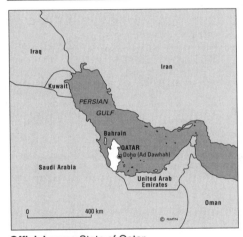

Official name State of Qatar
PEOPLE
Population 519,000. **Density** 118/mi² (45/km²).
Urban 90%. **Capital** Doha, 217,294. **Ethnic groups** Arab 40%, Pakistani 18%, Indian 18%, Iranian 10%. **Languages** Arabic, English.
Religions Muslim 95%. **Life expectancy** 73 female, 68 male. **Literacy** 76%.
POLITICS
Government Monarchy. **Parties** None. **Suffrage** None. **Memberships** AL, OPEC, UN.
Subdivisions 9 municipalities.
ECONOMY
GDP $8,800,000,000. **Per capita** $17,886.
Monetary unit Riyal. **Trade partners** Exports: Japan, Brazil, United Arab Emirates. Imports: U.K., Japan, U.S., Italy. **Exports** Petroleum, steel, fertilizer. **Imports** Food, beverages, animal and vegetable oils, chemicals, machinery.
LAND
Description Southwestern Asia. **Area** 4,412 mi² (11,427 km²). **Highest point** Aba al Bawl Hill, 344 ft (105 m). **Lowest point** Sea level.

People. Qatar's population is distinguished by a relatively high proportion of Iranians, Pakistanis, and Indians, who began arriving during the oil boom of the 1950s. Most Qataris are Sunni Muslims and live in or near Doha, the capital. In recent years the government has encouraged the nomadic Bedouins to take up settled lifestyles. Despite a political trend toward a modern welfare state, Qatar retains many elements of a traditional Islamic society.

Economy and the Land. Oil provides the great majority of Qatar's income, while extensive reserves of natural gas await exploitation. The government has made moves toward economic diversification, investing in agriculture and industry; fertilizer and cement are important new products. Most of Qatar is stony desert, and the climate is hot and arid.

History and Politics. No strong central government existed in Qatar before Saudi Muslims gained control in the late eighteenth century. Ottoman Turks occupied the region from 1872 to 1916, when Qatar became a British protectorate. Although oil was discovered in 1940 on the western side of Qatar's peninsula, the outbreak of World War II postponed exploitation for another nine years. Qatar became independent in 1971 after failing to agree on the terms of a union with eight Persian Gulf sheikdoms—today the United Arab Emirates and Bahrain. Oil revenues have been used to improve housing, transportation, and public health. ■

REUNION See FRANCE.

ROMANIA

Official name Romania
PEOPLE
Population 22,745,000. **Density** 248/mi² (96/km²). **Urban** 54%. **Capital** Bucharest,

2,064,474. **Ethnic groups** Romanian (mixed Latin, Thracian, Slavic, and Celtic) 89%, Hungarian 9%. **Languages** Romanian, Hungarian, German. **Religions** Romanian Orthodox 70%, Roman Catholic 6%, Protestant 6%. **Life expectancy** 73 female, 67 male. **Literacy** 96%.
POLITICS
Government Republic. **Parties** Democratic Convention, National Salvation Front, National Unity, Social Democracy. **Suffrage** Universal, over 18. **Memberships** NATO, UN. **Subdivisions** 40 counties, 1 municipality.
ECONOMY
GDP $63,700,000,000. **Per capita** $2,746.
Monetary unit Leu. **Trade partners** Exports: Former Soviet republics, Italy, Germany. Imports: Former Soviet republics, Iran, Egypt. **Exports** Machinery and transportation equipment; fuel, minerals, and metals. **Imports** Fuel, minerals, and metals; machinery and transportation equipment; chemicals.
LAND
Description Eastern Europe. **Area** 91,699 mi^2 (237,500 km^2). **Highest point** Moldoveanu, 8,346 ft (2,544 m). **Lowest point** Sea level.

People. The majority population of Romania belongs to the Romanian Orthodox church and traces its roots to Latin-speaking Romans, Thracians, Slavs, and Celts. Minorities, concentrated in Transylvania and areas north and west of Bucharest, are mainly Roman Catholic Hungarians and Germans. Other minorities include Gypsies, Serbs, Croats, Ukrainians, Greeks, Turks, and Armenians. Almost all inhabitants speak Romanian, although minority groups often speak other languages.

Economy and the Land. When Romania became a Communist country in the 1940s, the government began to turn the country from agriculture to industry. The economy is now based on such major products as iron and steel. Most agriculture is still collectivized, and corn and wheat are major crops. The transition to a market economy has been slow and troubled. The terrain is marked by a south-to-northeast plateau that curves around several mountain ranges, including the Carpathians, found in the northern and central regions. The climate is continental, with cold, snowy winters and warm summers.

History and Politics. First colonized by the Dacians, a Thracian tribe, around the fourth century B.C., the area became the Roman province of Romania in the second century A.D. Invading Bulgars, Goths, Huns, Magyars, Slavs, and Tartars followed the Romans. Between 1250 and 1350, the independent Romanian principalities of Walachia and Moldavia emerged. In the fifteenth and sixteenth centuries, Ottoman Turks conquered the principalities and, following a Russian-Turkish war, Russians occupied the states. In 1861 Walachia and Moldavia were united as Romania, in 1878 they gained independence, and in 1881 Romania was proclaimed a kingdom. Oppression and a concentration of land and wealth among the aristocracy marked the nation's government, and in 1907 its army quelled a rebellion. In 1919, after a World War I alliance with the Allies,

Romania gained Transylvania and other territories. Instability and dissatisfaction, spurred by worldwide economic depression, continued through the 1930s. With the cooperation of Romanian leadership, Germany occupied the country in World War II. In 1944 Soviet troops entered Romania, and the nation subsequently joined the Allies. A Communist government was established in 1945, and in 1947 the king was forced to abdicate and Romania officially became a Communist country. Initially Romania's policies were closely tied to those of the Soviet Union; but renewed nationalism in the sixties led to several independent policy decisions. Nicolae Ceausescu's twenty-four years of harsh, repressive leadership led to a popular revolt and his execution in 1989. An interim government held elections in 1990, which were won by the National Salvation Front (former Communists). The country approved a new constitution in December 1991 that allowed multiparty representation. There have been periodic riots over continued government failure to improve economic conditions. ■

RUSSIA

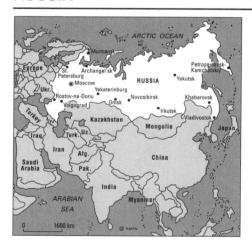

Official name Russian Federation
PEOPLE
Population 150,500,000. **Density** 23/mi^2 (8.8/km^2). **Urban** 74%. **Capital** Moscow, 8,801,500. **Ethnic groups** Russian 82%, Tatar 4%, Ukrainian 3%, Chuvash 1%. **Languages** Russian, Tatar, Ukrainian. **Religions** Russian Orthodox, Muslim. **Life expectancy** 74 female, 64 male. **Literacy** 99%.
POLITICS
Government Republic. **Parties** Democratic, Democratic Russia, Movement for Democratic Reforms, People's. **Suffrage** Universal, over 18. **Memberships** CIS, NATO, UN. **Subdivisions** 21 republics, 1 autonomous oblast, 49 oblasts, 6 krays, 10 autonomous okrugs, 2 cities.
ECONOMY
GDP $775,400,000,000. **Per capita** $5,152.

Monetary unit Ruble. **Trade partners** Western and eastern European countries, Japan. **Exports** Petroleum and natural gas, lumber, coal, nonferrous metals, chemicals. **Imports** Machinery and equipment, chemicals, consumer goods, grain, meat.

LAND

Description Eastern Europe and Northern Asia. **Area** 6,592,849 mi² (17,075,400 km²). **Highest point** Mt. Elbrus, 18,510 ft (5,642 m). **Lowest point** Caspian Sea, -92 ft (-28 m).

People. The Russians are a Slavic people who have occupied the land between the Baltic and Black seas for at least fifteen hundred years. Russia is also home to many other ethnic groups, including the Tatars, Yakuts, Ossetians, and Buryats. Many of the minority ethnic groups reside in their own autonomous regions. The Russian church is the largest of the Eastern Orthodox churches, and dates back to A.D. 988. Once discouraged under Communist rule, religion is now experiencing a revival. Russians are known for their many great contributions to the arts and sciences.

Economy and the Land. Before the fall of communism and subsequent breakup of the Soviet Union, the national government controlled the economy. Despite its strength as one of the world's industrial powers, the Soviet economy was plagued with low productivity, chronic shortages, and technological stagnation. The Soviet Union traded primarily with other Communist countries until the late 1980s, when economic reform led to greater trade with the West. Geographically, Russia is the largest nation in the world. Its terrain is widely varied and richly endowed with minerals. Though the country contains some of the world's most fertile land, long winters and hot, dry summers make agriculture difficult and risky.

History and Politics. Inhabited as early as the Stone Age, what is now Russia was much later invaded by the Scythians, Sarmatians, Goths, Huns, Bulgars, Slavs, and others. By A.D. 989 Byzantine cultural influence had become predominant. Various groups and regions were slowly incorporated into a single state. In 1547, Ivan the Terrible was crowned czar of all Russia, beginning a tradition of czarist rule and expansionism. The borders of all the Russian empire in the mid-1800s roughly approximated those of the former Soviet Union. Czarist rule continued until the 1917 Russian Revolution, when the Bolsheviks came to power and named Vladimir Lenin as head of the first Soviet government. The Bolsheviks established a new, experimental Communist state based on the works of economist Karl Marx. A bitter civil war ensued as all private property was seized by the government. Many areas that had been under the control of czarist Russia enjoyed a brief period of independence before Joseph Stalin succeeded Lenin as head of state, reclaimed the lost territories, and initiated a series of political purges that lasted through the 1930s. The Soviet Union became embroiled in World War II, siding with the Allies, losing over twenty million people, and suffering widespread destruction of its cities and countryside. It emerged from the war with extended influence, however, having annexed part of Finland and occupying many Eastern European nations. In the years following World War

II, the Soviet Union and the United States and their allies were engaged in a "cold war," which was characterized by escalating production of nuclear weapons and severe restrictions on travel and communications between the two sides. Mikhail Gorbachev took office in 1985 and introduced a new era of reform and government restructuring. The new political climate resulted in the end of the cold war and the ultimate breakup of the Soviet Union. Russia emerged as an independent state in late 1991. Russian president Boris Yeltsin rose to prominence as the leader of Russia and emphasized economic reform and closer ties with all Western nations. Political and economic instability continue to plague the new Russian state. ∎

RWANDA

Official name Republic of Rwanda

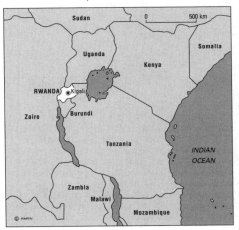

PEOPLE

Population 7,343,000. **Density** 722/mi² (279/km²). **Urban** 6%. **Capital** Kigali, 232,733. **Ethnic groups** Hutu 90%, Tutsi 9%, Twa (Pygmy) 1%. **Languages** French, Kinyarwanda, Kiswahili. **Religions** Roman Catholic 65%, Animist 25%, Protestant 9%. **Life expectancy** 48 female, 45 male. **Literacy** 50%.

POLITICS

Government Republic. **Parties** Democratic Republican, Liberal, Republican National Movement for Democracy and Development. **Suffrage** Universal adult. **Memberships** OAU, UN. **Subdivisions** 10 prefectures.

ECONOMY

GDP $6,800,000,000. **Per capita** $898. **Monetary unit** Franc. **Trade partners** Exports: Italy, Belgium, France. Imports: Belgium, Japan, Kenya. **Exports** Coffee, tea, tin, cassiterite, wolframite, pyrethrum. **Imports** Textiles, food, machinery, steel, petroleum, cement.

LAND

Description Eastern Africa, landlocked. **Area** 10,169 mi² (26,338 km²). **Highest point** Volcan

Karisimbi, 14,787 ft (4,507 m). **Lowest point** Along Ruzizi River, 3,117 ft (950 m).

People. Most Rwandans are Hutu, mainly farmers of Bantu stock. Minorities include the Tutsi, a pastoral people that dominated politically until a Hutu rebellion in 1959, and the Twa, Pygmies descended from the original population. Both French and Kinyarwanda are official languages, but most speak Kinyarwanda, a Bantu tongue. Roman Catholicism is the major religion, and minority groups practice indigenous beliefs as well as Protestantism and Islam. A high population density and a high birthrate characterize Rwanda.

Economy and the Land. Agriculture is the major activity, although plagued by the erosion and overpopulation of arable land. Many Rwandans practice subsistence farming, while coffee and tea are major export crops. The production and export of minerals, partly fueled by foreign investment, is also important. The country's landlocked position and underdeveloped transportation system hinder economic growth. The terrain consists mainly of grassy uplands and hills, with volcanic mountains in the west and northwest, while the climate is mild.

History and Politics. The Twa, the region's original inhabitants, were followed by the Hutu. The Tutsi most likely arrived about the fourteenth century, subjugating the weaker Hutu and becoming the region's dominant force. The areas of present-day Rwanda and Burundi became part of German East Africa in the 1890s. In 1919, following World War I, the region was mandated to Belgium as Ruanda-Urundi, and following World War II, Ruanda-Urundi was made a United Nations trust territory under Belgian administration. In 1959 a Hutu revolt against Tutsi domination resulted in the death of many Tutsi and the flight of many more. After gaining independence in 1962, the former territory split into the countries of Rwanda and Burundi. The military overthrew the nation's first president in 1973. Ethnic violence erupted after the death in April 1994 of President Habyarimana in a plane crash. The ruling Hutu tribe and the minority Tutsi engaged in horrific reprisals resulting in perhaps the greatest stream of refugees in Africa's history. ∎

ST. HELENA See UNITED KINGDOM.

ST. KITTS AND NEVIS

Official name Federation of St. Kitts and Nevis
PEOPLE
Population 42,000. **Density** 404/mi² (156/km²).
Urban 49%. **Capital** Basseterre, St. Christopher I., 14,725. **Ethnic groups** Black 94%, mixed 3%, white 1%. **Languages** English. **Religions** Anglican 33%, Methodist 29%, Moravian 9%, Roman Catholic 7%. **Life expectancy** 69 female, 63 male. **Literacy** 98%.
POLITICS
Government Parliamentary state. **Parties** Labor, People's Action Movement, Nevis Reformation.
Suffrage Universal, over 18. **Memberships** CW,

OAS, UN.
Subdivisions 14 parishes.
ECONOMY
GDP $163,000,000.
Per capita $3,881.
Monetary unit East Caribbean dollar.
Trade partners U.S., U.K., Trinidad and Tobago. **Exports** Sugar, clothing, electronics, postage stamps. **Imports** Food, manufactures, machinery, fuel.
LAND
Description Caribbean islands.
Area 104 mi² (269 km²). **Highest point** Mt. Liamuiga, 3,792 ft (1,156 m). **Lowest point** Sea level.

People. Most of the inhabitants of the islands of St. Kitts, often called St. Christopher, and Nevis are of black African descent. The primarily rural population is concentrated along the coast. English is spoken throughout the islands, and most people are Protestant, especially Anglican, evidence of former British rule.

Economy and the Land. Agriculture and tourism are the economic mainstays of St. Kitts and Nevis. Sugar cane is a major crop, cultivated mainly on St. Kitts Island, while Nevis Island produces cotton, fruits, and vegetables. Agriculture also provides for sugar processing, the major industrial activity. A tropical climate, beaches, and a scenic mountainous terrain provide an ideal setting for tourism.

History and Politics. The islands were first inhabited by Arawak Indians, who were displaced by the warlike Caribs. In 1493 Christopher Columbus sighted the islands, and in the 1600s British settlement of both islands began, along with French settlement on St. Christopher. Sugar plantations were soon established, and slaves were imported from Africa. Britain's control of the islands was recognized by the 1783 Treaty of Paris, and for a time St. Kitts, Nevis, and Anguilla were ruled as a single colony. Anguilla became a separate dependency of Britain in 1980, and St. Kitts and Nevis gained independence in 1983. ∎

ST. LUCIA

Official name St. Lucia
PEOPLE
Population 138,000. **Density** 580/mi² (224/km²).
Urban 44%. **Capital** Castries, 11,147. **Ethnic groups** Black 90%, mixed 6%, East Indian 3%.
Languages English, French. **Religions** Roman Catholic 90%, Protestant 7%, Anglican 3%. **Life expectancy** 72 female, 67 male. **Literacy** 67%.
POLITICS
Government Parliamentary state. **Parties** Labor, United Workers'. **Suffrage** Universal, over 18.

POLITICS
Government
Parliamentary state.
Parties Labor, United Workers'. **Suffrage** Universal, over 18.
Memberships CW, OAS, UN.
Subdivisions 11 quarters.
ECONOMY
GDP $433,000,000.
Per capita $2,830.
Monetary unit East Caribbean dollar.
Trade partners Exports: U.K., U.S., Dominica. Imports: U.S., U.K., Trinidad and Tobago. **Exports** Bananas, clothing, cocoa, vegetables, fruit, coconut oil. **Imports** Manufactures, machinery and transportation equipment, food, chemicals.
LAND
Description Caribbean island. **Area** 238 mi² (616 km²). **Highest point** Mt. Gimie, 3,117 ft (950 m). **Lowest point** Sea level.

People. St. Lucia's population is composed mainly of descendants of black African slaves, and minority groups include people of African-European descent, whites, and East Indians. During the colonial period, the island frequently shifted from British to French control, and its culture reflects both British and French elements. Although English is widely spoken, many St. Lucians speak a French dialect. Roman Catholicism is the main religion, and the Protestant minority includes Anglicans.

Economy and the Land. Agriculture remains important, and principal crops include bananas and cocoa. Tax incentives and relative political stability have caused an increase in industrial development and foreign investment, mainly from the United States. Tourism is becoming increasingly important, with visitors drawn by the tropical climate, scenic mountainous terrain, and beaches.

History and Politics. Arawak Indians arrived between the A.D. 200s and 400s and were conquered by the Caribs between the ninth and eleventh centuries. Dutch, French, and British rivalry for control began in the seventeenth century, but the Europeans were unable to subdue the Caribs. The first successful settlement was established by the French in 1651. After many years of alternating French and British control, St. Lucia came under British rule through the 1814 Treaty of Paris. The island gained full independence in 1979. ∎

ST. PIERRE AND MIQUELON See FRANCE.

ST. VINCENT AND THE GRENADINES

Official name St. Vincent and the Grenadines

PEOPLE
Population 110,000.
Density 733/mi² (284/km²). **Urban** 20%. **Capital** Kingstown, St. Vincent I., 15,466. **Ethnic groups** Black 82%, mixed 14%, East Indian 2%, white 1%. **Languages** English, French. **Religions** Anglican 42%, Methodist 21%, Roman Catholic 21%, Baptist 6%. **Life expectancy** 73 female, 70 male. **Literacy** 96%.
POLITICS
Government
Parliamentary state. **Parties** Labor, New Democratic. **Suffrage** Universal, over 18. **Memberships** CW, OAS, UN. **Subdivisions** 5 parishes.
ECONOMY
GDP $215,000,000. **Per capita** $1,870. **Monetary unit** East Caribbean dollar. **Trade partners** Exports: U.K., Trinidad and Tobago, U.S. Imports: U.S., U.K. **Exports** Bananas, eddoes and taro, arrowroot starch, tennis racquets, flour. **Imports** Food, machinery, chemicals, fuel.
LAND
Description Caribbean islands. **Area** 150 mi² (388 km²). **Highest point** Soufrière, 4,048 ft (1,234 m). **Lowest point** Sea level.

People. The people of St. Vincent are mainly descended from black African slaves. The colonial influences of Britain and France are evident in the languages and religions. English is the official language, though a French patois is also spoken. Most people are Anglican, Methodist, or Roman Catholic.

Economy and the Land. St. Vincent's economy is based on agriculture, especially banana production. Tourism also plays a role, both on the main island of St. Vincent and in the Grenadines. St. Vincent is the largest island, and about one hundred smaller islands make up the Grenadines. The terrain is mountainous, with coastlines marked by sandy beaches, and the climate is tropical.

History and Politics. The indigenous Arawak Indians were conquered by the Caribs about 1300. Christopher Columbus probably reached the area in 1498. Although the Caribs fought the Europeans, the British began settling St. Vincent in the 1760s. A period of French control began in 1779, and the islands were returned to the British in 1783. St. Vincent and the Grenadines remained under British rule until they gained independence in 1979. ∎

SAN MARINO

Official name Republic of San Marino
PEOPLE
Population 24,000. **Density** 1,000/mi² (393/km²).
Urban 92%. **Capital** San Marino, 2,794. **Ethnic groups** Sanmarinese (mixed Latin, Adriatic, and Teutonic), Italian. **Languages** Italian. **Religions** Roman Catholic. **Life expectancy** 85 female, 77 male. **Literacy** 96%.
POLITICS
Government Republic. **Parties** Christian Democratic, Progressive Democratic, Socialist, others. **Suffrage** Universal, over 18.
Memberships UN. **Subdivisions** 9 municipalities.
ECONOMY
GDP $370,000,000. **Per capita** $16.087.
Monetary unit Italian lira. **Trade partners** Italy.
Exports Building materials, lime, wood, chestnuts, wheat, wine. **Imports** Consumer goods.
LAND
Description Southern Europe, landlocked. **Area** 24 mi² (61 km²). **Highest point** Monte Titano, 2,425 ft (739 m). **Lowest point** Unnamed, 164 ft (50 m).

People. San Marino, completely surrounded by Italy, has strong ethnic ties to the Italians, combining Latin, Adriatic, and Teutonic roots. Italian is the main language, and Roman Catholicism the major religion. Despite San Marino's similarities to Italy, its tradition of independence has given its citizens a strong national identity.

Economy and the Land. Close economic ties between San Marino and Italy have produced a mutually beneficial customs union: Italians have no customs restrictions at San Marino's borders, and San Marino receives annual budget subsidiary payments from Italy. Most San Marinese are employed in agriculture; livestock raising is a main activity, and crops include wheat and grapes. Tourism and the sale of postage stamps are major economic contributors, as is industry, which produces construction materials for

export. Located in the Apennine Mountains, San Marino has a rugged terrain and a generally moderate climate.

History and Politics. San Marino is considered the world's oldest republic. Tradition has it that Marinus, a Christian stonecutter seeking religious freedom in a time of repressive Roman rule, founded the state in the fourth century A.D. Partly because of the protection afforded by its mountainous terrain, San Marino has been able to maintain continuous independence despite attempted invasions. In the 1300s the country became a republic, and the pope recognized its independent status in 1631. San Marino signed its first treaty of friendship with Italy in 1862. In its foreign relations, the country maintains a distinct identity and status. ∎

SAO TOME AND PRINCIPE

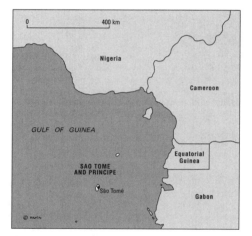

Official name Democratic Republic of Sao Tome and Principe
PEOPLE
Population 127,000. **Density** 341/mi² (132/km²).
Urban 42%. **Capital** São Tomé, São Tomé I., 5,245. **Ethnic groups** Black, mixed black and Portuguese, Portuguese. **Languages** Portuguese, Fang. **Religions** Roman Catholic, Evangelical Protestant, Seventh Day Adventist. **Life expectancy** 65 female, 61 male. **Literacy** 57%.
POLITICS
Government Republic. **Parties** Democratic Convergence-Reflection Group, Movement for the Liberation. **Suffrage** Universal, over 18.
Memberships OAU, UN. **Subdivisions** 7 districts.
ECONOMY
GDP $50,000,000. **Per capita** $407. **Monetary unit** Dobra. **Trade partners** Exports: Germany, Netherlands, China. Imports: Portugal, Germany, Angola, China. **Exports** Cocoa, copra, coffee, palm oil. **Imports** Machinery and electrical equipment.

LAND

Description Western African islands. **Area** 372 mi² (964 km²). **Highest point** Pico de São Tomé, 6,640 ft (2,024 m). **Lowest point** Sea level.

People. Descendants of African slaves and people of Portuguese-African heritage compose most of Sao Tome and Principe's population. Colonial rule by Portugal is evidenced by the predominance of the Portuguese language and Roman Catholicism. The majority of the population lives on São Tomé.

Economy and the Land. Cocoa dominates Sao Tome and Principe's economy. Copra and palm-oil production are also important, and fishing plays an economic role as well. Through the development of vegetable crops, the government hopes to diversify agricultural output, as much food must now be imported. Part of an extinct volcanic mountain range, Sao Tome and Principe have a mostly mountainous terrain. The climate is tropical.

History and Politics. When Portuguese explorers arrived in the 1400s, Sao Tome and Principe were uninhabited. Early settlers included Portuguese convicts and exiles. Cultivation of the land and importation of slaves led to a thriving sugar economy by the mid-1500s. In the 1800s, following slave revolts and the decline of sugar production, coffee and cocoa became the islands' mainstays, and soon large Portuguese plantations called *rocas* were established. Slavery was abolished by Portugal in 1876, but an international controversy arose in the early 1900s when it was found that Angolan contract workers were being treated as virtual slaves. Decades of unrest led to the 1953 Batepa Massacre, in which Portuguese rulers killed several hundred rioting African workers. A movement for independence began in the late 1950s, and following a 1974 change of government in Portugal, Sao Tome and Principe became independent in 1975. The country has established ties with other former Portuguese colonies in northern Africa since gaining independence. The first presidential elections were held in March 1990. ∎

SAUDI ARABIA

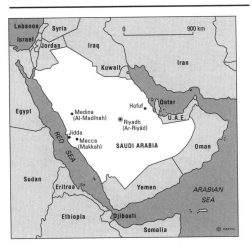

Official name Kingdom of Saudi Arabia
PEOPLE
Population 18,190,000. **Density** 22/mi² (8.5/km²). **Urban** 77%. **Capital** Riyadh, 1,250,000. **Ethnic groups** Arab 90%, Afro-Asian 10%. **Languages** Arabic. **Religions** Muslim 100%. **Life expectancy** 71 female, 68 male. **Literacy** 62%.
POLITICS
Government Monarchy. **Parties** None. **Suffrage** None. **Memberships** AL, OPEC, UN.
Subdivisions 14 emirates.
ECONOMY
GDP $194,000,000,000. **Per capita** $12,136.
Monetary unit Riyal. **Trade partners** Exports: Japan, U.S., Singapore. Imports: U.S., Japan, U.K. **Exports** Petroleum. **Imports** Manufactures, transportation equipment, construction materials, food.
LAND
Description Southwestern Asia. **Area** 830,000 mi² (2,149,690 km²). **Highest point** Mt. Sawda, 10,522 ft (3,207 m). **Lowest point** Sea level.

People. Saudi Arabia is inhabited primarily by Arab Muslims descended from Semitic peoples who settled in the region several thousand years ago. The petroleum industry has attracted a sizable minority of Arabs from other nations, Europeans, and non-Arab Muslims from Africa and Asia. The country's official language is Arabic, although English is used among educated Saudis in business and international affairs. Islam dominates Saudi life, and nearly all the people belong to the religion's Sunni branch. Various forms of Christianity and traditional religions are practiced among foreign workers and indigenous minority groups. Most live in urban areas, but some Bedouin tribes preserve their nomadic way of life.

Economy and the Land. The economy of Saudi Arabia has been shaped by its vast deserts and huge petroleum and natural gas reserves. The hot, mostly arid climate has prevented agricultural abundance and stability: the country must import nearly all its food. Oil was discovered in the 1930s, but the country did not begin rapid economic development until the reserves were aggressively exploited following World War II. Saudi Arabia is one of the world's leading exporters of petroleum, possessing the largest concentration of known oil reserves in the world. The government is seeking to diversify the economy, improve transportation and communication lines, and build agricultural output. Private enterprise and foreign investment are encouraged. Saudi Arabia is divided into the western highlands bordering the Red Sea, a central plateau, northern deserts, the huge Rub al Khali desert in the south, and the eastern lowlands. Only the coastal regions receive appreciable rainfall, and some inland desert areas may go without rain for several years.

History and Politics. Even though what is now Saudi Arabia established prosperous trade routes thousands of years ago, its history begins with the founding of Islam by Muhammad in the early 600s A.D. By the end of that century, Mecca and Medina were established as political and religious centers of Islam and remain so today. The territory split into numerous states that warred among themselves for over a thousand years. The Ottoman Turks gained control over the coastal region of Hejaz in the early 1500s, while Britain set up protectorates along the southern and eastern coasts of Arabia during the 1800s. The Saud family dynasty, founded in the 1400s, managed to remain a dominant religious and political force. Members of the dynasty fought to establish the supremacy of Islamic law and unite the various clans into one nation. In 1932 Ibn Saud proclaimed the Kingdom of Saudi Arabia and established a Saud monarchy that has continued despite dissension within the royal family. Since the 1960s Saudi Arabia has aggressively sought to upgrade local governments, industry, education, the status of women, and the standard of living, while maintaining Islamic values and traditions. Saudi Arabia is a dominant member of the Organization of Petroleum Exporting Countries (OPEC). Despite disagreements with the West and continuing conflicts with Israel, the country maintains strong diplomatic and economic ties with Western nations. During the Gulf War, Saudi Arabia received help from a coalition of nations to protect its borders from Iraqi invasion. The ruling family continues to resist both democratic and extreme fundamentalist influences. ∎

SENEGAL

Official name Republic of Senegal

PEOPLE
Population 8,862,000. **Density** 117/mi² (45/km²). **Urban** 40%. **Capital** Dakar, 1,490,450. **Ethnic groups** Wolof 44%, Fulani 23%, Serer 15%, Diola 6%, Malinke 5%. **Languages** French, Wolof, Fulani, Serer, indigenous. **Religions** Muslim 94%, Christian 5%. **Life expectancy** 50 female, 48 male. **Literacy** 38%.
POLITICS
Government Republic. **Parties** Democratic, Socialist, others. **Suffrage** Universal, over 18. **Memberships** OAU, UN. **Subdivisions** 10 regions.
ECONOMY

GDP $11,800,000,000. **Per capita** $1,503. **Monetary unit** CFA franc. **Trade partners** Exports: France, India, Mali, Italy. Imports: France, Nigeria, Italy. **Exports** Manufactures, fish, peanuts, petroleum products, phosphates. **Imports** Manufactures, food, petroleum, machinery.
LAND
Description Western Africa. **Area** 75,951 mi² (196,712 km²). **Highest point** Unnamed, 1,906 ft (581 m). **Lowest point** Sea level.

People. Most Senegalese are black Africans from many ethnic groups, each with its own customs and language. The country has many immigrants from other African nations. While French is the official language, Wolof is widely spoken. Islam is the religion of the vast majority. Senegal is mainly a rural nation of subsistence farmers.

Economy and the Land. The mainstays of the economy are petroleum, agriculture, fishing, and mining. Tourism is a rapidly growing new industry. Manufactured goods, fish, peanuts, and petroleum products rank as Senegal's primary exports. Agricultural output is often hurt by irregular weather patterns, and the country must import nearly all its energy. Senegal has one of the finest transportation systems in Africa. Small plateaus, low massifs, marshy swamps, and a sandy coast highlight the terrain, which is mainly flat. The climate is marked by dry and rainy seasons, with differing precipitation patterns in the south and the more arid north.

History and Politics. The area that is now Senegal has been inhabited by black Africans since prehistoric times. When Europeans first established trade ties with the Senegalese in the mid-1400s, the country had been divided into several independent kingdoms. By the early 1800s France had gained control of the region and in 1895 made Senegal part of French West Africa. In 1959 Senegal joined with French Sudan, or present-day Mali, to form the Federation of Mali, which became independent in 1960. However, Senegal withdrew from the federation later in the year to found the independent Republic of Senegal. The new government was plagued by coup attempts and an economy crippled by the severe droughts of the late 1960s and early 1970s. A socialist government has ruled the country since 1960. ∎

SEYCHELLES

Official name Republic of Seychelles
PEOPLE
Population 75,000. **Density** 429/mi² (166/km²). **Urban** 59%. **Capital** Victoria, Mahé I., 23,000. **Ethnic groups** Seychellois (mixed Asian, African, and European). **Languages** English, French, Creole. **Religions** Roman Catholic 90%, Anglican 8%. **Life expectancy** 73 female, 66 male. **Literacy** 85%.
POLITICS
Government Republic. **Parties** People's Progressive Front, Democratic. **Suffrage** Universal, over 17. **Memberships** CW, OAU, UN.

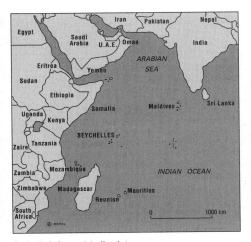

SIERRA LEONE

Subdivisions 21 districts.
ECONOMY
GDP $407,000,000. **Per capita** $5,899. **Monetary unit** Rupee. **Trade partners** Exports: France, Kuwait, Reunion. Imports: South Africa, U.K., Kuwait. **Exports** Fish, copra, cinnamon bark. **Imports** Manufactures, food, tobacco, beverages, machinery and transportation equipment.
LAND
Description Indian Ocean islands. **Area** 175 mi^2 (453 km^2). **Highest point** Mt. Seychellois, 2,969 ft (905 m). **Lowest point** Sea level.

People. The majority of Seychellois are of mixed African, European, and Asian ancestry. The islands' culture combines French and African elements, and although the official languages of French and English are widely spoken, most also speak a creole dialect of French. Many of the more than one hundred islands are coral atolls, unable to support human life. The population is concentrated on Mahé, the largest island, while the remainder live mainly on Praslin and La Digue islands.

Economy and the Land. The basis of the economy is tourism, with foreign visitors attracted by the tropical climate, white-sand beaches, and exotic flora and wildlife found on the granite islands. Mountainous granite islands, which contain fertile soils for growing cinnamon and coconuts, and flat coral islands comprise Seychelles.

History and Politics. The Portuguese reached the uninhabited islands in the early 1500s. For more than two hundred years, the islands served as little more than pirates' havens. France claimed them in 1756. By the 1770s white planters and African slaves had begun to settle Mahé. After a French-English war, France ceded the islands to Britain in 1814. Seychelles achieved independence in 1976. Opposition parties were legalized in 1991 and a new constitution was approved in 1993. ∎

SHETLAND ISLANDS
See UNITED KINGDOM.

Official name Republic of Sierra Leone
PEOPLE
Population 4,690,000. **Density** 168/mi^2 (65/km^2). **Urban** 32%. **Capital** Freetown, 469,776. **Ethnic groups** Temne 30%, Mende 30%, other African. **Languages** English, Krio, Mende, Temne, indigenous. **Religions** Muslim 30%, Animist 30%, Christian 10%. **Life expectancy** 45 female, 41 male. **Literacy** 21%.
POLITICS
Government Transitional military government. Parties. **Suffrage** Universal, over 18.
Memberships CW, OAU, UN. **Subdivisions** 3 provinces, 1 area.
ECONOMY
GDP $4,500,000,000. **Per capita** $1,017. **Monetary unit** Leone. **Trade partners** Exports: U.S., U.K., Netherlands. Imports: U.K., U.S., Germany. **Exports** Rutile, bauxite, cocoa, diamonds, coffee. **Imports** Machinery, food, petroleum, manufactures.
LAND
Description Western Africa. **Area** 27,925 mi^2 (72,325 km^2). **Highest point** Bintimani, 6,381 ft (1,945 m). **Lowest point** Sea level.

People. The population of Sierra Leone is divided into nearly twenty main ethnic groups. The two major groups are the Temne in the north and west and the Mende in the south. Descendants of freed American slaves, who settled in Freetown on the coast, make up a sizable Creole minority. English is the official language, but most of the people speak local African tongues. The Creoles speak Krio, a dialect of English. Most people practice Islam or various local religions, and a small number are Christian.

Economy and the Land. Sierra Leone is one of the world's largest producers of industrial and commercial diamonds. The nation also mines bauxite and rutile. Poor soil, a fluctuating tropical climate, and traditional farming methods keep crop yields low. Sierra Leone is one of Africa's poorest countries. Rice, coffee, and cocoa are important crops. To improve agricultural production, the government is clearing some of the coastal mangrove swamplands. The interior of Sierra Leone is marked by a broad coastal plain in the north and by mountains and plateaus that rise along the country's northern and eastern borders. During the wet season Sierra Leone receives heavy rainfall in the Freetown area and significantly less in the north.

History and Politics. When the Portuguese reached the region in 1460, they found the area inhabited by the Temne. The British followed the Portuguese in the 1500s. Europeans took slaves from the area for the New World until Britain abolished the slave trade. In 1787 Englishman Granville Sharp settled nearly four hundred freed black American slaves in what is now Freetown. Britain declared the peninsula a colony in 1808 and a protectorate in 1896. In 1961 Sierra Leone became an independent nation with a constitution and parliamentary form of government. A military takeover in 1967 was short-lived, and the constitution was rewritten in 1971 to make the country a republic. After years of corrupt one-party rule, the leaders of a military coup in 1992 promised to end corruption and organize democratic elections. Fighting against a strong rebel movement has killed 50,000 people since 1991 and been very destructive to the economy. ■

SINGAPORE

Official name Republic of Singapore
PEOPLE
Population 2,921,000. **Density** 11,874/mi²
(4,593/km²). **Urban** 100%. **Capital** Singapore,
2,921,000. **Ethnic groups** Chinese 76%, Malay 15%, Indian 6%. **Languages** Chinese (Mandarin), English, Malay, Tamil. **Religions** Taoist 29%, Buddhist 27%, Muslim 16%, Christian 10%, Hindu 4%. **Life expectancy** 77 female, 72 male.
Literacy 88%.
POLITICS
Government Republic. **Parties** Democratic, People's Action, Workers', others. **Suffrage** Universal, over 20. **Memberships** ASEAN, CW,

UN. **Subdivisions** None.
ECONOMY
GDP $42,400,000,000. **Per capita** $15,078.
Monetary unit Dollar. **Trade partners** Exports: U.S., Malaysia, Japan. Imports: Japan, U.S., Malaysia. **Exports** Petroleum, rubber, electronics, manufactures. **Imports** Machinery, petroleum, chemicals, manufactures, food.
LAND
Description Southeastern Asian island. **Area** 246 mi² (636 km²). **Highest point** Timah Hill, 545 ft (166 m). **Lowest point** Sea level.

People. Singapore is one of the most densely populated nations in the world. Most of the population is Chinese. A significant minority is Malay, and the remainder is European or Indian. Singapore's languages include Chinese, English, Malay, and Tamil. The main religions—Taoism, Buddhism, Islam, Christianity, and Hinduism—reflect the cultural diversity of the nation. A mixture of Western and traditional customs and dress characterize Singapore's society. Nearly all the population lives in the city of Singapore on Singapore Island.

Economy and the Land. Singapore is a leading Asian economic power. The city of Singapore is well known as a financial center and major harbor for trade. The nation's factories produce a variety of goods, such as chemicals, electronic equipment, and machinery, and are among the world leaders in petroleum refining. Singapore has few natural resources, however, and little arable land. Most agricultural output is consumed domestically; the country must import much of its raw materials and food. The nation consists of one main island, which is characterized by wet lowlands, and many small offshore islets. Cool sea breezes and a tropical climate make Singapore an attractive spot for tourists.

History and Politics. Present-day Singapore has been inhabited since prehistoric times. From the 1100s to the 1800s, Singapore served mainly as a trading center and refuge for pirates. The British East India Company, the major colonial force in India, realized Singapore's strategic importance to British trade and gained possession of the harbor in 1819. Singapore became a crown colony in 1826. As the port prospered, the island's population grew rapidly. Following World War II, the people of Singapore moved from internal self-government to independence in 1965. The government continues to work in partnership with the business community to further Singapore's growth. Singapore's standard of living is one of the highest in eastern Asia. The country's first presidential elections were held in August 1993. ■

SLOVAKIA

Official name Slovak Republic
PEOPLE
Population 5,353,000. **Density** 283mi² (109/km²).
Capital Bratislava, 441,453. **Ethnic groups** Slovak 86%, Hungarian 11%, Gypsy 2%.
Languages Slovak, Hungarian. **Religions** Roman Catholic 60%, Protestant 8%, Orthodox 4%. **Life expectancy** 77 female, 68 male.

POLITICS
Government Republic. **Parties** Christian
Democratic Movement, Democratic Left,
Movement for Democracy, Nationalist. **Suffrage**
Universal, over 18. **Memberships** NATO, UN.
Subdivisions 4 regions.
ECONOMY
GDP $31,000,000,000. **Per capita** $5,863.
Monetary unit Koruna. **Trade partners** Czech
Republic, former Soviet republics, Germany,
Poland. **Exports** Machinery and transportation
equipment; chemicals; fuels, minerals, and metals.
Imports Machinery and transportation equipment,
fuels and lubricants, manufactures.
LAND
Description Eastern Europe, landlocked. **Area**
18,933 mi² (49,035 km²). **Highest point**
Gerlachovka, 8,711 ft (2,655 m). **Lowest point**
Along Bodrog River, 308 ft (94 m).

People. The people of Slovakia are related to the
Czechs, but they are culturally linked to the Hungarians
rather than the Germans. The Slovak language is similar to Czech and has the same roots. Slovakia has
a large Hungarian minority, and Hungarians complain
that the Slovaks are trying to eliminate their language
and culture. Roman Catholicism is the main religion. The Slovaks are proud of the literary heritage
and their artistic achievements.

Economy and the Land. Slovakia suffers from both
high inflation and unemployment as it struggles to create a new economy in the aftermath of eastern
European communism. Although some industrialization
took place under communist rule, agriculture remains
an important economic activity. Most agriculture
takes place in the fertile Hungarian Plain in the
south. The nation has important mineral deposits, but
lacks any significant energy resources. Slovakia is
bounded on the north and east by the Carpathian
Mountains.

History and Politics. Slavic people settled Slovakia
in the fifth century, and were incorporated into the
Moravian state that was established in the ninth century. Slovakia fell under Hungarian rule in the early
tenth century, and little economic or social development
took place for three hundred years, until Hungary's
grasp on the region began to weaken and the
Slovaks began to make contact with the outside world.
Slovakia remained under Hungarian rule despite a
growing nationalist movement that gained momentum throughout the nineteenth century. After Austria-
Hungary was defeated in World War I, the Slovaks
and the Czechs were united to form the independent
nation of Czechoslovakia in 1918. The Slovaks,
who had envisioned a federal state, were angered
by the centrist government that was established
and extremists began demanding separation less than
ten years after the nation was formed. The Slovak
separatist movement remained active until it was obliterated by the communists who took over
Czechoslovakia after World War II. In 1968
Czechoslovakia adopted a liberal reform plan that
called for greater autonomy for Slovakia, but the invasion of the Warsaw Pact countries prevented the plan
from being implemented. Communist rule ended in
1989, and Slovakia gained full independence in
1993. Slovakia is moving very slowly towards democracy although the present government has privatized
as little as politically possible. ∎

SLOVENIA

Official name Republic of Slovenia
PEOPLE
Population 1,993,000. **Density** 255/mi² (98/km²).
Urban 49%. **Capital** Ljubljana, 233,200. **Ethnic
groups** Slovene 91%, Croat 3%, Serb 2%, Muslim
1%. **Languages** Slovenian, Serbo-Croatian.
Religions Roman Catholic 96%, Muslim 1%. **Life
expectancy** 78 female, 70 male. **Literacy** 99%.
POLITICS
Government Republic. **Parties** Christian
Democratic, Greens, Liberal Democratic, National
Democratic, Social Democratic, Socialist. **Suffrage**
Universal over 18; over 16 if employed.
Memberships NATO, UN. **Subdivisions** None.
provinces.
ECONOMY
GDP $15,000,000,000. **Per capita** $7,634.

Monetary unit Tolar. **Trade partners** Exports: Former Yugoslavian republics, Austria, Italy. Imports: Former Yugoslavian republics, Germany. **Exports** Machinery and transportation equipment, manufactures, chemicals, food. **Imports** Machinery and transportation equipment, manufactures, chemicals.
LAND
Description Eastern Europe. **Area** 7,820 mi^2 (20,253 km^2). **Highest point** Triglav, 9,396 ft (2,864 m). **Lowest point** Sea level.

People. The Slovenes managed to keep their own language and traditions only by resisting centuries of unrelenting pressure to adopt German culture. Most people are Roman Catholic, and their religion is an important part of their national identity. Slovenia is also home to small Croatian and Serbian minorities.

Economy and the Land. Slovenia has had a well-developed industrial sector since the mid-1800s. Most people are engaged in industry. Before it achieved independence in 1991, prosperity in Slovenia was greater than in the other Yugoslavian republics. Slovenia's economy is very well-rounded, and despite the mountainous terrain, agriculture is also an important activity. Major crops are potatoes, hops, hemp, and flax. Dairy farming is also an important agricultural activity. Coal and timber are produced in abundance.

History and Politics. Until the 1990s, Slovenia had never been an independent nation in modern times. Ancestors of the modern Slovenes are believed to have arrived in the region around A.D. 600. By the eighth century, they had been conquered by the Franks and were converted to Roman Catholicism by the emperor Charlemagne. The Slovenes were serfs under German feudal lords until the region came under the control of the Austro-Hungarian Hapsburg empire in the late 1200s. The Hapsburgs maintained control for seven hundred years, although the area was subjected to occasional Turkish raids. The German-speaking Hapsburg empire attempted to impose its language on the Slovenian people, who resisted and continued to speak their own Slavic language. Slovenia became part of Yugoslavia in 1918. During World War II, Slovenia was divided among Germany, Italy, and Hungary. Once again, the Germans attempted to eliminate Slovenian culture by killing the Slovenes in concentration camps or forcing them to migrate to other parts of Yugoslavia. Slovenia gained considerable autonomy after Yugoslavia was reconstituted as a federal Communist republic following the war. Under Communist rule, many Slovenians resented their obligation to support Serbia and the other poorer Yugoslavian republics. Without massive demonstrations or public unrest, the nation slowly moved towards a more peaceful separation from the rest of Yugoslavia. In June 1991, Slovenia, along with neighboring Croatia, declared its independence from Yugoslavia. Shortly after the announcement, the Yugoslavian army made a brief attempt to thwart the will of the people before ordering its troops out of Slovenia. Slovenia received international recognition in January 1992. A lack of public-sector reform has slowed economic development. ∎

SOLOMON ISLANDS

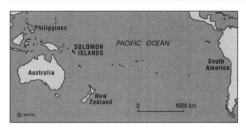

Official name Solomon Islands
PEOPLE
Population 393,000. **Density** 36/mi^2 (14/km^2). **Urban** 15%. **Capital** Honiara, Guadalcanal I., 30,413. **Ethnic groups** Melanesian 93%, Polynesian 4%, Micronesian 2%. **Languages** English, indigenous. **Religions** Anglican 34%, Roman Catholic 19%, Baptist 17%, United Church 11%. **Life expectancy** 73 female, 68 male.
POLITICS
Government Parliamentary state. **Parties** National Action, National Unity and Reconciliation, People's Alliance. **Suffrage** Universal, over 21. **Memberships** CW, UN. **Subdivisions** 7 provinces, 1 town.
ECONOMY
GDP $900,000,000. **Per capita** $2,795. **Monetary unit** Dollar. **Trade partners** Exports: Japan, U.K., Thailand. Imports: Australia, Japan. **Exports** Fish, wood, copra, palm oil. **Imports** Machinery, fuel, food.
LAND
Description South Pacific islands. **Area** 10,954 mi^2 (28,370 km^2). **Highest point** Mt. Makarakomburu, 8,028 ft (2,447 m). **Lowest point** Sea level.

People. Over 90 percent of the people are Melanesian, and the remainder are Polynesian, European, Chinese, and Micronesian. English is the official language, but some ninety local languages are also spoken. Most people are Anglican, Roman Catholic, Baptist, or other Protestants. The population is primarily rural, and much of its social structure is patterned on traditional village life.

Economy and the Land. The economy is based on subsistence farming and exports of fish, wood, copra, and some spices and palm-oil. Tourism, while small, is of growing importance. Food, machinery, gasoline, and manufactured goods must be imported. Terrain ranges from forested mountains to low-lying coral atolls. The climate is warm and moist, with heavy annual rainfall.

History and Politics. Hunter-gatherers lived on the islands as early as 1000 B.C. Because of disease and native resistance, early attempts at colonization failed, and Europeans did not firmly establish themselves until the mid-1800s. Britain declared the islands a protectorate in 1893. The area was the site of fierce battles between the Japanese and Allied forces during World War II, and following the war, moves were made toward independence. In 1978 the Solomon Islands adopted a constitution and became a sovereign nation. ∎

SOMALIA

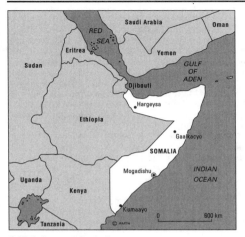

Official name Somalia
PEOPLE
Population 7,187,000. **Density** 29/mi² (11/km²).
Urban 24%. **Capital** Mogadishu, 600,000. **Ethnic groups** Somali 85%, Bantu. **Languages** Arabic, Somali, English, Italian. **Religions** Sunni Muslim. **Life expectancy** 49 female, 45 male. **Literacy** 24%.
POLITICS
Government None. **Parties** United Somali Congress. **Suffrage** Universal, over 18.
Memberships AL, OAU, UN. **Subdivisions** 18 regions.
ECONOMY
GDP $3,400,000,000. **Per capita** $567. **Monetary unit** Shilling. **Trade partners** Exports: Saudi Arabia, United Arab Emirates. Imports: Italy, Bahrain, U.K. **Exports** Bananas, livestock, fish, hides and skins. **Imports** Petroleum, food, construction materials.
LAND
Description Eastern Africa. **Area** 246,201 mi² (637,657 km²). **Highest point** Shimbiris, 7,897 ft (2,407 m). **Lowest point** Sea level.

People. Unlike the population in many African nations, the people of Somalia are remarkably homogeneous in their language, culture, and identity. Most are nomadic or seminomadic herders; only a quarter of the people have settled in permanent communities in southern Somalia. While Arabic and Somali are official languages, English and Italian are also spoken. Nearly all the Somali people are Sunni Muslims.

Economy and the Land. Somalia is a developing country that has not exploited its rich deposits of iron ore and gypsum. There is little manufacturing. The economy is agricultural, though activity is restricted to the vicinity of the rivers and certain coastal districts. A hot climate with recurring droughts, as well as a lack of railroads and paved highways, hamper economic development. The terrain ranges from central and southern flatlands to northern hills.

History and Politics. In the A.D. 800s or 900s, Arabs converted the ancestors of the Somalis who settled the region to Islam. They fought many religious wars with the Christian kingdom of Ethiopia between the 1300s and 1500s. The British, Italians, and French arrived in the region in the latter half of the 1800s and divided the Somali territory among themselves, with Ethiopia seizing Ogaden in the west. After World War II, Italy was made administrator of its former colony to prepare it for independence. In 1960 British Somaliland and Italian Somalia joined to form an independent republic. Since that time, Somalia has had many border clashes with Kenya and Ethiopia over the rights of Somalis living in these countries to determine their own destiny. Military leaders staged a successful coup in 1969, and subsequently changed the nation's name to Somali Democratic Republic and abolished all political parties. Military activity has since resulted in a civil war, famine, and the killing of thousands of civilians. Rebel forces overcame the government in January 1991, and Northern Somalia seceded in May 1991. Clan-based fighting led to mass starvation and the deaths of hundreds of thousands of people. In late 1992 the U.S. military intervened in an attempt to reduce chaos and enable world-wide relief efforts to proceed safely. The United Nations took over the operation in 1993, withdrawing in 1995. ∎

SOUTH AFRICA

Official name Republic of South Africa
PEOPLE
Population 44,500,000. **Density** 94/mi² (36/km²).
Urban 49%. **Capital** Pretoria (administrative), 525,583; Cape Town (legislative), 854,616; Bloemfontein (judicial), 126,867. **Ethnic groups** Black 70%, white 14%, mulatto (coloured) 9%, Indian 3%. **Languages** Afrikaans, English, Sotho, Tswana, Zulu, others. **Religions** Black Independent 19%, Dutch Reformed 14%, Roman Catholic 10%. **Life expectancy** 66 female, 60 male. **Literacy** 76%.

POLITICS

Government Republic. **Parties** African National Congress, Conservative, Democratic, National, others. **Suffrage** Universal, over 18. **Memberships** CW, OAU, UN. **Subdivisions** 9 provinces.

ECONOMY

GDP $171,000,000,000. **Per capita** $5,176. **Monetary unit** Rand. **Trade partners** Exports: Italy, Japan, U.S. Imports: Germany, Japan, U.K. **Exports** Gold, minerals and metals, food, chemicals. **Imports** Machinery, transportation equipment, chemicals, oil, textiles.

LAND

Description Southern Africa. **Area** 471,010 mi^2 (1,219,909 km^2). **Highest point** eNjesuthi, 11,306 ft (3,446 m). **Lowest point** Sea level.

People. South Africa's population consists of four groups: black, white, colored, and Asian. Black African groups make up the majority population. The minority whites are either Afrikaners—of Dutch, German, and French descent—or British. Coloreds, people of mixed white, black, and Asian heritage, and Asians, primarily from India, make up the remaining population. Afrikaans and English are the official languages, although the blacks, coloreds, and Asians speak their own languages as well. The dominant religions are Christian; however, many groups follow traditional practices. For decades the South African government enforced apartheid, a policy of racial segregation widely criticized for violating the rights of blacks, coloreds, and Asians.

Economy and the Land. The discovery of gold and diamonds in South Africa in the late 1800s shaped the nation's prosperous economy. Revenues from mining promoted industry, and today South Africa is one of the richest and most highly developed countries in Africa. Mining remains a mainstay, as does agriculture; the nation is almost self-sufficient in food production. Many effects of apartheid, including discriminatory systems of education and job reservation, kept the majority population from the benefits of national prosperity. The varied landscape features coastal beaches, plateaus, mountains, and deep valleys. The climate is temperate.

History and Politics. Southern Africa has been inhabited for many thousands of years. Ancestors of the area's present African population had settled there by the time Portuguese explorers reached the Cape of Good Hope in the late 1400s. The first white settlers, ancestors of today's Afrikaners, established colonies in the seventeenth century. Britain gained control of the area in the late eighteenth century, and relations between Afrikaners and the British soon became strained. To escape British rule, many Afrikaners migrated northward to lands occupied by black Africans. The discovery of gold and diamonds in the late 1800s brought an influx of Europeans and further strained relations between Afrikaners and the British, with both groups striving for control of valuable mineral deposits. Two wars broke out, and in 1902 the British defeated the Afrikaners, or Boers, and incorporated the Boer territories into the British Empire. The British also subdued black Africans, and in 1910 they formed the white-controlled Union of South Africa. Afrikaner nationalism grew in the early twentieth century and led to the formation of the National party, which gained control in 1924 and again in 1948. The party began the apartheid system of separation of the races in the late forties, and subsequent decades saw increasing apartheid legislation and racial tension. In 1951 South Africa embarked on a program to create a white majority by setting up "independent" black republics, or homelands, within its borders. During the 1980s, the government began to force blacks to move into the homelands and to renounce their citizenship, thereby sparking international outcry. Foreign and internal pressure forced the government to respond with reforms and to dismantle apartheid. The 1990 release of Nelson Mandela, leader of the African National Congress (ANC), after 27 years in prison paved the way for a new South Africa. Under the leadership of Mandela and President de Klerk, the country was led to relatively peaceful elections in April 1994. Mandela was elected president and an interim constitution abolishing the homelands was established. ∎

SOUTH GEORGIA
See UNITED KINGDOM.

SPAIN

Official name Kingdom of Spain
PEOPLE
Population 39,260,000. **Density** 201/mi^2 (78/km^2). **Urban** 78%. **Capital** Madrid, 3,102,846. **Ethnic groups** Spanish (mixed Mediterranean and Teutonic). **Languages** Spanish (Castilian), Catalan, Galician, Basque. **Religions** Roman Catholic 99%. **Life expectancy** 80 female, 75 male. **Literacy** 95%.
POLITICS
Government Constitutional monarchy. **Parties** Convergence and Unity, Popular, Social Democratic Center, Socialist Workers, United Left,

Places and Possessions of SPAIN

Entity	Status	Area	Population	Capital/Population
Balearic Islands (Mediterranean Sea)	Province	1,936 mi^2 (5,014 km^2)	714,000	Palma, 249,000
Canary Islands (North Atlantic; northwest of Africa)	Part of Spain (2 provinces)	2,808 mi^2 (7,273 km^2)	1,505,000	None
Spanish North Africa (Cities on northern coast of Morocco)	Five possessions	12 mi^2 (32 km^2)	146,000	None

reclaimed the country from the eleventh to the fourteenth centuries. Controlled by the three kingdoms of Navarre, Aragon, and Castile, Spain was united in the late 1400s under King Ferdinand and Queen Isabella. At the height of its empire, Spain claimed territory in North and South America, northern Africa, Italy, and the Canary Islands. However, a series of wars burdened Spain financially, and in the 1500s, under King Philip II, the country entered a period of decline. Throughout the 1700s and 1800s, the nation lost most of its colonial possessions through treaty or revolution. In 1936 a bitter civil war erupted between an insurgent fascist group and supporters of the republic. General Francisco Franco, leader of the successful insurgent army, ruled as dictator of Spain from the end of the war until his death in 1975. Spain has prospered but has had to grapple with separatist movements in Catalonia and the Basque region. Since Franco's death, King Juan Carlos has led the country toward a more democratic form of government. ∎

others. **Suffrage** Universal, over 18.
Memberships EU, NATO, OECD, UN.
Subdivisions 17 autonomous communities.
ECONOMY
GDP $498,000,000,000. **Per capita** $12,719.
Monetary unit Peseta. **Trade partners** Exports: U.S., Japan, U.K. Imports: Germany, U.S., U.K.
Exports Transportation equipment, manufactures, food, machinery. **Imports** Machinery, transportation equipment, fuel, manufactures, food.
LAND
Description Southwestern Europe. **Area** 194,885 mi^2 (504,750 km^2). **Highest point** Pico de Teide, 12,188 ft (3,715 m). **Lowest point** Sea level.

People. The population of Spain is a mixture of ethnic groups from northern Europe and the area surrounding the Mediterranean Sea. Spanish is the official language; however, several regional dialects of Spanish are commonly spoken. The Basque minority, one of the oldest surviving ethnic groups in Europe, lives mainly in the Pyrenees in northern Spain, preserving its own language and traditions. Since the 1978 constitution, Spain has not had an official religion, yet nearly all its people are Roman Catholic. Spain has a rich artistic tradition, blending Moorish and Western cultures.

Economy and the Land. Spain has benefited greatly from an economic-restructuring program that began in the 1950s. The nation has concentrated on developing industry, which now employs over 30 percent of the population. The chemical industry, high technology, electronics, and tourism are important sources of revenue. The agricultural contribution to the economy has declined to about half of peak production. Spain's terrain is mainly composed of a dry plateau area; mountains cover the northern section, and plains extend down the country's eastern coast. The climate in the eastern and southern regions is Mediterranean, while the northwest has more rainfall and less sunshine throughout the year.

History and Politics. Spain is among the oldest inhabited regions in Europe. A Roman province for centuries, Spain was conquered by the Visigoths in the A.D. 500s, only to change hands again in the 700s when the Arab-Berbers, or Moors, seized control of all but a narrow strip of northern Spain. Christian kings

SRI LANKA

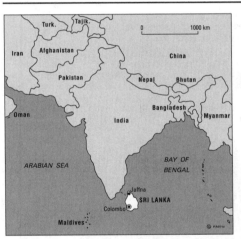

Official name Democratic Socialist Republic of Sri Lanka
PEOPLE
Population 18,240,000. **Density** 731/mi^2 (282/km^2). **Urban** 21%. **Capital** Colombo (designated), 612,000; Sri Jayawardenapura (seat of government), 108,000. **Ethnic groups** Sinhalese 74%, Ceylon Tamil 10%, Moor 7%, Indian Tamil 6%. **Languages** English, Sinhala, Tamil.
Religions Buddhist 69%, Hindu 15%, Muslim 8%, Christian 8%. **Life expectancy** 74 female, 70 male. **Literacy** 88%.
POLITICS
Government Socialist republic. **Parties** Freedom, Tamil Independents, United National, others.
Suffrage Universal, over 18. **Memberships** CW, UN. **Subdivisions** 8 provinces.
ECONOMY
GDP $53,500,000,000. **Per capita** $3,016.
Monetary unit Rupee. **Trade partners** Exports: U.S., Germany, U.K. Imports: Japan, Iran, U.S.

Exports Textiles and clothing, teas, petroleum, coconut, rubber. **Imports** Food, textiles, petroleum, machinery.

LAND

Description Southern Asian island. **Area** 24,962 mi^2 (64,652 km^2). **Highest point** Pidurutalagala, 8,281 ft (2,524 m). **Lowest point** Sea level.

People. The two principal groups in Sri Lanka are the majority Sinhalese and the minority Tamils. Other minorities include the Moors; Burghers, who are descendants of Dutch, Portuguese, and British colonists; Malays; and Veddah aborigines. Sinhala, Tamil, and English are official languages. Most Sinhalese are Buddhist, most Tamils are Hindu, and the majority of the Moors and Malays are Muslims.

Economy and the Land. Sri Lanka's economy is based on agriculture, which employs nearly half the people in producing tea, rubber, and coconuts. Sri Lanka also hopes to become self-sufficient in rice, thus reducing imports of this staple. Industrial production has increased, and major exports include rubber and textile products. The country also sponsors several internal-development programs. However, continuing high government subsidy and welfare policies threaten economic growth. A low coastal plain, mountainous and forested southern interior, and tropical climate characterize Sri Lanka.

History and Politics. The Sinhalese dynasty was founded by a northern Indian prince in about 500 B.C. Later, the Tamils from southern India settled in the north of Sri Lanka. European control began in the 1500s, when the Portuguese and Dutch ruled the island. It became a British possession in 1796 and the independent nation of Ceylon in 1948. In 1972 it changed its name to Sri Lanka. Tensions between the ruling Sinhalese and the minority Tamils resulted in violence. A ceasefire was signed in 1995. ∎

SUDAN

Official name Republic of the Sudan

PEOPLE

Population 25,840,000. **Density** 27/mi^2 (10/km^2). **Urban** 23%. **Capital** Khartoum, 473,597. **Ethnic groups** Black 52%, Arab 39%, Beja 6%. **Languages** Arabic, Nubian and other indigenous, English. **Religions** Sunni Muslim 70%, indigenous 25%, Christian 5%. **Life expectancy** 53 female, 51 male. **Literacy** 27%.

POLITICS

Government Provisional military government. **Parties** None. **Suffrage** None. **Memberships** AL, OAU, UN. **Subdivisions** 9 states.

ECONOMY

GDP $21,500,000,000. **Per capita** $748. **Monetary unit** Dinar. **Trade partners** Exports: Saudi Arabia, Thailand, Egypt. Imports: Saudi Arabia, U.K., Germany. **Exports** Cotton, sesame, gum arabic, peanuts. **Imports** Food, petroleum, manufactures, machinery, medicine and chemicals, textiles.

LAND

Description Eastern Africa. **Area** 967,500 mi^2 (2,505,813 km^2). **Highest point** Kinyeti, 10,456 ft (3,187 m). **Lowest point** Sea level.

People. Sudan's population is composed of two distinct cultures—black African and Arab. African blacks of diverse ethnicity are a majority and are concentrated in the south, where they practice traditional lifestyles and beliefs and speak indigenous languages. Arabic-speaking Muslims, belonging to several ethnic groups, live mainly in northern and central regions.

Economy and the Land. The economy is based on agriculture; and irrigation has made arid Sudan a leading producer of cotton, although the land is vulnerable to drought. Forests provide for production of gum Arabic, used in making candy and perfumes, while other crops include peanuts and sesame seeds. Economic activity is concentrated near the Nile River and its branches, as well as near water holes and wells. The mostly flat terrain is marked by eastern and western mountains; southern forests and savanna give way to swampland, scrubland, and northern desert. The climate varies from desert in the north to tropical in the south.

History and Politics. Egypt mounted repeated invasions of what is now northern Sudan beginning about 300 B.C. Sudan remained a collection of small independent states until 1821, when Egypt conquered and unified the northern portion. Egypt was unable to establish control over the south, which was often raided by slavers. In 1881 a Muslim leader began uniting various groups in a revolt against Egyptian rule, and success came four years later. His successor ruled until 1898, when British and Egyptian forces reconquered the land. Renamed the Anglo-Egyptian Sudan, the region was ruled jointly by Egypt and Britain, with British administration dominating. Since gaining independence in 1956, a series of military coups, a continuing civil war, and severe famine have burdened Sudan with political and economic instability. ∎

SURINAME

Official name Republic of Suriname
PEOPLE
Population 426,000. **Density** 6.7/mi² (2.6/km²).
Urban 48%. **Capital** Paramaribo, 241,000. **Ethnic groups** East Indian 37%, Creole 31%, Javanese 15%, black 10%, Amerindian 3%, Chinese 2%.
Languages Dutch, Sranan Tongo, English, Hindustani, Javanese. **Religions** Hindu 27%, Protestant 25%, Roman Catholic 23%, Muslim 20%. **Life expectancy** 73 female, 68 male. **Literacy** 95%.
POLITICS
Government Republic. **Parties** Democratic Alternative '91, New Democratic, New Front. **Suffrage** Universal, over 18. **Memberships** OAS, UN. **Subdivisions** 10 districts.
ECONOMY
GDP $1,170,000,000. **Per capita** $2,833. **Monetary unit** Guilder. **Trade partners** Exports: Norway, Netherlands, U.S. Imports: U.S., Netherlands Antilles, Trinidad and Tobago. **Exports** Alumina, bauxite, aluminum, rice, wood. **Imports** Machinery, petroleum, food, cotton, manufactures.
LAND
Description Northeastern South America. **Area** 63,251 mi² (163,820 km²). **Highest point** Juliana Mtn., 4,035 ft (1,230 m). **Lowest point** Sea level.

People. Descendants of East Indians and Creoles—of mixed European-black African heritage—compose Suriname's two major groups. Black African slaves and contract laborers, imported from the east, resulted in various ethnic populations. Minority groups include the Javanese; Bush Negroes, a black group; Amerindians, descendants of Arawak and Caribs; Chinese; and Europeans. Dutch is the official language, but most groups have preserved their distinct language, culture, and religion.

Economy and the Land. The economy is based on mining and metal processing, and bauxite and alumina are the major exports. Agriculture plays an economic role as well and, together with fishing and forestry, offers potential for expansion. A narrow coastal swamp, central forests and savanna, and southern jungle-covered hills mark the country's terrain. The climate is tropical.

History and Politics. Prior to the arrival of Europeans, present-day Suriname was inhabited by indigenous Indians. Christopher Columbus sighted the coast in 1498, but the area's lack of gold slowed Spanish and Portuguese exploration. The British established the first settlement in 1651, and in 1665 Jews from Brazil erected the first synagogue in the Western Hemisphere. In 1667 the British traded the area to the Netherlands for the Dutch colony of New Amsterdam—present-day Manhattan, New York. Subsequent wars and treaties shifted ownership of Suriname among the British, French, and Dutch until 1815, when the Netherlands regained control. In 1954 Suriname became an autonomous part of the Netherlands, with status equal to that of the Netherlands Antilles. Suriname gained independence in 1975. In 1980 the military seized power and established a military-civilian government soon after. However, the military has retained considerable control. A general election in May 1991 resulted in a degree of democratic representation. ∎

SWAZILAND

Official name Kingdom of Swaziland
PEOPLE
Population 889,000. **Density** 123/mi² (51/km²).
Urban 26%. **Capital** Mbabane (administrative), 38,290; Lobamba (legislative). **Ethnic groups** Swazi 97%, European 3%. **Languages** English, siSwati. **Religions** African Protestant and other Christian 60%, tribal religionist 40%. **Life expectancy** 60 female, 56 male. **Literacy** 64%.
POLITICS
Government Monarchy. **Parties** None. **Suffrage** None. **Memberships** CW, OAU, UN. **Subdivisions** 4 districts.

ECONOMY
GDP $2,300,000,000. **Per capita** $2,486.
Monetary unit Lilangeni. **Trade partners** Exports: South Africa, Western European countries, Canada. Imports: South Africa, Japan, Belgium. **Exports** Soft drink concentrates, sugar, wood, fruit. **Imports** Transportation equipment, machinery, petroleum, food, chemicals.

LAND
Description Southern Africa, landlocked. **Area** 6,704 mi^2 (17,364 km^2). **Highest point** Emlembe, 6,109 ft (1,862 m). **Lowest point** Along Usutu River, 70 ft (21 m).

People. About 95 percent of the people of Swaziland are black Africans called Swazi, though small minorities of white Europeans and Zulus also live in the country. The two official languages are English and siSwati. Government and official business is conducted primarily in English. More than half the Swazi belong to Christian churches, while others practice traditional African religions.

Economy and the Land. Most Swazi are subsistence farmers. Cattle are highly prized for their own sake but are being used increasingly for milk, meat, and profit. Europeans own nearly half the land in Swaziland and raise most of the cash crops, including fruits, sugar, tobacco, cotton, and wood. Although mining has declined in recent years, Swaziland has deposits of coal, pottery clay, gold, and tin. The country's mountains and forests have brought a growing tourist industry. The climate is temperate.

History and Politics. According to legend, the Swazi originally came from the area near Maputo. British traders and Dutch farmers from South Africa first reached Swaziland in the 1830s; more whites arrived in the 1880s when gold was discovered. Swazi leaders unknowingly granted many concessions to the whites at this time. After the Boer War, Britain assumed administration of Swaziland and ruled until 1967. Swaziland became independent in 1968. The British designed a constitution, but many Swazi thought it disregarded their traditions and interests. In 1973 King Sobhuza abolished this constitution, suspended the legislature, and appointed a commission to produce a new constitution. Sobhuza ruled until his death in 1982, and King Mswati III was installed in 1986. The king has committed to a greater degree of democracy but no political parties are allowed and 1993 elections were not considered open. ∎

SWEDEN

Official name Kingdom of Sweden
PEOPLE
Population 8,981,000. **Density** 52/mi^2 (20/km^2).
Urban 84%. **Capital** Stockholm, 674,452. **Ethnic groups** Swedish (Scandinavian) 92%, Finnish, Lapp. **Languages** Swedish, Lapp, Finnish.
Religions Lutheran (Church of Sweden) 94%, Roman Catholic 2%. **Life expectancy** 81 female, 75 male. **Literacy** 99%.
POLITICS
Government Constitutional monarchy. **Parties**

Center, Moderate, Liberal, Social Democratic, others. **Suffrage** Universal, over 18. **Memberships** EU, NATO, OECD, UN. **Subdivisions** 24 counties.

ECONOMY
GDP $153,700,000,000. **Per capita** $17,833.
Monetary unit Krona. **Trade partners** Exports: Germany, U.K., U.S. Imports: Germany, U.S., U.K. **Exports** Machinery, transportation equipment, paper, pulp and wood, iron and steel. **Imports** Manufactures, petroleum, chemicals, transportation equipment, food.

LAND
Description Northern Europe. **Area** 173,732 mi^2 (449,964 km^2). **Highest point** Kebnekaise, 6,926 ft (2,111 m). **Lowest point** Sea level.

People. The most significant minorities in the largely urban Swedish population are Swedes of Finnish origin and a small number of Lapps. Sweden is also the home of immigrants from other Nordic countries, Yugoslavia, Greece, and Turkey. Swedish is the main language, although Finns and Lapps often speak their own tongues. English is the leading foreign language, especially among students and younger people.

Economy and the Land. Sweden has one of the highest standards of living in the world. Taxes are also high, but the government provides exceptional benefits for most citizens, including free education and medical care, pension payments, four-week vacations, and payments for child care. The nation is industrial and bases its economy on its three most important natural resources—timber, iron ore, and water power. The iron and steel industry produces high-quality steel used in ball bearings, precision tools, agricultural machinery, aircraft, automobiles, and ships. Swedish farmers rely heavily on dairy products and livestock, and most farms are part of Sweden's agricultural-cooperative movement. Sweden's varied terrain includes mountains, forests, plains, and sandy beaches. The climate is temperate, with cold winters in the north. Northern Sweden lies in the "Land of the Midnight Sun" and experiences periods of twenty-four hours of daylight in summer and darkness in winter.

History and Politics. Inhabitants of what is now Sweden began to trade with the Roman Empire about 50 B.C. Sailing expeditions by Swedish Vikings began about A.D. 800. In the fourteenth century the kingdom came under Danish rule, but declared its independence in 1523. The Swedish king offered protection to the followers of Martin Luther, and Lutheranism was soon declared the state religion. By the late 1660s, Sweden had become one of the great powers of Europe; it suffered a military defeat by Russia in 1709, however, and gradually lost most of its European possessions. An 1809 constitution gave most of the executive power of the government to the king. Despite this, the power of the Parliament gradually increased, and parliamentary rule was adopted in 1917. A 1975 constitution reduced the king's role to a ceremonial one. Sweden remained neutral during both world wars. Except for 1976-82, when Sweden was run by a conservative coalition, the country had a Socialist government until February 1990, when it failed to carry Parliament in an economic reform bill. By 1994 the Socialist Party was back in power. ◾

SWITZERLAND

Official name Swiss Confederation
PEOPLE
Population 7,244,000. **Density** 454/mi²
(175/km²). **Urban** 62%. **Capital** Bern, 136,338.
Ethnic groups German 65%, French 18%, Italian 10%, Romansch 1%. **Languages** German, French, Italian, Romansch. **Religions** Roman Catholic 48%, Protestant 44%. **Life expectancy** 81 female, 75 male. **Literacy** 99%.
POLITICS
Government Republic. **Parties** Christian Democratic People's, People's, Radical Democratic, Social Democratic, others. **Suffrage** Universal, over 18. **Memberships** OECD.
Subdivisions 26 cantons.
ECONOMY
GDP $149,100,000,000. **Per capita** $21,773.
Monetary unit Franc. **Trade partners** Exports: Germany, France, Italy. Imports: Germany,

France, Italy. **Exports** Machinery, precision instruments, metals, food, clothing and textiles. **Imports** Agricultural products, machinery and transportation equipment, chemicals.
LAND
Description Central Europe, landlocked. **Area** 15,943 mi² (41,293 km²). **Highest point** Dufourspitze, 15,203 ft (4,634 m). **Lowest point** Lago Maggiore, 633 ft (193 m).

People. About seven hundred years ago, the Swiss began joining together for mutual defense, but preserved their regional differences in language and customs. The country has four official languages: German, French, Italian, and Romansch, which is spoken by a minority. Dialects often differ from community to community. The population is concentrated on a central plain located between mountain ranges.

Economy and the Land. The Alps and Jura Mountains cover nearly 70 percent of Switzerland, making much of the land unsuited for agriculture but a good basis for a thriving tourist industry. The central plain contains rich cropland and holds Switzerland's major cities and manufacturing facilities, many specializing in high-quality, precision products. Switzerland is also an international banking and finance center. Straddling the ranges of the central Alps, Switzerland features mountains, hills, and plateaus. The temperate climate varies with altitude.

History and Politics. Helvetic Celts inhabited the area of present-day Switzerland when Julius Caesar conquered the region, annexing it to the Roman Empire. As the Roman Empire declined, northern and western Germanic tribes began a series of invasions, and in the 800s the region became part of the empire of the Frankish king Charlemagne. In 1291 leaders of the three Swiss cantons, or regions, signed an agreement declaring their freedom and promising mutual aid against any foreign ruler. The confederation was the beginning of modern Switzerland. Over the next few centuries Switzerland became a military power, expanding its territories until 1515, when it was defeated by France. Soon after, Switzerland adopted a policy of permanent neutrality. The country was again conquered by France during the French Revolution; however, after Napoleon's final defeat in 1815, the Congress of Vienna guaranteed Switzerland's neutrality, a guarantee that has never been broken. ◾

SYRIA

Official name Syrian Arab Republic
PEOPLE
Population 14,100,000. **Density** 197/mi²
(76/km²). **Urban** 50%. **Capital** Damascus, 1,549,932. **Ethnic groups** Arab 90%, Kurdish, Armenian, and other 10%. **Languages** Arabic, Kurdish, Armenian, Aramaic, Circassian.
Religions Sunni Muslim 74%, other Muslim 16%, Christian 10%. **Life expectancy** 69 female, 65 male. **Literacy** 64%.
POLITICS
Government Socialist republic. **Parties** Arab

Socialist, Arab Socialist Resurrectionist (Baath), Communist. **Suffrage** Universal, over 18.
Memberships AL, UN. **Subdivisions** 14 districts.
ECONOMY
GDP $81,700,000,000. **Per capita** $5,807.
Monetary unit Pound. **Trade partners** Exports: Former Soviet republics, Italy, France. Imports: France, Germany, U.S. **Exports** Petroleum, agricultural products, textiles, phosphates. **Imports** Food, metals, machinery, textiles, petroleum.
LAND
Description Southwestern Asia. **Area** 71,498 mi² (185,180 km²). **Highest point** Mt. Hermon, 9,232 ft (2,814 m). **Lowest point** Near Sea of Galilee, -656 ft (-200 m).

People. Most Syrians are Arabic-speaking descendants of Semites, a people who settled the region in ancient times. The majority are Sunni Muslim, and Islam is a powerful cultural force. Only a small percentage are Christian. Non-Arab Syrians include Kurds and Armenians, who speak their own languages and maintain their own customs. French is widely understood, and English is spoken in larger cities. The population is evenly divided between urban and rural settlements.

Economy and the Land. Syria is a developing country with great potential for economic growth. Textile manufacturing is a major industry, and oil, the main natural resource, provides for expanding activity in oil refining. The plains and river valleys are fertile, but rainfall is irregular and irrigation is necessary to sustain agriculture. Most farms are small; cotton and wheat are their major products. The terrain is marked by mountains, the Euphrates River valley, and a semiarid plateau. The climate is hot and dry, with relatively cold winters.

History and Politics. Syria was the site of one of the world's most ancient civilizations, and Damascus and other Syrian cities were centers of world trade as early as 2500 B.C. Greater Syria, as the area was called until the end of World War I, originally included much of modern Israel, Jordan, Lebanon, and parts of Turkey. The region was occupied and ruled by several empires, including the Phoenician, Assyrian,

Babylonian, Persian, and Greek, before coming under Roman rule in 64 B.C. During subsequent years, Christianity arose in the part of Greater Syria called Palestine. In 636 the region fell to Arab Muslims, who governed until 1260, when Egypt gained control. Syria became part of the Turkish Ottoman Empire in 1516. During World War I, Syria aided Britain in defeating the Turks and Germans in return for independence. After the war, however, the League of Nations divided Greater Syria into four mandates—Syria, Lebanon, Palestine, and Transjordan—and placed Syria under French control. When Syria gained independence in 1946, many nationals wanted to reunite Greater Syria, but the United Nations made part of Palestine into the Jewish state of Israel. Tensions between Israel and Syria erupted in war in 1967 and 1973 and remain unresolved. In the 1980s Syria assumed a role in Lebanon's affairs and maintains a military presence there. ■

TAIWAN

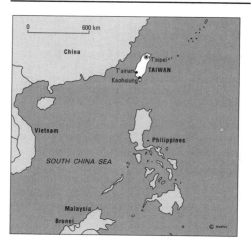

Official name Republic of China
PEOPLE
Population 21,150,000. **Density** 1,522/mi² (587/km²). **Urban** 71%. **Capital** T'aipei, 2,706,453.
Ethnic groups Taiwanese 84%, Chinese 14%, aborigine 2%. **Languages** Chinese (Mandarin), Taiwanese (Min), Hakka. **Religions** Buddhist, Confucian, and Taoist 93%, Christian 5%. **Life expectancy** 78 female, 72 male. **Literacy** 91%.
POLITICS
Government Republic. **Parties** Democratic Progressive, Kuomintang (Nationalist), others.
Suffrage Universal, over 20. **Memberships** None.
Subdivisions 16 counties, 7 municipalities.
ECONOMY
GDP $224,000,000,000. **Per capita** $10,674.
Monetary unit Dollar. **Trade partners** Exports: U.S., Japan. Imports: Japan, U.S., Germany.
Exports Machinery, textiles, metals, food, wood.
Imports Machinery, metals, chemicals, petroleum, food.

LAND

Description Eastern Asian island. **Area** 13,900 mi^2 (36,002 km^2). **Highest point** Yu Mtn., 13,114 ft (3,997 m). **Lowest point** Sea level.

People. The majority of Taiwan's inhabitants are descendants of Chinese who migrated from the coast of China in the eighteenth and nineteenth centuries. In 1949, when the Communists came to power in mainland China, many educated Chinese fled to Taiwan. A small group of aborigines, which lives in the mountains in central Taiwan, is most likely of Malay-Polynesian origin. Taiwan's languages are mainly various dialects of Chinese, a Fujian dialect, and a dialect known as "Hakka." Most religious practices combine Buddhist and Taoist beliefs with the Confucian ethical code.

Economy and the Land. Since World War II, Taiwan's economy has changed from agriculture to industry. A past emphasis on light industry, producing mainly consumer goods, has shifted to technology and heavy industry. Although only one-quarter of the island is arable, farmland is intensely cultivated, with some areas producing two and three crops a year. Though rice, sugar cane, fruits, tea, and fishing are important, much food must be imported. The island's terrain is marked by steep eastern mountains sloping to a fertile western region. The capital of T'aipei administers the Penghu Islands and about twenty off-shore islands as well as the island of Taiwan. The climate is maritime subtropical.

History and Politics. Chinese migration to Taiwan began as early as A.D. 500. Dutch traders claimed the island in 1624 as a base for trade with China and Japan. It was ruled by China's Manchu dynasty from 1683 until 1895, when China ceded Taiwan to Japan after the first Sino-Japanese war. Following World War II, China regained possession of Taiwan. A civil war in mainland China between Nationalist and Communist forces ended with the victory of the Communists in 1949. Nationalist leader Chiang Kai-shek fled to Taiwan, proclaiming T'aipei the provisional capital of Nationalist China. In 1971 the People's Republic of China replaced Taiwan in the United Nations. While the Republic of China still maintains that it is the legitimate ruler of all China, nearly all nations now recognize the mainland's People's Republic of China. While reunification talks between the two governments have taken place since 1993, there is a growing consensus among the Taiwanese that the island should remain independent. ■

TAJIKISTAN

Official name Republic of Tajikistan
PEOPLE
Population 6,073,000. **Density** 110/mi^2 (42/km^2). **Urban** 33%. **Capital** Dushanbe, 582,400. **Ethnic groups** Tajik 62%, Uzbek 24%, Russian 8%. **Languages** Tajik, Uzbek, Russian. **Religions** Sunni Muslim 80%, Shiite Musilm 5%. **Life expectancy** 71 female, 66 male. **Literacy** 96%.
POLITICS
Government Republic. **Parties** Democratic,

Islamic Renaissance, Rostakhez (Rebirth). **Suffrage** Universal, over 18. **Memberships** CIS, UN. **Subdivisions** 1 autonomous region, 3 regions.
ECONOMY
GDP $23,940,000,000. **Per capita** $4,654. **Monetary unit** Russian ruble. **Trade partners** Russia, Kazakhstan, Ukraine, Uzbekistan. **Exports** Aluminum, cotton, fruit, vegetable oil, textiles. **Imports** Chemicals, machinery and transportation equipment, textiles, food.
LAND
Description Central Asia, landlocked. **Area** 55,251 mi^2 (143,100 km^2). **Highest point** Communism Peak, 24,590 ft (7,495 m). **Lowest point** Along Syr Darya River, 984 ft (300 m).

People. The Tajik people are indistinguishable from the neighboring Uzbeks, although the country also includes many minority groups indigenous to the Pamir Mountains in the west. The Tajik language is closely related to Farsi, the principal language of Iran. The country is home to many people who were born in Uzbekistan, as well as many Russians. Islam has always been widely practiced in Tajikistan, even when the country was under Soviet rule. Most people live in small towns throughout the mountains. Folklore is important to the Tajiks, who are known for their colorful legends and poetry.

Economy and the Land. Cotton is among the country's principal crops, and irrigation allows production of fruits and grains. Cattle breeding is also an important agricultural activity. Tajikistan has many minerals, including coal, petroleum, uranium, lead, zinc, and others. Despite these significant resources, Tajikistan has the lowest standard of living of all of the former Soviet republics. The elevation of more than one-half of the country lies above ten thousand feet. The climate is harsh and precipitation is low. Earthquakes are common.

History and Politics. Iranian people are known to have lived in the region of Tajikistan since the first century B.C. Arabs brought Islam to the region between the seventh and eighth centuries A.D. Tajikistan came under Russian control in 1895 as part of a region known as Turkestan. There was substantial local resistance to the implementation of communism following the Russian Revolution, and several years of armed struggle ensued. The country became an Autonomous Republic within the Soviet Union in 1924 and a Soviet Socialist Republic in 1929. It declared its sovereignty in September 1991 and achieved full independence after the breakup of the Soviet Union during the following December. Communists and Islamic fundamentalists have been fighting for control of the country since 1992. ∎

TANZANIA

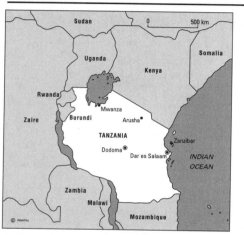

Official name United Republic of Tanzania
PEOPLE
Population 28,350,000. **Density** 83/mi² (32/km²).
Urban 21%. **Capital** Dar es Salaam (de facto), 1,096,000; Dodoma (legislative), 85,000. **Ethnic groups** African 99%. **Languages** English, Swahili, indigenous. **Religions** Animist 33%, Muslim 33%, Christian 33%. **Life expectancy** 52 female, 49 male. **Literacy** 46%.
POLITICS
Government Republic. **Parties** Revolutionary.
Suffrage Universal, over 18. **Memberships** CW, OAU, UN. **Subdivisions** 25 regions.
ECONOMY
GDP $16,700,000,000. **Per capita** $591.
Monetary unit Shilling. **Trade partners** Exports: Germany, U.K. Imports: U.K., Japan, Germany.
Exports Coffee, cotton, sisal, tea, cashews, meat, tobacco, diamonds, gold. **Imports** Manufactures, machinery and transportation equipment, cotton, petroleum, food.
LAND
Description Eastern Africa. **Area** 341,217 mi² (883,749 km²). **Highest point** Kilimanjaro, 19,340 ft (5,895 m). **Lowest point** Sea level.

People. The largely rural African population of Tanzania consists of more than 130 ethnic groups; most speak a distinct language. Religious beliefs are nearly evenly divided among Christian, Muslim, and traditional religions.

Economy and the Land. Agriculture accounts for the most export earnings and employs 80 percent of the work force. Yet two-thirds of the land cannot be cultivated because of lack of water and tsetse-fly infestation. Mainland farmers grow cassava, corn, and beans, while other cash crops include coffee and cashews. Zanzibar and Pemba islands are famous sources of cloves. Diamonds, salt, and iron are important mineral resources. Hot, humid coastal plains; an arid central plateau; and temperate lake and highland areas characterize mainland Tanzania. The climate is equatorial and includes monsoons.

History and Politics. The northern mainland has fossil remains of some of humanity's earliest ancestors. Subsequent early inhabitants were gradually displaced by Bantu farmers and Nilotes. Arabs were trading with coastal groups as early as the eighth century, and by the early 1500s the Portuguese had claimed the coastal region. They were displaced in the 1700s by Arabs, who subsequently established a lucrative slave trade. Germans began colonizing the coast in 1884 and six years later signed an agreement with Great Britain, which secured German dominance along the coast and made Zanzibar a British protectorate. After World War I, Britain received part of German East Africa from the League of Nations as a mandate and renamed it Tanganyika. The area became a trust territory under the United Nations following World War II. The country achieved independence in 1961, and two years later Zanzibar received its independence as a constitutional monarchy under the sultan. A 1964 revolt by the African majority overthrew the sultan, and Zanzibar and Tanganyika subsequently united and became known as Tanzania. Tanzania developed a special African brand of Socialism in the 1960s, which served as a model throughout the continent. In 1992 it moved from single to multiparty politics. ∎

TASMANIA See AUSTRALIA.

THAILAND

Official name Kingdom of Thailand
PEOPLE
Population 58,870,000. **Density** 302/mi² (117/km²). **Urban** 22%. **Capital** Bangkok, 5,620,591. **Ethnic groups** Thai 75%, Chinese 14%. **Languages** Thai, indigenous. **Religions** Buddhist 95%, Muslim 4%. **Life expectancy** 72 female, 67 male. **Literacy** 93%.
POLITICS
Government Constitutional monarchy. **Parties** Chart Thai, Democratic, Force of Truth (Palang Dharma), Justice Unity (Samakki Tham), New Aspiration. **Suffrage** Universal, over 21.
Memberships ASEAN, UN. **Subdivisions** 73 provinces.
ECONOMY
GDP $323,000,000,000. **Per capita** $5,566.
Monetary unit Baht. **Trade partners** Exports: U.S., Japan, Singapore. Imports: Japan, U.S.,

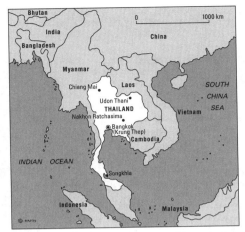

Singapore. **Exports** Machinery and manufactures, food, crude materials. **Imports** Machinery and manufactures, chemicals, fuel, crude materials.

LAND

Description Southeastern Asia. **Area** 198,115 mi^2 (513,115 km^2). **Highest point** Mt. Inthanon, 8,530 ft (2,600 m). **Lowest point** Sea level.

People. Thailand's society is relatively homogeneous. More than 80 percent of its people speak varying dialects of Thai and share a common culture and common religion, Buddhism. Chinese immigrants are a substantial minority. Thai society is rural, with most people living in the rice-growing regions. The government has sponsored a successful family-planning program, which has greatly reduced the annual birth rate.

Economy and the Land. With an economy based on agriculture, Thailand exports large quantities of rice each year. Forests produce teak and rattan, and tin is another valuable natural resource. Tourism is the largest source of foreign income. Future industrialization may hinge on deposits of coal and natural gas. Thailand is experiencing a period of prosperity and economic growth which provides an ideal climate for foreign investment. A mountainous and heavily forested nation, Thailand has a tropical climate, dominated by monsoons, high temperatures, and humidity.

History and Politics. Thai communities were established as early as 4000 B.C., although a Thai kingdom founded in the thirteenth century A.D. began the history of modern Thailand. In the late 1700s Burmese armies overwhelmed the kingdom. Rama I, founder of the present dynasty, helped to drive the invaders from the country in 1782. He subsequently renamed the nation Siam and established a capital at Bangkok. Siam allowed Europeans to live within its borders during the period of colonial expansion, but the nation never succumbed to foreign rule. As a result, Siam was the only South and Southeast Asian country never colonized by a European power. In 1932 a revolt changed the government from an absolute monarchy to a constitutional monarchy. Military officers assumed control in 1938, and the nation reverted to its former name, Thailand, in 1939. The coun-

try was invaded by Japan in World War II. Following the war, Thailand was ruled by military officers until 1973, when civilians seized control and instigated a period of democracy that ended in 1976, when the military again took control. In May 1992, soldiers opened fire on anti-government demonstrators, killing at least 50 people. Ensuing outrage led to the formation of a new, more democratic government. ∎

TOGO

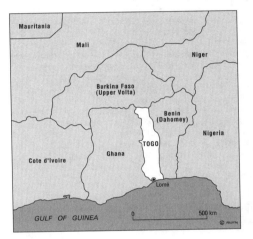

Official name Republic of Togo

PEOPLE

Population 4,332,000. **Density** 198/mi^2 (76/km^2). **Urban** 29%. **Capital** Lomé, 500,000. **Ethnic groups** Ewe, Mina, Kabye, others. **Languages** French, Ewe, Mina, Kabye, Dagomba. **Religions** Animist 70%, Christian 20%, Muslim 10%. **Life expectancy** 57 female, 53 male. **Literacy** 43%.

POLITICS

Government Provisional military government. **Parties** Rally of the People. **Suffrage** Universal adult. **Memberships** OAU, UN. **Subdivisions** 21 prefectures.

ECONOMY

GDP $3,300,000,000. **Per capita** $819. **Monetary unit** CFA franc. **Trade partners** Exports: Canada, France, Spain, Italy. Imports: France, Netherlands, Germany. **Exports** Phosphates, cocoa, coffee, cotton, manufactures, palm kernels. **Imports** Food, fuel, manufactures, machinery.

LAND

Description Western Africa. **Area** 21,925 mi^2 (56,785 km^2). **Highest point** Mont Agou, 3,235 ft (986 m). **Lowest point** Sea level.

People. Almost all the people of Togo are black Africans, coming primarily from the Ewe, Kabye, and Mina ethnic groups. Most of the population lives in the south and practices traditional religions. Significant Christian and Muslim minorities exist.

Economy and the Land. Togo is an agricultural country, but productive land is scarce. Fishing is a major industry in the coastal areas. Togo has one of the world's largest phosphate reserves. Much of Togo is mountainous, with a sandy coastal plain. The climate is hot and humid.

History and Politics. Togo's original inhabitants were probably the ancestors of the present-day central mountain people. Ewes entered the south in the 1300s, and refugees from war-torn northern countries settled in the north between the 1500s and 1800s. For two hundred years, European ships raided the coastal region in search of slaves. In 1884 Germany claimed the territory. After World War I Togoland became a League of Nations mandate governed by Britain and France. The mandate was made a United Nations trust territory following World War II and remained under British and French administration. British Togoland voted to join the Gold Coast and nearby British-administered territories in 1957 and became the independent nation of Ghana. French Togoland voted to become a republic in 1956 with internal self-government within the French Union, although the United Nations did not accept this method of ending the trusteeship. Togo peacefully severed its ties with France in 1960 and gained independence the same year. Internal political strife and military dominance of the government have characterized Togo's years of independence. ∎

TOKELAU See NEW ZEALAND.

TONGA

Official name Kingdom of Tonga
PEOPLE
Population 110,000. **Density** 382/mi² (147/km²).
Urban 35%. **Capital** Nuku'alofa, Tongatapu I., 21,265. **Ethnic groups** Tongan (Polynesian).
Languages Tongan, English. **Religions** Methodist 47%, Roman Catholic 16%, Free Church 14%, Church of Tonga 9%. **Life expectancy** 70 female, 66 male. **Literacy** 100%.
POLITICS
Government Constitutional monarchy. **Parties** None. **Suffrage** Literate adults, over 21 (males must be taxpayers). **Memberships** CW.
Subdivisions 3 island groups.
ECONOMY
GDP $200,000,000. **Per capita** $1,942. **Monetary unit** Pa'anga. **Trade partners** Exports: New Zealand, U.S., Australia. Imports: New Zealand, Australia, Fiji. **Exports** Coconut oil, copra, bananas, taro, vanilla beans, fruits and vegetables.
Imports Food, machinery and transportation equipment, manufactures, fuel.
LAND
Description South Pacific islands. **Area** 288 mi² (747 km²). **Highest point** Unnamed, 3,432 ft (1,046 m). **Lowest point** Sea level.

People. Almost all Tongans are Polynesian and follow Methodist and other Christian religions. About two-thirds of the population lives on the main island of Tongatapu.

Economy and the Land. Tonga's economy is dominated by both subsistence and plantation agriculture, while manufacturing is almost nonexistent. Most of the islands are coral reefs, and many have fertile soil. The climate is subtropical.

History and Politics. Tonga has been settled since at least 500 B.C. In the late 1700s, a civil war broke out among three lines of kings who sought to establish rulership. In 1822 Wesleyan Methodist missionaries converted one of the warring kings to Christianity. His faction prevailed, and he ruled as George Tupou I, founder of the present dynasty. Tonga came under British protection in 1900 but retained its autonomy in internal matters. The nation became fully independent in 1970. Elections in 1993 highlighted the growth of two movements, the status quo as a constitutional monarchy vs. a pro-democracy faction. ∎

TRINIDAD AND TOBAGO

Official name Republic of Trinidad and Tobago

PEOPLE
Population 1,281,000.
Density 647/mi² (250/km²). **Urban** 65%.
Capital Port of Spain, Trinidad I., 50,878.
Ethnic groups Black 41%, East Indian 41%, mixed 16%, white 1%.
Languages English, Hindi, French, Spanish.
Religions Baptist 40%, Anglican 19%, Methodist 16%, Church of God 11%. **Life expectancy** 74 female, 69 male. **Literacy** 95%.
POLITICS
Government Republic.
Parties National Alliance for Reconstruction, People's National Movement.
Suffrage Universal, over 18. **Memberships** CW, OAS, UN. **Subdivisions** 10 administrative areas.
ECONOMY
GDP $10,400,000,000. **Per capita** $7,957.
Monetary unit Dollar. **Trade partners** Exports: U.S., Barbados, Netherlands Antilles. Imports: U.S., Venezuela, U.K. **Exports** Petroleum, steel, fertilizer, sugar, cocoa, coffee, fruit. **Imports** Raw materials, machinery, manufactures.
LAND
Description Caribbean islands. **Area** 1,980 mi² (5,128 km²). **Highest point** El Cerro Del Aripo, 3,085 ft (940 m). **Lowest point** Sea level.

People. The two islands of Trinidad and Tobago form a single country, but Trinidad has nearly all the land mass and population. About 80 percent of all Trinidadians are either black African or East Indian, and about 20 percent are European, Chinese, and of mixed descent. Most Tobagonians are black African. The official language is English, and most people are Protestant.

Economy and the Land. Agriculture and tourism are important, but the economy is based on oil, which accounts for about 80 percent of the nation's exports. Trinidad is also one of the world's chief sources of natural asphalt and possesses supplies of natural gas. Tropical rain forests, scenic beaches, and fertile farmland characterize the islands.

History and Politics. Trinidad was occupied by Arawak Indians when Christopher Columbus arrived and claimed the island for Spain in 1498. The island remained under Spanish rule until 1797, when the British captured it and ruled for more than 150 years. Tobago changed hands among the Dutch, French, and British until 1814, when Britain took control. In 1888 Trinidad and Tobago became a single British colony, and achieved independence in 1962. The racially diverse society is beginning to agitate for a more balanced representation in the government. In August 1990 Muslim militants kidnapped a large number of government officials in an unfocused and failed attempt to force the Prime Minister to resign. However the militants retain a hold on the country's politics. ∎

TUNISIA

Official name Republic of Tunisia
PEOPLE
Population 8,606,000. **Density** 139/mi² (54/km²).
Urban 56%. **Capital** Tunis, 596,654. **Ethnic groups** Arab 98%, European 1%. **Languages** Arabic, French. **Religions** Muslim 98%, Christian 1%. **Life expectancy** 69 female, 67 male.
Literacy 65%.
POLITICS
Government Republic. **Parties** Constitutional

Democratic Rally, Movement of Democratic Socialists. **Suffrage** Universal, over 20.
Memberships AL, OAU, UN. **Subdivisions** 23 governorates.
ECONOMY
GDP $34,300,000,000. **Per capita** $4,038.
Monetary unit Dinar. **Trade partners** Exports: France, Italy, Germany. Imports: France, Italy, Germany. **Exports** Hydrocarbons, agricultural products, phosphates and chemicals. **Imports** Manufactures, petroleum, food.
LAND
Description Northern Africa. **Area** 63,170 mi² (163,610 km²). **Highest point** Mt. Chambi, 5,066 ft (1,544 m). **Lowest point** Chott el Gharsa, -56 ft (-17 m).

People. Tunisians are descended from a mix of Berber and Arab ethnic groups. Nearly all Tunisians are Muslim. Arabic is the official language, but French is widely spoken. Tunisia is a leader in the Arab world in promoting rights for women. A large middle class and equitable land distribution characterize its society.

Economy and the Land. Tunisia is an agricultural country; wheat, barley, citrus fruits, and olives are important crops. Oil from deposits discovered in the 1960s supplies domestic needs and serves as a major export, along with phosphates and other chemicals. Tourism is a growing industry, and despite an unemployment problem, Tunisia has a more balanced economy than many of its neighbors. Tunisia's terrain ranges from a well-watered and fertile northern area to more arid central and southern regions.

History and Politics. Phoenicians began the Carthaginian Empire in Tunisia about 1100 B.C. In 146 B.C. Romans conquered Carthage and ruled Tunisia for six hundred years. Arab Muslims from the Middle East gained control of most of North Africa in the seventh century, influencing the religion and overall culture of the region. Tunisia became part of the Turkish Ottoman Empire in the late 1500s, and in 1881 France succeeded in establishing a protectorate in the area. Nationalistic calls for Tunisian independence began before World War I and gained momentum by the 1930s. When Tunisia gained independence in 1956, more than half of the European population emigrated, severely damaging the economy. A year later Tunisia abolished its monarchy and became a republic. The first multiparty parliament was elected in March 1994. Muslim fundamentalist parties are banned. ∎

TURKEY

Official name Republic of Turkey
PEOPLE
Population 62,030,000. **Density** 206/mi² (80/km²). **Urban** 61%. **Capital** Ankara, 2,559,471. **Ethnic groups** Turkish 80%, Kurdish 20%. **Languages** Turkish, Kurdish, Arabic. **Religions** Muslim. **Life expectancy** 70 female, 65 male.
Literacy 81%.

a vast empire for six hundred years. Mustafa Kemal founded the Republic of Turkey in 1923, after the collapse of the Ottoman Empire. In 1960 the Turkish government was overthrown by Turkish military forces, who subsequently set up a provisional government, adopted a new constitution, and held free elections. In the 1960s and 1970s, disputes with Greece over Cyprus, populated by majority Greeks and minority Turks, flared into violence, and radical groups committed terrorist acts against the government. Turkey's generals assumed power in 1980 and restored order to the country. The government returned to civilian rule in 1984 and in 1993 elected its first woman prime minister. The militant Kurdish minority insurrection continues to defy military and political resolution. Militant fundamentalist Muslims are also a threat to stability. ■

POLITICS
Government Republic. **Parties** Correct Way, Motherland, Social Democratic Populist. **Suffrage** Universal, over 21. **Memberships** NATO, OECD, UN. **Subdivisions** 74 provinces.
ECONOMY
GDP $312,400,000,000. **Per capita** $5,329.
Monetary unit Lira. **Trade partners** Exports: Germany, Italy, U.S. Imports: Germany, U.S., Italy.
Exports Steel, chemicals, fruits, vegetables, tobacco, meat products. **Imports** Petroleum, machinery, transportation equipment, metals, chemicals.
LAND
Description Southeastern Europe and southwestern Asia. **Area** 300,948 mi^2 (779,452 km^2).
Highest point Mt. Ararat, 16,804 ft (5,122 m).
Lowest point Sea level.

People. Most Turks are descended from an Asian people who migrated from Russia and Mongolia around A.D. 900. About half the Turkish population lives in cities and half in rural areas. Kurds, the largest minority, live in the country's mountainous regions. Arabs and whites compose smaller minorities. The population is mainly Sunni Muslim. The changing status of women and the influence of Islam on daily life are key issues in Turkish society.

Economy and the Land. More than half the workers in this developing country are farmers, but industrialization has increased greatly since 1950. The most productive lands are in the mild coastal regions, although wheat and barley are grown in the desertlike plateau area. The government owns or controls many important industries, transportation services, and utilities, while most small farms and manufacturing companies are privately owned. The climate is Mediterranean along the coast, but temperature extremes are typical in the inland plateau.

History and Politics. Hittites began to migrate to the area from Europe or central Asia around 2000 B.C. Successive dominant groups included Phrygians, Greeks, Persians, and Romans. Muslims and Christians battled in the area during the Crusades of the eleventh and twelfth centuries. In the 1300s Ottoman Turks began to build what would become

TURKMENISTAN

Official name Turkmenistan
PEOPLE
Population 4,035,000. **Density** 21/mi^2 (8.3/km^2).
Urban 45%. **Capital** Ashkhabad, 412,200. **Ethnic groups** Turkmen 73%, Russian 10%, Uzbek 9%, Kazakh 2%. **Languages** Turkmen, Russian, Uzbek. **Religions** Muslim 87%, Eastern Orthodox 11%. **Life expectancy** 69 female, 61 male.
Literacy 97%.
POLITICS
Government Republic. **Parties** Democratic.
Suffrage Universal, over 18. **Memberships** CIS, NATO, UN. **Subdivisions** 4 oblasts.
ECONOMY
GDP $13,000,000,000. **Per capita** 3,347.
Monetary unit Manat. **Trade partners** Russia, Ukraine, Uzbekistan. **Exports** Natural gas, oil, chemicals, cotton, textiles, carpets. **Imports** Machinery and parts, plastics and rubber, consumer durables, textiles.
LAND
Description Central Asia, landlocked. **Area** 188,456 mi^2 (488,100 km^2). **Highest point**

Unnamed, 10,299 ft (3,139 m). **Lowest point** Akdzhakaya Basin, -266 ft (-81 m).

People. Almost three-quarters of the people are Turkmen, although there are Russian and Uzbek minorities. Before the Russian Revolution, the Turkmen were nomads who were organized into tribes and clans. Under Communist rule, many people turned to agriculture. The Turkmen speak a Turkish dialect of the same name.

Economy and the Land. Most of Turkmenistan is a vast desert. Like most deserts, the climate is characterized by extreme variations in temperature. Agriculture takes place in the country's river valleys and oases, and cotton is the most significant crop. Grapes, melons, and vegetables are also grown. Animal husbandry is a traditional activity, and sheep, horses, and camels are raised. The sheep provide wool for the country's famous handmade Oriental carpets. Petroleum and natural gas are among Turkmenistan's most important mineral resources. Only 10 percent of the people of Turkmenistan are engaged in industry.

History and Politics. In ancient times, Turkmenistan was part of the Persian Empire. Arabs invaded the region in the eighth century, bringing Islam. Turkic tribes conquered Turkmenistan in the tenth century, followed by the Mongols and the Uzbeks. The area was incorporated into Russian Turkestan in 1881. In 1925, Turkestan became a Soviet Socialist Republic within the Soviet Union. Turkmenistan was slow to make its claim to independence from the Soviet Union following the abortive coup against President Mikhail Gorbachev and the subsequent disbanding of the Soviet Communist party. The country gained full independence with the rest of the former Soviet republics in December 1991. Communists continue to dominate Turkmenistan's politics, and democratic institutions have not been established. With no opposition, the incumbent Turkmen Democratic Party was returned to power in 1994 and President Saparmurad Niyazov's term was extended to 2002. Turkmenistan is one of the few former Soviet republics that has not experienced internal ethnic strife. ■

TURKS AND CAICOS
ISLANDS See UNITED KINGDOM.

TUVALU

Official name Tuvalu
PEOPLE
Population 10,000. **Density** 1,000/mi² (385/km²). **Capital** Funafuti, Funafuti I., 2,191. **Ethnic groups** Tuvaluan (Polynesian). **Languages** Tuvaluan, English. **Religions** Congregationalist (Church of Tuvalu) 97%. **Life expectancy** 64 female, 61 male.
POLITICS
Government Parliamentary state. **Parties** None. **Suffrage** Universal, over 18. **Memberships** CW. **Subdivisions** 1 town council, 7 island councils.

ECONOMY
GNP $6,4000,000. **Per capita** $727. **Monetary unit** Dollar, Australian dollar. **Trade partners** Exports: Fiji, Australia, New Zealand. Imports: Australia, New Zealand, U.K. **Exports** Copra. **Imports** Food, animals, fuel, machinery, manufactures.
LAND
Description South Pacific islands. **Area** 10 mi² (26 km²). **Highest point** Unnamed, 16 ft (5 m). **Lowest point** Sea level.

People. The small island nation of Tuvalu has a largely Polynesian population centered in rural villages. Tuvaluans speak the Tuvaluan language, derived from Polynesian, and many also speak English, reflecting ties with England.

Economy and the Land. The soil of the Tuvaluan coral-reef islands is poor, and there are few natural resources other than coconut palms. Copra and developed film are the primary exports, and many Tuvaluans weave mats and baskets for export. Tuvalu has minimal manufacturing and no mining. The nation consists of nine islands, most of them atolls surrounding lagoons. The climate is tropical.

History and Politics. Tuvalu's first inhabitants were probably Samoan immigrants. The islands were not seen by Europeans until 1568 and came under British control in the 1890s. Then called the Ellice Islands by Europeans, they were combined with the nearby Gilbert Islands in 1916 to form the Gilbert and Ellice Islands Colony. The island groups were separated in 1975. The Ellice Islands were renamed Tuvalu and gained independence in 1978. One year later, the Gilbert Islands became part of independent Kiribati. ■

UGANDA

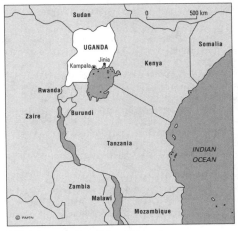

Official name Republic of Uganda
PEOPLE
Population 18,270,000. **Density** 196/mi² (76/km²). **Urban** 11%. **Capital** Kampala, 773,463.

Ethnic groups Ganda, Nkole, Gisu, Soga, Turkana, Chiga, Lango, Acholi. **Languages** English, Luganda, Swahili, indigenous. **Religions** Roman Catholic 33%, Protestant 33%, Muslim 16%, Animist. **Life expectancy** 43 female, 41 male. **Literacy** 48%.

POLITICS

Government Republic. **Parties** National Resistance Movement. **Suffrage** Universal, over 18. **Memberships** CW, OAU, UN. **Subdivisions** 33 districts.

ECONOMY

GDP $24,100,000,000. **Per capita** $1,384. **Monetary unit** Shilling. **Trade partners** Exports: U.S., U.K., France. Imports: Kenya, U.K., Italy. **Exports** Coffee, cotton, tea. **Imports** Petroleum products, machinery, textiles, metals, transportation equipment.

LAND

Description Eastern Africa, landlocked. **Area** 93,104 mi² (241,139 km²). **Highest point** Margherita Pk., 16,763 ft (5,109 m). **Lowest point** Along Albert Nile River, 2,000 ft (610 m).

People. Primarily a rural nation, Uganda has a largely African population, which is composed of various ethnic groups. Numerous differences divide Uganda's peoples and have traditionally inspired conflict. Though English is the official language, Luganda and Swahili are widely used, along with indigenous Bantu and Nilotic languages. Most Ugandans are Christian, but Muslims and followers of traditional beliefs compose significant minorities.

Economy and the Land. Despite attempts to diversify the economy, the country remains largely agricultural. Uganda meets most of its own food needs and grows coffee, cotton, and tea commercially. Copper deposits account for most mining activity. Though Uganda straddles the equator, temperatures are modified by altitude. Most of the country is plateau, and Uganda benefits from its proximity to several major lakes.

History and Politics. Arab traders who traveled to the interior of Uganda in the 1830s found sophisticated kingdoms that had developed over several centuries. Trying to track the source of the Nile River, British explorers arrived in the 1860s and were followed by European missionaries. Britain quickly became a dominant force in eastern Africa, and part of modern Uganda became a British protectorate in 1894. Subsequent border adjustments brought Uganda to its present boundaries in 1926. After increasing demands for independence, moves toward autonomy began in the mid-1950s. Independence came in 1962, followed by internal conflicts and power struggles. In 1971 Major General Idi Amin Dada led a successful coup against President Obote and declared himself president. His dictatorship was rife with corruption, economic decline, and disregard for human rights, and he was driven into exile in 1979. In July 1993 the ancient kingdom of Buganda was symbolically restored and Ronald Mutebi crowned as king. A Constituent Assembly was elected in 1994 to draft a constitution. ■

UKRAINE

Official name Ukraine

PEOPLE

Population 52,140,000. **Density** 224/mi² (86/km²). **Urban** 67%. **Capital** Kiev (Kyyiv), 2,635,000. **Ethnic groups** Ukrainian 73%, Russian 22%. **Languages** Ukrainian, Russian, Romanian, Polish. **Religions** Ukrainian Orthodox, Ukrainian Catholic. **Life expectancy** 75 female, 75 male. **Literacy** 97%.

POLITICS

Government Republic. **Parties** Democratic Rebirth, Green, Peasant Democratic, People's, Republican, Social Democratic, Ukrainian Socialist. **Suffrage** Universal, over 18. **Memberships** CIS, NATO, UN. **Subdivisions** 1 republic, 24 oblasts.

ECONOMY

GDP $205,400,000,000. **Per capita** $3,951. **Monetary unit** Karbovanets. **Trade partners** Russia, Belarus, Kazakhstan. **Exports** Coal, electricity, metals, chemicals, machinery, transportation equipment. **Imports** Machinery, transportation equipment, chemicals, textiles.

LAND

Description Eastern Europe. **Area** 233,090 mi² (603,700 km²). **Highest point** Mt. Hoverla, 6,762 ft (2,061 m). **Lowest point** Sea level.

People. The size of the population of newly independent Ukraine is second only to Russia among the former Soviet republics. Although there are more than one hundred minority groups, ethnic Ukrainians account for almost three-quarters of the population. Ukrainians are Slavic people, and their language is closely related to Russian and Belorussian. The Ukrainians are proud of their traditional stories, music, and art.

Economy and the Land. The land is almost entirely flat plains. The topography and the extremely fertile soils combine to make Ukraine one of the world's most outstanding agricultural areas. Major crops include grain, potatoes, meat, and milk. The country is also rich in mineral resources, including petroleum, coal, iron ore, and manganese. Industry is well developed in the eastern part of the country, and Ukraine boasts powerful steel and chemical industries. The coast of the Crimean Peninsula on the Black Sea is a famous resort area owing to its warm Mediterranean climate. Unlike many former Soviet republics, Ukraine has a very well developed transportation system.

History and Politics. Ukraine's first inhabitants were agricultural tribesmen who made their homes in the fertile river valleys. Slavic people found their way to the area around the fourth century A.D. In the ninth century, a dynasty centered at Kiev, called the Kievan Rus, was founded by the Scandinavian Varangians. This kingdom is considered the foundation of both the modern Ukrainian and Russian states. Kiev was destroyed during the Tatar-Mongol invasion in 1237. In the late 1300s Ukraine was part of the Lithuanian empire, and was later governed by Poland. The Ukrainians were made serfs under Polish rule, and religious rivalry between the Orthodox Ukrainians and the Roman Catholic Poles exacerbated the situation. Ukrainians who rebelled and fled from serfdom came to be known as Cossacks. The Cossacks established their own colonies and led several revolts against Polish rule and also against the Tatars. Eventually, the Cossacks turned to the Russians for protection and the first treaty was signed in 1654. By the late 1700s the Cossacks began to chafe under czarist rule, but the Russians managed to keep the territory under its control despite numerous revolts. Ukraine declared its independence after the Russian Revolution in 1917, but the new nation was soon invaded by Germany. Bolshevik troops drove the Germans out and the country became a Soviet Socialist Republic in 1922. In the 1930s agricultural land was seized by the government and devastating political purges followed. Most of the farmers were killed, and millions of people died in the ensuing famine. Ukraine was again ravaged during the German invasion of the Soviet Union during World War II. The country prospered in the years after the war, but nationalist sentiments were revived during the upheaval accompanying Gorbachev's rule. The nuclear accident at the Chernobyl nuclear power plant in 1986 contributed to the people's growing desire for greater control over their own territory. A referendum in Ukraine in early December 1991 called for complete independence from the Soviet Union and ultimately prompted the final collapse of the USSR in late 1991. Anger over rampant inflation and general economic chaos resulted in a 1994 presidential election promising reform. Crimea continues to press for independence. ■

UNITED ARAB EMIRATES

Official name United Arab Emirates
PEOPLE
Population 2,855,000. **Density** 88/mi² (34/km²).
Urban 81%. **Capital** Abu Dhabi, 242,975. **Ethnic groups** South Asian 50%, native Emirian 19%, other Arab 23%. **Languages** Arabic, Farsi, English, Hindi, Urdu. **Religions** Sunni Muslim 80%, Shiite Muslim 16%. **Life expectancy** 74 female, 70 male. **Literacy** 68%.

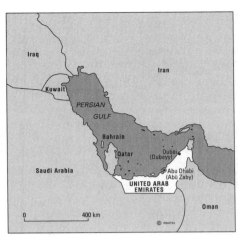

POLITICS
Government Federation of monarchs. **Parties** None. **Suffrage** None. **Memberships** AL, OPEC, UN. **Subdivisions** 7 emirates.
ECONOMY
GDP $63,800,000,000. **Per capita** $24,633.
Monetary unit Dirham. **Trade partners** Exports: Japan, France, U.S. Imports: Japan, U.K., U.S.
Exports Petroleum, natural gas, dried fish, dates.
Imports Food, manufactures, machinery.
LAND
Description Southwestern Asia. **Area** 32,278 mi² (83,600 km²). **Highest point** Mt. Yibir, 6,346 ft (1,934 m). **Lowest point** Sea level.

People. The United Arab Emirates is a predominantly urban federation of seven independent states, each with its own ruling emir. The indigenous population is mostly Arab and Muslim, but only a small percentage of residents are United Arab Emirates citizens. Other groups include foreigners attracted by jobs in industry, especially Asians and Western Europeans. Arabic is the official language, but Farsi and English are widely spoken. The nation's population enjoys one of the highest per capita incomes in the world, as well as free medical and educational facilities.

Economy and the Land. Most of the United Arab Emirates is desert, which explains agriculture's small economic role. However, the federation is rich in oil, and major deposits—primarily in Abu Dhabi—account for nearly all of the Emirian national budget. The United Arab Emirates has tried to diversify its economy through production of natural gas, ammonia, and building materials. To attract tourists, airport expansion and hotel development are also on the rise.

History and Politics. Centuries ago, Arab rulers gained control of the region, formerly called the Trucial Coast, and Islam spread to the area in the A.D. 600s. In 1820 Arabian emirs signed the first of a number of treaties with the United Kingdom. Mutual self-interest led to an 1892 treaty that granted Britain exclusive rights to Trucial territory and government activity in return for military protection. Britain formally withdrew from Trucial affairs in 1971, and six of the Trucial emirates entered into a loose federation called the United Arab Emirates, which included

Abu Dhabi, Dubai, Ash Shāriqah, 'Ajmān, Umm al Qaywayn, and Al Fujayrah. The seventh, Ra's al Khaymah, joined in early 1972. Because each emirate has a great deal of control over its internal affairs and economic development, the growth of federal powers has been slow. Defense spending is on the increase, however, and growing Arab nationalism may lead to a more centralized government. ∎

UNITED KINGDOM

Official name United Kingdom of Great Britain and Northern Ireland
PEOPLE
Population 58,430,000. **Density** 620/mi² (239/km²). **Urban** 89%. **Capital** London, England, 6,574,009. **Ethnic groups** English 82%, Scottish 10%, Irish 2%, Welsh 2%. **Languages** English, Welsh, Scots Gaelic. **Religions** Anglican 47%, Roman Catholic 9%, Presbyterian 3%, Methodist 1%. **Life expectancy** 79 female, 74 male. **Literacy** 99%.
POLITICS
Government Parliamentary monarchy. **Parties** Conservative, Labor, Liberal Democratic, others. **Suffrage** Universal, over 18. **Memberships** CW, EU, NATO, OECD, UN. **Subdivisions** 2 countries, 1 principality, 1 province.
ECONOMY
GDP $980,200,000,000. **Per capita** $16,932. **Monetary unit** Pound sterling. **Trade partners** Exports: U.S., Germany, France. Imports: Germany, U.S., France. **Exports** Manufactures, machinery, fuel, chemicals, transportation equipment. **Imports** Manufactures, machinery, food.
LAND
Description Northwestern European islands. **Area** 94,249 mi² (244,101 km²). **Highest point** Ben Nevis, 4,406 ft (1,343 m). **Lowest point** Holme

Fen, England, -9 ft (-3 m).

People. The ancestry of modern Britons reflects many centuries of invasions and migrations from Scandinavia and the European continent. Today Britons are a mixture of Celtic, Roman, Anglo-Saxon, Norse, and Norman influences. English is the predominant language, although Celtic languages such as Welsh and Scottish Gaelic are also spoken. Anglican is the dominant religion in England, while many Scots practice Presbyterianism. A sizable minority is Roman Catholic. The population is primarily urban and suburban, with a significant percentage living in the southeastern corner of England.

Economy and the Land. A land of limited natural resources, the United Kingdom has relied on trading and, more recently, manufacturing to achieve economic strength. Access to the sea is a traditional economic and political asset. The country maintains a large merchant fleet, which at one time dominated world trade. The industrial revolution developed quickly in Great Britain, and the country continues to be a leading producer of transportation equipment, metal products, and other manufactured goods. Although climate and limited acreage have hindered agricultural development, intensive, mechanized farming methods have allowed the nation to produce half of its food supply. Livestock raising is especially important. Additional contributors to the country's industry are extensive deposits of coal and iron, which make mining important. London is well known as an international financial center. The United Kingdom includes Scotland, England, Wales, Northern Ireland, and several offshore islands. The varied terrain is marked by several mountain ranges, moors, rolling hills, and plains. The climate is tempered by the sea and is subject to frequent changes. Great Britain administers many overseas possessions.

History and Politics. Little is known of the earliest inhabitants of Britain, but evidence such as Stonehenge indicates the existence of a developed culture before the Roman invasion in the 50s B.C. Britain began to trade with the rest of Europe while under Roman rule. The Norman period after A.D. 1066 fostered the establishment of many cultural and political traditions that continue to be reflected in British life. Scotland came under the British Crown in 1603, and in 1707 England and Scotland agreed to unite as Great Britain. Ireland had been conquered by the early seventeenth century, and the 1801 British Act of Union established the United Kingdom of Great Britain and Ireland. Although colonial and economic expansion had taken Great Britain to the Far East, America, Africa, and India, the nation's influence began to diminish at the end of the nineteenth century as the industrial revolution strengthened other nations. World War I significantly weakened the United Kingdom and during the period following World War II, which saw the demise of an empire, many colonies gained independence. The Conservative party has governed the country since 1979. The issue of peace for Northern Ireland continues to dominate the country's political scene. ∎

Places and Possessions of the UNITED KINGDOM

Entity	Status	Area	Population	Capital/Population
Anguilla (Caribbean island)	Dependent territory	35 mi^2 (91 km^2)	7,000	The Valley, 1,042
Ascension (South Atlantic island)	Dependency of St. Helena	34 mi^2 (88 km^2)	1,000	Georgetown
Bermuda (North Atlantic islands; east of North Carolina)	Dependent territory	21 mi^2 (54 km^2)	61,000	Hamilton, 1,100
British Indian Ocean Territory (Indian Ocean islands)	Dependent territory	23 mi^2 (60 km^2)	None	None
Cayman Islands (Caribbean)	Dependent territory	100 mi^2 (259 km^2)	32,000	George Town, 12,921
Channel Islands (Northwestern European)	Dependent territory	75 mi^2 (194 km^2)	150,000	None
Falkland Islands (South Atlantic; east of Argentina)	Dependent territory	4,700 mi^2 (12,173 km^2)	2,100	Stanley, 1,557
Gibraltar (Southwestern Europe; peninsula on Spain's southern coast)	Dependent territory	2.3 mi^2 (6.0 km^2)	32,000	Gibraltar, 32,000
Guernsey (Northwestern European islands)	Crown dependency	30 mi^2 (78 km^2)	64,000	St. Peter Port, 16,648
Hong Kong (Eastern Asia; islands and mainland area on China's southeastern coast)	Chinese territory under British administration	414 mi^2 (1,072 km^2)	5,927,000	Hong Kong (Victoria) 1,250,993
Isle of Man (Northwestern European island)	Crown dependency	221 mi^2 (572 km^2)	72,000	Douglas, 22,214
Jersey (Northwestern European island)	Crown dependency	45 mi^2 (116 km^2)	86,000	St. Helier, 28,123
Montserrat (Caribbean island)	Dependent territory	39 mi^2 (102 km^2)	13,000	Plymouth, 1,568
Orkney Islands (North Atlantic)	Part of Scotland	377 mi^2 (976 km^2)	20,000	Kirkwall, 5,713
Pitcairn (South Pacific islands)	Dependent territory	19 mi^2 (49 km^2)	100	Adamstown, 100
Shetland Islands (North Atlantic)	Part of Scotland	553 mi^2 (1,433 km^2)	23,000	Lerwick, 6,333
South Georgia and the South Sandwich Islands (South Atlantic)	Dependent territory	1,450 mi^2 (3,755 km^2)	None	None
St. Helena (South Atlantic islands)	Dependent territory	121 mi^2 (314 km^2)	7,000	Jamestown, 1,413
Tristan da Cunha (South Atlantic islands)	Dependency of St. Helena	40 mi^2 (104 km^2)	300	Edinburgh
Turks and Caicos Islands (Caribbean)	Dependent territory	193 mi^2 (500 km^2)	14,000	Grand Turk, 3,691
Virgin Islands, British (Caribbean islands)	Dependent territory	59 mi^2 (153 km^2)	13,000	Road Town, 2,479

UNITED STATES

Official name United States of America
PEOPLE
Population 262,530,000. **Density** 69/mi^2 (27/km^2). **Urban** 75%. **Capital** Washington, D.C., 606,900. **Ethnic groups** White 84%, black 12%, Asian 3%. **Languages** English, Spanish. **Religions** Baptist and other Protestant 56%, Roman Catholic 28%, Jewish 2%. **Life expectancy** 79 female, 73 male. **Literacy** 98%.
POLITICS
Government Republic. **Parties** Democratic, Republican. **Suffrage** Universal, over 18. **Memberships** NATO, OECD, OAS, UN.

Subdivisions 50 states, 1 district.
ECONOMY
GDP $6,379,000,000,000. **Per capita** $24,877.
Monetary unit Dollar. **Trade partners** Exports: Canada, Japan, Mexico. Imports: Canada, Japan, Mexico. **Exports** Machinery, automobiles, raw materials, manufactures, agricultural products. **Imports** Petroleum, machinery, automobiles, manufactures, raw materials, food.
LAND
Description Central North America. **Area** 3,787,425 mi^2 (9,809,431 km^2). **Highest point** Mt. McKinley, 20,320 ft (6,194 m). **Lowest point** Death Valley, California, -282 ft (-86 m).

People. The diverse population of the United States is mostly composed of whites, many descended from eighteenth-and nineteenth-century immigrants; blacks, mainly descended from African slaves; peoples of Spanish and Asian origin; and indigenous Indians, Inuit, and Hawaiians. Religions encompass the world's major faiths, but Christianity predominates. English is the predominant language, though Spanish is spoken by many, and other languages are often found in ethnic enclaves.

Economy and the Land. The United States is an international economic power, and all sectors of the economy are highly developed. Fertile soils produce high crop yields, with considerable land under cultivation. Mineral output includes petroleum and natural gas, coal, copper, lead, and zinc; but high consumption makes the United States dependent on foreign oil. The country is a leading manufacturer, with a well-developed service sector. Mountains, prairies,

woodlands, and deserts mark its vast terrain. The climate varies regionally, from mild year-round along the Pacific coast and in the South to temperate in the Northeast and Midwest. In addition to forty-eight contiguous states, the country includes the subarctic state of Alaska and the tropical state of Hawaii, an island group in the Pacific.

History and Politics. Thousands of years ago, Asiatic peoples, ancestors of American Indians, crossed the Bering Strait land bridge and spread across North and South America. Vikings reached North America around A.D. 1000, and Christopher Columbus arrived in 1492. Following early explorations by Portugal and Spain, England established a colony at Jamestown, Virginia, in 1607. Thirteen British colonies waged a successful war of independence against England from 1775 to 1783. United States expansion continued westward throughout the nineteenth century. The issues of black slavery and states' rights led to the American Civil War from 1861 to 1865, a struggle that pitted the South against the North and resulted in the end of slavery. Opportunities for prosperity accompanied the industrial revolution in the late nineteenth century and led to a large influx of immigrants. From 1917 to 1918 the country joined with the Allies in World War I. A severe economic depression began in 1929, and the United States did not really recover until World War II stimulated industry and the economy in general. In 1945 the use of the atomic bomb on Japan ended the war and changed the course of history. The Civil Rights Act of 1964 and the Vietnam War, 1961–75, ushered in an era of great social progress and turmoil in the United States. Technological advances were unparalleled with man's entry into space and the first landing on the moon in 1969. The 1980s saw increasing concern with a deteriorating environment and the nuclear arms race. Unemployment, a sluggish economy, a trade deficit, crime, and health care reform were the greatest concerns of Americans in the early 1990s. ∎

Places and Possessions of the UNITED STATES

Entity	Status	Area	Population	Capital/Population
American Samoa (South Pacific islands)	Unincorporated territory	77 mi^2 (199 km^2)	56,000	Pago Pago, 3,518
Guam (North Pacific island)	Unincorporated territory	209 mi^2 (541 km^2)	152,000	Agana, 1,139
Johnston Atoll (North Pacific island)	Unincorporated territory	0.5 mi^2 (1.3 km^2)	1,300	None
Midway Islands (North Pacific)	Unincorporated territory	2.0 mi^2 (5.2 km^2)	500	None
Navassa Island (Caribbean Sea)	Unincorporated territory	1.9 mi^2 (4.9 km^2)	None	None
Northern Mariana Islands (North Pacific)	Commonwealth	184 mi^2 (477 km^2)	51,000	Saipan (island)
Palau (Belau) (North Pacific islands)	Republic in free association with the U.S.	196 mi^2 (508 km^2)	17,000	Koror (de facto) and Melekeok (future), 9,018
Puerto Rico (Caribbean island)	Commonwealth	3,515 mi^2 (9,104 km^2)	3,625,000	San Juan, 426,832
Virgin Islands of the United States (Caribbean Sea)	Unincorporated territory	133 mi^2 (344 km^2)	97,000	Charlotte Amalie, 12,331
Wake Island (North Pacific)	Unincorporated territory	3.0 mi^2 (7.8 km^2)	300	None

URUGUAY

Official name Oriental Republic of Uruguay

PEOPLE
Population 3,317,000.
Density 48/mi^2
(19/km^2). **Urban** 89%.
Capital Montevideo,
1,251,647. **Ethnic
groups** White 88%,
mestizo 8%, black 4%.
Languages Spanish.
Religions Roman
Catholic 66%,
Protestant 2%, Jewish
2%. **Life expectancy**
76 female, 69 male.
Literacy 96%.
POLITICS
Government Republic.
Parties Broad Front,
Colorado, National
(Blanco). **Suffrage**
Universal, over 18.

Memberships OAS, UN. **Subdivisions** 19 departments.
ECONOMY
GDP $19,000,000,000. **Per capita** $6,030.
Monetary unit Peso. **Trade partners** Exports:
Brazil, U.S., Germany. Imports: Brazil, Argentina,
U.S. **Exports** Hides and leather goods, beef, wool,
fish, rice. **Imports** Fuel, metals, machinery, transportation equipment, chemicals.
LAND
Description Eastern South America. **Area** 68,500
mi^2 (177,414 km^2). **Highest point** Cerro Catedral,
1,686 ft (514 m). **Lowest point** Sea level.

People. Most Uruguayans are white descendants of
nineteenth- and twentieth-century immigrants from
Spain, Italy, and other European countries. Mestizos,
of Spanish-Indian ancestry, and blacks round out the
population. Spanish is the dominant language, and
Roman Catholicism is the major religion, with small
Protestant and Jewish minorities. About one-third of
all Uruguayans claim to follow no religion.

Economy and the Land. Uruguay's fertile soil,
grassy plains, and temperate climate provide the basis
for agriculture and are especially conducive to livestock raising. The country has virtually no mineral
resources, and petroleum exploration has been
unrewarding. However, refinement of imported fuel
is a major industry, and Uruguay has significant
hydroelectric potential.

History and Politics. Uruguay's original inhabitants
were Indians. In the 1680s the Portuguese established
the first European settlement, followed by a Spanish
settlement in the 1720s. By the 1770s Spain had gained
control of the area, but in the 1820s Portugal once
again came to power, annexing present-day Uruguay
to Brazil. When nationalistic feelings in the early
nineteenth century led to an 1828 war by Uruguayan
patriots and Argentina against Brazil, the country
achieved independence. Political unrest, caused in
part by economic depression, resurfaced in the
1970s, leading to military intervention in the government
and the jailing of thousands of political prisoners. The
country restored its civilian government in 1985.
The first democratic elections in twenty years were
won by the centrist Colorado party which is expected to introduce economic reforms. ∎

UZBEKISTAN

Official name Republic of Uzbekistan
PEOPLE
Population 22,860,000. **Density** 132/mi^2
(51/km^2). **Urban** 41%. **Capital** Tashkent,
2,113,300. **Ethnic groups** Uzbek 71%, Russian
8%, Tajik 5%, Kazakh 4%. **Languages** Uzbek,
Russian. **Religions** Muslim 88%, Eastern
Orthodox 9%. **Life expectancy** 72 female, 65
male. **Literacy** 97%.
POLITICS
Government Republic. **Parties** ERK, People's
Democratic. **Suffrage** Universal, over 18.
Memberships CIS, NATO, UN. **Subdivisions** 1
republic, 11 oblasts.
ECONOMY
GDP $53,700,000,000. **Per capita** $2,454.
Monetary unit Som. **Trade partners** Russia,
Ukraine, eastern European countries. **Exports**
Cotton, gold, textiles, fertilizers, vegetable oil.
Imports Machinery, manufactures, grain and other
food.
LAND
Description Central Asia, landlocked. **Area**
172,742 mi^2 (447,400 km^2). **Highest point**
Unnamed, 15,233 ft (4,643 m). **Lowest point**
Mynbulak Basin, -39 ft (-12 m).

People. The third most populous of the former
Soviet republics, Uzbekistan is a land of many ethnic groups. Ethnic Uzbeks account for more than 70
percent of the population. Other ethnic groups
include Russians, Tajiks, Kazakhs, and Tatars. The
Uzbeks speak a Turkish dialect and adhere to Islam.

Economy and the Land. Irrigation allows for the production of cotton, and Uzbekistan is one of the world's largest producers although they hope to diversify their economy and end their dependence on cotton. Fruit and silk are produced in the mountain valleys. Gold, uranium, natural gas, and other minerals are mined in abundance. Western Uzbekistan is a flat desert that rises to mountains in the eastern part of the country. Most of the population and economic activity is based in valleys that cross eastern Uzbekistan. Uzbekistan exports electricity to other former Soviet central Asian republics, and it is the region's largest machinery producer.

History and Politics. Uzbekistan was inhabited as far back as the Stone Age. The area was much later conquered by the Turks, the armies of Alexander the Great, the Arabs, and the Mongols. Uzbekistan was under the rule of the Mongol-Turk Tamerlane dynasty from the thirteenth to the sixteenth centuries. Various sovereign khanates ruled the land until Russia annexed Uzbekistan in 1885 as part of the region then known as Turkestan. After the Russian revolution, Uzbekistan attempted to establish a western-style democracy, but the Soviets took over in 1924, and it was admitted to the Soviet Union the following year. Uzbekistan gained independence in 1991, following the dissolution of the Soviet Union. At first Uzbeks struggled to establish a new economy and form of government, but rising Islamic fundamentalism in neighboring Tajikistan has prompted a return to conservative government policies and a moratorium on reform. A new constitution, adopted December 1992, promised freedom and multiparty democracy. However, on the same day several opposition politicians were arrested. Elections in 1994 proved that power is still firmly in the hands of ex-communists and a centralized economic system. Economic reform has been moderately effective. ∎

VANUATU

Official name Republic of Vanuatu
PEOPLE
Population 161,000. **Density** 34/mi^2 (13/km^2).
Urban 19%. **Capital** Port-Vila, Efate I., 18,905.
Ethnic groups Ni-Vanuatu (Melanesian) 92%, European 2%, other Pacific Islander 2%.
Languages Bislama, English, French. **Religions** Presbyterian 37%, Anglican 15%, Roman Catholic 15%, other Protestant. **Life expectancy** 61 female, 57 male. **Literacy** 53%.
POLITICS
Government Republic. **Parties** National (Vanua'aku Pati), Union of Moderate Parties, others. **Suffrage** Universal, over 18. **Memberships** CW, UN. **Subdivisions** 11 island councils.
ECONOMY
GDP $142,000,000. **Per capita** $979. **Monetary unit** Vatu. **Trade partners** Exports: Netherlands, Japan, France. Imports: Australia, New Zealand, Japan. **Exports** Copra, cocoa, meat, fish, timber. **Imports** Transportation equipment, food, manufactures, raw materials, chemicals.

LAND
Description South Pacific islands. **Area** 4,707 mi^2 (12,190 km^2). **Highest point** Mont Tabwémasana, 6,165 ft (1,879 m). **Lowest point** Sea level.

People. The majority of Vanuatuans are Melanesian. Europeans and Polynesians compose minorities. Languages include English and French, the languages of former rulers; and Bislama, a mixture of English and Melanesian. Most Vanuatuans are Christian, although indigenous religions are also practiced.

Economy and the Land. The economy is based on agriculture, and copra is the primary export crop. Fishing is also important, as is the growing tourist business. Narrow coastal plains, mountainous interiors, and a mostly hot, rainy climate characterize the more than eighty islands of Vanuatu.

History and Politics. In 1606 Portuguese explorers encountered indigenous Melanesian inhabitants on islands that now compose Vanuatu. Captain James Cook of Britain charted the islands in 1774 and named them the New Hebrides after the Hebrides islands of Scotland. British and French merchants and missionaries began to settle the islands in the early 1800s. To resolve conflicting interests, Great Britain and France formed a joint naval commission to oversee the area in 1887 and a condominium government in 1906. Demands for autonomy began in the 1960s, and the New Hebrides became the independent Republic of Vanuatu in 1980. The first national election since independence was held in 1991. ∎

VATICAN CITY

Official name State of the Vatican City
PEOPLE
Population 1,000. **Density** 5,000/mi^2 (2,500/km^2).
Urban 100%. **Capital** Vatican City, 1,000. **Ethnic groups** Italian, Swiss, other. **Languages** Italian, Latin, other. **Religions** Roman Catholic. **Literacy** 100%.
POLITICS
Government Monarchical-sacerdotal state.
Parties None. **Suffrage** Roman Catholic cardinals less than 80 years old. **Memberships** None.
Subdivisions None.
ECONOMY
Monetary Unit Lira.
LAND
Description Southern Europe, landlocked (within the city of Rome, Italy). **Area** 0.2 mi^2 (0.4 km^2).
Highest point Unnamed, 249 ft (76 m). **Lowest point** Unnamed, 62 ft (19 m).

People. The Vatican City, the smallest independent state in the world, is the administrative and spiritual center of the Roman Catholic church and home to the pope, the church's head. The population is composed of administrative and diplomatic workers of more than a dozen nationalities; Italians and Swiss predominate. A military corps known as the Swiss Guard also resides here. Roman Catholicism is the only religion. The official language is Italian, although acts of the Holy See are drawn up in Latin.

Economy and the Land. The Vatican City does not engage in commerce per se; however, it does issue its own coins and postage stamps. In addition, it is the destination of thousands of tourists and pilgrims each year. Lying on a hill west of the Tiber River, the Vatican City is an urban enclave in northwestern Rome, Italy. The Vatican City enjoys a mild climate moderated by the Mediterranean Sea.

History and Politics. For centuries the popes of the Roman Catholic church ruled the Papal States, an area across central Italy which included Rome. The popes' temporal authority gradually was reduced to the city of Rome, which itself was eventually annexed by the Kingdom of Italy in 1870. Denying these rulings, the pope declared himself a prisoner in the Vatican, a status that lasted fifty-nine years. The Vatican City has been an independent sovereign state since 1929, when Italy signed the Treaty of the Lateran in return for papal dissolution of the Papal States. The pope heads all branches of government, though day-to-day responsibilities are delegated to staff members. ∎

VENEZUELA

Official name Republic of Venezuela
PEOPLE
Population 21,395,000. **Density** 61/mi² (23/km²).
Urban 91%. **Capital** Caracas, 1,822,465. **Ethnic groups** Mestizo 67%, white 21%, black 10%, Indian 2%. **Languages** Spanish, Amerindian.
Religions Roman Catholic 96%, Protestant 2%.
Life expectancy 74 female, 67 male. **Literacy** 88%.
POLITICS
Government Republic. **Parties** Democratic Action, Movement Toward Socialism, Social Christian, others. **Suffrage** Universal, over 18.
Memberships OAS, OPEC, UN. **Subdivisions** 20 states, 2 territories, 1 dependency, 1 district.
ECONOMY
GDP $161,000,000,000. **Per capita** 8,436.

Monetary unit Bolivar. **Trade partners** Exports: U.S., Japan, Colombia, Netherlands. Imports: U.S., Germany, Italy. **Exports** Petroleum, bauxite and aluminum, iron ore, agricultural products. **Imports** Food, chemicals, manufactures, machinery and transportation equipment.
LAND
Description Northern South America. **Area** 352,145 mi² (912,050 km²). **Highest point** Pico Bolívar, 16,427 ft (5,007 m). **Lowest point** Sea level.

People. Spanish colonial rule of Venezuela is reflected in its predominantly mestizo population, people of Spanish-Indian blood, and its official language of Spanish. Minorities include Europeans, blacks, and Indians, who generally speak local languages. Nearly all Venezuelans are Roman Catholic, further evidence of former Spanish domination. Protestants and lesser numbers of Jews and Muslims compose small minorities, and traditional religious practices continue among some Indians.

Economy and the Land. Since the expansion of the petroleum industry in the 1920s, Venezuela has experienced rapid economic growth, but unevenly distributed wealth, a high birthrate, and fluctuations in the price of oil have hampered the economy. Partly because of the emphasis on oil production, agriculture has declined; its contribution to the gross national product is minimal, and Venezuela must import much of its food. Manufacturing and hydroelectric power are being developed. The varied Venezuelan landscape is dominated by the Andes Mountains, a coastal zone, high plateaus, and plains, or llanos. The climate is tropical, but temperatures vary with altitude. Most of the country experiences rainy and dry seasons.

History and Politics. The original inhabitants of modern Venezuela included Arawak and Carib Indians. In 1498 Christopher Columbus was the first European to visit Venezuela. The area became a colony of Spain and was briefly under German rule. Independence was achieved in 1821 under the guidance of Simón Bolívar, Venezuela's national hero. Venezuela became a sovereign state in 1830. The nineteenth century saw political instability and revolutionary fervor, followed by a succession of dictators in the twentieth century. Since 1958, Venezuela has tried to achieve a representative form of government and has held a number of democratic elections. The fall in oil prices, for a country heavily dependent upon oil export, has been an economic hardship in recent years. Abortive coups and presidential corruption have underscored Venezuela's continuing political instability. ∎

VIETNAM

Official name Socialist Republic of Vietnam
PEOPLE
Population 73,760,000. **Density** 579/mi² (223/km²). **Urban** 20%. **Capital** Hanoi, 905,939.
Ethnic groups Kinh 87%, Hao 2%, Tay 2%.
Languages Vietnamese, French, Chinese, English, Khmer, indigenous. **Religions** Buddhist,

Taoist, Roman Catholic, indigenous, Islamic. **Life expectancy** 66 female, 62 male. **Literacy** 88%.
POLITICS
Government Socialist republic. **Parties** Communist. **Suffrage** Universal, over 18.
Memberships UN. **Subdivisions** 50 provinces, 3 municipalities.
ECONOMY
GNP $72,000,000,000. **Per capita** $1,034.
Monetary unit Dong. **Trade partners** Japan, Singapore, Thailand, eastern European countries.
Exports Agricultural products, handicrafts, coal, minerals. **Imports** Petroleum, steel, railroad equipment, chemicals, pharmaceuticals, cotton.
LAND
Description Southeastern Asia. **Area** 127,428 mi² (330,036 km²). **Highest point** Phan Si Pang, 10,312 ft (3,143 m). **Lowest point** Sea level.

People. Despite centuries of foreign invasion and domination, the people of Vietnam remain remarkably homogeneous; ethnic Vietnamese compose the majority of the population. Chinese influence is seen in the major religions of Buddhism and Taoism. Most people live along two rivers, the Red in the north and the Mekong in the south, separated by mountains. The official language is Vietnamese, but a history of foreign intervention is reflected in wide use of French, English, Chinese, and Russian.

Economy and the Land. The Vietnamese economy has struggled to overcome the effects of war and the difficulties inherent in unifying the once-divided country. Agriculture, centered in the fertile southern plains, continues to employ nearly 70 percent of the people. Vietnam intends to expand its war-damaged mining industry, which has been slowed by lack of skilled personnel and a poor transportation network. Vietnam's economic picture is not likely to improve until the country can resolve its political and social problems. The landscape of Vietnam ranges from mountains to plains, and the climate is tropical.

History and Politics. The first Vietnamese lived in what is now northern Vietnam. After centuries of Chinese rule, Vietnam finally became independent in the 1400s, but civil strife continued for nearly two centuries. French missionary activity began in the early

seventeenth century, and by 1883 all of present-day Vietnam, Cambodia, and Laos were under French rule. When Germany occupied France during World War II, control of French Indochina passed to the Japanese until their defeat in 1945. The French presence continued until 1954, when Vietnamese Communists led by Ho Chi Minh gained control of North Vietnam. United States aid to South Vietnam began in 1961 and ended, after years of conflict, with a cease-fire in 1973. Communist victory and unification of the country as the Socialist Republic of Vietnam was achieved in 1975. Vietnamese military policy resulted in fighting with China and the occupation of Cambodia until 1989. A U.S. economic embargo was lifted in 1994, and the economic picture is likely to improve as the country attracts foreign investors. ∎

VIRGIN ISLANDS, BRITISH
See UNITED KINGDOM.

VIRGIN ISLANDS, UNITED STATES See UNITED STATES.

WAKE ISLAND See UNITED STATES.

WALLIS AND FUTUNA
See FRANCE.

WESTERN SAHARA

Official name Western Sahara
PEOPLE
Population 215,000. **Density** 2.1/mi² (0.8/km²).
Urban 57%. **Capital** El Aaiún, 93,875. **Ethnic groups** Arab, Berber. **Languages** Arabic.
Religions Muslim. **Life expectancy** 46 female, 44 male.
POLITICS
Government Occupied by Morocco.
Memberships None. **Subdivisions** None.
ECONOMY
GNP $60,000,000. **Per capita** $300. **Monetary unit** Moroccan dirham. **Trade partners** Morocco.
Exports Phosphates. **Imports** Fuel, food.
LAND
Description Northwestern Africa. **Area** 102,703 mi² (266,000 km²). **Highest point** Unnamed, 2,640 ft (805 m). **Lowest point** Sea level.

People. Most Western Saharans are nomadic Arabs or Berbers. Because these nomads often across national borders in their wanderings, the population of Western Sahara is in a constant state of flux. Islam is the principal religion, and Arabic is the dominant language.

Economy and the Land. Most of Western Sahara is desert, with a rocky, barren soil that severely limits agriculture. Mining of phosphate deposits began in 1972, and phosphates are now the primary export. Western Sahara is almost completely arid; rainfall is negligible, except along the coast.

History and Politics. By the fourth century B.C. Phoenicians and Romans had visited the area. Spain explored the region in the sixteenth century and gained control of the region in 1860, but Spanish Sahara was not designated a province of Spain until 1958. When Spanish control ceased in 1976, the area became known as Western Sahara. Mauritania and Morocco subsequently divided the territory, and Morocco gained control of valuable phosphate deposits. Fighting soon broke out between an independence movement, the Polisario Front, and troops from Morocco and Mauritania. In 1979 Mauritania gave up its claim to the area and withdrew. After years of conflict, Morocco and the Polisario Front agreed in 1988 to a cease-fire and a referendum to offer Western Saharans a choice between independence and integration with Morocco. The U.N.'s attempts to organize a referendum have been consistently frustrated. ∎

WESTERN SAMOA

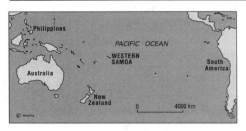

Official name Independent State of Western Samoa
PEOPLE
Population 172,000. **Density** 157/mi² (61/km²). **Urban** 22%. **Capital** Apia, Upolu I., 34,126. **Ethnic groups** Samoan (Polynesian) 93%, mixed European and Polynesian 7%. **Languages** English, Samoan. **Religions** Congregational 50%, Roman Catholic 22%, Methodist 16%, Mormon 8%. **Life expectancy** 70 female, 65 male. **Literacy** 97%.
POLITICS
Government Constitutional monarchy. **Parties** Human Rights Protection, National Development. **Suffrage** Universal, over 21. **Memberships** CW, UN. **Subdivisions** 11 districts.
ECONOMY
GDP $115,000,000. **Per capita** $639. **Monetary unit** Tala. **Trade partners** Exports: New Zealand, Australia. Imports: New Zealand, Australia, Japan. **Exports** Coconut oil, taro, copra, cocoa. **Imports**

Manufactures, food, petroleum, machinery.
LAND
Description South Pacific islands. **Area** 1,093 mi² (2,831 km²). **Highest point** Mt. Silisili, 6,096 ft (1,858 m). **Lowest point** Sea level.

People. Most Western Samoans are of Polynesian descent, and a significant minority are of mixed Samoan and European heritage. Most of the population is Christian and practices a variety of faiths introduced by European missionaries and traders. Samoan and English are the principal languages.

Economy and the Land. The tropical climate of Western Samoa, which is composed of volcanic islands, is suited for agriculture—the country's chief economic support. Bananas, coconuts, and tropical fruits are the most important crops.

History and Politics. Polynesians settled the Samoan islands more than two thousand years ago. Dutch explorers visited the islands in the early 1700s, and English missionaries arrived in 1830. Rivalry between the islands' royal families increased, along with competition among the United Kingdom, the United States, and Germany. In 1900 the United States annexed Eastern Samoa, and Germany obtained Western Samoa. By the end of World War I, New Zealand had gained control of Western Samoa. Growing demand for independence led to United Nations intervention and gradual steps toward self-government. The islands became fully independent in 1962. The nation maintains friendly relations with New Zealand and neighboring Pacific islands. ∎

YEMEN

Official name Republic of Yemen
PEOPLE
Population 12,910,000. **Density** 63/mi² (24/km²). **Urban** 29%. **Capital** Sana, 427,150. **Ethnic groups** Arab, Afro-Arab, south Asians. **Languages** Arabic. **Religions** Muslim, Jewish, Christian, Hindu. **Life expectancy** 53 female, 52 male. **Literacy** 38%.

POLITICS

Government Republic. **Parties** Alliance for Reform, General People's, Socialist. **Suffrage** Universal, over 18. **Memberships** AL, UN. **Subdivisions** 17 governorates.

ECONOMY

GDP $9,000,000,000. **Per capita** $737. **Monetary unit** Rial. **Trade partners** Exports: Italy, Saudi Arabia. Imports: Japan, Saudi Arabia, U.K. **Exports** Oil, cotton, coffee, hides, vegetables, fish. **Imports** Textiles, consumer goods, oil, sugar, grain, flour, food, cement, machinery.

LAND

Description Southwestern Asia. **Area** 203,850 mi^2 (527,968 km^2). **Highest point** Mt. Nabi Shuayb, 12,008 ft (3,660 m). **Lowest point** Sea level.

People. Most inhabitants of Yemen are Arab, with small minorities of Indians, Pakistanis, and East Africans. Islam is the predominant religion, while Arabic is the language of Yemen. The population includes both Sunni and Shiite Muslims. Small numbers of Christians, Hindus, and Jews also exist. Most of the population lives in the western part of the country.

Economy and the Land. Much of northwestern Yemen has a terrain suited for agriculture, the backbone of the nation's economy. However, ineffective agricultural techniques combined with regional instability often hinder production. Industrial activity is growing slowly, with production based on domestic resources, but exploitation of oil, iron ore, and salt deposits is financially prohibitive at this time. Subsistence farming and nomadic herding characterize the drier, eastern part of the country. Yemen varies from arid lowlands to fertile, well-cultivated highlands. The climate is temperate in the highlands and hot and dry in the lowlands.

History and Politics. Between 1200 B.C. and 525 A.D., trade empires occupied the area of present-day Yemen, and it was part of the Kingdom of Sheba in the 900s B.C. Christian and Jewish societies thrived before the seventh century, when Islam was introduced. The region's flourishing economy made it a focal point in the development of Islam. The country was divided since the early sixteenth century, when the Ottoman Empire conquered northwestern Yemen. The Turks stayed in power until 1918, when the Turkish military withdrew and gave control to the Zaidis, who established a monarchy. The Imam Badr was overthrown in 1962, when the Yemeni army proclaimed creation of the Yemen Arab Republic. Meanwhile, Aden and the southeastern part of the country were under British domination since 1839, and became a protectorate in the 1930s. By the mid-1960s, Aden had become the focus of Arab nationalists, and in 1967 Britain granted independence to the People's Republic of South Yemen. After a coup by a Marxist faction in 1970, the country's name changed to the People's Democratic Republic of Yemen. Border clashes between the two Yemens were frequent during the 1970s but relations improved throughout the 1980s, and the two countries merged to form the Republic of Yemen in 1990. Four years later civil war broke out, fueled by dual military forces. It was won by the North and unity was restored. ∎

YUGOSLAVIA

Official name Socialist Federal Republic of Yugoslavia

PEOPLE

Population 10,765,000. **Density** 273/mi^2 (105/km^2). **Capital** Belgrade, 1,136,786. **Ethnic groups** Serb 63%, Albanian 14%, Montenegrin 6%, Hungarian 4%. **Languages** Serbo-Croatian 95%, Albanian 5%. **Religions** Orthodox 65%, Muslim 19%, Roman Catholic 4%. **Life expectancy** 75 female, 69 male. **Literacy** 89%.

POLITICS

Government Republic. **Parties** Former Communist, Serbian Radical, Serbian Renewal. **Suffrage** Universal, over 18; over 16 if employed. **Memberships** None. **Subdivisions** 2 republics (2 autonomous provinces).

ECONOMY

GDP $10,000,000,000. **Per capita** $937. **Monetary unit** Dinar. **Trade partners** Exports: Former Yugoslav republics, former Soviet republics. **Exports** Machinery and transportation equipment, manufactures, chemicals, food. **Imports** Machinery, fuels and lubricants, manufactures, chemicals, food.

LAND

Description Eastern Europe. **Area** 39,449 mi^2 (102,173 km^2). **Highest point** Daravica, 8,714 ft (2,656 m). **Lowest point** Sea level.

People. The population of Yugoslavia is mainly Serbs, although there are important Montenegrin, Albanian, and Hungarian minorities. Relations between the Orthodox Serbs and the Muslim Albanians are particularly tense in Kosovo province, where the Albanians form the majority.

Economy and the Land. Before the breakup of Yugoslavia in 1991, most industry was located in the republics of Croatia and Slovenia. As a result, the new Yugoslavia is struggling to improve its industrial base and move away from an agricultural economy. Economic conditions, which improved rapidly after World War II, are now poor as a result of political instability and failed economic restructuring. The nation has many mineral resources, including coal. Much of the land is hilly or mountainous, although there are broad, fertile river valleys.

History and Politics. The area now known as Yugoslavia was originally inhabited by the Thracians and the Illyrians, who were eventually conquered by the Roman Empire. These people were in turn overtaken by Slavs who migrated to the area from Poland and Russia in the seventh century. Orthodox Christianity came to the area in the tenth century. In the thirteenth century, Serbia was established as an independent kingdom, and it was then that it gained control over Montenegro. The Ottoman Turks conquered the region in the mid-1300s, and Turkey held the area for almost five hundred years. The nation gained its independence in 1878, but was politically and economically dominated by Austria. Calls for Slavic unity began in the early 1800s. In 1914, a Slavic patriot assassinated Archduke Ferdinand of Austria-Hungary and triggered World War I. The Kingdom of Serbs, Croats, and Slovenes was formed in 1918. Fighting among the various groups encouraged King Alexander I to declare himself dictator in 1929 and change the country's name to Yugoslavia, which was retained after Alexander's assassination in 1934. Germany and the other Axis powers invaded Yugoslavia during World War II. After the war, Josip Broz Tito assumed leadership, and Yugoslavia became a Communist republic. Tito's policy of nonalignment caused the Soviet Union to break off diplomatic relations from 1948 to 1955. After Tito's death in 1980, the country was governed by a presidency rotating amongst the republics. In June 1991, the federation began to break apart as Croatia and Slovenia declared their independence, followed by Macedonia and then Bosnia and Herzegovina, leaving Serbia and Montenegro as the remaining Yugoslav republics. Continuing aggression against its neighboring former republics has led to international economic sanctions and an economy in a shambles. By 1994 sanctions were eased as Yugoslavia vowed to end support to Bosnian Serbs. However, the summer of 1995 saw renewed hostilities that left the U.N. and NATO questioning their future roles as peace-keepers. ∎

ZAIRE

Official name Republic of Zaire
PEOPLE
Population 43,365,000. **Density** 48/mi^2 (18/km^2).
Urban 28%. **Capital** Kinshasa, 3,000,000. **Ethnic groups** Kongo, Luba, Mongo, Mangbetu-Azande, others. **Languages** French, Kikongo, Lingala, Swahili, Tshiluba, Kingwana. **Religions** Roman Catholic 50%, Protestant 20%, Kimbanguist 10%, Muslim 10%. **Life expectancy** 53 female, 50 male. **Literacy** 72%.
POLITICS
Government Republic. **Parties** Popular Movement of the Revolution, others. **Suffrage** Universal, over 18. **Memberships** OAS, UN. **Subdivisions** 10 regions, 1 independent town.

ECONOMY
GDP $21,000,000,000. **Per capita** $528.
Monetary unit Zaire. **Trade partners** Exports: U.S., Belgium, Germany. Imports: Belgium, Brazil, France. **Exports** Copper, coffee, diamonds, cobalt, petroleum. **Imports** Manufactures, food, machinery, transportation equipment, fuel.
LAND
Description Central Africa. **Area** 905,355 mi^2 (2,344,858 km^2). **Highest point** Margherita Pk., 16,763 ft (5,109 m). **Lowest point** Sea level.

People. The diverse population of Zaire is composed of over two hundred African ethnic groups, with Bantu peoples in the majority. Belgian settlers introduced French, but hundreds of indigenous languages are more widely spoken. Much of the population is Christian, another result of former European rule. Many non-Christians practice traditional or syncretic faiths such as Kimbanguism. The majority of Zairians are rural farmers.

Economy and the Land. Zaire is rich in mineral resources, particularly copper, cobalt, diamonds, and petroleum; mining has supplanted agriculture in economic importance and now dominates the economy. Agriculture continues to employ most Zairians, however, and subsistence farming is practiced in nearly every region. Industrial activity—especially petroleum refining and hydroelectric production—is growing. Zaire's terrain is composed of mountains and plateaus. The climate is equatorial, with hot and humid weather in the north and west, and cooler and drier conditions in the south and east.

History and Politics. The earliest inhabitants of modern Zaire were probably Pygmies who settled in the area thousands of years ago. By the A.D. 700s, sophisticated civilizations had developed in what is now southeastern Zaire. In the early 1500s, the Portuguese began the forced emigration of black Africans for slavery. Other Europeans came to the area as the slave trade grew, but the interior remained relatively unexplored until the 1870s. Belgian King Leopold II realized the potential value of the region, and in 1885 his claim was recognized. Belgium took control from Leopold in 1908, renaming the colony the Belgian Congo. Nationalist sentiment grew until rioting broke out in 1959. The country, which was then called the Congo, gained independence in 1960, and a weak government assumed control. Violent civil disorder, provincial secession, and a political assassination characterized the next five years. The country stabilized under the rule of President Mobutu Sese Seko, a former army general. However, widespread charges of corruption have strengthened the cause of rebels based in Angola and forced the government to institute minor reforms. Serious ethnic fighting in 1993 left thousands dead. By 1994 the country teetered on the brink of anarchy. A new transition government under President Mobutu promises reform and free elections. ■

ZAMBIA

Official name Republic of the Zambia
PEOPLE
Population 8,809,000. **Density** 30/mi² (12/km²).
Urban 42%. **Capital** Lusaka, 982,362. **Ethnic groups** African 99%, European 1%. **Languages** English, Tonga, Lozi, other indigenous. **Religions** Christian 50-75%, Muslim and Hindu 24-49%. **Life expectancy** 45 female, 44 male. **Literacy** 73%.
POLITICS
Government Republic. **Parties** Movement for Multiparty Democracy, United National Independence. **Suffrage** Universal, over 18. **Memberships** CW, OAU, UN. **Subdivisions** 9 provinces.
ECONOMY
GDP $7,300,000,000. **Per capita** $861. **Monetary unit** Kwacha. **Trade partners** Exports: Japan, Germany, U.K. Imports: South African countries, U.K., U.S. **Exports** Copper, zinc, cobalt, lead, tobacco. **Imports** Machinery, transportation equipment, food, fuel, manufactures.
LAND
Description Southern Africa, landlocked. **Area** 290,586 mi² (752,614 km²). **Highest point** Unnamed, 7,100 ft (2,164 m). **Lowest point** Along Zambezi River, 1,081 ft (329 m).

People. Virtually all Zambians are black Africans belonging to one of more than seventy Bantu-speaking ethnic groups. Besides the indigenous Bantu languages, many speak English, a reflection of decades of British influence. Although most Zambians are Christian, small minorities are Hindu, Muslim, or hold indigenous beliefs. Many Zambians are subsistence farmers in small villages; however, the mining industry has caused many people to move to urban areas, where wages are rising.

Economy and the Land. The economy is based on copper, Zambia's major export. In an attempt to diversify the economy, the government has emphasized the development of agriculture to help achieve an acceptable balance of trade. Zambia is a subtropical nation marked by high plateaus and great rivers.

History and Politics. European explorers in the nineteenth century discovered an established society of Bantu-speaking inhabitants. In 1888 Cecil Rhodes and the British South Africa Company obtained a mineral-rights concession from local chiefs; and Northern and Southern Rhodesia, now Zambia and Zimbabwe, came under British influence. Northern Rhodesia became a British protectorate in 1924. In 1953 Northern Rhodesia was combined with Southern Rhodesia and Nyasaland, now Malawi, to form a federation, despite African-nationalist opposition to the white-controlled minority government in Southern Rhodesia. The federation was dissolved in 1963, and Northern Rhodesia became the independent Republic of Zambia in 1964. In late 1991 the first multiparty election in decades brought a landslide victory for democratic forces, as well as a sound rejection of socialism. Zambia is now undergoing a painful conversion to capitalism. ■

ZIMBABWE

Official name Republic of Zimbabwe
PEOPLE
Population 11,075,000. **Density** 73/mi² (28/km²).
Urban 29%. **Capital** Harare, 681,000. **Ethnic groups** Shona 71%, Ndebele 16%, white 1%.